Revives My Soul Again

Revives My Soul Again

The Spirituality of Martin Luther King Jr.

LEWIS V. BALDWIN AND VICTOR ANDERSON

FORTRESS PRESS
MINNEAPOLIS

REVIVES MY SOUL AGAIN
The Spirituality of Martin Luther King Jr.

Cover design: Alisha Lofgren

Print ISBN: 978-1-5064-2470-5
eBook ISBN: 978-1-5064-2471-2

The paper used in this publication meets the minimum requirements of American National Standard for Information Sciences — Permanence of Paper for Printed Library Materials, ANSI Z329.48-1984.

Manufactured in the U.S.A.

For the poor in spirit,
and for
Dale P. Andrews, PhD,
Cornelius Vanderbilt Chair and
Distinguished Professor
of Homiletics, Social Justice, and Practical Theology at
Vanderbilt University Divinity School; teacher, scholar,
mentor, friend, and colleague; prophet of justice,
truth to power, and beloved community.
Gone too soon.

There are two lives, the natural and the spiritual, and we must lose the one before we can participate in the other.

—William James, *The Varieties of Religious Experience* (1902)

Yes, sometimes I feel discouraged and feel my work's in vain. But then the Holy Spirit revives my soul again.

—Martin Luther King Jr., "Why Jesus Called a Man a Fool" (1967)

Contents

Contributors

Victor Anderson is the Oberlin Theological School Professor of Ethics and Society at Vanderbilt University Divinity School, and he also serves as a professor in the Program of African American and Diaspora Studies and Religious Studies in the College of Arts and Sciences at Vanderbilt. He is the author of *Creative Exchange: A Constructive Theology of African American Religious Experience* (2008), *Pragmatic Theology: Negotiating the Intersection of an American Philosophy of Religion and Public Theology* (1999), *Beyond Ontological Blackness: An Essay on African American Religious and Cultural Criticism* (1995), and numerous articles and book chapters.

Lewis V. Baldwin is professor emeritus of religious studies, Vanderbilt University. He is the author of *Behind the Public Veil: The Humanness of Martin Luther King, Jr.* (2016), *Never to Leave Us Alone: The Prayer Life of Martin Luther King, Jr.* (2010), *The Voice of Conscience: The Church in the Mind of Martin Luther King, Jr.* (2010), *Toward the Beloved Community: Martin Luther King, Jr. and South Africa* (1995), *To Make the Wounded Whole: The Cultural Legacy of Martin Luther King, Jr.* (1992), and *There Is a Balm in Gilead: The Cultural Roots of Martin Luther King, Jr.* (1991); a coauthor of *Between Cross and Crescent: Christian and Muslim Perspectives on Malcolm and Martin* (2002), *The Legacy of Martin Luther King, Jr.: The Boundaries of Law, Politics, and Religion* (2002), and *Freedom Is Never Free: A Biographical Portrait of E. D. Nixon, Sr.* (1992); editor of *"Thou, Dear God": Prayers That Open Hearts and Spirits—The Reverend Dr. Martin Luther King, Jr.* (2012) and *"In a Single Garment of Destiny": A Global Vision of Justice—Martin Luther King, Jr.* (2012); a coeditor of *The Domestication of Martin Luther King, Jr.: Clarence B. Jones, Right-Wing Conservatism, and the Manipulation of the King Legacy* (2013) and *"In an*

Inescapable Network of Mutuality": Martin Luther King, Jr. and the Globalization of an Ethical Ideal (2013); and the author of numerous articles and book chapters.

Stewart Burns is professor of ethical and creative leadership and Martin Luther King Jr. Studies, Union Institute and University, North Adams, Massachusetts, and a former editor of the Martin Luther King Jr. Papers Project at Stanford University. He is the author of *"We Will Stand Here Till We Die": Freedom Movement Shakes America, Shapes Martin Luther King, Jr.* (2013), *To the Mountaintop: Martin Luther King, Jr.'s Mission to Save America, 1955–1968* (2004), *Daybreak of Freedom: The Montgomery Bus Boycott* (1997), and *Social Movements of the 1960s: Searching for Democracy* (1990); editor of *Cosmic Companionship: Spirit Stories of Martin Luther King, Jr.* (Kindle Edition, 2013) and *American Messiah: Martin Luther King, Jr.'s Ultimate Journey!* (Kindle Edition, 2008); and a contributing editor to *The Papers of Martin Luther King, Jr., Volume III: Birth of a New Age, December 1955–December 1956* (1997).

Walter Earl Fluker is the Martin Luther King Jr. Professor of Ethical Leadership, the director of the Martin Luther King Jr. Initiative for the Development of Ethical Leadership (MLK-IDEAL), and the editor of the Howard Thurman Papers at Boston University's School of Theology. He is the author of *The Ground Has Shifted: The Future of the Black Church in Post-Racial America* (2016), *Ethical Leadership: The Quest for Character, Civility, and Community* (2009), and *They Looked for a City: A Comparative Analysis of the Ideal of Community in the Thought of Howard Thurman and Martin Luther King, Jr.* (1989); editor of a multivolume series on the works of Howard Thurman, among which are *The Papers of Howard Washington Thurman: The Soundless Passion of a Single Mind, June 1949–December 1962*, vol. 4 (2017); *The Papers of Howard Washington Thurman: The Bold Adventure, September 1943–May 1949*, vol. 3 (2015); *The Papers of Howard Washington Thurman: "Christian, Who Calls Me Christian?," April 1936–August 1943*, vol. 2 (2012); and *The Papers of Howard Washington Thurman: My People Need Me, June 1918–March 1936*, vol. 1 (2009); a coeditor of *A Strange Freedom: The Best of Howard Thurman on Religious Experience and Public Life* (1998); and the author of numerous articles and book chapters.

Diana L. Hayes is professor emerita of systematic theology at Georgetown University. In addition to a PhD in religious studies, she holds the juris doctorate in law and a doctorate of sacred theology (STD). She is the author of *Forged in the Fiery Furnace: African American Spirituality* (2012), *Standing in the Shoes My Mother Made: A Womanist Theology* (2010), *Were You There? Stations of the Cross* (1999), *Taking Down Our Harps: Black Catholics in the United States* (1998), *And Still We Rise: An Introduction to Black Liberation Theology* (1996), *Trouble Don't Last Always: Soul Prayers* (1995), and *Hagar's Daughters: Womanist Ways of Being in the World (Maldeleva Lecture in Spirituality)* (1995); a coeditor of *Many Faces, One Church: Cultural Diversity and the American Catholic Experience (Catholic Studies)* (2004); and the author of numerous articles and book chapters.

Aaron J. Howard, a PhD in religion, ethics, and society from Vanderbilt University, has either taught or assisted in teaching a number of courses on the life and thought of Martin Luther King Jr., has given numerous presentations on King's thought and activism at the American Academy of Religion Meetings and in other venues, and is the recipient of numerous honors and awards. He is the author of "Beyond Belief: Ethnography, the Supernatural and Hegemonic Discourse," *Practical Matters*, no. 6 (2013), and his dissertation is titled "Incommensurable Paradigms: The Competing Theological Claims of Black Pietism and Black Liberationism" (2017).

Beverly J. Lanzetta is a theologian, an authority on global spirituality, and a spiritual teacher who is widely praised and celebrated for her wisdom, eloquence, and mystical insight. She is the author of *Path of the Heart: A Spiritual Guide to Divine Union* (exp. ed., 2014), *Nine Jewels of Night: One Soul's Journey into God* (2014), *40 Day Journey with Joan Chittister* (2007), *Emerging Heart: Global Spirituality and the Sacred* (2007), *Radical Wisdom: A Feminist Mystical Theology* (2005), and *The Other Side of Nothingness: Toward a Theology of Radical Openness* (2001); and a coauthor of *Embracing Solitude: Women and New Monasticism* (2013).

Michael Brandon McCormack is a professor in Pan-African Studies at the University of Louisville, with a secondary appointment in the Division of Humanities (Religious Studies). His research interests focus on the intersections of African American religion and cultural studies. His dissertation examined and analyzed the contested relationships between the prophetic tradition in black religion, black moral panic, and the cultural productions of the hip-hop generation. He teaches a range of courses in African American religion and the religions of the African diaspora.

Nichole R. Phillips is a practical theologian and social scientist of religion, and is also an assistant professor of sociology, religion, and culture at Candler School of Theology, Emory University. Before joining the Candler faculty in 2013, she was a postdoctoral fellow in the Practical Theology and Religious Practices Program at Candler, which functioned in collaboration with Emory's Graduate Division of Religion. A recipient of numerous honors and awards, her research interests rest at the intersection of religion and American public life, with a focus on community and congregational studies, where she investigates the moral commitments and vision of community and congregational members. Her first monograph, *Patriotism Black and White: The Color of American Exceptionalism* (2018), is a study of blacks and whites in a rural southern community and their shifting interpretations of American national identity with the election of Barack H. Obama, the first black president, at the height of the wars in Iraq and Afghanistan. The volume further considers the implications of these patriotic and exceptionalist meanings under the Trump administration.

Mervyn A. Warren is professor emeritus of preaching (homiletics) at Oakwood University in Huntsville, Alabama, where he also served as dean of the school of religion, provost, and interim president. He has done extensive research on Martin Luther King Jr. as preacher and pastor, and is the author of *King Came Preaching: The Pulpit Power of Dr. Martin Luther King, Jr.* (2001). He is also the author of *Black Preaching: Truth and Soul* (1977) and is a contributor to a major work on Seventh Day Adventism titled *The Enduring Legacy of Ellen G. White and Social Justice* (2017).

Acknowledgments

Every book is the product of a collective endeavor, and *Revives My Soul Again* is no exception. This volume has come to fruition because of the resources and sources of persons who believe that the life, thought, activities, and legacy of Martin Luther King Jr. are still meaningful for our times. We are only two of many people who worked together to make the final product something that appeals to a broad readership. Needless to say, we have accumulated many debts, and we now have the great pleasure of finally acknowledging them in this space.

The stimulus for pursuing and completing *Revives My Soul Again* was a special roundtable event celebrating the advancement of Martin Luther King Jr. studies, which has taken on global significance. Held at Vanderbilt University on May 5–6, 2016, the event provided opportunities for invigorating conversations between the established and emerging King scholars who contributed chapters to this book. The event was successful due to the encouragement, support, and contributions of a number of sources and persons. The Kelly Miller Smith Institute at Vanderbilt Divinity School, headed by Forrest Harris, generously provided funds. Dean Emilie Townes made the reading room at the divinity school available for the reception on the first day of the event and was supportive the whole way. Frank Dobson and his staff at the Bishop Joseph H. Johnson Black Cultural Center at Vanderbilt provided space for the roundtables. Tamyron Moore set up the entire reception, and prepared delicious food and drinks for all involved over the two-day period. All of these persons contributed to the kind of congenial environment that made the roundtable event a truly enlightening and pleasurable experience, and for their efforts, expertise, and goodwill, we owe them a great debt of gratitude.

A hearty word of thanks is extended to the stellar group of established and rising scholars from various fields of study, who wrote chapters for this volume. We are not only academics but faith-inspired people who are sensitive to the need for more interdisciplinary work on Dr. King, and *Revives My Soul Again* allowed the ten of us to show in writing, from our own distinctive perspectives, how spirituality and social justice activism came together in the consciousness and life of this phenomenal figure. The probing questions, the rich insights, and the deep social conscience that each contributor brought to bear on our roundtable discussions and the content of this book are highly commendable, and we are most appreciative and grateful. Each contributor has left his or her mark on *Revives My Soul Again.*

We are heavily indebted to the late Dale P. Andrews, the Cornelius Vanderbilt Chair and Distinguished Professor of Homiletics, Social Justice, and Practical Theology at the Vanderbilt University Divinity School, who was with us from the very beginning of this scholarly venture. Dale unhesitatingly contributed some of his own grant money, which helped enable us to follow through with the special roundtable event, and some of the provocative insights in *Revives My Soul Again* can be attributed to him. Sadly, rapidly declining health prevented him from completing his chapter for the book. Dale was a model of humane collegiality and intellectual rigor. His death on June 23, 2017 deeply affected us, but we are inspired by the memories of his exemplary collegiality, his unflagging support and friendship, and his commitment to the life of the mind and spirit. This book is dedicated with love, gratitude, and respect to Dale's memory, and with the acknowledgment that he did so much to make *Revives My Soul Again* possible. A word of thanks also goes to Sha'Tika Brown, the program and events coordinator at Vanderbilt Divinity School, for her efforts in facilitating lines of communication between Dale and some of the other contributors to this book.

We appreciate very much the stimulating group of graduate students who showed up and participated in our roundtable event at Vanderbilt. Their attentiveness, searching questions, and thoughtful comments came at a time when we were actually conceptualizing *Revives My Soul Again,* and they helped frame many of the ideas and insights that ultimately factored into the content of this work. We owe them a great intellectual debt.

Warmest thanks to Stephanie Y. Mitchem and Barbara A. Holmes for their contributions to our book. Dr. Mitchem, a professor in the department of religious studies at the University of South Carolina, graciously accepted our invitation to write the foreword. Dr. Holmes, president emerita of the United Theological Seminary of the Twin Cities, was equally gracious in agreeing to write the afterword. Both Dr. Mitchem and Dr. Holmes are highly accomplished teachers and scholars with sterling publishing records, and we are honored to have secured their involvement with *Revives My Soul Again.*

We also acknowledge our enormous debt to Michael Gibson, our editor at Fortress Press, for his enthusiastic encouragement and patient support. A young man of amazing talent and ability, Mike was always there when we had questions about content and style relative to our book, and he was flexible when we could not meet deadlines. He actually met and conversed at length with the group of contributors at the American Academy of Religion Meetings in San Antonio in November 2016, and we benefitted immensely from the exchange of ideas with him.

Last, but not least, *Revives My Soul Again* is offered as a gift to the poor of spirit, or those who feel spiritual emptiness in these times of crisis and gripping insecurity and uncertainty. It is also a gift to faith-inspired people who are committed to social justice, human rights, and peace. We hope that people from all walks of life will find some enlightenment and inspiration in this book, and that it will stimulate discussion in the academy, in religious circles, and in the larger public sphere. If this happens, the time, energy, and resources that went into it will not be meaningless.

Foreword

"Are you woke yet?"

From kitchen table to street corner to pulpit, this question ranges across black American communities in response to state sanctioned violence, voting suppression, vocal white supremacists, and the daily microaggressions that dehumanize anyone marked *Other*. Being woke is more than a state of physically *not* sleeping. Rather, this is a call for an alert focus with vigilance and attentiveness to the moment. There have been many who write and talk about the shape of protest today, especially with the expansion of social media. Both human rights and civil rights are at stake and responses are needed. How do we learn? From Dr. Martin Luther King Jr.? Significant, thoughtful explorations of Dr. King's spirituality have been missing from the literature. *Revives My Soul Again* fills that void and is critical to understanding the challenges of, and responses to, our present moment.

As the editors of this volume point out, Dr. King used his own spirituality as bedrock for his activism, gathering people in order to achieve the task of calling us back, as the introduction reminds us, from "approaching spiritual death." Since King's assassination April 4, 1968, the seductions toward spiritual death have been upon us. The seduction of money. The longing to achieve the American dream. Fears of loneliness. Reality programs invite views of love, hip hop, singing competitions, modeling success, or vapid stories of real housewives.

Yet, past the slick, pretty wrappings, an undercurrent of violence flows against people of color, poor people, Muslims, and Jews. We have names of Trayvon, Sandra, Dontae, Alberta, Eric, Tanisha, Tamir, Shantel, and Walter. Refugees are targeted as terrorists. Immigrants are labeled drug dealers. White hate groups expand their bases. Approaching spiritual death, indeed.

To discuss the richness of Dr. King's spiritual life and strength is to recognize African American intellectual history. Too often, the "intellectual" is defined as existing only within the halls of universities and colleges. Here, we are told, we will find the best and brightest minds. Yet the scholarly canon was set in white, European-focused tones. That is not the end of the story, though.

During enslavement, African Americans were forbidden to read or write, for the most part. Therefore, education became critically important in black communities after emancipation in 1863. The concept of anything good coming from black minds was a joke enforced by Jim Crow, segregation, sharecropping, rape, and lynching.

We can point to a black folk wisdom, born from people who perhaps had only fourth-grade educations. Practical knowledge and mother wit provided information past the surfaces of life, otherwise how would we have lived? How would we have survived when white people were telling us that we weren't even humans? Knowledge of the arts and appreciation for the beautiful might be expressed in home care but might be recognized at a moment watching a brilliant sunrise. Reading and discussion happened in smaller community-based groups: W. E. B. Du Bois, Ida B. Wells, Kelly Miller, Mary Church Terrell, and an assortment of black newspapers were sources of information. Black churches provided community centers where people could share what they had learned and could encourage others, even as discussions and analyses of daily events occurred. Justice was understood as needed in this world but not separate from our souls. Prayer was connected to life, not shut in sterile buildings and accessed once a week. Or, as one old auntie used to say, "Get up off your knees and do something." We had hard lives, but also a wisdom tradition that informed our intellectual lives.

This is the intellectual tradition that Rev. Martin Luther King Jr. could access. He knew that beyond book learning, there was emotional intelligence to be gleaned. He could learn the spiritual wisdom of the community even as he recognized the embodied suffering and material deprivation experienced by black and poor Americans. He was fully woke.

Anyone who has read the texts of Dr. King's sermons can recognize his academic brilliance. But hearing the recorded words of Dr. King in full preacher mode is to recognize that this was not a dry academic. Instead, the intensity of the emotional, spiritual, and scholarly dimensions does not point toward unconnected dimensions of his personality but shows us the way to wholeness. How might we learn about the depth of his spiritual wisdom? How did Dr. King continue in the face of seemingly insurmountable odds?

Today we know that we have not arrived at some post-racial utopia. It would seem that there are forces seeking to return us to an America that makes black people invisible again. But going back is not an option. The National Museum of African American History and Culture is now open on the Mall in Washington, DC. In 2017, a noose was left in a gallery inside the museum, clearly hoping to intimidate someone. But this is not the past, and a noose, despite the history of black lynchings, is not the same.

One lesson to learn from Dr. King is that solo acts will not bring deep social change. While we look at one man, we must recognize that there were communities of folk who were involved and supported the work. Today, social scientists talk about the "theory of change" and recognize the simultaneous need for focus and flexibility. Social theorists talk about "systems theory" because they recognize that no single person can make changes but that we must work in community together. We can learn how Dr. King drew people around him but let other people take the lead as needed. We can learn that social change is connected to our moral and spiritual lives as communities.

Too often, the "I Have a Dream" sermon becomes the central and only mention of Rev. King's spirituality. The small section of the sermon that is quoted functions to caricature the complex realities of the man's faith; too often, that dream is held up as a black-people-need-to-do-what-they're-told instruction, one that seeks to reduce spiritual strivings to some prescribed and docile content of character. The context keeps getting yanked out of the Rev. Dr. Martin Luther King's story.

What did "revive" Rev. Martin Luther King Jr.'s soul? Dr. King was fully human, not mythic. His journey to spiritual strength was not a fluke and is not able to be domesticated, but it is also not divorced from his race, culture, and region. That this dimension of his being has not been explored has served to diminish his strength to a strange, one-off occurrence. There had been a nagging absence of the serious study of Dr. King's spirituality.

But now, Lewis V. Baldwin and Victor Anderson have collected a stellar group of scholars to explore aspects of Dr. King's spirituality. Prayer and ritual practice interweave with issues of oppression and leadership. Material connections are made for understanding a life in spirit.

This book shows the realities of Dr. King's powerful spirituality, and enfleshes and embodies the theories about King's political genius. The various scholars connect the idea of beloved community with public service and prayer. Stated another way, spirituality is made material, which is consistent with the traditional holistic spirituality of black Americans. At the same time, the essays in this book expand our concepts and give deeper meaning to spirituality. In that way, they expand the idea of justice even as they remind us of the global dimensions—the universalizing aspects—of Rev. Dr. King's profound spirituality.

I celebrate this long-needed collection of essays that forever ends the silences and simplistic discussions of Dr. King's powerful, spiritual life that was lived in our public eyes.

Are we woke yet?

Stephanie Y. Mitchem
Department of Religious Studies
University of South Carolina

Introduction

Martin Luther King Jr.'s commitment to the creation of the beloved community dovetailed well with his deep engagement with the life of the spirit. King was consistently driven by the demands of inner truth, and he never allowed the voices of the world to silence his own inner voice. This is why Gardner C. Taylor described King as "the one true spiritual genius which this land has produced,"[1] and Harry Belafonte, in a similar vein, declared that King "was the first pure spiritual force I'd met."[2] The point is that the essence of the person that was Martin Luther King Jr. ultimately inhered not so much in his exemplary public leadership, the dynamic speeches he gave, and the many marches he led, but, rather, in the quality of his own spiritual journey and how he sought to rescue humanity from what he termed an "approaching spiritual death" or a perpetual "death of the spirit."[3]

This book treats King's life as a paradigm of a deep, vital, engaging, and contagious spirituality. While not ignoring his towering

1. At another point, Taylor called King "the only authentic spiritual genius America has produced." See Gardner C. Taylor, *The Words of Gardner Taylor: Special Occasion and Expository Sermons*, compiled by Edward L. Taylor (Valley Forge, PA: Judson, 2001), 4, 16, and 103; and Gardner C. Taylor, "An Heir of the Heroic Lineage of a People," recording of a sermon on Martin Luther King Jr.'s birthday, Colgate-Rochester Divinity School, Rochester, New York (15 January 1974).

2. Referring at greater length to King, Belafonte noted: "And while I kept my doubts, his spirituality changed my life" and "nourished by soul." Wyatt Tee Walker, another King aide, essentially agreed with Belafonte's point about the impact of King's spirituality, while also identifying King as "that great spirit." See Harry Belafonte, *My Song: A Memoir*, with Michael Shnayerson (New York: Alfred A. Knopf, 2011), 297; and Wyatt Tee Walker, "Spirituality as an Instrument of Social Change," unpublished essay (2015), 1–3 and 5–8.

3. Martin Luther King Jr., *Where Do We Go from Here: Chaos or Community?* (Boston: Beacon, 1968; originally published in 1967), 188; and Martin Luther King Jr., "Address to a Joint Convention of the Two Houses of the General Court of Massachusetts," Boston, Massachusetts (22 April 1965), unpublished version, Library and Archives of the Martin Luther King Jr. Center for Nonviolent Social Change, Inc. (KCLA), Atlanta, Georgia, 13.

significance as a civil rights leader, it concludes nonetheless that King was first and foremost a spiritual leader with an unwavering commitment to faithful Christian service. The commitment itself was clearly made in childhood,[4] when King was growing up in Ebenezer Baptist Church in Atlanta, Georgia, but the precise form of that service would be defined during his Morehouse College years, 1944–1948, when he, still a teenager, felt called "to serve God and humanity."[5] From that point, King increasingly embraced a spiritual life that took seriously the personal, interpersonal, and sociopolitical aspects of the Christian faith, and, in time, figured prominently in recasting the very definition of spirituality for his generation.

Even so, the scholarship on King is seriously lacking in terms of richly nuanced and revelatory accounts of his spirituality and spiritual life. Only fleeting attention has been given to the subject even in the best articles and books on King. Lewis V. Baldwin's works on King's churchmanship and prayer life, and also his edited collection of King's prayers,[6] are an exception, and so are Frederick L. Downing's exploration of the faith pilgrimage that King followed from his early years in Atlanta to martyrdom in Memphis,[7] and Stewart Burns's treatments of the ways in which King's spirituality was thoroughly intertwined with his prophetic witness and activism against social injustice.[8] In any case, this kind of

4. See Martin Luther King Jr., *Daddy King: An Autobiography* (New York: William Morrow, 1980), 109; and Mrs. Alberta King, "Dr. Martin Luther King, Jr.: Birth to Twelve Years Old by His Mother," Ebenezer Baptist Church, Atlanta, Georgia, KCLA Recording (18 January 1973).

5. Clayborne Carson et al., eds., *The Papers of Martin Luther King, Jr.: Advocate of the Social Gospel, September 1948–March 1963* (Berkeley: University of California Press, 2007), 6:368; Clayborne Carson et al., eds., *The Papers of Martin Luther King, Jr.: Called to Serve, January 1929–June 1951* (Berkeley: University of California Press, 1992), 1:121; and Martin Luther King Jr., *The Autobiography of Martin Luther King, Jr.*, ed. Clayborne Carson (New York: Warner, 1998), 14–16.

6. Lewis V. Baldwin, *The Voice of Conscience: The Church in the Mind of Martin Luther King, Jr.* (New York: Oxford University Press, 2010), 51–122 and 217–49; Lewis V. Baldwin, *Never to Leave Us Alone: The Prayer Life of Martin Luther King, Jr.* (Minneapolis: Fortress, 2010), 1–89; and Martin Luther King Jr., *"Thou, Dear God": Prayers That Open Hearts and Spirits—The Reverend Dr. Martin Luther King, Jr.*, ed. Lewis V. Baldwin (Boston: Beacon, 2012), ix–xxii and 3–233.

7. Downing uses the psychosocial theories of Erik Erikson and James Fowler's stages of faith development to frame and reinforce his perspectives concerning the transformative power of religion, faith, and/or spirituality in Dr. King's life experiences. Portraying King as a preacher and a prophet on a faith journey, Downing concludes that faith and life were inseparable for King. See Frederick L. Downing, *To See the Promised Land: The Faith Pilgrimage of Martin Luther King, Jr.* (Macon, GA: Mercer University Press, 1986), 6–286.

8. Burns views King as a moral leader and nonviolent apostle who was not only inspired and motivated by spiritual values, but also on essentially a spiritual mission to redeem the soul of America. See Stewart Burns, *To the Mountaintop: Martin Luther King, Jr.'s Sacred Mission to Save America: 1955–1968* (New York: HarperCollins, 2004), 12–482; Stewart Burns, ed., *American*

neglect explains, perhaps more than anything else, why it is so difficult for scholars to hold the *real* Martin Luther King Jr. in proper perspective. It also feeds into the widely held and misguided assumption that King's spiritual leadership and his civil rights leadership remained separate entities; that they were not in any sense extensions of each other.[9] The works of Baldwin, Downing, and Burns dispel much of this mass confusion over King's identity and sense of mission and purpose, while also raising important questions and challenges for the direction that this book is taking on the issue of King's spirituality.

Revives My Soul Again addresses and corrects a serious pattern of omission in the scholarship on King; namely, the all too pervasive tendency to highlight King's social justice advocacy and civil and human rights activism without serious attention to critical aspects of his spirituality. Viewing King as the quintessential model of what Donal Dorr calls "a balanced spirituality,"[10] this book has a manifold purpose. First, to explore the roots of King's spirituality in the history and traditions of the black church. Second, to examine the dimensions of King's spirituality as revealed in his prayer life, his preaching, his employment of mythical stories, ritual and language, and selected pieces of his writings, while also making the case for King as a prominent spiritual leader. Third, to explain how King's spirituality embodied not only the personal life of prayer, meditation, and fasting, but also an effective and enduring commitment to social justice, equal rights, and peace. Fourth, to highlight the ways in which King applied spirituality as a category of human experience to the whole of human life. Fifth, to trace King's interest in and contributions to the shaping of a vibrant pluralist spirituality, a spirituality that is inclusive and respectful of the rich mosaic of human life in this age of unprecedented global connectivity. Finally, to assess how King's spiritual journey may itself serve as a kind of pedagogy for people of different faith traditions and sociopolitical persuasions in the twenty-first

Messiah: Martin Luther King, Jr.'s Ultimate Journey (Kindle Edition, 2008), 1–100; and Stewart Burns, ed., *Cosmic Companionship: Spirit Stories of Martin Luther King, Jr.* (Kindle Edition, 2013), 1–144.

9. King himself repeatedly denied such claims. See Martin Luther King Jr., "Doubts and Certainties Link: Transcript of an Interview," unpublished, London, England (Winter, 1968), KCLA, 3; and James M. Washington, ed., *A Testament of Hope: The Essential Writings and Speeches of Martin Luther King, Jr.* (San Francisco: HarperSanFrancisco, 1991), 345, 408, and 480–81.

10. Here Dorr has in mind the kind of spirituality that demands that "we walk humbly with our God," "love tenderly," and "act justly"—a spirituality that embraces the "personal, interpersonal," and also the "public or political aspects of the Christian faith." Strangely, Dorr makes no mention of King in his treatment of the subject. See Donal Dorr, *Spirituality and Justice* (Maryknoll, NY: Orbis, 1987), 8–18.

century, and especially those who are in search of new spiritual direction.

Some scholars make a sharp distinction between spirituality and religion, and this was the subject of some discussion as *Revives My Soul Again* was being conceptualized. Specific references were made to Diana Butler Bass, who identifies spirituality with experience, connection, transcendence, doubt, searching, openness, prayer, meditation, nature, energy, wisdom, inclusiveness, and the inner life, and religion with institution, organization, rules, order, dogma, authority, beliefs, buildings, structure, defined principles, hierarchy, orthodoxy, boundaries, and certainty.[11] This volume takes a different approach, concluding that "spirituality" and "religious experience" cross-pollinate in terms of their meanings. Also, King himself used the words "spirituality" and "religion" interchangeably, to refer to a particular category of human experience. He seldom spoke of spirituality without also mentioning religion or religious experience, so these were essentially indistinguishable in his thinking. He saw spiritual growth as a necessary component of a healthy and vital religion, and spoke of religion as essentially an expression of spirituality.[12] *Revives My Soul Again* takes seriously King's tendency to view "spirituality" as an empirical marker of "religious experience" or "religious piety."

Revives My Soul Again includes pieces from a stellar cast of both established and rising scholars from various disciplines or academic fields. In chapter 1, Victor Anderson, a religious ethicist, philosopher, and cultural critic, turns to the worlds of religious experience and the religious affections as motivational structures in King's soul life and calling. Anderson draws on two thinkers far separated in time for framing this chapter. The first is William James. King was well acquainted with James's psychology and philosophy, and often evoked and/or quoted James. As Anderson indicates, William James treated spirituality and religious experience as crucial dimensions of everyday human life, and he was particularly inter-

11. Diana B. Butler, *Christianity after Religion: The End of Church and the Birth of a New Spiritual Awakening* (New York: HarperCollins, 2012), 3–6, 22, 28, 33–35, 67–71, 91–94, 97–99, 142–43, 234, and 278n2; and Clay Stauffer, "Spirituality and Religion Must Be Linked: Message of the Week," *The Tennessean*, Nashville, Tennessee (13 October 2012): 3B.

12. Carson et al., eds., *Papers*, 6:223 and 534; Baldwin, *Voice of Conscience*, 201–16; and King, *"Thou, Dear God,"* 45. This sense of the overlapping meanings of "spirituality" and "religious experience" in King's consciousness was evident as far back as his seminary years, when he, in a paper in November 1949, insisted that "religious experience" is "not an intellectual formulation about God," but rather, "the awareness of the presence of the divine" and "a lasting acquaintance with God." Throughout most of his life, King evidently had a clear sense of "spirituality" and "religious experience" as coextensive, or as extensions of each other. See Carson et al., eds., *Papers*, 1:232–33.

ested in the feelings, acts, and experiences of persons in their moments of solitude. This point is essential in highlighting the fact that King experienced profound spiritual realities not only within the church and in the midst of the many social, economic, and political crises he faced, but also when he was alone and engaging God or the supernatural realm in silence, as in the case of his "Kitchen Vision."[13] Anderson's chapter is all the more interesting since King himself reflected at times on James's work, drawing on it in his own references to "mystical experience" as an "immediate experience with what is believed to be the source of value," and to religious experience as "a thou experience" or as an experience of "the 'I' seeking the 'thou.'"[14] Anderson makes particular use of James's conceptions of human conscious life as a stream of consciousness and religious experience as the experiencing of the *MORE* disclosed in human engagement with cosmic events.

Anderson then turns even further backward in time to Jonathan Edwards's classic "Treatise on the Religious Affections" to understand the power of the affections for "moving" or "inclining" the wills of people toward works of piety. He focuses on the transformative power of the religious affections to turn moments of grief, dismay, and doubts into an assurance that issues in faith, hope, and love. Anderson then explores the affections of doubt and assurance as developmental motivations in King's spirituality from childhood to his death on April 4, 1968. He takes two episodes in King's life of intense grief and doubt to frame his discussion; namely, the death of his maternal grandmother, Jennie C. Parks Williams, and the death and eulogy of Birmingham's children martyrs. In the end, Anderson argues that in such moments of grief and doubt, King's blessed assurance was most acute in giving shape to his spiritual endurance and the work ahead, as he both envisioned and undertook it.

Chapter 2, written by Diana L. Hayes, a systematic theologian, treats King as both a product and exemplar of what she calls an "African American spirituality." According to Hayes, King was rooted in "the

13. This calls to mind what Wyatt Tee Walker termed "King's self-imposed day of silence," during which he "abstained from the distractions of daily life, including the telephone, television, and radio," while also praying, meditating, and "developing a rigorous discipline of 'think time.'" See Clayborne Carson and Peter Holloran, eds., *A Knock at Midnight: Inspiration from the Great Sermons of Reverend Martin Luther King, Jr.* (New York: Warner, 1998), 159–63; and Baldwin, *Never to Leave Us Alone*, vii and 123n5.

14. Interestingly enough, King once noted: "William James was once asked to give his definition of spirituality. After a moment's hesitation he answered that he was not sure he could give the meaning in words, but he could point to a person who was it—Phillips Brooks." See Carson et al., *Papers*, 1:233, 246–47, and 428; and Clayborne Carson et al., eds., *The Papers of Martin Luther King, Jr.: Rediscovering Precious Values, July 1951–November 1955* (Berkeley: University of California Press, 1994), 2:108.

religious and spiritual traditions of the African American church," traditions that were "forged in the fiery furnace of slavery" and segregation "in the United States." Hayes goes on to explain that King helped "rekindle Black America's faith" in a personal God who acts in history to bring the disjointed elements of humanity into a harmonious whole. In Hayes's estimation, King lived "African American spirituality" not only in his preaching and prayer life, but also in his struggle to eliminate the evil and unjust institutions and laws that negatively impacted the quality of "black life" in particular and human life as a whole.[15] This bears out this book's contention that King looked beyond spirituality as merely an experience that is individualistic and subjective while practicing an engaging, balanced, and wholistic spirituality. Clearly, King was interested not only in spirituality, but also in how it gets translated from personal experience to certain kinds of social justice activism. At the same time, Hayes is quite mindful of a point that William D. Hart brilliantly and repeatedly makes in his insightful study of the spirituality of Malcolm X, Julius Lester, and Jan Willis; namely, that "the black spiritual imagination—religious, political, and personal—cannot be limited to the Standard Narrative of Black Religion as the Black Church."[16]

Hayes captures King's sense of those traditions that grounded his spirituality, noting the importance of reading King in context. This is significant because King's biography functions as something more than the story of an individual life. King was part of a history, a heritage, a people, and a place in which the rhythm of human life was accentuated through spirituality. His spirituality illuminated that rich spiritual heritage so central to black religion and the black church.

Chapter 3 explains how King employed the language of the *spiritual* in describing the supernatural realm, his own inner self, inner search, and inner life, the human quest for a sense of the divine or supernatural, the nature of the church, and the state of our nation and the world. Here Victor Anderson and Lewis V. Baldwin, a religious and cultural historian, probe the depths of King's sermons, mass meeting speeches, and writings, which are saturated with words and/or terms like "spirit," "spiritual beings," "spiritual body," "spiritual journey," "spiritual life," "spiritual experience," "spiritual values," "spiritual might," "spiritual problem," "spiritual lift," "spiritual progress," "spiritual genius," "spiritual responsibility," "spiritual movement," "spiritual doom," "spiritual death," "spir-

15. Diana L. Hayes, *Forged in the Fiery Furnace: African American Spirituality* (Maryknoll, NY: Orbis, 2012), 2 and 120–23.

16. William D. Hart, "Personal Statement," Religious Studies Faculty and Staff, The University of North Carolina at Greensboro, https://tinyurl.com/yd3ptfsz, 1. Also see William D. Hart, *Black Religion: Malcolm X, Julius Lester, and Jan Willis* (New York: Palgrave Macmillan, 2008).

itual means," and "spiritual ends." The point is to examine how this terminology revealed King's tendency to relate the spiritual to not only God and/or the supernatural sphere, but to the whole of humanity, life, the universe, and, indeed, what he saw as "the interrelated structure of all reality."[17] This chapter concludes with reflections on King's tendencies toward what James W. Fowler calls "universalizing faith," or, in more precise terms, looking beyond "self as the center of experience" to participate "in God or ultimate reality" as "the center of experience."[18]

What King's use of the language of the *spiritual* reflected about his own spirituality, spiritual life, and importance as a spiritual leader is covered here in relationship to what he sought to achieve through nonviolent creative dissent and activism. Spirituality for King never encouraged passivity in the face of social evil and a retreat into otherworldly values. He was convinced that spirituality and religion, in varying degrees, had to do not only with the "inescapable ultimate concern" of humanity, of saving souls and integrating humans with God, but also with improving the social, economic, and political conditions that damn, strangle, and cripple the mind, body, and soul.[19] Thus, chapter 3 also builds on the idea that courses through *Revives My Soul Again*; namely, that King was both a proponent and practitioner of a spirituality that was in essence powerful, engaging, balanced, and genuinely inclusive.

Chapter 4 examines King's conception of the Holy Spirit, which is seriously neglected in even the most impressive scholarship on King's theology.[20] Here Aaron J. Howard, an emerging young scholar in the

17. Martin Luther King Jr., *The Trumpet of Conscience* (New York: Harper & Row, 1987; originally published in 1967), 69–70.

18. The term "universalizing spirituality" might also be used here. See James W. Fowler, *Stages of Faith: The Psychology of Human Development* (New York: HarperOne, 1995; originally published in 1981), 199–210.

19. Martin Luther King Jr., *Stride toward Freedom: The Montgomery Story* (New York: Harper & Row, 1958), 36.

20. The lack of any careful attention to King's idea of the Holy Spirit is quite evident in virtually all of the major works on the theology of the civil rights leader. See, for examples, John Colin Harris, "The Theology of Martin Luther King, Jr.," PhD diss., Duke University (1974); Joseph Milburn Thompson, "Martin Luther King, Jr. and Christian Witness: An Interpretation of King Based on a Theological Model of Prophetic Witness," PhD diss., Fordham University (1981); Noel Leo Erskine, *King among the Theologians* (Cleveland: Pilgrim, 1994); and Luther D. Ivory, *Toward a Theology of Radical Involvement: The Theological Legacy of Martin Luther King, Jr.* (Nashville: Abingdon, 1997). Fleeting but important attention is devoted to the subject in Richard Wayne Wills Sr., *Martin Luther King, Jr. and the Image of God* (New York: Oxford University Press, 2009), 75, 105, 108–10, and 152. Interestingly enough, the absence of attention to King's thinking regarding the Holy Spirit is quite obvious even in works that treat him in relation to black theology and the southern revivalist tradition. See, for examples, Paul Russell Garber, "Martin Luther King, Jr.: Theologian and Precursor of Black Theology," PhD diss., The Florida State University (1973); and Edward L. Moore, "Billy Graham and Martin Luther

fields of religion, ethics, and society, challenges the view, advanced by black liberation theologian J. Deotis Roberts Sr., that King "failed to accentuate the importance of the guidance and power of the Holy Spirit" in his theological perspective. In contrast, Howard argues "that King's writings and speeches evince a deep awareness of and attention to the work of the Holy Spirit." Howard further elaborates the point, noting that King's sense of the Holy Spirit was rooted in his views concerning the immanence and activity of God in history and in human experience—that it was not only personal and historical, but also had social and political implications, particularly in that it was intimately connected to his civil rights campaigns.[21]

Howard's focus on King's pneumatology further reveals the depth and vitality of both King's spirituality and his definition of what constituted a disciplined and meaningful spiritual life. We learn more about King's spiritual wisdom, spiritual vision, and sense of spiritual truths, and also about those elements of King's spirituality that encouraged and inspired radical civil disobedience in the face of social evil and injustice. As Howard's chapter suggests, King brought new meaning to his conception of the Holy Spirit by insisting that the "Lo, I will be with you always" language in the New Testament does not mean that believers should passively wait on God alone to act in history, but that they should strive vigorously themselves, as co-workers and co-sufferers with God, for the actualization of the beloved community, which is the ethical equivalent of both the theological ideal of the kingdom of God on earth and the socio-economic and political ideal of the democratic socialist society.[22]

Stewart Burns, civil rights movement historian and King biographer, focuses in chapter 5 on Martin Luther King Jr.'s spiritual odyssey, during which his religious foundation in the black Social Gospel and personalist

King, Jr.: An Inquiry into White and Black Revivalist Traditions," PhD diss., Vanderbilt University (1979).

21. See Aaron J. Howard, "Casting out Demons of Injustice: A Pneumatological Interpretation of Martin Luther King, Jr.'s Passive Resistance," unpublished paper presented at the American Academy of Religion, San Francisco, California (21 November 2011), 1–14. Here Howard disagrees with J. Deotis Roberts while siding with the theological ethicist Rufus Burrow Jr. See J. Deotis Roberts, *Bonhoeffer and King: Speaking Truth to Power* (Louisville: Westminster John Knox, 2005), 128; and Rufus Burrow Jr., "Bonhoeffer and King: Speaking Truth to Power: A Book Review," *Encounter*, 67, no. 3 (2006): 330.

22. Martin Luther King Jr., *Strength to Love* (Philadelphia: Fortress, 1981; originally published in 1963), 131–32 and 154–55; Kenneth L. Smith and Ira G. Zepp Jr., *Search for the Beloved Community: The Thinking of Martin Luther King, Jr.* (Valley Forge, PA: Judson, 1998; originally published in 1974), 101, 111, 142–43, and 153–54; and Kenneth L. Smith, "The Radicalization of Martin Luther King, Jr.: The Last Three Years," *Journal of Ecumenical Studies* 26, no. 2 (Spring 1989): 270–88.

philosophy confronted cascading crises that marked a crucial turning point in American history. According to Burns, this confrontation over five years (1963–1968) begot "a lived theology" that steeled King to face psychic assaults from all sides and from within, even as he put forth his most courageous and farsighted leadership.[23] Burns goes on to assert that King's lived theology emerged after his most severe crisis, the annihilation of four girls in a Birmingham church in 1963, which brought on the depression that plagued King for the rest of his life. King's deep suffering and fierce nonviolent combat, Burns continues, forged upon his spiritual foundation a theology of action, thus showing how shared suffering inspirits the souls of sufferers and connects them to form the beloved community, leading ultimately toward a union of humanity and divinity. With this in mind, Burns carefully examines King's growing belief that transforming himself, his community, his adversaries, and the American people as a whole called for immersion in darkness as well as light. In other words, the point is that healing the soul-sickness of self and society required, in King's judgment, going through a "dark night of the soul."

Burns's chapter grows out of his earlier scholarship, which "sought to integrate the spiritual and political realms of Martin Luther King Jr.'s life and work." Burns rightly contends that this synthesis is missing in most works on King, in part because King never found the time to draw together his political mission and his spiritual revelations into a coherent theology. Burns is apparently mindful of King's significance as a theologian, but he is more interested in sharpening the picture of King as fundamentally a spiritual leader and practitioner of an inclusive, enlightened spirituality open to all peoples.[24] Even so, Burns's focus on the wedding of the "spiritual" and the "political" in King's consciousness and activities clearly supports the growing contention that King's legacy must be considered in any serious study of both political theology and American civil religion.[25]

23. See Charles Marsh et al., eds., *Lived Theology: New Perspectives on Method, Style, and Pedagogy* (New York: Oxford University Press, 2016).

24. Burns, *To the Mountaintop*, 12–482; and Burns, ed., *Cosmic Companionship*, 7.

25. See Lewis V. Baldwin, "The Political Theology of Martin Luther King, Jr.," Shaun Casey and Michael Kessler, eds., *The Oxford Handbook of Political Theology* (New York: Oxford University Press, forthcoming); John D. Elder, "Martin Luther King, Jr. and American Civil Religion," *Harvard Divinity Bulletin*, n.s. 1, no. 3 (Spring 1968): 17–18; Robert N. Bellah and Phillip E. Hammond, *Varieties of Civil Religion* (New York: Harper & Row, 1980), 15, 171–72, 175, and 194–95; Andrew M. Manis, *Southern Civil Religions in Conflict: Civil Rights and the Culture Wars* (Macon, GA: Mercer University Press, 2002), 4 and 9–10; and Lewis V. Baldwin, et al., *The Legacy of Martin Luther King, Jr.: The Boundaries of Law, Politics, and Religion* (Notre Dame: University of Notre Dame Press, 2002), 42–51.

In chapter 6, Lewis V. Baldwin discusses King's prayer life as the most critical component of his spirituality. For Baldwin, King's discipline and practice of prayer were reflective of his sense that spirituality functions both vertically and horizontally; that it not only connects humans with God, but also humans with themselves, each other, and the world. This was ultimately King's point in his celebrated sermon, "The Three Dimensions of the Complete Life,"[26] and also what he was trying to convey when speaking about "the interrelated structure of all reality."[27] Baldwin makes this clear while highlighting King's sense of the place and significance of prayer in the civil rights movement and in the struggles of the oppressed and marginalized worldwide. Mindful of the role that prayer assumed in King's personal life and his public ministry, Baldwin concludes that King saw prayer as both a kind of "self-purification" and a "creative energy" that invigorated civil and human rights movements. In other words, prayer figured prominently into the structuring of King's own religious life and in how he translated faith into human possibilities.

Much of Baldwin's emphasis is not only on the ways in which King drank from the wellsprings of the black prayer tradition, but also on the genius he displayed in living out and building on or expanding that tradition.[28] Central to the discussion is King's creative use of various forms of prayer, and especially the phenomenon of the prayer circle, which constituted a direct link to King's ancestors in Africa and on the plantations of the American South. The prayer circle was an important ritual for African slaves and free Africans who met in the cabins, the praise houses, the brush harbors, and at events such as the annual August Quarterly festival in Wilmington Delaware, and, under King's leadership, it was reclaimed and united with the picket line, thus becoming perhaps the most important ritual of the civil rights movement of the 1950s and '60s.[29] In any case, chapter 6 is yet another reminder that King's spiritu-

26. Carson and Holloran, eds., *Knock at Midnight*, 117–19 and 122–40.

27. King, *Trumpet of Conscience*, 69–70.

28. See Baldwin, *Never to Leave Us Alone*, 20–23.

29. Sterling Stuckey rightly argues that the ring shout was "the most important African ritual in antebellum America," but it is also clear in the case of the August Quarterly meetings, which dated back to 1813, that the ring shout and the prayer circle came together and were often inseparable in the consciousness and practices of people of African descent during worship. This blending process extended into the late nineteenth and early twentieth centuries. See Sterling Stuckey, *Slave Culture: Nationalist Theory and the Foundations of Black America* (New York: Oxford University Press, 1987), viii; *Every Evening*, Wilmington, Delaware (28 August 1882): 1; *The Delaware State Journal*, Wilmington, Delaware (30 August 1883): 1; Lewis V. Baldwin, *"Invisible" Strands in African Methodism: A History of the African Union Methodist Protestant and Union American Methodist Episcopal Churches, 1805–1980* (Metuchen, NJ: Scarecrow, 1983), 137–41; and Baldwin, *Never to Leave Us Alone*, 21–22.

ality must be understood not only phenomenologically, but also in both a historical and cultural context.

Chapter 7 explores the relationship between King's spirituality and his preaching, based on a selective use and reading of some of his sermons. Written by Mervyn A. Warren, emeritus professor of preaching (homiletics) at Oakwood University, it concludes that much of King's spirituality and sense of the spiritual life found expression in his preaching. Looking beyond the power and dynamism of King's preaching, the mysterious quality of his rhetorical wisdom and rare gift of oratory and conversational resonance, the melodic and poetic quality of his sermonic language, and his mastery of a certain kind of pulpit style and manner, Warren tells us that King's preaching provided timeless and practical guides for living out the Christ-centered spiritual life. Throughout this chapter, Warren is also sensitive to King's struggle to become the message that he shared in his sermons, especially insofar as his own enduring spiritual search was concerned.

Warren's chapter dispels any notion that King, like so many other preachers in his time, was merely a spiritual merchant who marketed a certain brand of impotent and escapist Christianity through his proclamations.[30] Warren insists instead that the messages echoing through King's sermons were, from a spiritual standpoint, always inviting, enlightening, illuminating, liberating, and empowering. His sermons gave voice to the most complex and necessary facets of the spiritual quest and the authentic spiritual life, and also exposed his gifts as perhaps the most important, inspiring, and well-known spiritual leader of his generation. But, at the same time, Warren reminds us, in ways subtle and not so subtle, that the spirituality of King's preaching was never devoid of that call for active human involvement in bringing the kingdom of God to earth.

In chapter 8, Nichole R. Phillips, an assistant professor of sociology, religion, and culture, explains King's use of a "spirituality of improvisation" in the form of mythical stories, rhetoric, and ritual in his "I Have a Dream" speech to redefine America. Beginning with the sermonic tone of "I Have a Dream" and the responses it generated from the audience who heard it, including the larger world that was exposed to it, Phillips, in more specific terms, analyzes the ways in which King employed language, religious myth, ritual, and American religious history in the speech to reframe America's national identity or to reenvision

30. Here Warren echoes the position set forth in Gayraud S. Wilmore, *Black Religion and Black Radicalism: An Interpretation of the Religious History of African Americans* (Maryknoll, NY: Orbis, 1998), 204.

"a new America."[31] Phillips's chapter is particularly instructive in view of King's own efforts, largely through his Southern Christian Leadership Conference (SCLC), to heal and transform the nation not only socially, politically, and economically, but spiritually as well. Thinking in terms of a more collective effort in this regard, involving the mass of his people, King envisioned this as a struggle "to redeem the soul of America," or to "bring a special spiritual and moral contribution to American life."[32]

Phillips's chapter is actually suggestive of how religious myth and ritual as a "spirituality of improvisation," harnessing the creative nature of the spirit, were related in King's consciousness and activities, for both are about probing the deeper meanings of life while envisioning a higher and better state of human existence. Clearly, King turned to both religious myth and spiritual language to articulate and define his dream, a dream that he, according to Phillips, mapped onto ritual behavior in the form of his public speaking and preaching.

Walter E. Fluker, a social ethicist, begins chapter 9 "with operational definitions of spirituality, ethics, and leadership." From that point, he integrates King into the discussion with an eye toward fulfilling a threefold purpose. First, to "build upon the discussion of leadership literature that incorporates spirituality and ethics with a model of discourse" he calls "ethical leadership," which "finds resonance with King's transformed nonconformity formulation." Second, to "examine the ways in which" King's "dialectical appropriation of knowledge, faith, and practice informed his view of transformed nonconformity." Finally, to "recommend a conceptual grid for black church leadership that captures the inherent tensions in the *doubleness* of black life and offers directions for new subversive possibilities utilizing the triune ethical constructs of character, civility, and community." Generally speaking, Fluker shows that so much of what King believed, said, and did was grounded in both

31. Nichole R. Phillips, "The Role of Religious Myth in Shifting Martin Luther King, Jr.'s 'I Have a Dream' Speech to the Greatest Prophetic and Perduring Political Sermon in Perpetuity," unpublished paper, Vanderbilt University (13 December 2005), 1–36. Much of what Phillips says about King's "I Have a Dream" oration is supported by the insights of the religious commentator Ray Waddle. Waddle sees the speech as not only "a political reckoning for the cause of racial harmony," but also as a masterpiece that "marked a spiritual turning"—as "one of the last public religious moments to touch the national soul under the imagery of biblical religion." "Our politics haven't been the same since," Waddle concludes. See Ray Waddle, "Message of the Week: King Wielded a Spiritual Maturity We Rarely See," *The Tennessean,* January 19, 2013, 3B.

32. "To redeem the soul of America" was actually the motto of King's SCLC, and it obviously carried spiritual implications. Martin Luther King Jr. to Dr. P. J. Ellis, unpublished version of a letter (6 February 1960), KCLA, 1; Washington, ed., *Testament of Hope*, 317; and Adam Fairclough, "The Southern Christian Leadership Conference and the Second Reconstruction, 1957–1973," *The South Atlantic Quarterly* 8, no. 2 (Spring 1981): 178.

"a profound sense of spirituality" and a "searching ethical awareness," and he provides rich and fresh insights into the connection between spirituality, ethics, and leadership in King's thinking and praxis.[33]

Fluker shows how King's leadership modeled the relationship between spirituality and social transformation. It was "King's spiritual genius," Fluker concludes, that provided him with "the essential assets and tools" to lead a nonviolent revolution of values that moved America beyond "parochially applied democratic principles to concrete proposals for inclusiveness and action." Thus, King became, in Fluker's estimation, a supreme embodiment of the black Christian tradition of spirituality and social transformation.[34]

In chapter 10, Beverly J. Lanzetta, a theologian and spiritual teacher, treats King as a social mystic who was also representative of a pluralist or global spirituality. Based on a reading of Lanzetta's piece, one senses that King was very much like the Indian leader Mohandas K. Gandhi, the American Catholic monk and mystic Thomas Merton, the Jewish rabbi Abraham J. Heschel, the African American theologian Howard Thurman, the Buddhist monk Thich Nhat Hanh, and other celebrated pioneers of a global spirituality,[35] especially in the sense that King combined a disciplined spiritual life with a commitment to and engagement with the needs of humanity and the world. Lanzetta evidently feels that there were some continuities and discontinuities between the spiritual journeys of King and these other figures, and that they all shared a conception of a world that is globally interrelated and interdependent, an understanding of spirituality as lived experience encompassing all faith traditions, a sense of spirituality as involving a life of service to humanity, a belief in nonviolence as a spiritual discipline that leads to wholeness and community, and a continuing quest for a spirituality that affords ultimate meaning, inner peace, human fulfillment, purpose, and transcendence. But Lanzetta, the author of some seven books on global spirituality, is essentially concerned with King's own personal engagement with the life of the spirit and how that informed his love ethic, his discipline of nonviolence, and his efforts for social change.

Lanzetta's chapter supports the notion that it was largely King's interfaith vision and view of himself as "a citizen of the world"[36] that made his

33. Walter E. Fluker, "Transformed Nonconformity: Spirituality, Ethics, and Leadership in the Life and Work of Martin Luther King Jr.," *The Princeton Seminary Bulletin* 25, n.s., no. 1 (2004): 28, 35, and 53.

34. Fluker, "Transformed Nonconformity," 34–35.

35. See Beverly Lanzetta, *Emerging Heart: Global Spirituality and the Sacred* (Minneapolis: Fortress, 2009), 1–160.

36. King, *Trumpet of Conscience*, 31; and Martin Luther King Jr., *"In a Single Garment of Des-*

spirituality and his spiritual life so genuine, alive, and dynamic. In other words, King felt that he was so much a part of humanity as a whole that he could not realize the fullness of what God created him to be until all other humans realized the fullness of what God created them to be. His spirituality, Lanzetta concludes, was sensitive to religious and cultural pluralism. He also had much to say about the "spiritual power that the Negro," or his own people, could "radiate to the world" through "love, understanding, good will, and nonviolence."[37] This was the profundity of both King's global spirituality and his theological vision. Lanzetta's stress on King's global spirituality comports with much of the content of *Revives My Soul Again*, which is not merely about re-centering King in our renderings of a Christian spirituality, but also about reclaiming his significance as one who envisioned and contributed to a spiritual reality that affirmed the essential unity and oneness of divine creation and the timeless truths in all faith traditions. Spirituality is that one category of human experience that had the greatest impact on how King perceived the world around him. Clearly, King, as Lanzetta suggests at points, offered a paradigm for how spirituality in different forms might best intersect with a global rights culture and agenda.[38]

In the eleventh and final chapter of *Revives My Soul Again,* Michael Brandon McCormack, an authority in African American religion and cultural studies, takes the discussion in a decidedly different direction, giving careful consideration to the continuities and discontinuities between Kingian spirituality and what he terms the "nonconformist" or "deviant" spirituality of the contemporary Black Lives Matter movement (BLM). Beginning with the question, "What would Martin Luther King Jr. say about the Black Lives Matter Movement?," McCormack concedes that King's engagement and/or exchanges with the black power movement in his own time are suggestive of how he might deal with BLM today. McCormack goes on to argue that BLM's failure to conform to the politics of black middle-class religious respectability, as exempli-

tiny": A Global Vision of Justice—Martin Luther King, Jr., ed. Lewis V. Baldwin (Boston: Beacon, 2012), 190–209.

37. King, *Stride toward Freedom*, 224; King, *Where Do We Go from Here?,* 57; Martin Luther King Jr., "Untitled Column on European Tour," typed version prepared for *New York Amsterdam News* (September 17, 1964), KCLA, 2; and Coretta Scott King, *My Life with Martin Luther King, Jr.* (New York: Henry Holt, 1993; originally published in 1969), 96 and 239. In his very last essay, "A Testament of Hope," published posthumously, King declared that "in another sense we are both Americans and Africans. Our very bloodlines are a mixture. I hope and feel that out of the universality of our experience, we can help make peace and harmony in this world more possible." See Washington, ed., *Testament of Hope*, 318.

38. Here Lanzetta adds significantly to her discussion of those rich traditions of a global spirituality that constitute the core of her outstanding book, *Emerging Heart* (2007).

fied by Martin Luther King Jr. and the civil rights movement in the 1950s and '60s, does not necessarily amount to a rejection of either "spirituality" or the spirituality of King, but, rather, a reimagining and renegotiation of both "spirituality" and "King" by young, poor, female, queer, tattooed, and angry activists in BLM. In a stunning conclusion, McCormack insists that that there are "compelling connections" and/or "continuities" between King's spirituality and the non-traditional and non-black church-based spirituality of the Black Lives Matter movement.

McCormack's chapter reaffirms a point that echoes through parts of this volume; namely, that King's spirituality still holds some meaningfulness and/or relevance for social activists in the twenty-first century. At the same time, McCormack is mindful of those points at which King is not so relevant. He feels that the very existence and spirit of the Black Lives Matter movement expose the need for a critical approach that scrutinizes "the spirituality of Martin Luther King Jr." in public debates about the spiritual, moral, and sociopolitical status of vulnerable black youth involved in BLM.

Clearly, *spirituality* is the unifying theme of *Revives My Soul Again*. It shows that King had a life-long interest in spirituality and the spiritual life, and that this is what compelled him to study sociology, religion, theology, history, philosophy, ethics, metaphysics, and logic during his college, seminary, and graduate school years. He found in these disciplines tools to describe spiritual beings, the spiritual journey, and the spiritual life. What King got from these disciplines, and what he gained through the prism of daily experience, aided his spiritual odyssey over the course of virtually his entire life, and particularly his endless struggle with core questions that undergird every spiritual search: Who am I? Where did I originate? What is my relationship to transcendent, spiritual reality, and how should that figure into my connections to natural social reality? How should I live my life? What is the ultimate goal of life? As this volume indicates, King came to see that spirituality, which he equated with religious experience, is not simply about participating in some organized religion—that it is about the power and workings of what he called "our own inner being," or that process through which humans seek inner peace, ultimate meaning, purpose, and transcendence. King's sense of the spiritual journey as an ongoing discovery of the self and its relationship to other selves, and of spirituality as *lived experience* rooted in service to both God and humanity,[39] never gets lost in this book.

39. Carson et al., eds., *Papers*, 1:232–34, 246–51, and 408–13; Carson et al., eds., *Papers*, 2:87–88; Clayborne Carson et al., eds., *The Papers of Martin Luther King, Jr.: To Save the Soul*

Another point regarding spirituality as the unifying theme of this volume should also be made here. A number of the chapters either mention or focus at some length on Martin Luther King Jr.'s "kitchen vision," which occurred in Montgomery, Alabama, on January 27, 1956, but the treatments are complementary with very different purposes. Thus, the fact that some of the chapters draw on common quotes or episodes, especially when highlighting King's "kitchen vision," is not really problematic. This merely establishes the point that the "kitchen vision"— which involved silence, meditation, prayer, a deep sense of the divine presence, and "the quiet assurance of an inner voice"—was perhaps the pivotal experience, and even the defining moment, in King's spirituality and spiritual life.[40]

Revives My Soul Again is quite timely because it speaks to the kind of personal, spiritual, and ethical challenges that King's spirituality and spiritual life still present for humans as a whole, and especially those who are either questioning or turning away from organized, established, and institutionalized religion, or seeking some new avenues to spiritual guidance.[41] In fact, this book concludes that the story of King's spiritual life is perennially available and relevant for this contemporary age, and is thus capable of informing our own inward journeys. Perhaps his story can help enliven our pilgrimages toward a healthier and more inclusive, vital, and engaging spirituality. The contributors to this volume firmly believe that a creative appropriation of many of King's spiritual insights and practices are needed in these times, in which there is so much uncertainty and insecurity, and such a quickening of the pulse of life.

Revives My Soul Again is also timely in light of the ongoing conver-

of America, January 1961–August 1962 (Berkeley: University of California Press, 2014), 7:576; and Washington, ed., *Testament of Hope*, 231. King also spoke in terms of the "inner strength and integrity" of the self, which carried obvious implications in terms of the *spiritual*. He had in mind much of what the great theologian and philosopher of religion Howard Thurman, whom he read, called "the inward journey." See Alex Ayres, ed., *The Wisdom of Martin Luther King, Jr.: An A-to-Z Guide to the Ideas and Ideals of the Great Civil Rights Leader* (New York: Penguin, 1993), 36; and Howard Thurman, *The Inward Journey: Meditations on the Spiritual Quest* (Richmond, IN: Friends United, 1977; originally published in 1961), 14–155. Drawing on Thurman, I used "The Inward Journey" as the title of chapter 1 in my book, *Never to Leave Us Alone*, which chronicles King's prayer life.

40. See King, *Stride toward Freedom*, 134–35; and Carson and Holloran, eds., *Knock at Midnight*, 159–64. As part of his quest for "self-purification," King often combined moments of silence, meditation, and prayer with what he called "my quiet day of reading" and "endless self-analysis." See Washington, ed., *Testament of Hope*, 372 and 376.

41. Ray Waddle, "Spiritual, but Not Religious Is Becoming a Common Refrain," *The Tennessean*, March 7, 2015, 10A; Saritha Prabhu, "Spirituality in U.S. Is Evolving," *The Tennessean*, September 1, 2013, 17A; Lauren Markoe, "More Americans Reject Religion, but Believers Firm in Faith, Study Says," *The Tennessean*, November 4, 2015, 2B; and Ray Waddle, "Poetry Provides Ancient, Unfettered Spiritual Solace," *The Tennessean*, April 20, 2013, 3B.

sations about the role of religion and spirituality in public life. King's words and actions anticipated this discussion on many levels, and the vitality of religion and spirituality in public life should be accounted as a fundamental aspect of the legacy of both King and the civil rights movement.[42] King was determined to break down those seemingly impenetrable walls—not only social, political, and economic but also spiritual—that hindered progress toward peace, understanding, cooperation, and wholeness, and, to achieve this goal, he put his spirituality to the service of invigorating an impulse toward radical Christian action. At the root of his spirituality was a desire to know, love, learn, and significantly change humanity for the better. He knew that humanity's problem was deeper than entrenched racial structures and attitudes, political and economic systems, and the law—that it was ultimately a problem of the human heart—and that the hearts of people had to be changed before his sustained efforts for peace, social justice, and equal rights could be fully translated into practical reality, or into the kind of public policy initiatives that benefitted the common good.

This is essentially what *Revives My Soul Again* is all about. King's deep, vital, engaging, balanced, contagious, and wholistic spirituality is presented here with a vigor and power fresh for our generation. Although this is a book about King's continuing relevance, it is not meant to suggest that King is *the* authoritative source when it comes to every spiritual challenge we face in the twenty-first century.[43] We view him, first and foremost, as an example and an inspiration, but not as the great leader with all the answers. In short, we only hope this collaborative effort will stand as an eloquent, provocative, and timely testimony to the enduring power and relevance of certain aspects of the legacy of Martin Luther King Jr.

42. For an essay that advances this thesis while placing King at the center of the conversation, see Lewis V. Baldwin, "The Public Perversion of Religion," *Orbis* 5, no. 7 (April 2006): 12–13 and 18.

43. Traci C. West rightly cautions us against overburdening King with the role of "the great man" with "the answers" to so many of today's problems. She sees many sweeping statements about King and his "supposed current political positions'" as indicative of "the misuse of King," "of an overly inflated image of King," "of a kind of deification of King," and "of a disturbing, masculinist pattern." See Traci C. West, "Gay Rights and the Misuse of Martin," in Lewis V. Baldwin and Rufus Burrow Jr., *The Domestication of Martin Luther King, Jr.: Clarence B. Jones, Right-Wing Conservatism, and the Manipulation of the King Legacy* (Eugene, OR: Cascade, 2013), 145–46 and 156.

1.

Blessed Assurance: Martin Luther King Jr. and the Consolation of the Soul

VICTOR ANDERSON

> God is able to give us interior resources to confront the trials and difficulties of life. Each of us faces circumstances in life which compel us to carry heavy burdens of sorrow. Adversity assails us with hurricane force. Glowing sunrises are transformed into darkest nights. Our highest hopes are blasted and our noblest dreams are shattered.
>
> —Martin Luther King Jr.[1]

> Rock o' my soul in the bosom of Abraham
> Rock o' my soul in the bosom of Abraham
> Rock o' my soul in the bosom of Abraham
> Oh rock o' my soul
> Why don't you rock o' my soul?
>
> —Negro spiritual[2]

The following philosophical reflections center on affective dynamics in Martin Luther King Jr.'s spiritual experience. They focus on pervasive doubt, the will to believe, and the assurance that faith brings as consolation to the soul. Turning to affectivity will excite distrust in some King scholars. It seems to diminish to sentimentality King's robust and daring confrontations with and prophetic witness to power. Others may worry that a focus on the affective dynamics of King's religious experience, rather than on his critical consciousness, brackets his heroic lead-

1. Martin Luther King Jr., *Strength to Love* (Philadelphia: Fortress, 1981; originally published in 1963), 111.

2. William Francis Allen et al., eds., *Slave Songs of the United States* (New York: Peter Smith, 1951; originally published in 1867), 73; and Miles Mark Fisher, *Negro Slave Songs in the United States* (New York: Citadel, 1990; originally published in 1953), 100.

ership and intellectual and strategic consciousness as clues to his political acumen and civil rights successes. These worries are not lost to King scholars such as Baldwin, Burrow, Burns, and others.[3] They have written extensively on the intellectual, cultural, and critical consciousness early manifested in King's scholarly journey from Morehouse to Boston University, which are evident in his speeches, sermons, interviews, debates, hearings, and engagements with student movements, religious leaders, and political powers.

But, King spoke of *the whole self.* He directed his social witness in sermons and speeches to whole selves who were self-alienated, fractured, anxiety ridden, blunted in conscience, feelings, and moral disregard, stricken by the banality of the evils of segregation, or resigned to the feelings of futility and toward eradicating it.[4] And to these *whole selves,* he says, "For religion is like a mighty wind that knocks down doors and breaks down walls and makes that possible, and even easy, which seems difficult and impossible. It is religion; it is a proper faith that is the answer to the tensions of life."[5] After reading Walter Rauschenbusch's *Christianity and Social Crisis*, King says,

> The gospel at its best deals with the whole man, not only his soul but also his body, not only his spiritual well-being, but his material well-being. Any religion that professes to be concerned about the souls of men and is not concerned about the slums that damn them, the economic conditions that strangle them and the social conditions that cripple them, is a spiritually moribund religion.[6]

In as much as King wielded powers of description, explanation, and analysis to open up critical consciousness on our social problems, he did so with the whole self as the clue to repentance and redemption of individual souls and of the soul of the nation.

King did not divorce the behaviors, actions, or habits of people from their affections of trepidation, indifference, fear or hate. And he did not urge the individual or collective toward walking up freedom's road

3. See, for example, Lewis V. Baldwin, *There Is a Balm in Gilead: The Cultural Roots of Martin Luther King, Jr.* (Minneapolis: Fortress, 1991); Rufus Burrow Jr., *God and Human Dignity: The Personalism, Theology, and Ethics of Martin Luther King, Jr.* (Notre Dame: University of Notre Dame Press, 2006); and Stewart Burns, *To the Mountaintop: Martin Luther King, Jr.'s Sacred Mission to Save America, 1955–1968* (San Francisco: HarperSanFrancisco, 2004).

4. Clayborne Carson et al., eds, *The Papers of Martin Luther King, Jr.: Advocate of the Social Gospel, September 1948–March 1963* (Berkeley: University of California Press, 2007), 6:262.

5. Carson et al., eds., *Papers,* 6:264.

6. Martin Luther King Jr., *Stride toward Freedom: The Montgomery Story* (New York: Harper & Row, 1958), 36; and King, *Strength to Love*, 150.

without appealing to the affections of love, *agape*, and the sense of divine companionship as spiritual and moral norms for living nonviolence, not only as a strategy of social change but as a form of life:

> In struggling for human dignity the oppressed people of the world must not succumb to the temptation of becoming bitter or indulging in hate campaigns. To retaliate with hate and bitterness would do nothing but intensify the existence of hate in our world. We have learned through the grim realities of life and history that hate and violence solve nothing. They only serve to push us deeper and deeper into the mire. Violence begets violence; hate begets hate; and toughness begets a greater toughness. It is all a descending spiral, and the end is destruction—for everybody. Along the way of life, someone must have sense enough and morality enough to cut off the chain of hate by projecting the ethic of love to the center of our lives.[7]

These philosophical reflections are but a small look into the affective shapes of doubt and assurance as motivating structures of King's soul life. To be sure, his soul life was deep and expansive, and heightened at times to the greatest degree by sorrows and joys, excitement and dismay, confidence and doubts, euphoria and grief, which are brought on by his just getting on with the daily ordinary living and by the trials and persecutions of life brought by his calling. As Jonathan Edwards below reminds us, with anyone, the affections of the soul admit powers of emotion, feeling, and senses, some clear and others dull. They admit dull indifference and intense desires, feelings of sadness and overwhelming grief, faint laughter and joy overflowing, the dull sense of confusion of mind and the burdening of the soul with doubt. However, King knew all too well that where inquiry and belief may settle confusions of the mind, faith satisfies the anguish of doubt with blessed assurance. Remembering Mother Pollard, a dear dedicated participant in the Montgomery Movement and a great consoler of King's soul when he found his back against the wall, King recalls:

> Mother Pollard has now passed on to glory and I have known very few quiet days. I have been tortured without and tormented within by the raging fires of tribulation. I have been forced to muster what strength and courage I have to withstand howling winds of pain and jostling storms of adversity. But as the years have unfolded the eloquently simple words of Mother Pollard have come back again and again to give me light and peace and guidance to my troubled soul. "God's gonna take care of you."[8]

7. Quoted in James M. Washington, ed., *A Testament of Hope: The Essential Writings and Speeches of Martin Luther King, Jr.* (San Francisco: Harper & Row, 1986), 87–88.

8. Carson, et. al., eds., *Papers*, 6:544.

These philosophical reflections on doubt and assurance as motivational structures of King's spiritual life begin with a short excursion into the ideas of religious experience and religious affections derived from William James and Jonathan Edwards. They then consider these affective structures of doubt and assurance in light of two critical existential situations in King's soul life where his faith is tested to the highest degree. Of course, there are many entry points, which might have been chosen over the course of his life. But throughout his life, King's struggles with doubt and assurance seem most acute when confronted by senses of futility that tend to accompany death and the threat of death. Disappointedly, the needs of this volume do not permit more expanded reflections on the many occasions. So, these reflections focus on the shapes of doubt and assurance surrounding the death of King's grandmother, Jennie C. Parks Williams, in May 1941, and the eulogy of the martyred children of Sixteenth Street Baptist Church in Birmingham in September 1963.[9] Selecting these two episodes, from the many, is perhaps most determined by the present religious situation, where despair, doubt, and senses of futility are normative in so many young souls and have led many to suicide and early deaths by street and police violence. King held firm to the idea of the immortality of the soul as a belief content of his blessed assurance. Perhaps, then, the immortal souls of our martyred children may have something to say to us.

PHILOSOPHICAL EXCURSUS

At first glance, it may seem weird to begin these reflections with two thinkers so separated by time and by temperaments, William James (1842–1910) and Jonathan Edwards (1703–1758). The one belongs to the modern scientific age and the other the Puritan age and the Great Awakening. Both were philosophers and scientists concerned with religious experience and with human souls. Edwards was willing to be damned for the salvation of souls from divine judgment and hell. James was concerned with the equilibrium of the psychic life. What invites them into these reflections is their empirical accounting for religious experience and the affections as motiving structures of human actions and purposes.

9. Frederick L. Downing's pastoral theology perspective is valuable for his discussion of these two episodes in light of James Fowler's classic, *Stages of Faith: The Psychology of Human Development and the Quest for Meaning* (1981). See Frederick L. Downing, *To See the Promised Land: The Faith Pilgrimage of Martin Luther King, Jr.* (Macon, GA: Mercer University Press, 1986), 97–120 and 228–34.

As a student, King indicated a high regard for Edwards's preaching genius, the potency of his use of metaphors, his powers of suasion in converting the souls, which were often accompanied by ecstatic joy or remorse in hearing his famous "Sinners in the Hands of an Angry God."[10] King was also well acquainted with the philosophy and psychology of William James, his conception of stream of consciousness and view of knowledge by acquaintance.[11] King felt that James's most recognized work "was quite in line with facts when he [also] entitled his Gilford lecture, *The Varieties of Religious Experience*; for the strictest fact about religious experience is its variety."[12]

In any talk about human "experience," we will most likely stumble into pervasive ambiguity. The word "experience" is not so troubling. American pragmatists, like James, insist that we are acted upon by cosmic events, which affect human life. So, when talking about experience, this is just our way of coming to terms, quite literally, with our being acted upon, undergoing, and participating in cosmic events. However, what these cosmic events mean is not given in the "immediate experiencing" of them. When James is thinking about experience, he has in mind nothing short of the act of "*actual experiencing*," being acted upon, undergoing or participating in an event, or, "as he liked to put it, the 'particular go' of the thing," says Smith.[13] To see just how the meaning of an experience lies in its interaction with a stream of consciousness at work in stabilizing our everyday "getting about," Smith takes us to James's example of the experiencing of a clap of thunder:

> The experience of thunder is not exhausted as an instantaneous datum of sound, a sensible simple or impression, but is part of a temporal episode, which James sought to represent by the use of hyphens. What is experienced is a sudden, sharp booming which breaks in upon a preceding silence making us vividly aware of the interruption and the contrast so that, if we may so say, we now "hear" the silence which was shattered since, as part of the familiar, prevailing situation, we had no occasion to notice it before. *The experience has the character of an event and belongs to the ongoing biography of the one who has it* [my emphasis]; to abstract from the total episode the bare sense quality of sound and call that the delivery of "experience" is, in James's view, to confuse the concrete experiencing with the abstraction and one

10. Clayborne Carson, et al., eds., *The Papers of Martin Luther King, Jr.: Called to Serve, January 1929–June 1951* (Berkeley: University of California Press, 1992), 1:345–47.

11. Carson et al., eds. *Papers*, 1:233, 246–47, 336, 345–67, and 428.

12. "William James," The King Center digital archives, https://tinyurl.com/yag9jamd.

13. John E. Smith, "The Re-conception of Experience in Pierce, James and Dewey," *The Monist: The Nature of Experience* 68, no. 4 (October 1985): 546.

> which has been dictated by the demand that experience be preeminently sensory in character.[14]

The thunder clap example highlights two things; one, we notice the clap of thunder as an in-breaking into an ongoing stream of conscious life, in this case, the silence; and, two, we would have no recognition of the clap of thunder that now breaks the silence were it not qualitatively felt as a startling experience to my silence. Thus, having an experience is not the same thing as explaining one, but recognizing this or that actual experience as falling within the stream of consciousness as this or that. This is what James means by knowledge by acquaintance with the facts of our experience.

However, James also points us to the reality of our being sensuous animals and sensuously related to planetary events. This fact did not go unnoticed by a philosopher such as Ludwig Feuerbach who says, "I differ *toto cello* from those philosophers who pluck out their eyes that they may see better; for my thought, I require the senses, especially sight; I found my ideas on materials which can be appropriated only through the activity of the senses; I do not generate the object from the thought, but the thought from the object."[15]

In trying to excavate the sphere of affectivity, Feuerbach and James are suggesting that in relation to planetary events we are not passive cogs in a machine but responsible beings. Events strike us, evoking from us corresponding responses. However, in this back and forth between cosmic events and human responses, all that we have learned and acquired in the duration of our evolutionary history has become, for us, taken for granted, acknowledged, and settled. Again, this is what James has in mind when talking about the stream of consciousness. Much of what we know from our long stream of experiential knowledge remains dormant

14. Smith, "Re-conception of Experience," 546. William James explains the stream of consciousness and interjecting jolts in his *Principles of Psychology* (1890): "The confusion is between the thoughts themselves, taken as subjective facts, and the things of which they are aware. It is natural to make this confusion, but easy to avoid it when once put on one's guard. The things are discrete and discontinuous; they do pass before us in a train or chain, making often explosive appearances and rending each other in twain. But their comings and goings and contrasts no more break the flow of the thought that thinks them than they break the time and the space in which they lie. A silence may be broken by a thunder-clap, and we may be so stunned and confused for a moment by the shock as to give no instant account to ourselves of what has happened. But that very confusion is a mental state, and a state that passes us straight over from the silence to the sound. The transition between the thought of one object and the thought of another is no more a break in the thought than a joint in a bamboo is a break in the wood. It is a part of the consciousness as much as the joint is a part of the bamboo." William James, *Complete Works of William James* (Kindle Locations 5584–93). Minerva Classics. Kindle Edition.

15. Ludwig Feuerbach, *The Essence of Christianity,* trans. George Eliot (New York: Harper & Row, 1957), xxxiv.

until, like a clap of thunder, we are now startled and awakened to new experiences. Who would not be unsettled by the sheer magnitude that planetary events inject into our nicely settled worlds of everyday experience? We at times may be thrown into *senses* of curiosity and bewilderment. However, our sensuous nature may also *feel* surprise. One might even inwardly experience a heightened sense of a newness of life or a sense of being born again by the weight of an in-breaking experience.

Still other cosmic events *affect* our already settled world of experiences with feelings of repulsion or perhaps of beauty. In this case, one is aesthetically affected. Cosmic events call forth in human experience a profound sense of others, the sense of not being alone. And this feeling, however vague, evokes a sense of kinship with others. This is a social sense, which swells up, arousing in us other senses of responsibility and obligations toward others. James Q. Wilson describes this as the "moral sense." "People have a natural moral sense, a sense that is formed out of the interaction of their innate dispositions with their earliest familiar experiences. To different degrees among different people, but to some important degree in almost all people, that moral sense shapes human behavior and the judgments people make of the behavior of others."[16]

From what has been said thus far, it is quite easy to identify different senses or feelings aroused by cosmic events and that produce *affectivities* of doubting and believing (cognitive experience), the beautiful and repulsive (aesthetic experience), kinship with the familiar and alien (social experience), and responsibility and obligations (moral experience). But is there anything in cosmic events that correspond to the "religious sense" and hence, religious experience in the same way that we may speak of the other senses? James finds in the case files that make up *The Varieties of Religious Experience* a faint, vague "quality" in human experience corresponding to the religious sense. And he describes it as a profound sense of the *more* or *the ineffable* in cosmic events. It enlarges our perceptions that we are more than meat, brain, neurons, chemical effects, and complexes. This is not to discount that there is no conscious life independent of bodies. But this felt quality of experience forms effervescent feelings of harmonious union with the *more* of the universe. What emerges in this harmonious unity between the material and immaterial, between body and mind, is the soul life.

In the soul life, James says, the believer "becomes conscious with . . . *more* of the same quality, which is operative in the universe outside of him, and which he can keep in working touch with, and in a fashion get on board of and save himself when all his lower being has gone to

16. James Q. Wilson, *The Moral Sense* (New York: The Free Press, 1993), 2.

pieces in a wreck."[17] It involves "a change of personal centre and the surrender of the lower self."[18] People undergoing or experiencing such a change, James observes, "express the appearance of exteriority of the helping power and yet account for our sense of union with it; and they fully justify our feelings of security and joy."[19] "Spiritual strength *really* increases in the subject when he has them, a new life opens for him, and they seem to him a place of conflux where the forces of two universes meet."[20]

Religious experience thus reveals in cosmic events creative transformations, an opening of particular experiences to a wider harmony of experience, and profound appreciation for the complexity of shared human experience. Religious experience reveals our sensuous vulnerability to felt qualities of the universe in what Jonathan Edwards calls "Religious Affections." For Edwards, the "religious affections" are qualitatively distinct responses to life's trials.[21] His essay is based on his commentary on 1 Peter 1:8, written to the faithful suffering persecution and whose trials evoked love to Christ and joy unspeakable in Christ:

> The world was ready to wonder, what strange principle it was, that influenced them to expose themselves to so great sufferings, to forsake the things that were seen, and renounce all that was dear and pleasant, which was the object of sense. . . . Although there was nothing that the world saw, or that the Christian themselves ever saw with their bodily eyes, that thus influenced and supported them, yet they had a supernatural principle of love to something *unseen;* they loved Jesus Christ, for they saw him spiritually, whom the world saw not, and whom they themselves had never seen with bodily eyes.[22]

Edwards is not degrading ordinary love, which we experience profoundly in ordinary living. Rather, he describes the love of persecuted Christians as qualitatively heightened to the greatest degree by life's trials. Edwards then describes the affection of joy as a qualitative mode of experience:

17. William James, *The Varieties of Religious Experience: A Study of Human Nature* (New York: Macmillan, 1961), 394.

18. James, *Varieties*, 394.

19. James, *Varieties*, 394.

20. James, *Varieties*, 394.

21. Jonathan Edwards, "A Treatise Concerning the Religious Affections," in *Jonathan Edwards: Basic Writings*, ed. Ola Elizabeth Winslow (New York: New American Library, 1966), 184–95.

22. Edwards, "Religious Affections," 186.

> There are two things, which the apostle takes notice of in the text concerning joy. 1. The manner in which it raises, the way in which Christ, though unseen, is the foundation of it, viz. by *faith*; which is the evidence of things not seen; In *whom, though now ye see him not, yet BELIEVING, ye rejoice.* 2. The nature of joy; unspeakable and full of glory. Unspeakable in the kind it is; very different from worldly joys and carnal delights; of a vastly pure, sublime, and heavenly nature, something supernatural, and truly divine, and so ineffably excellent! The sublimity and exquisite sweetness of which there were no words to set forth. Unspeakable also in degree; it having pleased God to give them this joy with a liberal hand, in the state of persecution.[23]

Edwards concludes, "True religion, in great part, consists in holy affections."[24] It consists in love and joy, which through the trials of life are refined in tastes, sentiment, and most affectively in the vitality of the soul. "The affections are no other than the more vigorous and sensible exercise of the inclination and will of the soul."[25] The affections incline or move the soul to action. They invigorate the soul in heightened senses of what Edwards calls "sensible exercises" of the soul that include not only pleasures, happiness, and the beautiful and sublime, but also in their opposites—displeasure, grief, and repulsion, even hate. Most striking in Edwards's account of the religious affections is their union in the soul. "Take away all love and hatred, all hope and fear, all anger, zeal, and affectionate desire and the world would be, in a great measure, motionless and dead."[26] Thus, when enlarged in the greatest degree of vitality by the religious experiencing of James's *more* or Edwards's Christ, the religious affections invigorate the soul, which has become dull in sympathy, inclined toward mediocrity, full of venom, and debased with hate, and they revive the soul again with love and joy unspeakable, glorious praise, and Martin Luther King Jr.'s blessed assurance that "God is able, God's gonna take care of you," and that there is a "cosmic companion" acting in this universe.

BLESSED ASSURANCE

In religious experience, the religious affections move and incline the soul toward shapes of piety toward God and other selves, which may include dependence and gratitude, obligation and responsibility, and repentance

23. Edwards, "Religious Affections," 186.
24. Edwards, "Religious Affections," 187.
25. Edwards, "Religious Affections," 187.
26. Edwards, "Religious Affections," 192–93.

and direction. If, as Edwards insists, the religious affections are most acute in life trials, then King's soul life manifests a plenitude of being.

Charles Sanders Peirce spoke of the irritation of doubt.[27] And this mental itch can run deep in the soul life of believers. It may affect what they believe and what they feel, their capacity for sympathy with others, or how they orient their lives to everyday events, tragedies, and social systems. For Peirce, the remedy of this nagging itch was inquiry, interrogating one's own belief and the belief of others until the itch is resolved by a process of clarifying our ideas. King certainly engaged this process throughout his life as he was devoted to critical study, beginning in Sunday school, and later at Morehouse College, Crozer Theological Seminary, and Boston University.[28] But the irritation of doubt that most plagued King was felt in his life as pastor and religious leader, on whom the souls of so many were dependent for consolation and assurance that the aims and purposes of the movement could not be stopped by death and the threat of death. Still, at such moments, King's soul was full of such moments of doubt.[29]

King's early young life was characterized by a plenitude of affections of care and love, which he received from filial bonds of family and church life. These sources of filial care and love were deeply seeded in his young maturing soul. They fostered in him profound senses of comfort and assurance. While a student at Crozer, he recalls:

> It is quite easy for me to think of a God of love mainly because I grew up in a family where love was central and where lovely relationships were ever present. It is quite easy for me to think of the universe as basically friendly mainly because of my uplifting hereditary and environmental circumstances. It is quite easy for me to lean more toward optimism than pessimism about human nature mainly because of my childhood experiences.[30]

Further, King found in the life of the church a sense of home, of belonging, and the confidence that would be the bedrock of his young faith:

27. Charles Sanders Peirce, "How to Make Our Ideas Clear," in *Values in a Universe of Chance: Selected Writings of Charles S. Peirce (1839–1914)*, ed. Philip P. Wiener (Garden City, NY: Doubleday, 1958), 118–19.

28. Martin Luther King Jr., *The Autobiography of Martin Luther King, Jr.*, ed. Clayborne Carson (New York: Warner, 1998), 1–33; and Martin Luther King Jr., "An Autobiography of Religious Development," in Carson et al., eds., *Papers,* 1:359–63.

29. Martin Luther King Jr., "Doubts and Certainties Link: Transcript of an Interview," unpublished, London (1968), Library and Archives of the Martin Luther King Jr. Center for Nonviolent Social Change (KCLA), 2.

30. Carson et al., eds., *Papers*, 1:360.

> The church has always been a second home for me. As far back as I can remember I was in church every Sunday. My best friends were in Sunday school, and it was the Sunday school that helped me to build the capacity for getting along with people. I guess this was inevitable since my father was the pastor of my church, but I never regretted going to church until I passed through a stage of skepticism in my second year of college.[31]

King was clear that what skepticism he held toward church was rooted in his *discomfort* with what he describes as its fundamentalist tendencies. His struggles with doubt were between what he came to consider simplistic, literalistic readings of the Bible and a burgeoning theological liberalism.

> The lessons which I was taught in Sunday school were quite in the fundamentalist line. None of my teachers ever doubted the infallibility of the Scriptures. Most of them were unlettered and had never heard of biblical criticism. Naturally, I accepted the teachings as they were being given to me. I never felt any need to doubt them—at least at that time I didn't. I guess I accepted biblical studies uncritically until I was about twelve years old. But this uncritical attitude could not last long, for it was contrary to the very nature of my being. I had always been the questioning and precocious type. At the age of thirteen, I shocked my Sunday school class by denying the bodily resurrection of Jesus. Doubts began to spring forth unrelentingly.[32]

The recounts above describe ambiguities early formed in a young soul where childhood comfort and assurance anticipate irritating doubts, which are often evoked and resolved by crises. King's doubt surrounding the bodily resurrection of Jesus may be appreciated as the resolve of his soul to a child's first grief.

A CHILD'S FIRST GRIEF

In early adolescence, King learns of his grandmother Jennie Williams's death on May 18, 1941. Frederick L. Downing has discussed this episode at great length with significant importance to the faith life of King.[33] King is twelve and attempts suicide twice. The first episode surrounds an incident where he and his brother A. D. are playing in the house. A. D. slides down the banister of the house to the first level. Upon his landing to bottom floor, he accidentally knocked Grandmother Williams to the floor. She is motionless. Young King supposes that she is dead,

31. Carson, et al., eds., *Papers*, 1:361–62; and King, *Autobiography*, 6.
32. King, *Autobiography*, 6.
33. Downing, *To See the Promised Land,* 97–120.

killed by his brother, and he does nothing to prevent it. He runs back upstairs to the second floor and jumps out the window to the ground below. Like Grandmother Williams, he, too, is motionless. He remains there motionless on the ground until hearing the good news that Grandmother Williams is very much alive.

However, on May 18, only a few months after this incident, Grandmother Williams prepares to speak at the Mount Olive Baptist Church in Atlanta. Young King is expected to be home doing homework. Being the precocious child he admits to being, he is downtown, watching a parade. What heightened sense of euphoria graces his young soul. It brings about a sense of forgetfulness of chores undone and parental directives. Then, like a clap of thunder breaking into silence, his affectivities of excitement, happiness, and joy are shattered when someone brings word to him that Grandmother Williams has fallen ill and that he should come straight home. His soul fills with anxiety, fear, and a heightened sense of urgency. Arriving to the house, he sees people already gathered. Grandmother Williams has died. Downing reports, "he again ran upstairs and leaped from the window, apparently trying to follow his grandmother to another world. But when he landed with a jolt on the hard ground on the front yard below, he was shaken but still alive. Both his guilt and his grief were still with him."[34]

Martin Luther King Sr. remembers that his son "cried off and on for several days afterward, and was unable to sleep at night."[35] With Grandmother Jennie's death in mind, King himself later recalls: "I was particularly hurt by this incident because of the extreme love I had for her. . . . She assisted greatly in raising all of us."[36] Affectivities of grief and despair overwhelm him. His parents intervene to comfort and assure him that bodily death is not the end. King Sr. explains, death "'was a part of life that was difficult to get used to' and that God had 'His own plan and His own way, and we cannot change or interfere with the time He chooses to call any of us back to Him.'"[37] Downing describes this episode as "The Loss of Mythic-Literal Faith."[38] The lessons King learned at home and in Sunday school Bible classes, and the stories he heard in sermons of God's power to intervene in the affairs of life, miracles of turning water into wine, healing the sick, raising the dead, and even the bodily resurrection of Jesus were all taken for granted in King's developing stream of con-

34. Carson, et al., eds., *Papers*, 1:362.
35. Carson et al., eds., *Papers,* 1:34 and 362.
36. Carson et al., eds., *Papers,* 1:34.
37. Carson et al., eds., *Papers,* 1:34.
38. Downing, *To See the Promised Land,* 99.

sciousness. "Yet the serious questioning of that faith evident in this story implies that a transition may be in store for him," says Downing.[39]

Grandmother Williams's death startled young King from the soul, like a clap of thunder startles silence. It breaks into the stream of consciousness of King's everyday of familiar care and assurances. He must now attune himself at age twelve to the precariousness of life, but also to a hard, uneasy assurance that death is not the end; that the soul has an enduring life. "It was after this incident for the first time," says King, "that I talked at any length on the doctrine of immortality. My parents attempted to explain it to me and I was assured that somehow my grandmother still lived."[40] What a faint, dull consolation to King's young soul, occasioning his revelation to his Sunday school class that he could no longer believe in the bodily resurrection of Jesus. In his mature soul life, looking back on a child's first grief and the hope of meeting Grandmother Williams again soul to soul, King's piety affirms, "I guess this is why today I am such a strong believer in personal immortality."[41]

With time, this blessed assurance, offered by a belief in the personal immortality of the soul, revives young King's soul, easing the irritation of doubt that the death of a loved one often brings. The religious affections of comfort and assurance, as motivational structures of King's soul life, incline King's soul in piety to consent to the ways of God, which may in religious experience evoke in our souls affectivities or senses of loss, grief, and despair. Consent to God's ways is a shape of piety that lifts King's soul into the blessed assurance that even death opens up to James's "*MORE*" in human experience and the ineffable in cosmic events. As King matures, the trials of life would test this blessed assurance many times over. But perhaps, none more deeply than the senses of doubt, loss, despair, and grief that Birmingham would manifest in the fall of 1963.

AUGUST 28, 1963

On the most commemorated day of the civil rights movement, and climatic in the journey of King's soul life from Montgomery to Washington, DC., King describes his euphoria:

> In the summer of 1963, a great shout for freedom reverberated across the land. It was a shout from the hearts of a people who had been too patient, too long. It was a shout which arose from the North and from the South. It was a shout which reached the ears of a President and stirred him to

39. Downing, *To See the Promised Land,* 99.

40. Carson, et al., eds., *Papers*, 1:362.

41. Carson, et al., eds., *Papers*, 1:362; and King, *Autobiography*, 6.

> unprecedented statesmanship. It was a shout which reached the halls of Congress and brought back to the legislative chambers a resumption of the Great Debate. It was a shout which awoke the conscience of millions of white Americans and caused them to examine themselves and to consider the plight of twenty million black disinherited brothers. It was a shout which brought men of God down out of their pulpits, where they had been preaching only a Sunday kind of love, out into the streets to practice a Monday kind of militancy. Twenty million strong, militant marching blacks, flanked by legions of white allies, militant in an army which had a will and a purpose—the realization of a new and glorious freedom.[42]

The day was the celebrated March on Washington. And King's soul is bursting with religious affections, which Edwards describes as "joy unspeakable and glorious praise." King recalls, "We had strength because there were so many of us, representing so many more. We had dignity because we knew our cause was just. We had no anger, but we had a passion—a passion for freedom. So we stood there, facing Mr. Lincoln and facing ourselves and our own destiny and facing the future and facing God."[43] Then he spoke these words, which reverberate into the future: "I Have a Dream!" On Edwards's account of the religious affections, King's greatest speech closes with no greater intensity of religious affections and piety than glorious praise: "Free at Last, Free at Last, Thank God Almighty, we are free at last!"[44]

DARK NIGHT OF THE SOUL

The religious affections of the soul, the joy unspeakable and glorious praise, roused by this monumental moment in cosmic history was shattered quickly and violently with despairing news and overwhelming grief swelling up from Birmingham. The blessed assurance, which King first experienced at age twelve with the death of his grandmother and later in his "Kitchen table testimony" only days before his home was bombed in Montgomery; the blessed assurance, which accompanied his many releases from jail sentences and incarcerations, and which burst

42. Martin Luther King Jr., "A Summer of Discontent," chap. 7, unpublished draft for *Why We Can't Wait* (September 1963), Martin Luther King Jr. Papers, Special Collections, Mugar Memorial Library, Boston University, Boston, Massachusetts; Martin Luther King Jr., "Address at the March on Washington for Jobs and Freedom," unpublished version, Washington, DC (28 August 1963), Southern Christian Leadership Conference Tapes; and King, *Autobiography*, 218–19.

43. King, *Autobiography*, 222–23.

44. King, *Autobiography*, 227.

into joy unspeakable and glorious praise at the March on the Washington Mall, would be tested once more by the fire.

In the *Washington Post* dated September 16, 1963, the headline reads, "Six Dead after Church Bombing: Blast Kills Four Children: Riots Follow, Two Youths Slain; State Reinforces Birmingham Police." The glorious March that symbolized the new Negro and hope for a new South was tested in the fire of persecution. King recalls, "I shall never forget the grief and bitterness I felt on that terrible September morning. I think of how a woman cried out crunching through broken glass, 'My God, we're not even safe in church.' I think of how that explosion blew the face of Jesus Christ from a stained glass window. I can remember thinking, was it all worth it? Was there any hope?"[45]

Doubt, grief, rage, and despair are all appropriate affectivities of the soul. And if as James insists, knowledge is always knowledge by acquaintance, then King's soul was fully acquainted with these affections of the soul. After all, he experienced them many times, breaking in on his stream of consciousness as leader of SCLC and the civil rights movement. But this moment appears monumental in his soul life even as was the euphoria he experienced only weeks earlier on the Washington Mall. His blessed assurance explodes, louder than a clap of thunder, in the bombing and rioting, the burning of black businesses and the death of six black youths, and the civil carnage that was Birmingham in 1963. King's soul cries out in anguish, "Was it all worth it? Was there any hope?" He explained further: "In Birmingham, which we believed to be a city redeemed, a crucifixion had taken place. The children were the victims of a brutality which echoed around the world. Where was God in the midst of falling bombs?"[46]

In all the trials of his life, King learned that cosmic events and human experience vex the soul, bringing it close to the edge of sheer cynicism when overwhelmed by human moral failures. He says,

> Perhaps the poverty of conscience of the white majority in Birmingham was most clearly illustrated at the funeral of the child martyrs. No white official attended. No white faces could be seen save for a pathetically few courageous ministers. More than children were buried that day; honor and decency were also interred. Our tradition, our faith, our loyalty were taxed that day as we gazed upon the caskets which held the bodies of those children. Some of us could not understand why God permitted death and destruction to come to those who had done no man harm.[47]

45. King, *Autobiography*, 230.
46. King, *Autobiography*, 230.
47. "Epitaph and Challenge," *SCLC Newsletter* (November–December 1963); Martin Luther

During this dark night of the soul, King does not come face to face with Mr. Lincoln, humanity, or destiny, which just days earlier he hailed passionately with glorious praise. He is face to face with the precariousness and tragic face of human wickedness and yet mystery operative in cosmic events. His soul turns concretely to the experience of ancestors who also lived with their backs against a wall.

Like Howard Thurman, King, too, would come to understand that the Negro spirituals do not only speak of sorrow, as W. E. B. DuBois once described them as "sorrow songs."[48] Rather, they intonate shapes of freedom in the experience of predecessors. Thurman's soul was attuned to the senses of ambiguity evoked by the spirituals, contending that they speak of life and of death:

> What, then, is the fundamental significance of all these interpretations of life and death? What are these songs trying to say? They express the profound conviction that God was not done with them; that God was not done with life. The consciousness that God had not exhausted His resources did not ever leave them. This is the secret of their ascendancy over circumstances and *the basis of their assurances* [my emphasis] concerning life and death. The awareness of the presence of a God who was personal, intimate, and active was the central fact of life and around it all the details of life and destiny were integrated.[49]

Birmingham 1963 brings King face-to-face with the ambiguities of religious experience when confronting life and death. It is in and through life and death that the reality of God comes forth in blessed assurance of a God affecting his soul personally, intimately, and active; "God was not done with life!" This blessed assurance stirs up a plenitude of piety in King's soul: responsibility, obligation, repentance, and direction.

King's soul has been preparing for such moments in the trials of life that had taken Medgar Evers in June 1963 and William Lewis Moore two months earlier. But what could have prepared his soul for this slaughter of innocent, non-voluntary participants in struggles they did not choose for themselves and in battles into which they were baptized by laws and systems of racial hatred of which they had no full weight of conscience for becoming martyrs? Still, King conceives the dying of the

King Jr., "Eulogy for the Martyred Children," unpublished version (18 September 1963), KCLA; and King, *Autobiography*, 230–31.

48. See W. E. B. DuBois, "The Sorrow Songs," *The Souls of Black Folk*, in *DuBois: Writings*, ed. Nathan Huggins (New York: The Library of America, 1986), 536–46.

49. Howard Thurman, "The Negro Spirituals Speak of Life and Death," in *African American Religious Thought: An Anthology*, ed. Cornel West and Eddie Glaude Jr. (Louisville: Westminster John Knox, 2003), 41.

four girls vicariously. And he now stands in the subject position of Saint Paul, not writing to the persecuted Philippians, whose religious affections and piety inspire Edwards, but to the persecuted of Birmingham:

> In every battle for freedom there are martyrs whose lives are forfeited and whose sacrifice endorses the promise of liberty. The girls died as a result of the Holy Crusade of black men to be free. . . . So, children are a glorious promise, and no one could tell what those children could have become —another Mary Bethune or Mahalia Jackson. But, they became the most glorious that they could have become. They became symbols of our crusade. They gave their lives to insure our liberty. They did not do it deliberately. They did it because something strange, something incomprehensible to man is reenacted in God's will, and they are home today with God.[50]

Affections of the soul experienced so long ago at age twelve return to revive King's soul again. The blessed assurance that God is not done with life overwhelms him. And now this blessed assurance must revive the souls of a tragedy-ridden community. It comes forth from the immortal souls of slain children through the power of speech: "So they have something to say to us in their death," says King.[51] They speak judgment to all those whom King had only a few weeks earlier lifted in glorious praise: "to every minister of the gospel who has remained silent behind the safe security of stained-glass windows," to "every politician who has fed his constituents the stale bread of hatred and the spoiled meat of racism," to the "federal government that has compromised with the undemocratic practices of Southern Dixiecrats and the blatant hypocrisy of right-wing Northern Republicans," and to "every Negro who passively accepts the evil system of segregation and stands on the sidelines in the midst of a mighty struggle for justice."[52]

The immortal souls of the slain children speak to the soul of the nation not only in judgment and of repentance. "They say to each of us, black and white, that we must substitute courage for caution" and direct our concerns from who murdered them to the "systems, the way of life, and the philosophy that produced the murderers." Their immortal souls revive the souls of the community in grief to heightened senses of obligations and direction. "Their death says to us that we must work passionately and unrelentingly to make the American dream a reality," to "substitute an aristocracy of character for an aristocracy of color," "to transform the negative extremes of a dark past into a positive extreme of

50. "Epitaph and Challenge"; "Eulogy for the Martyred Children"; and King, *Autobiography*, 230.

51. King, *Autobiography*, 231–32.

52. King, *Autobiography*, 231.

a bright future," and to "cause the white South to come to terms with its conscience."[53]

Much more can be said concerning the affections of King's soul life, which journeyed with him from his birth in Atlanta on January 15, 1929, to his death in Memphis on April 4, 1968. But that is the work of the community of interpreters who make up this volume. These philosophical reflections on religious experience through the religious affections touch on emotions, which are all too human, growing and working in King's soul and forming his religious sense of life and death. The spirituality of King was surely acquainted with despair, grief, loss, and agitating, nagging doubts through a life of trials and persecution. But cosmic events also startled his soul to shapes of piety, which were filled with joy unspeakable, glorious praise and the blessed assurance that *God is not done with life*. Now King's immortal soul extends that message of blessed assurance to the future:

> God is able to conquer the evils of history. His control is never usurped. If at times we despair because of the relatively slow progress being made in ending racial discrimination and if we become disappointed because of the undue cautiousness of the federal government, let us gain new heart in the fact that God is able. In our sometimes difficult and often lonesome walk up freedom's road, we do not walk alone. God walks with us.[54]

To conclude, Birmingham 1963 seems a long way off from our twenty-first-century social realities. William James insisted that the stream of consciousness passes from one generation to another. So too the jolts and bolts of anti-black racism, segregation, lynching, bombings, death and the threat of death are not only the reality of the mournful souls of that city, lamenting for its children; it is also the reality of our present religious situation. We, too, live with systemic social forces of anti-black racism, and our souls are all too acquainted with the nagging irritations of debilitating doubt when mass incarceration of our young, promising men and women deprive them of life and freedom, and targets for extinction the glorious promise of our children.

If knowledge is knowledge by acquaintance, our religious situation is well acquainted with the morbid pervasive reality of the death of our young and mature slain by police shootings, while in police custody or apprehension, while driving black, and by the internal disintegration of community within US cities. King's soul life was well acquainted with the affectivity of irritating doubt, which threatened his own young soul

53. King, *Autobiography,* 231–32.

54. Washington, ed., *Testament of Hope,* 507.

twice with suicidal weight. From youth to maturity, this burden and irritation of doubt was present but not crippling of his spiritual life. The religious affections of his soul found consolation in a blessed assurance, which formed the motivational structures of his spirituality. King's great consolation was in knowing by acquaintance that "God Is Able," "God Is Not Done with Life," and, in Mother Pollard's simple words, "God's Gonna Take Care of You." Closing his eulogy for Birmingham's children martyrs, King admonishes, "Let this daring faith, this great invincible surmise, be your sustaining power during these trying days."[55]

55. King, *Autobiography*, 232.

2.

A Great Cloud of Witnesses: Martin Luther King Jr.'s Roots in the African American Religious and Spiritual Traditions

DIANA L. HAYES

> Therefore, since we are surrounded by so great a cloud of witnesses, let us also lay aside every weight, and sin which clings so closely, and let us run with perseverance the race that is set before us.
>
> —Hebrews 12:1

> Our mothers and fathers knew that it was God that would bring them over. . . . Our mothers and fathers were able to get over the dark days of slavery and the dark days of segregation because religion gave them something within. It was the only way that they were able to live with that system.
>
> —Martin Luther King Jr.[1]

Where did Martin Luther King Jr. find the strength to love those who opposed him and sought to overcome his dream of the Beloved Community? How did he gather the strength and courage to persevere on the perilous journey he embarked on at such an early age, a journey that he came to realize could very well, and actually did, end in his premature death? In common with his ancestors, who were enslaved, and his family, friends, and community, King found that strength in his faith, faith in a God of love and justice, a righteous God opposed to the hate-filled, racist traditions that persisted in the South in which he grew up. As with those who came before him and led the way, the source of his

1. Martin Luther King Jr., "Discerning the Signs of History," unpublished version of a sermon, Ebenezer Baptist Church, Atlanta, Georgia (15 November 1964), Library and Archives of the Martin Luther King Jr. Center for Nonviolent Social Change (KCLA), Atlanta, Georgia, 4–5.

faith, of his wisdom, of his ability to find "a way out of no way" came from the Christian religion in which he had been immersed from birth as well as the religious traditions of Africa in which he and his community were grounded. It was a living spirituality expressed in a religious faith, the Baptist faith. That faith nurtured and sustained King as it had countless others of African descent in the United States. King was buoyed up, watched over, and guided by his faith in a "wonder working" God, the same God that brought his ancestors out of slavery with the promise that they, too, would one day enter the promised land of freedom.

Richard Lischer reveals aspects of this interconnectedness in his description of a mural on a wall in the Dexter Avenue Baptist Church, King's first pastorate:

> The mural symbolizes the thickness of King's spiritual environment. In the formative period of his life, he was encompassed by a series of concentric circles: first Mother Church, next by the tradition of the black preachers and reformers who came before him, and finally by the circle of mentors and teachers who guided his preparation for ministry. If there were a text beneath the mural, it might well be from the Book of Hebrews, "Since we are surrounded by so great a cloud of witnesses . . . "[2]

What is missing from this mural, however, is the circle encompassing King's African ancestry.

In this chapter, I will explore, define, and situate the spirituality of Dr. Martin Luther King Jr. within the history, traditions, and ongoing activism of the black church and the spirituality of African Americans. To do so requires that I not only delve into the history of the black church but also its historically liberating role in the African American community in the United States, especially in the South. This will necessitate, in turn, an exploration of the history and traditions of that church in its social context and location. The black church is made up of the diverse community of persons of African descent in the United States, a people brought to this country in chains over 400 years ago. They are a people still engaged in fighting for the freedoms that Dr. King also fought for, the struggle for liberation from injustice, prejudice, and discrimination, and for equal rights and citizenship in the land of their birth. As we shall see, the black church was both a liberating and conservative force in the lives of African Americans.

Dr. Stacey Floyd-Thomas affirms that "the black church emerges from the religious, cultural, and social experience of black people. With its

2. Richard Lischer, *The Preacher King: Martin Luther King Jr. and the Word That Moved America* (New York: Oxford University Press, 1995), 15.

roots on the continent of Africa and the Middle Passage, the black church provided structure and meaning for African people and their descendants in the Americas who struggled to survive the ravages and brutality of slavery and racial oppression."[3] The black church "was the center of Black life, culture, and heritage for much of the history of the African American experience in North America."[4] King emerged from one of the oldest branches of that church, the Baptist church, but the black church itself is pluralistic, including both Protestant and Catholic faithful who identify with the black struggle for freedom.

After King's death, most scholars focused on his graduate academic studies in liberal and personalist theologies as the foundation for his public speeches and actions, as he himself did in his some of his published works. This gave the false impression, however, that King had abandoned the heritage in which he was shaped and formed, that of the black church and the extended black community. Fortunately, in recent years, thanks to the work of scholars such as James H. Cone, Clayborne Carson, and Lewis V. Baldwin, the focus has turned to illuminate all of the influences on King's vocation, but especially his cultural roots which trace back to his enslaved ancestors and to Africa itself.[5]

What these scholars have begun and what is still needed is a more holistic perspective on King, in keeping with the African roots of black spirituality and black faith. This spirituality and faith sees no separation between the secular and the sacred, resulting in an action-oriented understanding of one's faith, a faith that can "move mountains" in its efforts to end the racial, political, and economic injustice that has been the fate of African Americans since their arrival in the United States. For King, this holistic perspective encompasses African and African American religious traditions, the people in all their diversity who make up the black community in the United States, the more immediate extended family of Ebenezer Baptist Church and his own family, as well as the

3. Stacey Floyd-Thomas et al., *Black Church Studies: An Introduction* (Nashville: Abingdon, 2007), xxiii.

4. Floyd-Thomas et al., *Black Church Studies*, xxiii.

5. See Clayborne Carson, "The Georgia Roots of Martin Luther King, Jr.," 1989 Georgia Week Lecture (Atlanta: Georgia Humanities Council, 1989), 1–19; Clayborne Carson et al., eds., *The Papers of Martin Luther King, Jr.: Called to Serve, January 1929–June 1951* (Berkeley: University of California Press, 1992), 1:1–57; James H. Cone, "Martin Luther King, Jr., Black Theology—Black Church," *Theology Today*, 40, no. 4 (January 1984): 409–11; Lewis V. Baldwin, "Martin Luther King, Jr., the Black Church, and the Black Messianic Vision," *The Journal of the Interdenominational Theological Center* 12, nos. 1–2 (Fall 1984/Spring 1985): 93–108; and Lewis V. Baldwin, *There Is a Balm in Gilead: The Cultural Roots of Martin Luther King, Jr.* (Minneapolis: Fortress, 1991), 15–339.

European-American intellectual knowledge that he acquired at Crozer Theological Seminary and Boston University.

All of these factors were critical for the personal, religious, psychological, and political development of this young man from Sweet Auburn in Atlanta, Georgia, who became the prophetic leader of his people in the 1950s. They helped to propel him into leadership and to withstand the forces, positive and negative, arrayed against him. Arguably, the black church not only gave King and others in the civil rights movement a foundational basis upon which to launch their sit-ins, pray-ins, and marches, it also gave them the theological and spiritual language in which they could ground their calls for civil, social, and economic liberation for persons of African descent. Because of this, King was able "to harness the moral authority and organizing power of the black churches" through the Southern Christian Leadership Conference (SCLC) to "the service of Civil Rights reform."[6]

King's spirituality is, indeed, deeply rooted in the spirituality of those in whose midst he spent his entire life, his immediate and extended family, his church (both the Baptist church and the larger black Christian community), and the black community of the American South. King had a "Southern sense of place" that served to anchor him throughout his life. Although he left the South for a number of years to study in the North, especially Chester, Pennsylvania, and Boston, Massachusetts, he could not and did not want to escape from the land of his birth. He was the son, grandson, and great grandson of Baptist ministers, standing in the footsteps of his forefathers going back at least four generations into slavery. Thus, in many ways, his calling as a minister in the Baptist church, especially in the South, was foreordained. Although initially he sought a vocation as a lawyer or a physician, God had too firm a grip on him. By age eighteen, he answered the call "to serve God and humanity,"[7] was ordained and served in his father's congregation, Ebenezer Baptist, a church pastored by his maternal grandfather, Adam D. Williams, as well. After ordination, King never looked back, increasingly embracing "a spiritual life that took seriously the personal, interpersonal, and socio-political aspects of the Christian faith, and, in time, recasting the very definition of spirituality for his generation."[8]As he stated often: "I was born and raised in the black church and am a product of it. At heart, I am simply a clergyman, a Baptist preacher."[9] This church

6. Floyd-Thomas et al., *Black Church Studies*, 31.

7. Baldwin, *There Is a Balm in Gilead*, 30–44; and Lewis V. Baldwin and Victor Anderson's introduction to this volume.

8. Baldwin and Anderson, introduction, 2.

9. Martin Luther King Jr., "The Un-Christian Christian," *Ebony* 20, no. 10 (August 1965),

was noted in Atlanta and the South both for its adherence to a fundamentalist perspective of Christianity and its fervently preaching pastors. It was also, however, a church that saw social activism on behalf of the poor and oppressed as a necessary part of faith.[10]

No one, however, could have foreseen the path that young King would take in his life, a path that, in some ways, was reminiscent of those African American men and woman who had been seen as "race" leaders for their people. They sought liberation from racism and a better life for their people as did he. His path, however, was a very different one in that it laid the foundations for the remaking of life from what it had been for blacks for centuries before, especially in the southern United States.

Dr. King, like most persons of African descent, was raised in a religious and spiritual milieu that gave him life, laid a foundation of love, and helped him understand himself and his place in the world around him. To give justice to King and his journey to become "the Preacher King,"[11] as Lischer describes him, known not only for his rhetorical skills but also for his intellectual acumen and a deep and abiding faith in humankind regardless of race or ethnicity, we must begin in Africa from which African American spirituality has its source.

The religious tradition into which King was born stretches over the Atlantic to sub-Saharan Africa, then back again over that same ocean to the American colonies where his ancestors toiled for centuries. He, like all African Americans, had African roots that grew, over centuries, into American branches, a coming together of peoples, languages, and religious beliefs to form a new people who established tight-knit and caring communities of Christian faith that enabled them to survive more than four hundred years of enslavement and the racism and discrimination that evolved from their enslavement.

AFRICAN SPIRITUALITY

African American spirituality was forged in the fiery furnace of slavery in the United States. The ore was African in origin, in worldview, in culture and traditions. The coals were laid in the bowels of ships named after Jesus and Christian virtues, which carried untold numbers of Africans to the Americas. The fire was stoked on "seasoning" islands

77; Lee E. Dirks, "'The Essence is Love': The Theology of Martin Luther King, Jr.," *National Observer* (30 December 1963): 1 and 12.

10. Martin Luther King Sr., *Daddy King: An Autobiography*, with Clayton Riley (New York: William Morrow, 1980), 71, 82–83, and 89.

11. See Lischer, *Preacher King*, 3.

of the Caribbean or the "breeding" plantations of the South, where men, women, and children of Africa were systematically and efficiently reduced to beasts of burden and items of private property. Yet, those who came forth from these fires were not what they seemed. Despite the oppressive and ungodly forces applied against them, they were able to forge a spirituality that encouraged hope and sustained faith, which enabled them to build communities of love and trust and to persevere in their persistent efforts to be the free men and women God had created them to be.[12]

African spirituality places special significance on the understanding and importance of community, one that includes everyone in a village, tribe, and beyond. There is no life without the community and there is no community without the active participation of all. As a well-known African proverb states: "I am because we are." That is, unlike in Western society, it is not the individual but the community that is of critical importance.[13] The smallest component of the community is the family, whose lives are intertwined and who support and sustain each other. There are no strangers in the community or family, as those who come from elsewhere are welcomed and integrated into both family and community as happened in the Americas.

Just as family and community are vital aspects of life, religion is as well. There is no word in any African language for religion as such, for it is not seen as a separate entity in which people choose to participate or not, as in Western society. Rather, religion is an integral part of life without which there can be no viable life. Thus, African spirituality is grounded in the very lives and activities of the African people. They live it, breathe it, walk it, sing it, and dance it. There is no life without religion, the interconnection of all people, all created things, and God:

> Spirituality for the people of Africa is not a passive "given"; it is played out in day-to-day life, through observance of moral codes, rites and rituals, and patterns of relationships. Relationships among all elements of creation . . . are the essence of African spirituality, because Africans believe

12. See Diana L. Hayes, *Forged in the Fiery Furnace: African American Spirituality* (Maryknoll, NY: Orbis, 2012), 1–2.

13. A slight variation is offered in Archbishop Desmond Tutu's description of Ubuntu: "I am what I am because of who we all are." Martin Luther King Jr. echoed this view in his assertion that "The self cannot be self without other selves." See Desmond Tutu, *The Words of Desmond Tutu*, selected by Naomi Tutu (New York: Newmarket, 1989), 71–79; and Martin Luther King Jr., *Where Do We Go from Here: Chaos or Community?* (Boston: Beacon, 1968; originally published in 1967), 180.

> that only through harmonious relationships is cosmic existence possible and its vital force preserved.[14]

This vital force or power is a critical aspect of human life as it affects one's very being for good or ill. *Ntu* or vital power causes an "ontic change" in a person as a result, for example, of his/her elevation to a new position or role in the community of which he or she is a part. That elevation triggers "a profound transformation resulting in a new form of being that causes a person to act in a manner and style that befits the new situation or status."[15] This understanding remained with the Africans through the ordeal of the Middle Passage to the Caribbean and on to the American colonies. It provided them with the strength and ability to adapt to the new circumstances to which they were being exposed, often with great violence, and to remain whole and human. It, as a result, helped raise among them leaders whose soul force strengthened them and enabled them, as a people, to survive.

An extension of this understanding can be found in that of *Ubuntu* (other names are used by different African peoples) in terms of ultimate or accomplished humanness. "A person with *Ubuntu* (full humanity) is open and available to others, affirming of others, does not feel threatened that others are able and good."[16] As Laurenti Magesa affirms: "A person with Ubuntu embraces those qualities in others, 'for he or she has a proper self-assurance that comes from knowing that he or she belongs to a great whole and is diminished when others are humiliated or diminished, when others are tortured or oppressed.'"[17] What Ubuntu underscores is "'the vital importance of mutual recognition and respect complemented by mutual care and sharing in the construction of human relations.' Ubuntu is manifested in self-giving and readiness to cooperate and communicate with others."[18]

This understanding of community, of vital force, and of Ubuntu or full humanity lies at the heart of King's efforts to develop the Beloved Community, which he saw as that "period of social harmony and universal brotherhood that would follow the current social struggle."[19] At that

14. Laurenti Magesa, *What Is Not Sacred?: African Spirituality* (Maryknoll, NY: Orbis, 2013), 195.

15. Hayes, *Forged in a Fiery Furnace*, 17. Also see Vincent Mulago, "Traditional African Religions and Christianity," in Jacob K. Olupona, *African Traditional Religion in Contemporary Society* (Saint Paul, MN: Paragon, 1991), 119.

16. Desmond Tutu as cited in Magesa, *What Is Not Sacred?,* 13.

17. Magesa, *What Is Not Sacred?,* 13.

18. Magesa, *What Is Not Sacred?,* 13.

19. Lischer, *Preacher King*, 234.

time, blacks and whites would be reconciled and able to walk together as a family of brothers and sisters without racial strife or disharmony.

AFRICAN AMERICAN SPIRITUALITY

These emphases on community and family, as well as the significance of full humanity and vital force, accompanied by belief in a God who created all things and participates in the lives of that creation, were brought from Africa through the Middle Passage to become a vital part of the lives and worldviews of those who were enslaved. They widened the circle of relationship beyond blood lines because of their perilous situation. Old enemies became new brothers and sisters, aunts and uncles, parents and grandparents, sharing in the horrors of slavery and enabling survival.[20] This was an experience that King shared under much different circumstances. During his graduate school years, and wherever he studied, there were black families that took him in and treated him as one of their own.

African American spirituality is a result of the encounter of a particular people with their God. It is their communal rather than individual response to God's action in their history in ways that revealed to them the meaning of God for themselves, as well as provided them with an understanding of themselves as beings created by God. Thus, African American spirituality cannot be understood without the knowledge and understanding of who African Americans are, how they came into being, and why they have been able to grow, develop, mature, and persevere as a people of faith in the face of seemingly insurmountable odds. African American spirituality is the result of their encounter with Jesus Christ, who enabled them to find a "way out of no way," justified their self-understanding as children of God, and thus enabled them to persist in their belief that one day they would be free. They believed that God saw them as human, created in God's own image and likeness, and intended them to be a free people. They acted on that belief in countless rebellions, escape efforts, and other activities toward freedom.

That spirituality is contemplative, holistic, joyful, and communitarian.[21] This means that it is expressed in prayer and a deeply conscious prayer life that is not passive. Unlike Western tradition, but in keeping with their African ancestry, there is no separation between the sacred

20. Hayes, *Forged in the Fiery Furnace*, 1–7 and 9–28.

21. See "Our Spirituality and Its Gifts," in *What We Have Seen and Heard: A Pastoral Letter on Evangelization from the Black Bishops of the United States* (Cincinnati: St. Anthony Messenger, 1984) 8–11.

and secular worlds, which are interwoven and lived as one holistic way of being in the world. African American spirituality calls forth the joy of loving God and acknowledges receiving the grace of God in sermon, song, story, dance, and other expressive and emotion-filled ways. It is also communitarian in that it helps to weave together a community of those who are connected not merely by kinship or blood ties but by ties of shared oppression and denigration of its humanity. This community is revealed both in worship and in other activities that give life to the community.

African American spirituality is born of the pride and the pain, the horror and the hope of a people whose eyes have always been watching God and whose hands stayed firm on the plow as they fought their way to freedom. It is a spirituality forged in the fiery furnace of four hundred-plus years of slavery, segregation, and racism, but grounded in a history, thousands of years old, of a people who always believed in someone greater than themselves and who, because of that belief, built civilizations and cities, raised families and created communities, gave birth to leaders and warriors, and passed on their hope to those who came after them, long after them, in a different land and facing far different circumstances. Theirs is a spirituality which emerges from and is sustained by their love of God, love of self, and love of each other long before they heard of Jesus's Great Commandment. This spirituality sustained and nurtured them, enabled them to hold their heads up and "keep on keeping on" when all and everything else seemed opposed to their forward movement. It is a spirituality expressed in song, in dance, in prayer, in preaching, and, most importantly, in living each day as best they could in solidarity with one another and their God over against the principalities and powers of their time.

There are several aspects of African spirituality that particularly resonate with African American spirituality and can be seen reflected in the life and ministry of Martin Luther King Jr. For Magesa and other scholars of African religions and spirituality, such as Benjamin C. Ray, Benezet Bujo, Jacob K. Olupona, and Mercy Amba Oduyoye, African spirituality is rooted in the lives and experiences of the ancestors, those who have gone before. It is not passive, as noted earlier, but calls everyone to act morally, ritually, and relationally. Theirs is a moral worldview in which all are related and are nurtured and engaged in efforts to aid humanity. All are welcome; there are no strangers or "others" to be ostracized or left out of the community, for all carry the "spark of divine, 'spiritual' life." Dialogue is valued over forced conversion and a holistic view of life is encouraged. To seek the "good life" is the goal of African spirituality, seen, however, not as a monetary or materialistic goal but as an effort to bring all of creation harmoniously working together.[22]

Lewis V. Baldwin speaks of King's spirituality in somewhat similar terms, naming "a sense of place" as of vital importance to King's self-understanding, a sense of community of which he was a part so he was not working or acting on his own, and a Christian optimism that fed his mission and understanding that "God will ultimately emerge triumphant over evil and bring liberation and salvation (the good life) to all."[23] As well, the understanding of *ntu* or "life force or vital power" is certainly reflected in King's own journey from a young, inexperienced minister just out of graduate school to the prophetic and charismatic leader of a movement for civil and human rights that changed America in ways many had not thought possible. King had not trained for this exalted role as such but was able to adapt and evolve into the person most suited for the role he undertook. His was certainly an experience of *Ubuntu*, the development of a person's full humanity, one that was lived not for himself but for others not just in America but throughout the world.

The spirituality of Martin Luther King Jr. was expressed in his preaching style, his intense life of prayer, and his life-long emphasis on the liberation of his people. It was at the heart of his efforts to develop the Beloved Community and his refusal to accept any restrictions placed on his effort to engage people of faith in the struggle for the elimination of racial prejudice and discrimination. King became the person, the prophet, whom persons of African descent in the United States needed to overcome the life of segregation and oppression under which they had been forced to live for more than a century after slavery's end.

This vital power was the source, the foundation, for King's spirituality, the ingredient that urged him on to fight for the rights, civil and human, of his own people and also in time for all people as he sought the Beloved Community of Jesus or the kingdom of God on earth. Over the course of his life, King came to understand the interconnection of all humanity, recognizing with Peter Paris that "Unity in diversity is another metaphor for African (and therefore African American-DLH) spirituality,"[24] and thus a metaphor for his actions and mission:

> I am cognizant of the interrelatedness of all communities and states. I cannot sit idly by in Atlanta and not be concerned about what happens in Birmingham. Injustice anywhere is a threat to justice everywhere. We are caught

22. Magesa, *What Is Not Sacred?,* 195–97.

23. Baldwin, *There Is a Balm in Gilead*, 4–5.

24. Peter Paris, *The Spirituality of African Peoples: The Search for a Common Moral Discourse* (Minneapolis: Fortress, 1994), 22.

> in an inescapable network of mutuality, tied in a single garment of destiny. Whatever affects one directly affects all indirectly. Never again can we afford to live with the narrow, provincial "outside agitator" idea. Anyone who lives inside the United States can never be considered an outsider anywhere in this country.[25]

That understanding is true also for the spirituality in which King grew up, a spirituality shaped, formed, and embodied in his father's church and the Sweet Auburn community in which he lived. That unity came together in many ways with people of African ancestry across the United States, forging a new people who, although treated as less than human, could take the false and distorted Christianity imposed upon them and retrieve the liberating truth of the gospel message—that message that God saw them as they saw themselves, human beings worthy of the dignity and respect accorded all of God's creation. This unifying and life-affirming message was renewed every Sunday in the lives of black Christians, and King was clearly influenced by it. King saw in the people with whom he interacted a vibrant people of God called to serve as the messengers of hope for a transformed and better world, or a beloved community for all of humanity.

THE BLACK CHURCH AND THE BLACK SOCIAL GOSPEL

The period between 1955 and 1968 in the United States was a time of radical change, the coming to fruition of the spiritual and physical struggle of the African American people. They had toiled and labored, struggled and climbed, and kept their faith alive for over 400 years in the face of all obstacles. God, they believed, could be seen, once again, acting in their lives as they fervently believed God had done throughout their sojourn in the United States, but especially at slavery's end. Once again, God was clearly on their side as the hated Black Codes and Jim Crow laws and their dehumanizing restrictions began to tumble and fall. They were stepping out on their faith and not allowing anything or anyone to turn them around.[26] And, as during slavery, God sent men and women to help them walk forth into freedom, men such as Martin Luther King Jr. and others. They were preachers and teachers, adults and children, ordinary men and women who believed the time had finally come to stand

25. Quoted in James M. Washington, ed., *A Testament of Hope: The Essential Writings and Speeches of Martin Luther King, Jr.* (San Francisco: Harper and Row, 1986), 290.

26. Hayes, *Forged in the Fiery Furnace*, 102–10.

up for justice and righteousness in God's name on behalf of their brother and sister co-sufferers.

The civil rights movement did not just spring up from nothing and nowhere. It was deeply rooted in all that had taken place in the history of people of African descent in the United States. The movement was the fruit of African roots and American branches and had to be woven together by the hearts, minds, and spirits of many into the immensely powerful tapestry of love and resistance that it became. There has always been one constant thread in the hearts and minds of African Americans throughout the centuries of their sojourn in the United States, and that is the desire to experience a true physical and spiritual freedom. For them, this meant not only breaking the chains of slavery, but also the chains of feudalism that were quickly forged, especially in the southern states, to re-enslave them in all but name. They sought to regain that which had been promised at the end of the Civil War and with the passage of the thirteenth and fourteenth amendments. They sought the freedom to do as they desired with their lives, their minds, their bodies, and their spirits; to live where they chose; to vote for whomever they desired; to educate themselves and their children in any school they desired. They sought to do so without having to live in fear of their lives being forfeited because they had unwittingly broken one of the arcane laws of Jim Crow segregation, the uniquely American form of apartheid that continued to persevere for more than a hundred years after legal slavery's official end.[27]

It is in the South, the former states of the Confederacy, where the full extent and weight of the Jim Crow laws persisted with their stranglehold on the lives and livelihoods of thousands of men, women, and children of African descent. In many ways, it is truly miraculous that African Americans survived yet another hundred years of slavery in all but name. The peculiar institution of slavery may have ended, but the even more peculiar system, peculiar because it was never formally acknowledged as such, of Jim/Jane Crow bound blacks to land they still did not own, forcing them to work in the fields and factories of their former slave masters and their descendants. This is the world that King grew to adulthood in,[28] a world of prejudice and discrimination but also a world of love, caring, and compassion within the black community, a community of faith, resourcefulness, and resistance.

27. Hayes, *Forged in the Fiery Furnace*, 102–10; and Washington, ed., *Testament of Hope*, 5–6 and 135–37.

28. King himself saw southern Jim Crow as "a form of slavery disguised by certain niceties of complexity," and he, too, understood the spiritual, physical, and psychological pain that it visited upon his people. See Martin Luther King Jr., *Why We Can't Wait* (New York: The New American Library, 1964), 23.

The black church was of critical importance to the sharecroppers as well as urban blacks in the South and elsewhere after Reconstruction. It served as an escape from the indignities of daily life and as an anchor in what often seemed to be a stormy sea. The black church was a refuge, a spiritual haven and oasis, a place of education and inspiration, a source of hope and a site of dignity for many. In the haven of the church, children could indulge their youthful mischievousness under the watchful eyes of stern but loving elders who acted as "moms and dads" to any and every black child who crossed their paths, much as King and his siblings did. They were taught how to pray to the Jesus who loved them as they were, a lesson of particular importance in Georgia, where segregation reigned. Their budding talents were nurtured, and they were provided a respite from the demands of life in a world where, even in the North, black children were seen as "less than" and "less capable" than white children. Black parents, teachers, and extended family reminded their children on an almost daily basis that they were as good as if not better than those who opposed their success.[29]

The black church served an important civic and political function in the black community, as it was the only place where people of African ancestry could define themselves and their spirituality without hindrance. It was in the church that leadership skills were taught. As Stacey Floyd-Thomas affirms, "during the Civil Rights era, from the mid-1950's to the early 1970's, the Black Church, especially in the South, was an important mobilizing force in black community political activity."[30] King, especially, as he often noted, was raised and nurtured in the bosom of the black church, and largely at Ebenezer Baptist in Atlanta, Georgia. Here he learned and developed his oratorical and pastoral skills while, at the same time, receiving an education and practical lessons in the role of the pastor as activist.

King was deeply influenced by his father's and grandfather's activism in the church. They participated in the activities of the NAACP and other civil and human rights entities in the Atlanta area, while opposing as best they could the limitations and restrictions placed on persons of color across the South. Also, King Jr. from youth had rebelled against these restrictions, harboring for a short time an intense hatred of whites, which he was, over time, able to overcome. He was firmly entrenched in Gayraud S. Wilmore's understanding of the radical branch of Christianity, seeing its message as one of action and not passivity. Wilmore speaks

29. Carson et al., eds., *Papers*, 1:360; and Martin Luther King Jr., *The Autobiography of Martin Luther King, Jr.*, ed. Clayborne Carson (New York: Warner, 1998), 3–4.

30. Floyd-Thomas et al., *Black Church Studies*, 106–7.

of a certain dualism in black religious life that has historically expressed itself in two "divergent tendencies . . . , the first tending toward radicalism, the other toward hypocritical compromise." Both, Wilmore asserts, express "two strands of a survival tradition" that enabled blacks to survive and thrive despite the often-life-threatening obstacles in their paths.[31] King himself spoke of the shortcomings of the black church often, especially its emotionalism and "other-worldly" gospel, which he felt had little to no bearing on the reality of the world around them.[32]

Both King's father and grandfather were products of the black Social Gospel tradition that emerged in the mid- to late nineteenth century.[33] Ministers like Henry McNeil Turner, Reverdy C. Ransom, and others were pioneers in this progressive movement that emerged in the aftermath of Reconstruction's end. They preached a gospel that proclaimed God was on the side of the marginalized and oppressed and that the black church had a responsibility to act in love to alleviate injustice and to ensure the human and civil rights of black folk.

Despite the resistance of many in the black church who felt their role was to preach an otherworldly salvation rather than to get involved in the issues of contemporary society, black Social Gospel advocates acted to make a difference. Those of the second generation included many of King's mentors and teachers, such as Benjamin E. Mays, Howard Thurman, George D. Kelsey, and his own father and paternal grandfather, Martin Luther King Sr. and Adam D. Williams. These men taught King "to harvest the social justice potential of the churches."[34] His father and grandfather were active participants in this movement, encouraging their congregations to register to vote, and working with Atlanta government officials to improve educational opportunities and other actions that brought Jesus's message of liberation into direct contact with the needs and concerns of ordinary blacks.

The founders and proponents of the black Social Gospel tradition addressed economic, social, and political issues "very differently from white progressives," whose perspective on race was that of the supremacy and superiority of whiteness.[35] For black ministers like King

31. Gayraud S. Wilmore, *Black Religion and Black Radicalism: An Interpretation of the Religious History of Afro-American People*, 2nd ed. (Maryknoll, NY: Orbis, 1983), 259.

32. King, *Autobiography,* 15.

33. Carson et al., eds., *Papers,* 1:10–18. This tradition is explored at considerable length in Gary Dorrien, *Breaking White Supremacy: Martin Luther King, Jr. and the Black Social Gospel* (New Haven: Yale University Press, 2018), 1–504.

34. Gary Dorrien, "What We Don't Know about Black Social Gospel: A Long-Neglected Tradition Is Reclaimed," in *Religion Dispatches* (9 November 2015): 3; Carson et al., eds., *Papers,* 1:10–18; and King, *Daddy King,* 82.

35. Dorrien, "What We Don't Know," 4.

Sr. and A. D. Williams, racial oppression trumped everything in the African American context and refigured how other problems were experienced.

These black Social Gospelers started "something imminently important, refusing to be denigrated."[36] They taught that God was for the oppressed and excluded; they preached equality, democracy, peacemaking, and Jesus's love for all children.[37] They kept the hope of the death of white supremacy alive for the black faithful and tapped into what Kelly Brown Douglas calls a "spirituality of resistance" that lay at the heart of black spiritual life in the United States:

> Historically, a *spirituality of resistance* has been central to black people's survival and wholeness in a society that demeans their very black humanity. Such spirituality is characterized by a sense of connection to one's own heritage as well as to the divine. As such, it provides black men and women with a buffer of defense against white cultural characterizations of them as beings unworthy of freedom, dignity, even life. At the same time, a spirituality of resistance grants them, especially black women, a sense of control over their own bodies.[38]

King saw Christianity and, therefore, Jesus Christ as radically present in the struggle for the civil rights of African Americans and was impacted by a number of influences, including the liberal Social Gospel of Reinhold Niebuhr, the non-violent teachings of Gandhi, and the religious and spiritual traditions of the African American church. Out of these, he forged a theology of Christian nonviolent disobedience that helped to re-radicalize the black community and the black church and, in so doing, profoundly changed the United States. King, a deeply spiritual man, believed that Jesus, the Son of God, was in solidarity with those historically oppressed and downtrodden. In the United States, that meant black Americans who were confronted with racism everywhere. God was a God of the poor and meek, that ever-present force which empowered them to fight their own battle of liberation guided by Jesus the liberator:

> Nonviolence is the answer to the crucial political and moral questions of our time—the need for mankind to overcome oppression and violence without resorting to violence and oppression. Civilization and violence are antithetical concepts. . . . Sooner or later all the people of the world will have to

36. Dorrien, "What We Don't Know," 5.
37. Dorrien, "What We Don't Know," 5.
38. Kelly Brown Douglass, *What's Faith Got to Do with It? Black Bodies, Christian Souls* (Maryknoll, NY: Orbis, 2005), 172.

> discover a way to live together in peace, and thereby transform this pending cosmic elegy into a creative psalm of brotherhood. If this is to be achieved, man . . . must evolve for all human conflict a method which rejects revenge, aggression and retaliation. The foundation of such a method is love.[39]

For King, God "was both a comforting personal presence and a powerful spiritual force acting in history for righteousness."[40] His immersion in the black religious experience as well as his theological training helped him to look at life and the church very differently. It can be said that he "possessed an activist spirituality that had an intense concern for sociopolitical and economic justice. King approached the issues of racism, poverty, militarism, materialism, and consumerism not only as social and political concerns, but also as fundamentally moral-theological crises."[41] In today's understanding, King would be considered both a liberation and a practical theologian because of his emphasis on liberation from all forms of oppression and the necessity of living out one's faith in terms of action on behalf of those marginalized and oppressed: "The gospel deals with the whole man, not only his soul, but his body; not only his spiritual well-being, but his material well-being. . . . Any religion which professes to be concerned about the souls of men and is not concerned about the social and economic conditions that scar the soul, is a spiritually moribund religion only waiting for the day to be buried."[42]

King helped to rekindle black America's faith in a God who walked and talked with them, and who sent His Son on their behalf to guide them into the new kingdom of God on earth, or the beloved community, where all of humanity lived, worked, and played in harmony one with another. King lived his spirituality in his preaching and prayer life and also in his everyday life, and he called forth a response that in time overwhelmed the South's restrictive laws and limitations on black life. He was the catalyst that set the river of black frustration flowing in a nonviolent and organized manner. King saw the black church as instrumental in the black struggle for rights, a struggle he, during his life time, realized went beyond civil rights to encompass the rights of all of humanity. Facing opposition from his parishioners as well as from lead-

39. Martin Luther King Jr., "Nobel Peace Prize Acceptance Speech" (1964), https://tinyurl.com/y9txdf7q.

40. Clayborne Carson, "Martin Luther King Jr. and the African American Social Gospel," in *African American Religious Thought: An Anthology*, ed. Cornel West and Eddie S. Glaude Jr. (Louisville: Westminster John Knox, 2003), 711.

41. Luther D. Ivory, *Toward a Theology of Radical Involvement: The Theological Legacy of Martin Luther King Jr.* (Nashville: Abingdon, 1997), 86.

42. Martin Luther King Jr., *Stride toward Freedom: The Montgomery Story* (New York: Harper & Row, 1958), 36, 91.

ing churchmen and women of his own and other denominations and religious faiths, he sought to bring the liberating church of the past to new and renewed life, calling it to witness to God's demand for justice and righteousness for all, regardless of skin color or economic class. "Injustice anywhere is a threat to justice everywhere," King declared. He further explained: "We are caught in an inescapable network of mutuality, tied to a single garment of destiny. Whatever affects one directly, affects all indirectly."[43]

Various aspects of black spirituality, passive and radical, came together in the civil rights movement of the 1960s, catalyzed by the Montgomery bus boycott of 1955–1956. The movement could be said to be the final stoking of the furnace that forged the African American Christian faithful into a living army of God. In the words of gospel singer and composer James Cleveland, they would soon "come forth as pure gold."[44]

Black spirituality, with its emphasis on God (God-centeredness) and Scripture (biblical rootedness), with its Spirit-filled naturalness that is joyful, holistic, and contemplative, with its focus on community, and with its orientation toward liberation and justice, became once again the foundation upon which African Americans in this period built all their hopes and dreams. This spirituality was expressed in powerful liturgies that emphasized prayer, song, fervent preaching and testifying, and, above all else, soul-stirring music that lifted the participants out of their seats to dance in ecstatic joy and praise of God.

The mass meetings at various black churches throughout the South, many of which were bombed and/or burned to the ground afterward, gathered the dispersed threads of black spirituality and wove them once again into a tight, embracing, protective garment that clothed the nonviolent demonstrators with the armor of God as they stepped out in their marches, boycotts, sit-ins, and pray-ins. Participants prayed for deliverance from the hell of Jim/Jane Crow; they prayed for the safety of those marching in defiance of the laws; they prayed for an end to this strife. As Coretta Scott King recounted: "Prayer was a wellspring of strength and inspiration during the civil rights movement. Throughout the movement, we prayed for greater human understanding. We prayed for the safety of our compatriots in the freedom struggle. We prayed for victory in our nonviolent protest, for brotherhood and sisterhood among people

43. King, *Why We Can't Wait*, 77.

44. Line from James Cleveland's gospel song, "Please Be Patient with Me, God Is Not Through with Me Yet."

of all races, for reconciliation and the fulfillment of the Beloved Community."[45]

Both the radical and passive branches of the black church, as denoted by Gayraud Wilmore, were galvanized into action by the fires and bombings as well as the spirit-filled example of men and women, and children as young as six, who stepped into the hands of danger as they peacefully demonstrated in the face of vicious police dogs, cattle prods, and water hoses. By so doing, they affirmed and authenticated their faith and their spirituality as the movement brought together people from all classes and across racial and gender lines for a common cause; namely, freedom:

> The absolute criterion of authentic black spirituality is its impact on the quality of the believer's life. It assumes that the true nature of our faith is reflected in the way in which we relate to other human beings and the created order, and that our concern for others will naturally generate witness and actions directed toward the realization of freedom for all human beings to live a liberated and joyful life, energized by the power of the Spirit. Authentic black spirituality leads to prophetic action on behalf of justice, a justice that requires liberation from sin and its effects. . . . A person imbued with the life-force at the center of black spirituality—with the Spirit of God—is willing to struggle for this liberation.[46]

All of those who were engaged in the struggle with King found themselves inspired and motivated by this young man who seemed to walk with God through all types of trials and tribulations. King's call to do ministry in the service of all of God's creation, regardless of race, creed, or skin color, gave him the courage, buoyed up on prayer, to engage the principalities of this world in a struggle literally to the death. He succeeded against many odds, with the inspiration and support of those engaged in the struggle with him, to finally overcome.

Although King was critical of the black church for its emotionalism, fundamentalism, and "otherworldly" emphasis, he also saw it "as an agent of redemption because it continues to live as a 'colony of heaven' in an alien world." It continues to enact the Christian story and has not rationalized away the harder demands of the prophets and Jesus. It still understands that the church is called to heal the brokenhearted, preach

45. See Coretta Scott King, foreword to *Standing in the Need of Prayer: A Celebration of Black Prayer* (New York: Free Press, 2003), x.

46. Jamie T. Phelps, "Black Spirituality," in *Spiritual Traditions for the Contemporary Church*, ed. Robin Maas and Gabriel O'Donnell (Nashville: Abingdon, 1990), 344–45.

deliverance to captives, and to announce the acceptable year of the Lord, much unlike the white church.[47]

Yet there were times when King experienced doubt and fear at the events that had so rapidly taken over his life. This is precisely when he turned in faith to the God who had brought him so far; that God who remained the source of his strength. Over and over, in times of crisis, King found himself turning not to the liberal theology he had studied in the North but to that "old-time religion" in which he had been immersed his entire life, a religious faith that provided him with the strength to continue in the struggle. It was the faith of his fathers and mothers, the people from whom he emerged as a prophet. They were what revived his soul again and again and enabled him to carry on to his journey's end, a journey that was life and breath to him.[48] They were that "great cloud of witnesses" who surrounded him at birth, nurtured and sustained him throughout his life, and grieved together at his untimely death. King's spirituality was indeed a spirituality of resistance to any and all principalities that sought to deter the efforts of African Americans toward a full and precious freedom, one they had been fighting for for centuries. They never gave up and neither would he, for the journey was too valuable and the end so near.

At the same time, there were problems within these sources of King's spirituality. The black church and the black Social Gospel tradition were not perfect. The church was and is a human institution with all too many human faults and failings. It was in many instances a place of middle-class elitism, both South and North, where a person's acceptance was based on the color of their skin, their education, and the types of work they did. The churches were often divided along class and color lines, and those that had the most affluent members were the ones who often preached maintenance of the status quo and discouraged stirring up trouble. With this in mind, Gayraud Wilmore speaks of a "dark and contrary side of black religion as it developed under the most trying circumstances":[49]

> The dark and contrary side of black religion must be understood as an alternative form of spirituality. It is a fundamental aspect of what we may call the survival tradition. . . . Although it was often expressed as a curiously divergent form of black spirituality, it is not to be equated with the kind of pietism that can be translated into social reform. It often had, rather, a bitter

47. Lischer, *Preacher King,* 239.

48. Clayborne Carson and Peter Holloran, eds., *A Knock at Midnight: Inspiration from the Great Sermons of Reverend Martin Luther King, Jr.* (New York: Warner, 2000), 159–64.

49. Wilmore, *Black Religion and Black Radicalism,* 257.

unsentimentality about it. It was more often cynical, manipulative, and at the very least, ambivalent about spiritual things.[50]

In keeping with Howard Thurman's critique of Christianity, for its failure to address issues of racism in the United States, womanist theologian Stacey Floyd-Thomas asks: "How can the Black church be so politically assertive on questions of race and representation yet remain conservative (and, in some cases, reactionary) regarding gender, the role of women, and sexual orientation as they relate to church membership and leadership?"[51]

It is, in many ways, the fault of that same historical tradition that shaped and formed King himself. Although seen by many as a radical institution that fought for the freedom of its people, the truth is that neither during slavery, or its aftermath, Reconstruction and Jim Crow, was the church as radically active as many believed. It was, rather, a conservative voice that mostly stressed good behavior and other-worldly perspectives. Despite his legacy position in the National Baptist Convention, King himself discovered that he was unable to garner the support or even respect of Reverend Joseph Jackson, the president. Instead, he and those who supported his efforts to bring the church in line with the social and economic needs of persons of African descent were forced in the early 1960s to start a new convention, the Progressive Baptists, to carry out their goals.[52]

It must be acknowledged that King was a product of his times and was unable or unwilling to change his own attitude on certain issues, and especially those regarding the role and involvement of women. He was indeed influenced by his upbringing in the black Christian community and the black church, both of which were staunchly conservative and patriarchal. Although his mother and grandmother were active members of Atlanta's Ebenezer Baptist Church, they had no significant leadership roles other than those historically open to women, such as the music department, the Sunday school, and various women's auxiliary groups. It was the men who ruled from the pulpit and within the home, and this was not apparently questioned by King. Rather, he instituted the same patriarchal hierarchy in his own home and in the SCLC, where Ella Baker, founding member and secretary, was eventually ousted for being too assertive (aggressive) in seeking a role in decision-making. It is truly ironic that King's growth and development, which expanded over

50. Wilmore, *Black Religion and Black Radicalism*, 257–58.

51. Floyd-Thomas et al., *Black Church Studies*, 107.

52. Charles H. King, "Quest and Conflict: The Untold Story of the Power Struggle between King and Jackson," *Negro Digest*, May 1967, 6–9 and 71–79.

time to include action against economic injustice and the Vietnam War, never reached the level of understanding needed to include the equality of women and of LGBTQ persons, an understanding his widow, Coretta Scott King, did achieve. Then again, he did not have the time to further develop his perspective as his wife did. This patriarchal and hierarchical understanding of men and women in the black church persists to the present day, despite the growing involvement in the church of women ordained into the ministry.

King was undoubtedly a man of his times, with the problems and promises of that time. However, as I have tried to show in this chapter, he was also clearly a man ahead of his time, one who, in keeping with his ancestral traditions, was empowered by *ntu,* the awesome life-force (spiritual power) of African and African American spirituality, to become so much more than he may have initially seemed capable of becoming. The young inexperienced minister blended the academic knowledge that he attained in the academy with the spirituality of his African/African American religious tradition and forge a renewed understanding of church engagement in the world around it that resonated in the hearts of millions, black and white.

As Lewis V. Baldwin and Victor Anderson point out in the introduction to this work, "King was part of a history, a heritage, a people, and a place in which the rhythm of human life was accentuated through spirituality."[53] For King, there was no separation of the secular and spiritual. As with his African ancestors, religion was a foundational part of all life and could not be envisioned apart from all of life. All of life is religious, therefore all of life is necessarily spiritual. King's entire life was a spiritual quest for the betterment of not only the lives of African Americans, but those of all Americans, irrespective of race, creed, or class. His understanding of the interconnectedness of all life and its value can be traced all the way back to the Africa of his ancestors. King was truly a product of his upbringing in the black Christian community of the South and the black church, with its emphasis on the Social Gospel. He embodied African American religious and spiritual traditions in the totality of his life, a life dedicated to changing the lives of countless others for the better, and he succeeded on many levels. His journey of faith is a model and inspiration for others who seek to create a better world from our present world, and to bring all of us into that beloved community that Jesus challenged us to build in our midst.

53. Baldwin and Anderson, introduction, 4, 8.

3.

The Promptings of Some Beneficent Force: Dimensions of the "Spiritual" in the Life and Language of Martin Luther King Jr.

LEWIS V. BALDWIN AND VICTOR ANDERSON

> Several incidents in my life have convinced me of spiritual interposition—of the promptings of some beneficent force outside ourselves, which tries to help us where it can.
>
> —Sir Arthur Conan Doyle[1]

> This is the time of year when we come to see that the most powerful forces in the universe are not those forces of military might but those forces of spiritual might.
>
> —Martin Luther King Jr.[2]

The African belief that spirits inhabit the whole of creation and the universe survived slavery in one form or another in the United States, while also impacting the thinking of generations of blacks in the American South up to and even beyond the time of Martin Luther King Jr. Born in 1929 in Atlanta, Georgia, and raised in an environment in which ex-slaves and their immediate descendants functioned as principal protagonists and/or sources of culture, King was exposed very early to certain ideas concerning the spiritual world, and especially the notion of the surviving spirits of ancestors that continue to dwell among and influence

1. Quoted in John Bartlett, *The Shorter Bartlett's Familiar Quotations: A Collection of Passages, Phrases, and Proverbs Traced to Their Sources in Ancient and Modern Literature*, ed. Christopher Morley and Louella D. Everett (New York: Pocket, 1964), 111.

2. Martin Luther King Jr., "Palm Sunday Sermon on Mohandas K. Gandhi," in Clayborne Carson et al., eds., *The Papers of Martin Luther King, Jr.: Threshold of a New Decade, January 1959–December 1960* (Berkeley: University of California Press, 2005), 5:145.

the affairs of the living.[3] This culture and worldview were foundational for King in later years as he crafted language to explain his own sense of the dimensions of spiritual reality.

This chapter highlights King's use of the language of the *spiritual* not only in reference to his own inner self, inner journey, and inner life, but also in describing what he termed "the interrelated structure of all reality,"[4] and particularly the nature of God and humanity, the human quest for a sense of the divine or supernatural realm, the nature of the church, the state of the nation and the world, and humanity's essential and relentless struggle for freedom. In other words, the focus is on King's tendency to relate the phenomena of the *spiritual* to the whole of life, existence, and the universe. Attention is also devoted to what King's employment of the language of the *spiritual* revealed about his own spirituality, spiritual life, spiritual leadership, and efforts to "save" or "redeem the soul" of his own nation and the world.[5] This chapter closes

3. King Jr.'s belief in a spirit or soul that survives the body after death was evident as early as 1941, as he, at age twelve, struggled with the death of his maternal grandmother, Jennie C. Parks Williams. The youngster "was particularly hurt by this incident," and "for the first time" discussed at length with his parents, Martin Luther Sr. and Alberta Williams King, "the doctrine of immortality." From that point, King Jr. never really doubted that the spirits of ancestors survive while maintaining a relationship with living descendants. He made the point in a paper outline prepared in 1949, while he was a seminarian, noting that "death is the cessation of the physical life" but not the cessation of "the spirit"—that "The spiritual leaves the material body, but lives on, and enters new scenes of action." See Clayborne Carson et al., eds., *The Papers of Martin Luther King, Jr.: Called to Serve, January 1929–June 1951* (Berkeley: University of California Press, 1992), 1:250, 362, and 398; Sterling Stuckey, *Slave Culture: Nationalist Theory and the Foundation of Black America* (New York: Oxford University Press, 1987), 5 and 333–34; and Lewis V. Baldwin, "'A Home in Dat Rock': Afro-American Folk Sources and Slave Visions of Heaven and Hell," *The Journal of Religious Thought* 41, no. 1 (Spring–Summer 1984): 50.

4. See Martin Luther King Jr., *Where Do We Go from Here: Chaos or Community?* (Boston: Beacon, 1968; originally published in 1967), 181; and Martin Luther King Jr., *The Trumpet of Conscience* (New York: Harper & Row, 1987; originally published in 1967), 69–70.

5. After the successful outcome of the Montgomery bus boycott (1955–1956), King often spoke of his mission in terms of the redemption or salvation of America's soul. The motto of his Southern Christian Leadership Conference (SCLC)—a South-wide organization founded in 1957 "to serve as a channel through which local protest organizations in the South could coordinate their protest activities, and to give the total struggle a sense of Christian and disciplined direction"—was "to save" or "to redeem the soul of America." I submit that as King increasingly gained international prominence, in terms of his stature, vision, and social justice outreach, he thought more and more in terms of *saving* and/or *redeeming* not simply America's soul, but the soul of humanity and the world as a whole. During his thirteen years in the public limelight, King never really made a distinction here. This is not surprising since he always thought of America's problems in relation to, and as a reflection of, world problems. His description of himself "as a citizen of the world" in those latter years of his public life and career clearly suggests that he understood himself and his mission in universal terms, and this carried prophetic and spiritual as well as social, political, and economic implications. See Carson et al., eds., *Papers*, 5:370 and 546; Clayborne Carson et al., eds., *The Papers of Martin Luther King, Jr.: To Save the Soul of America, January 1961–August 1962* (Berkeley: University of California Press,

with some reflections on how King embodied certain tendencies toward what James W. Fowler terms "universalizing faith," or, more specifically, moving beyond "self as the center of experience" to entertain "a participation in God or ultimate reality" as "the center of experience."[6]

ON BEINGS OF SPIRIT: THINKING IN THEOCENTRIC, CHRISTOCENTRIC, AND HUMANOCENTRIC TERMS

Martin Luther King Jr.'s sense of "spirit" or the "spiritual" related very much to the supernatural realm, and was deeply rooted in his conception of God as "a being of spirit," as "the only perfect personality," as "the Supreme Cause," and as "the central and most creative person" of "the universe," ideas he inherited through his upbringing in black church culture and his later exposure to Crozer Theological Seminary, Boston University, and the personalist school of philosophical theology. Drawing on these sources, and to a great extent on his reading of the Scriptures, King viewed God as "spirit" or "spiritual being," and he at times spoke of "the living Spirit," "the Holy Spirit," "God's spirit," "the spirit of God," "the presence of the Divine," "something spiritual in the cosmos," "a creative personal power in the universe" that "cannot be explained in materialistic terms," or "the personal spirit, perfectly good, who in love creates, sustains, and orders all."[7] "The God I worship is not a body," King declared.

2014), 7:237, 297, and 596; King, *Where Do We Go from Here?,* 167–91; and King, *Trumpet of Conscience,* 31 and 67–78. Adam Fairclough consciously and brilliantly treats King's mission in terms of the redemption of America's soul, giving major attention to SCLC's "inner dynamics," but he largely ignores how that vision of America's redemption and world redemption was always one and the same in King's moral vision and in his efforts to create what he called "the beloved community." See Adam Fairclough, *To Redeem the Soul of America: The Southern Christian Leadership Conference and Martin Luther King, Jr.* (Athens: University of Georgia Press, 1987), 1–8 and 13–405.

6. In his exploration of spiritual development, Fowler developed a theoretical framework embracing six stages of faith through which people who practice both traditional faiths and alternative expressions of spirituality go. "Universalizing faith" is the sixth stage, and it relates to persons who devote their lives to the service of others without worries, doubts, or reservations. One could also use the term "universalizing spirituality." See James W. Fowler, *Stages of Faith: The Psychology of Human Development* (New York: HarperOne, 1995; originally published in 1981), 199–210.

7. Martin Luther King Jr., "Who Are We?," unpublished version of a sermon, Ebenezer Baptist Church, Atlanta, Georgia (5 February 1966), Library and Archives of the Martin Luther King Jr. Center for Nonviolent Social Change (KCLA), Atlanta, Georgia, 3; Martin Luther King Jr., "Training Your Child in Love," unpublished version of a sermon, Ebenezer Baptist Church, Atlanta, Georgia (8 May 1966), KCLA, 10; Carson et al., eds., *Papers,* 1:243–44, 248–51, 254, and 257; Carson et al., eds., *Papers,* 5:425; Alex Ayres, ed., *The Wisdom of Martin Luther King, Jr.: An A-to-Z Guide to the Ideas and Ideals of the Great Civil Rights Leader* (New York: Penguin, 1993), 247; Clayborne Carson and Peter Holloran, eds., *A Knock at Midnight:*

"He is pure spirit, lifted above the categories of time and space."[8] Here King had in mind "spirit" as related to the miraculous or "spirit" as a form of existence outside and beyond the natural, material, visible, observable, and quantifiable world, and as a being inexplicable solely in terms of the findings of science and natural law and phenomena.[9] Speaking of God in the context of the time factor, King asserted that "all reality has spiritual control"—that "History is ultimately guided by spirit, not matter." "This simply means," King wrote, "that we must rediscover the principle that there is a God behind the process of life, and that He has supreme control over His creation." "In our age of materialism," he added, "we have gotten away from this principle."[10] His Christian faith led him to the view that history is in large measure a spiritual conflict "between God and Satan," or "good and evil," with "good eventually" emerging "as victor."[11] King gradually teased out and embraced many of these essential points of theology in the period from the mid-1940s to the mid-1950s, as he pursued his studies in sociology and religion at Morehouse College, and in systematic and philosophical theology at Crozer Theological Seminary and Boston University.

King never really doubted the idea of God as the one and only purely spiritual being, but questions remain about how he understood what he termed "the divine sonship of Jesus" in relation to this purely spiritual being. While in his teens, King actually struggled with traditional concepts of the divinity or deity of Jesus Christ. More specifically, the youngster expressed doubts concerning the virgin birth and the resur-

Inspiration from the Great Sermons of Martin Luther King, Jr. (New York: Warner, 1998), 164; Carson et al., eds., *Papers,* 7:387 and 442; Clayborne Carson et al., eds., *The Papers of Martin Luther King, Jr.: Advocate of the Social Gospel, September 1948–March 1963* (Berkeley: University of California Press, 2007), 6:223, 293, 302, 528, 534, and 574; and Martin Luther King Jr., *Stride toward Freedom: The Montgomery Story* (New York: Harper & Row, 1958), 92.

8. Martin Luther King Jr., *The Measure of a Man* (Philadelphia: Fortress, 1988; originally published in 1959), 12–13; and King, *Stride toward Freedom,* 92.

9. King, "Who Are We?," 3; King, *Measure of a Man,* 12–13; and King, *Stride toward Freedom,* 92.

10. At other points in his writings, King referred to God as "the ultimate ground of the historical process," or as that being that "reveals himself progressively through human history." At the same time, he categorically rejected Communism's "materialistic interpretation of history," mainly because it is "avowedly secularistic and materialistic," and "has no place for God." See Carson and Holloran, eds., *Knock at Midnight,* 15; Ayres, ed., *Wisdom of Martin Luther King, Jr.,* 107; King, *Stride toward Freedom,* 92; Carson et al., eds., *Papers,* 1:250–51 and 294; Carson et al., eds., *Papers,* 6:162; and Clayborne Carson et al., eds., *The Papers of Martin Luther King, Jr.: Birth of a New Age, December 1955–December 1956* (Berkeley: University of California Press, 1997), 3:348.

11. "Sunday with Martin Luther King," unpublished, WAAF-AM, Chicago, Illinois (10 April 1966), KCLA, 1.

rection,[12] and, by implication, the concept of Jesus as supernatural being or essence in the same sense as God. In his academic papers at Crozer and Boston, King stressed the "genuine humanity" and the "divine sonship of Jesus"—that Jesus was a mysterious integration of body, mind, soul, and spirit—but his continuing struggle with what the "bodily resurrection" and "the virgin birth" meant in both spiritual and rational terms precluded any possibility of him embracing the view that Jesus, like God, was "a being of pure spirit."[13] As late as 1963, when King had become well-established as pastor, civil rights leader, and world figure, he explained that "the traditional issues of theology"—meaning "the divinity of Christ, the virgin birth, His bodily resurrection"—"are peripheral," and he rejected "the virgin birth of Christ as a literal fact." "The early Christians had noticed the moral uniqueness of Jesus," he held, and "to make this uniqueness appear plausible, they devised a mythological story of Jesus's biological uniqueness." In King's judgment, then, what "set Jesus apart" was his "unique goodness." "I don't think anyone can be Jesus," he continued. "He was one with God in purpose. He so submitted His will to God's will that God revealed His divine plan to man through Jesus. In this sense, Jesus was divine." The suggestion here is that Jesus's divinity meant that he was in some special sense "a being of spirit," but not inherently "pure spirit."[14]

The conviction that Jesus uniquely achieved a unity of spirit with both God and humanity courses through the interviews, writings, and sermons of King, but his references to "the spirit of Jesus," "the spiritual genius of Jesus," "Jesus as a personal spirit," "the living Savior," "the spirit of Jesus's teaching," and "Jesus as the absolute" and "highest revelation of God" meant as much and considerably more than this when considered in relation to what he called "the workings of the Holy Spirit."[15] King

12. Carson et al., eds., *Papers*, 1:361; Martin Luther King Jr., *The Autobiography of Martin Luther King, Jr.*, ed. Clayborne Carson (New York: Warner, 1998), 6; and Keith D. Miller, *Voice of Deliverance: The Language of Martin Luther King, Jr. and Its Sources* (New York: The Free Press, 1992), 40.

13. Carson et al., eds., *Papers*, 1:226–29, 246–49, 263–67; and Clayborne Carson et al., eds., *The Papers of Martin Luther King, Jr.: Rediscovering Precious Values, July 1951–November 1955* (Berkeley: University of California Press, 1994), 2:102–3, 131–32, 178–91, and 215.

14. Lee E. Dirks, "'The Essence Is Love': The Theology of Martin Luther King, Jr.," *National Observer* (30 December 1963): 1 and 12. As a seminary student, King had argued that "The true significance of the divinity of Christ lies in the fact that his achievement is prophetic and promissory for every other true son of man who is willing to submit his will to the will and spirit of God." See Carson et al., eds., *Papers*, 1:246 and 257.

15. Carson et al., eds., *Papers*, 5:146–47; Carson et al., eds., *Papers*, 7:205 and 442; Carson et al., eds., *Papers*, 6:177; King, "Who Are We?," 6; Carson et al., eds., *Papers*, 1:246–49; and Clayborne Carson et al., eds., *The Papers of Martin Luther King, Jr.: Symbol of the Movement, January 1957–December 1958* (Berkeley: University of California, 2000), 4:472.

believed that Jesus was not only begotten of the Holy Spirit, baptized in the name of the Holy Spirit, anointed and led by the Holy Spirit, and offered as a sacrifice under the power of the Holy Spirit, but also commanded his disciples to teach and baptize in the name of the Holy Spirit, and is one through whom "the Spirit of God works today."[16] The Holy Spirit works through Christ, King concluded, so that we might not only "seek God," but also in order that "we might differentiate between right and wrong," commit to "truth," choose "the right," and become "efficient instruments of the divine energy" in "bringing about" the "moral transformation within the individual" and society.[17]

A sense of "spirit" or the "spiritual" figured similarly and in other ways into King's understanding of humanity, especially as he probed the question of the human relationship to the divine. He moved from the premise that humans embody not only body and mind, but soul and spirit as well. Based on the *imago dei* concept, or humans created in the image of God, he discounted the notion, advanced by naturalists, that "man is a cosmic accident" whose "whole life can be explained by matter in motion," or that man is merely "an animal" or "a biological being" with "a physical body" and a "kinship with animate nature." King also challenged humanists who, struck by humanity's "noble, spiritual powers," and especially "the power of reason," tended to "lift man almost to the position of a god."[18] Avoiding the extremes of what he termed "a pessimistic naturalism" and "an optimistic humanism," King approached the issue in true Hegelian fashion, or through the process of dialectical thinking, insisting that humans are both biological beings as well as spiritual beings. As a reflection of the divine image, he declared, "man is a being of spirit," but "not God" nor "pure spirit" because "some of the image of God" was "scarred" and "left us" due to "our sinfulness." Quoting the psalmist, King, addressing the question, "What is man?," in spiritual terms, noted that "Thou hast made him a little lower than the angels and crowned him with glory and honor" (Ps 8:4–5).[19] King's most

16. King obviously rejected the idea, advanced in the circles of Oneness Pentecostalism, that Jesus is Father, Son, and Holy Spirit. See Carson et al., eds., *Papers*, 5:146–47; Carson et al., eds., *Papers,* 7:205 and 442; Carson et al., eds., *Papers*, 2:215; and Carson et al., eds., *Papers*, 1:245–51.

17. Interestingly enough, when King mentioned "individuals who greatly reveal the working of the Spirit of God," he included the names of David Livingstone, Mahatma Gandhi, and Albert Schweitzer alongside the name of Jesus of Nazareth. See Carson et al., eds., *Papers,* 1:248–49.

18. King, *Measure of a Man*, 9–13; and King, "Who Are We?," 6–7. The best secondary sources on this subject are Garth Baker-Fletcher, *Somebodyness: Martin Luther King, Jr., and the Theory of Dignity* (Minneapolis: Fortress, 1993), 79–184; and Richard W. Wills, *Martin Luther King, Jr. and the Image of God* (New York: Oxford University Press, 2009), 59–136.

19. King, *Measure of a Man,* 9–14; King, "Who Are We?," 6–7; Carson et al., eds., *Papers,*

analytical and insightful statement on the spiritual side of human nature is set forth in his book, *The Measure of a Man* (1959), though he also discussed the subject at points in some of his interviews, speeches, sermons.[20]

But what did this image of humans as "spiritual beings" or "beings of spirit" mean in more specific terms for King, aside from the fact that they are "more than flesh and blood" and "crowned with glory and honor?" Writing at length concerning "the spiritual element in man," King stated the following: "This is ultimately that which distinguishes man from his animal ancestry. He is in time, yet above time. He is in nature, yet above nature."[21] King went on to point out that much unlike humans, other animals cannot write "a Shakesperian play," discuss "intricate problems concerning the political and economic structures of a society," speculate "on the nature and destiny of the universe," "think a poem and write it," "think a symphony and compose it," or "imagine a great civilization and create it." For King, "the spiritual element," "the human spirit," or the creative inner power in humans, accounted in large measure for "man's amazing capacity for memory and thought and imagination," and also his ability to "leap oceans" and "break through walls," to "have communion with the past," to "rise above the limitations of time and space," to "entertain ideals" that "become his inspiration," to choose "his supreme end," to "embrace the uncertainties of the future," to "be a hero or a fool," and to "be true or false to his nature."[22] Thus, "the highest expression of man's spiritual quality," King concluded, "is freedom." Despite oppression, King sensed that "we are all free in the sense that freedom is the inner power that drives us to achieve freedom."[23] At other points in his speeches and interviews, he spoke of such a human spirit in terms of "a certain kind of inner hope," "an inner faith," or "an 'in-spite of' quality."

6:177–78 and 334; Carson et al., eds., *Papers*, 7:442; and John J. Ansbro, *Martin Luther King, Jr.: The Making of a Mind* (Maryknoll, NY: Orbis, 1982), 90. In a Graduate Record Examination in March 1951, King examined the "essential religious belief" that "man is a soul or spiritual being." See Carson et al., eds., *Papers*, 1:412.

20. See, for example, King, "Who Are We?," 3–4.

21. Here King had in mind what he labeled humanity's "self-transcending quality." At other points, he spoke of humanity's "readjusting qualities." Carson et al., eds., *Papers*, 6:177–79; King, "Who Are We?," 6–7; and Martin Luther King Jr., "Doubts and Certainties Link: Transcript of an Interview," unpublished, London, England (Winter 1968), KCLA, 2.

22. Carson et al., eds., *Papers*, 6:177–78; Carson et al., eds., *Papers,* 1:244; and King, *Measure of a Man,* 11–21.

23. Martin Luther King Jr., "Moving to Another Mountain," *The Wesleyan University Alumnus* 52, no. 4 (May 1968): 3; Martin Luther King Jr., "See You in Washington," unpublished version, SCLC Staff Retreat Ebenezer Baptist Church, Atlanta, Georgia (17 January 1968), 11; King, *Where Do We Go from Here?,* 171; and King, "Doubts and Certainties Link," 2–3.

King felt that humanity's spiritual quality or essential inner nature inhered, perhaps more importantly, in its unique power and capacity to communicate and fellowship with God. "Man is a spiritual being born to have communion with the eternal God of the universe"—"with that which is eternal and everlasting," King wrote. "God creates every individual for a purpose—to have fellowship with Him." He elaborated further: "This is the ultimate meaning of the image of God. It is not that man as he is in himself bears God's likeness, but rather that man is designated for and called to a particular relation with God. The concept of the image of God assures us that we, unlike our animal ancestry and the many inanimate objects of the universe, are privileged to have fellowship with the divine."[24] For King, this is what affirmed in the loftiest of terms the ultimate meaning of life and human existence.

But the chief spiritual crisis of the modern world consisted, in King's estimation, in humanity's common and seemingly inescapable tendency to choose the path of sin and evil, which leads to self-estrangement and estrangement from other selves, and, perhaps more importantly, estrangement from God. "Whenever man looks deep into the depths of his nature," King maintained, "he becomes painfully aware of the fact that the history of life is the history of a constant revolt against God."[25] As far as King was concerned, this, perhaps more than anything else, accounted for the nagging, ongoing spiritual hunger that haunts human beings, a hunger with which Saint Augustine, the great church father, was struggling when he declared: "Thou madest us for Thyself, and our heart is restless, until it repose in Thee," and, "Lord, make me pure but not yet."[26] These words resonated well with King because they spoke to his own enduring spiritual quest as a flawed and finite human being. He always spoke in terms of "the primacy of the spiritual,"[27] and continuously sought refuge in that "being of pure spirit" that responds "to the deepest yearnings of the human heart"—that "living reality" that is "validated in the experiences of everyday life," that "works in the world to bring goodness to pass," that becomes coworkers with "human beings" in the struggle "to achieve a social order that is moral in nature and capable of expressing love." "When I am physically overburdened and find that my spiritual lamp is growing somewhat dim," King

24. Carson et al., eds., *Papers,* 6:177–78.

25. King, *Measure of a Man,* 21–27; and Carson et al., eds., *Papers,* 6:178.

26. Carson et al., eds., *Papers*, 6:190, 335, and 424; King, *Measure of a Man*, 22; Carson et al., eds., *Papers,* 5:579; and Martin Luther King Jr., *"Thou, Dear God": Prayers That Open Hearts and Spirits—The Reverend Dr. Martin Luther King, Jr.,* ed. Lewis V. Baldwin (Boston: Beacon, 2012), 221–23.

27. King, *Where Do We Go from Here?,* 171; Carson et al., eds., *Papers,* 6:176.

asserted, "I remember one of my favorite Biblical passages from the Book of Psalms: 'I will look to the hills from whence cometh my help. My help cometh from the Lord'" (Ps 121:1–2).[28] "We may not be able to see Him with our eyes," King proclaimed in a sermon in May 1966, "but I tell you this morning that I feel the pull of God." "I felt the pull of God "every time I noticed beauty," "every time I noticed truth," "every time I saw goodness in the universe." This sense of an intangible, divine, undying, "loving presence that binds all life" was both the source of King's own spiritual security and the force behind his efforts to significantly improve the human condition.[29]

The need for humans to connect with their spiritual selves was equally important for King. "Each of us lives in two realms, the internal and the external," said he in his sermon, "The Man Who Was a Fool." "The internal is the realm of spiritual ends expressed in art, literature, morals, and religion," he further stated. "The external is that complex of devices, techniques, mechanisms, and instrumentalities by means of which we live. These include the house we live in, the car we drive, the clothes we wear, the economic resources we acquire—the material stuff we have to exist." In King's estimation, humans, like the man Jesus called "a fool" in Luke 12:20, always face the danger of allowing the material means by which they live to replace the spiritual ends for which they live, and, in such instances, "the internal" gets lost "in the external."[30] Thus, it is critically significant to "keep a line of distinction between means and ends, between structure and destiny." Otherwise, the richer persons become "materially," the poorer they become "intellectually and spiritually." "Western civilization is particularly vulnerable at this moment," he further argued, "for our material abundance has brought us neither peace of mind nor serenity of spirit." For King, such an indictment was disturbingly inescapable, and it further underscored the pressing need for humans to "move out of the mountain of practical materialism," which

28. Martin Luther King Jr., "Interview during Chicago Gathering with CCCO," unpublished, Chicago, Illinois (18 March 1966), KCLA, 1; Carson and Holloran, eds., *Knock at Midnight*, 159–64; Frederick L. Downing, *To See the Promised Land: The Faith Pilgrimage of Martin Luther King, Jr.* (Macon, GA: Mercer University Press, 1986), 279–93; and Wyatt Tee Walker, "Spirituality as an Instrument of Social Change," unpublished essay (2015), 1–3.

29. Martin Luther King Jr., *Strength to Love* (Philadelphia: Fortress, 1981; originally published in 1963), 4 and 154–55; Carson et al., eds., *Papers*, 1:386, 408, and 413; Carson et al., eds., *Papers*, 7:576; Carson et al., eds., *Papers*, 2:88, 96, and 294; and King, "Training Your Child in Love," 10.

30. King went on to explain that the man was a fool "because he minimized the within and maximized the without," "because he failed to keep a line of distinction between him and his," "because he allowed his life to be submerged in the rolling waters of his livelihood." See King, *Strength to Love*, 67–68; and King, "Moving to Another Mountain," 3–4.

encourages "the tendency of living as if all life can be reduced to material values" or "judged in a materialistic context."[31]

ESCAPING "SPIRITUAL DOOM": HEALING THE NATION'S HEART PROBLEM

The language of "the spiritual" proved quite useful for Martin Luther King Jr. as he diagnosed the condition of the oppressed in the United States and sought to offer and implement prescriptions for much-needed social, political, and economic change. Convinced that the predicament his own people faced was ultimately spiritual in nature, he routinely began his analysis of social justice issues with a careful and insightful focus on what he termed "the heartbreaking problem of race." "Modern man has strayed to the far countries of secularism, materialism, sexuality, and racial injustice," King lamented, as he reflected upon the state of his own country and much of the world in 1966. And perhaps with the parable of the prodigal son in the New Testament in mind, he added: "The journey has brought moral and spiritual famine in Western civilization but it is not too late to return home." He called upon the nation, and especially "white southerners," to realize "that the treatment of Negroes is a basic spiritual problem."[32] In other words, racism or white supremacy was, in King's judgment, a deep spiritual malady, or "spiritual deformation," for it undermined and ultimately threatened the very essence of *who* and *what* "we are" as human beings, as beings of spirit, and indeed as reflections of the divine image. Taking aim at Jim Crow in the American South, King held that discrimination "distorts the personality," "assails the spirit," and "scars the soul of both the segregator and the segregated." "This is the ultimate tragedy of segregation," he wrote. "It not only harms one physically, but it injures one spiritually."[33] He estimated that the vast majority of white people, perhaps unconsciously, were afflicted with a spiritual and moral disconnect, which made all too many of them incapable of thinking rationally, or distinguishing between right and wrong, when it came to questions regarding race in

31. King, *Strength to Love*, 68–69; King, "Moving to Another Mountain," 3; and King, *Where Do We Go from Here?,* 171–72.

32. Carson et al., eds., *Papers*, 4:103, 105, and 462; Carson et al., eds., *Papers*, 5:120; Carson et al., eds., *Papers*, 7:164; and "Sunday with Martin Luther King," unpublished, WAAF-AM, Chicago, Illinois (17 April 1966), KCLA, 5.

33. James M. Washington, ed., *A Testament of Hope: The Essential Writings and Speeches of Martin Luther King, Jr.* (New York: HarperCollins, 1991), 311; Carson et al., eds., *Papers*, 4:186 and 460; and Martin Luther King Jr., "Nonviolence: The Christian Way in Human Relations," *Presbyterian Life* 11 (February 1958): 12.

America.[34] Of particular concern for King was the lingering and devastating impact that racial discrimination and injustice had upon children, black and white, who were always the most vulnerable under such systems. The nagging "spiritual problem" children faced, he believed, was to grow up "with suspicion, distrust, fear, anxiety, and vindictiveness," a circumstance that no sane, inclusive, and progressive society could realistically value nor tolerate. This is why King had so much to say about the roles of family, religious institutions, and educational structures in shaping the minds and hearts of children and youth.[35]

King had essentially the same perspective on the impact of poverty, economic injustice, and violence and human destruction, which he included among the "Sins of the spirit."[36] Drawing on Jesus's parable of the rich man Dives and the poor man Lazarus in Luke 16:19–31, King pointed to the vast gulf between rich and poor in America and abroad. "Dives went to hell because he forgot about the poor," thus becoming "a conscientious objector in the war on poverty," King declared. King went on to admit that he shuddered at the thought of the rich "going to a kind of spiritual degenerate hell," simply because they allowed the poor "to become invisible" while passing them "by every day." Such a nation, he felt, was "purchasing its own spiritual death through an installment plan."[37] The same applied in the case of violence and human destruc-

34. Martin Luther King Jr., "America's Chief Moral Dilemma," unpublished version of a speech, United Church of Christ—General Synod, Palmer House, Chicago, Illinois (6 July 1965), KCLA, 15 and 19; and Carson et al., eds., *Papers*, 5:120.

35. Here King spoke from experience and with authority, for he himself resented whites during much of his childhood. See Carson et al., eds., *Papers,* 6:354; Carson et al., eds., *Papers*, 7:164; and King, *Autobiography*, 7. King challenged all Americans with the willingness to "pay the price of physical death" in order to free children from "a permanent life of psychological" and spiritual death. He felt that "nothing could be more Christian." See Carson et al., eds., *Papers*, 5:355; King, "Training Your Child in Love," 1–10; Martin Luther King Jr., "The Negro Family," an address at the University of Chicago, Chicago, Illinois, unpublished version (27 January 1966), KCLA, 1–7; King, *Stride toward Freedom,* 21 and 33; Martin Luther King Jr., "What a Mother Should Tell Her Child," unpublished version of a sermon, Ebenezer Baptist Church, Atlanta, Georgia (12 May 1963), KCLA, 1–6; Martin Luther King Jr., "Dives and Lazarus," unpublished version of a sermon, WILD SND, Atlanta, Georgia (10 May 1963), KCLA: 1–10; and Martin Luther King Jr., "To Serve the Present Age," unpublished version of a sermon, Victory Baptist Church, Los Angeles, California (25 June 1967), KCLA: 1–8.

36. Here King drew a sharp distinction between what he labeled "Sins of the flesh" (drunkenness, adultery, stealing, gambling, profanity, etc.) and "Sins of the spirit" (envy, jealousy, self-centeredness, social callousness, etc.). See Carson et al., eds., *Papers*, 6:274 and 372.

37. Martin Luther King Jr., "Pre-Washington Campaign," unpublished version of a speech, St. Thomas AME Church, Birmingham, Alabama (15 February 1968), KCLA, 9; Carson et al., eds., *Papers*, 5:248; King, "Nonviolence: The Christian Way," 12; Gary G. Kohls, "MLK's Warning of America's Spiritual Death," *Consortium News* (19 July 2014), consortium news.com/2014/01/19/mlks-warning-of-americas-spiritual-death/, 1–11; King, "America's Chief Moral Dilemma," 5; and King, *Where Do We Go from Here?,* 186 and 188.

tion, which, in his judgment, also reflected the sinister side of the American spirit. "Our nation is sick with militarism," King noted. "Any nation that spends some seventy or eighty billion dollars on military pursuits is headed toward its spiritual doom."[38] With "great anxiety and agony and anguish of spirit," he estimated that the war in Vietnam, for example, was "damaging the soul of our nation."[39] Needless to say, these were the sentiments of a man deeply troubled about not only the acrimonious state of his country's spiritual and moral life, but its political and/or public life as well.

Clearly, King extended his analysis beyond race, economics, and violence to make a larger point about the state of the nation's soul or spiritual health. America, he maintained, suffered from an extreme spiritual sickness, spiritual deficiency or "bankruptcy," and perhaps even "spiritual famine," as revealed most prominently in the racist and segregated practices of white churches.[40] In other words, America had a "heart problem," and was in dire need of a new humanity, or what he called "a

38. Martin Luther King Jr., "The Meaning of Hope," typed version of a sermon, Dexter Avenue Baptist Church, Montgomery, Alabama (10 December 1967), KCLA, 5. King made essentially the same point about the nation's failure "to achieve civil rights." At another point, King reasoned that "the democratic ideal of freedom and equality will be fulfilled for all—or all human beings will share in the resulting social and spiritual doom." See "Issues and Answers: Martin Luther King, Jr.," unpublished version, ABC Radio and Television Program (18 January 1967), KCLA, 13; King, *Where Do We Go from Here?*, 188; Washington, ed., *Testament of Hope*, 631; and Ayres, ed., *Wisdom of Martin Luther King, Jr.*, 57. Gary G. Kohls rightly concludes that King saw "the disease of violence" as "poisoning America's soul." By publicly advancing this viewpoint, or this kind of "prophetic vision," Kohls continues, King was in effect "signing his own death warrant." See Kohls, "MLK's Warning of America's Spiritual Death," 2–4. With Vietnam in mind, King had planned to preach a sermon titled, "America Too Is Going to Hell," in early April 1968, but was assassinated a week or so before doing so. Notes from this sermon poignantly speak to a nation trapped in a sort of spiritual hell—a nation in danger of completely losing its soul.

39. Martin Luther King Jr., "Transcript of a Press Conference," Biltmore Hotel, Los Angeles, California (12 April 1967), unpublished version, KCLA, 7.

40. Washington, ed., *Testament of Hope*, 355; and "Sunday with Martin Luther King, Jr.," transcript of a taped sermon, WAAF-AM Radio, Chicago, Illinois (17 April 1966), unpublished version, KCLA, 5. King's thoughts on this matter have been repeatedly expressed by both religious leaders and politicians since his death. Speaking of the race problem in America and South Africa in 1973, the evangelist Billy Graham, who was influenced by King, asserted that "we all need a new heart," but his stress on conversion alone, to the exclusion of direct action, would not have been embraced by King. In July 2016, while eulogizing the five police officers who were killed by a sniper in Dallas, Texas, President Barack Obama alluded to the nation's need for "a new heart." The president also had in mind the healing of America around its racial ills. See King, *Where Do We Go From Here?*, 186; and "'We All Need a New Heart': Rev. Graham to S. Africa," in *Jet* 44, no. 2 (5 April 1973): 13. At a number of points in speeches, King insisted that "the habits, if not the hearts of people, have been and are being altered everyday by legislative acts, judicial decisions, and executive orders." "Judicial decrees may not change the heart," he declared, "but they can restrain the heartless." See King, "America's Chief Moral Dilemma," 15; and Carson and Holloran, *Knock at Midnight*, 196.

new kind of man," with a heart open to the suffering and struggles of others. "If America was to fulfill her dream of an integrated, just, and peaceful society," King argued, this "must come by change of the heart and through persuasion."[41] For King, this had long entailed, to a great extent, "conversion to God," which he equated with an "internal revolution" of the spirit. "There is no greater revolution in the world than conversion to God," he once wrote. While he believed in the power of conversion, and especially prayer, to "soften" the "hearts" of oppressors, he felt that, in addition to religion, which worked on the heart, education was needed to change minds, and legislation and court action and nonviolent direct action were required to transform and regulate behavior patterns.[42] In any case, King never completely surrendered to the idea that his country lacked the inner spiritual strength or "resources" to redirect its culture toward genuine and sustainable community. But he was equally clear and compelling when insisting that the Negro, whose greatest gift to America had always been essentially spiritual in nature,[43] should form the vanguard in such a spiritual and moral quest. "We feel that we are the conscience of America—we are its troubled soul," King maintained, "and we will continue to insist that right be done because

41. King, "Doubts and Certainties Link," 5; and "Press Conference USA: Interview with Martin Luther King, Jr.," Transcript from a Video Tape Recording, unpublished (5 July 1963), KCLA, 6. King also spoke of "the heart faith in God," or "a trusting act of self-surrender to God," which, along with "the mind faith in God," or the belief that "there is a God," brings positive change on both the individual and societal levels. See Martin Luther King Jr., "Answer to a Perplexing Question," unpublished version of a sermon, Atlanta, Georgia (3 March 1963), KCLA, 13–14.

42. Nothing was more important for King since white America, like the Pharisee in "the parable of the Pharisee and the Publican" in Luke 18:9–14, stood in danger of being increasingly victimized by an "inordinate spiritual pride"—or "the sin of engaging in evil so long that you lose the capacity of knowing that you are doing evil." See King, *Stride toward Freedom*, 33–34; Carson et al., eds., *Papers,* 6:84; Martin Luther King Jr., "Pharisee and Publican," unpublished version of a sermon, Atlanta, Georgia (9 October 1966), KCLA, 4; and Martin Luther King Jr. and Ralph Abernathy, "Why Our Prayer Vigil: Group Statement of the Negotiating Committee of the Albany Movement and Its Chief Consultants," unpublished, Albany, Georgia (1962), KCLA, 2.

43. Here King was echoing the thinking of W. E. B. DuBois, whom he had read at some length from the time he was at Morehouse College. DuBois highlighted the creative genius of blacks in virtually every sphere of American life and culture, giving considerable attention to their gift of the *spiritual* to the nation's history and culture. See the sections on W. E. B. DuBois, "Of Our Spiritual Strivings," "Of the Faith of the Fathers," and "Of the Sorrow Songs," in *The Souls of Black Folk in Three Negro Classics*, ed. John Hope Franklin (New York: Avon, 1965; originally published in 1903), 213–21, 337–49, and 377–87; and chap. 7, "The American Folk Song," and chap. 9, "The Gift of the Spirit," in W. E. B. DuBois, *The Gift of Black Folk: The Negroes in the Making of America* (Garden City, NY: Square One, 2009), 127–34 and 151–62; King, "Pre-Washington Campaign," 12; Lewis V. Baldwin, *Behind the Public Veil: The Humanness of Martin Luther King, Jr.* (Minneapolis: Fortress, 2016), 186–87; and Martin Luther King Jr., "Honoring Dr. DuBois," *Freedomways* 8, no. 2 (Spring 1968): 104–11.

both God's will and the heritage of our nation speak through our echoing demands."[44] King believed that the Negro's willingness to suffer and even die to change America for the better poignantly revealed not only "the texture and quality of his soul" and the indomitability of the human spirit, but also the potential "effectiveness of a creative minority who serve the state by resisting it with the intention of improving it."[45] If the Negro failed to assume the leadership role in providing the transforming impulse for America, he said in early 1968, "it's going straight to hell." "Cities are burning down every summer," he remarked, as he pondered the race riots, "and there's the war in Vietnam." "Everywhere we look," he continued, "things are confused and messed up. And it's all because our white brothers have not learned how to be just. And we've got to make them just."[46] Wisdom gleaned through experience had convinced King that "physical death is the price that some must pay to free their children and their white brothers from a permanent death of the spirit." He felt that "nothing can be more redemptive!"[47]

Convinced that both the oppressors and the oppressed had to have "the right heart" before much-needed, positive change could be manifested in the social, political, and economic structures of society, King, through his social justice advocacy and direction action campaigns, set out to appeal to the heads and especially the hearts of the American people.[48] The motto of his Southern Christian Leadership Conference (SCLC), founded in 1957 to coordinate local protest activities and to

44. Martin Luther King Jr., "Negro Gains in Rights—1965," Atlanta Press Club, Atlanta, Georgia (10 November 1965), unpublished, KCLA, 18–19.

45. Here King echoed the position of Henry David Thoreau on "the creative minority," whom Thoreau felt provided the greatest opportunity and/or potential for constructive change in any society. See Ansbro, *Martin Luther King, Jr.*, 111; King, *Stride toward Freedom*, 51; King, *Autobiography*, 14 and 54; and Lewis V. Baldwin, *The Voice of Conscience: The Church in the Mind of Martin Luther King, Jr.* (New York: Oxford University Press, 2010), 112–13.

46. King, "Nonviolence: The Christian Way," 12; and Martin Luther King Jr., "Address at a Mass Meeting," unpublished, Laurel, Mississippi (19 March 1968), KCLA, 4. King repeatedly warned white Americans that "The democratic ideal of freedom and equality will be fulfilled for all—or all human beings will share in the resulting social and spiritual doom." See Ayres, ed., *Wisdom of Martin Luther King, Jr.*, 57; and King, *Stride toward Freedom*, 196.

47. Martin Luther King Jr., "Address to a Joint Convention of the Two Houses of the General Court of Massachusetts," Boston, Massachusetts (22 April 1965), unpublished version of a speech, KCLA, 13; and Carson et al., eds., *Papers*, 5:248.

48. At times, King raised the need for "a transformation and change of heart" in America, for "our white brothers" are "carrying it more and more to destruction and damnation." See King, *Stride toward Freedom*, 99; Ayres, ed., *Wisdom of Martin Luther King, Jr.*, 173; Martin Luther King Jr., "A Proposed Statement to the South," unpublished version, presented at the Southern Negro Leaders Conference on Transportation and Nonviolent Integration, Atlanta, Georgia (10–11 January 1957), The King Papers Project, Special Collections, Mugar Memorial Library, Boston University, Boston, Massachusetts, 3; Carson et al., eds., *Papers*, 7:596; and Carson and Holloran, eds., *Knock at Midnight*, 196.

"give the total struggle a sense of Christian and disciplined direction," was "to save" or "redeem the soul of America." After all, America was, in King's mind, rapidly becoming a nation without a soul, and King and his people's intention was not necessarily to *Christianize* but to *humanize* the nation—to ultimately bring into being "the new Detroit, the new Atlanta, the new Chicago, the new New York, and the new America."[49] By taking to the streets and offering practical lessons in democracy's faults and limitations, King felt that his people were, "without writing books or articles," forcing a critical reexamination of the true meaning of both American democracy and the Christian ethic.[50] Noting that King "believed that *white* Christianity had failed to act in accordance with its teachings," Coretta Scott, King's wife, reported that "my husband felt not that the Christian ethic must be rejected, but that those who failed Christianity must be brought—through love, to brotherhood, for their own redemption as well as ours." She added: "He believed that there was a great opportunity for black people to redeem Christianity in America."[51]

This mission to save the nation's soul, which embodied not only spiritual but social, political, and economic implications from the time of the Montgomery bus boycott in 1955–1956,[52] had a powerful, binding

49. Here King was calling for a spiritual renewal of the culture, a kind of conversion experience, but not necessarily the type of "crisis conversion" routinely encouraged in the context of church life, and particularly in fundamentalist and evangelical circles. "America, you must be born again!," King cried, on a number of occasions in his sermons, mass meeting speeches, and writings. Clearly, King understood that the saving of individual souls had to be coupled with the redemption of the nation's soul—that one without the other was essentially meaningless. See Martin Luther King Jr. to Dr. P. J. Ellis, unpublished version of a letter (6 February 1960), The King Papers Project, Boston University, 1; King, "Who Are We?," 5; Carson et al., eds., *Papers,* 6:332; Washington, ed., *Testament of Hope*, 251; Carson et al., eds., *Papers,* 7:237, 529, and 596; Carson et al., eds., *Papers*, 5:370 and 546; King, *Strength to Love*, 57, 68, and 75; Baldwin, *There Is a Balm in Gilead*, 192; and Baldwin, *Voice of Conscience*, 96.

50. Martin Luther King Jr., "The Negro Gains in Rights—1965," unpublished version of a speech, Atlanta, Georgia (10 November 1965), KCLA, 18–19.

51. Coretta Scott King, *My Life with Martin Luther King, Jr.* (New York: Henry Holt, 1993; originally published in 1969), 239. King advanced this position further, insisting that the Negro was "in a destiny-making moment in history, not for ourselves alone but to save the soul of America." He suggested that "the Negro" was "God's instrument" for such a noble cause. See Martin Luther King Jr., "Speech Made in Savannah," unpublished version, Savannah, Georgia (1 January 1961), KCLA, 7 and 9; and Baldwin, *There Is a Balm in Gilead*, 231–43. With King's sense of his people's role as both a Christianizing and humanizing force in mind, C. Eric Lincoln wrote: "King's moral leadership and eventual martyrdom did more to re-establish credibility and interest in the faith than all of the councils and pronouncements of the last hundred years." See C. Eric Lincoln, "The Black Church and a Decade of Change," part 2, *Tuesday at Home* (March 1976): 7.

52. In his first mass meeting speech during the boycott, delivered at the Holt Street Baptist Church in Montgomery, King speculated that "when the history books are written in the future, somebody will have to say, 'There lived a race of people, a *black* people, "fleecy locks

effect on black Americans. This is why King framed and articulated the goals of the civil rights movement in these terms. The mission entailed uniting and inspiring blacks and well-meaning whites in an effort to heal the national divide along the lines of race, ethnicity, culture, class, and religion, and King variously referred to the movement as "a spiritual movement," "a spiritual explosion," "a spiritually rooted movement," "a movement depending on moral and spiritual forces," "a great and creative spiritual venture," "the burning spirit of this new period," and "a movement of essentially revolutionary quality."[53] King obviously viewed the movement in light of the spirit of the people who comprised and launched it, and especially "the New Negro," who were engaging in a reevaluation of self, who had "a new sense of somebodiness and self-respect," who embraced "a new sense of destiny," and who had "a new determination to achieve freedom and human dignity" even at the risk of life and limb.[54] Thus, King could also speak of "spiritual responsibility," of "the spirit of our movement," of "the spiritual and moral dimensions of the desegregation movement," of "the spirit of our nonviolent direct action program," and of movement foot soldiers who were "rich in spirit" and driven by "a divine dissatisfaction," "a new spirit," "this indomitable spirit," "a radiant spirit," "a fighting spirit," "the spirit of prayer," "the spirit of God," "a great spirit," "a dedicated spirit," and a determination "to inject new spiritual blood into the veins of" the soci-

and black complexion," a people who had the moral courage to stand up for their rights. And thereby they injected new meaning into the veins of history and of civilization.'" "And we're gonna do that," he added. "God grant that we will do it before it is too late." See Carson et al., eds., *Papers,* 3:74.

53. See Ayres, ed., *Wisdom of Martin Luther King, Jr.,* 33; Washington, ed., *Testament of Hope*, 52, 84, 162, and 170; "Glenn Smiley Interview with Martin Luther King Jr. Regarding the Montgomery Bus Boycott," unpublished version (February–March, 1956), KCLA, 1–2; Carson et al., eds., *Papers,* 3: 92, 200, and 280; Carson et al., eds., *Papers*, 7:212; and Carson et al., eds., *Papers,* 5:328. Michael Long's claim that King saw the civil rights movement not "as mostly political," but "primarily as a prayerful event" is also relevant to this discussion. See Michael G. Long, "A Review of Lewis V. Baldwin, *Never to Leave Us Alone: The Prayer Life of Martin Luther King, Jr.* (New York: Oxford University Press, 2010)," in *Interpretation: A Journal of Bible and Theology* 66, no. 1 (January, 2012): 110. Such images of the movement support Albert Raboteau's claim that King drew upon and appropriated "the spiritual tradition of black suffering Christianity." Raboteau argues that King, "better than any other leader," articulated "the religious meaning of civil rights for the nation." See Albert J. Raboteau, *A Sorrowful Joy: The Spiritual Journey of an African-American Man in Late Twentieth-Century America* (Mahwah, NJ: Paulist Press, 2002), 29 and 50; and Albert J. Raboteau, "Martin Luther King, Jr. and the Tradition of Black Religious Protest," in Rowland A. Sherrill, ed., *Religion and the Life of the Nation: American Recoveries* (Urbana: University of Illinois Press, 1990), 47.

54. Washington, ed., *Testament of Hope*, 101, 108, and 137; Martin Luther King Jr., "An Address to the National Press Club," Washington, DC, unpublished version (9 July 1962), KCLA, 6–7; Carson et al., *Papers*, 4:77, 126, and 326; and Carson et al., eds., *Papers,* 3:238, 283, and 285, 301, and 456.

ety, thus "transforming its jangling discords into meaningful symphonies of spiritual harmony."[55]

The church as "spiritual body" or "the body of Christ" figured prominently in King's understanding of the civil rights cause. While he alluded frequently to "the inner spiritual church," "the spiritual church," "the spiritual blessings of the church," "the Holy Spirit and the church," and "the spiritual life of the church," his sense of "the true *ekklesia*" entailed much more than a gathering of believers who "transcend the hurly-burly of everyday life" by dwelling "in a transcendent realm" or immersing themselves in the "great resources of power in prayer and worship."[56] When describing the movement as "an extension of the church's mission in the world," as "people dedicated by faith and moved by the Christian spirit," as "the Holy Crusade of black men to be free," and as "a cross that we must bear," and the church as "a community of service" and "a moral and persuasive authority in the Negro's movement towards equality," King actually had in mind radical Christian discipleship—people who consciously combined experiences of a liturgical nature and a belief in the truths of Scripture with theological substance, pragmatic realism, and a well-informed and sustained social activism.[57] He was never oblivious to what Bryan N. Massingale calls "the intrinsic connection between

55. Washington, ed., *Testament of Hope,* 170, 251, 357, and 363; Carson et al., eds., *Papers,* 7:166, 379, 416, and 576; Carson et al., eds., *Papers,* 3:151, 381, 428, and 430; Carson et al., eds., *Papers,* 2:580; Carson et al., eds., *Papers,* 4:413; and Carson et al., eds., *Papers,* 5:166–67, 185, 243, and 425. Interestingly enough, King spoke of the Protestant Reformation in similar terms, viewing it as "that great spiritual movement which gave birth to the Protestant concern for moral and spiritual freedom," but he never meant to suggest that the Protestant Reformation and the civil rights movement were essentially the same in terms of outlook, focus, and goals. See King, *Strength to Love,* 130. C. Douglas Weaver concludes that "The outer piety of Martin Luther King Jr.'s spirituality was social action manifested in the Civil Rights Movement." See C. Douglas Weaver, "The Spirituality of Martin Luther King, Jr.," in *Baylor University: Perspectives in Religious Studies* 31, issue 1 (Spring 2004): 55–70.

56. Washington, ed., *Testament of Hope,* 345–46; Carson et al., eds., *Papers,* 2:232 and 582; Carson et al., eds., *Papers,* 5:172; Carson et al., eds., *Papers,* 4:504; Carson et al., eds., *Papers,* 1:249; Carson et al., eds., *Papers,* 6:225; "Press Conference USA: Interview with Martin Luther King, Jr.," 6; Carson and Holloran, eds., *Knock at Midnight,* 29–31; Martin Luther King Jr., "Emancipation—1963," *Renewal 3* (4 June 1963):2–3; and Martin Luther King Jr., *Why We Can't Wait* (New York: The New American Library, 1963), 91–92.

57. Martin Luther King Jr. to Dr. Truman Douglas, unpublished version of a letter (28 June 1965), KCLA, 1; "Press Conference USA: Interview with Martin Luther King, Jr.," 6–7; Martin Luther King Jr., "An Ambitious Dream Confronts Reality," unpublished version prepared for *New York Amsterdam News* (23 June 1965), KCLA, 1; Martin Luther King Jr., "Eulogy for the Martyred Children," offprint and unpublished version, Birmingham, Alabama (22 September 1963), KCLA, 2; Martin Luther King Jr. "People to People: Meaning of Georgia Elections," *New York Amsterdam News* (3 July 1965): 16; and Carson et al., eds., *Papers,* 4:258.

authentic religious piety," "intellectual ability," and "committed social action."[58]

On some levels, King was critiquing much of the old ecclesial order and traditions while simultaneously calling for a new paradigm for church-world relations. Frustrated by the church's obsession with "creeds," "pious irrelevancies," and "sanctimonious trivialities"—and indeed by its flimsy, vague, superficial, impotent, self-absorbed, and misguided spirituality—King consistently challenged that institution to reclaim "the sacrificial spirit of the early church" while also addressing "the spiritual and physical needs" of people.[59] He felt that the church had both a mandate and an opportunity to "exhibit moral authority" and to model the spiritual life at its best, and he, by word and deed, projected fresh images of what that meant in terms of the *church gathered*, the *church universal*, and the *church sent out to serve*.[60] In other words, King, through his civil rights crusade, was setting forth a compelling new vision for the church as well as practical strategies for implementing that vision. He really believed in the possibility of the emergence of a new ecclesial ideal, and this is why he, in 1965, could even speak of "a spirit within the white churches which had been growing since the early days of the movement and which had really begun to bear fruit following the Birmingham movement."[61] When it came to the potential of the church as a transformational influence on the country, and indeed the world, negativity and hopelessness were not an option for King. "A hopeless individual is a dead individual," he often said. "And if one loses hope, he may still be alive physically, but he's dead spiritually and psychologically." "And he may go on and live another thirty, forty, or fifty years," King continued, "but the cessation of breathing in his life will merely be the belated

58. See Bryan N. Massingale, "Book Explores King's Living Faith," *National Catholic Reporter* 47, no. 6 (7 January 2011): 18.

59. Washington, ed., *Testament of Hope,* 251 and 300; King, *Why We Can't Wait,* 90 and 92; Carson et al., eds., *Papers,* 6:219, 223, 274, 295, 351, and 528; King, "America's Chief Moral Dilemma," 2–3; and Baldwin, *Voice of Conscience*, 51–100. King occasionally criticized some black churches for confusing "spirituality with muscularity" and all too many white churches with confusing spirituality with doctrinal conformity and emotionalism. See King, *Strength to Love,* 63; Carson et al., eds., *Papers,* 6:500; and King, "Pharisee and Publican," 2.

60. King says at a number of points in his writings that "The true Church is the spiritual Church." See Carson et al., eds., *Papers,* 6:219; and Carson et al., eds., *Papers,* 2:232.

61. King's hopefulness at this point seemed misplaced and very difficult to understand, especially since white churches as a collectivity had done so little to really promote the civil rights cause. He was obviously being more diplomatic than realistic when referring to the changing spirit in white churches. The hope he expressed relative to the role of black churches made more sense and is much easier to digest. See King, "America's Chief Moral Dilemma," 13–14 and 19.

announcement of an earlier death of the spirit. He died when he lost hope."[62]

The church acting in the spirit of Jesus Christ and the Sermon on the Mount is largely what King was thinking when referring to the highest ecclesial ideal. He noted on one occasion that the movement "received its spirit and its inspiration from Christ" long before his people "heard the names of Mohandas K. Gandhi or Mahatma Gandhi," and that that movement was "based on the Christian ethic of love" as expressed in the Sermon on the Mount and other parts of the New Testament.[63] Here King found evidence of the power of *agape* or altruistic love, nonviolence, and the redemptive possibilities of unearned suffering. He believed that "somehow when love begins to move out, it finds a kindred spirit, and a responding spirit," and he held that "the deep spirit of Christian love" was "the regulating ideal" in his people's struggle to redeem the soul of the oppressor. "But even as a boycott," he asserted, "we do it with a loving spirit because we somehow know that a boycott is not an end within itself, but merely a means to awaken a sense of shame within their hearts."[64] In King's mind, this was the case with not only boycotts but also marches, demonstrations, voter registration drives, sit-ins, kneel-ins, prayer vigils, and other nonviolent means which, as he put it, constituted "love in action" or "Christianity in action."[65] Clearly, King regarded nonviolence as primarily a spiritual discipline rather than a political tactic, and he made frequent references to "Christian nonviolence," "the nonviolent spirit," or "the spirit of nonviolence." The "qualities of courage, perseverance, unity," and "sacrifice, plus a nonviolence

62. King also maintained that "people who lose hope become bitter. And people who become bitter become spiritually blind." See King, "Meaning of Hope," 13–14.

63. Carson et al., eds., *Papers*, 7:198, 352, 484, 491, 503, and 598; and Carson et al., eds., *Papers*, 5:229. At age fifteen, King had spoken about "the spirit of Christ," which he often said was "the right spirit," or "that spirit" which "promised mercy to the merciful," and which "lifted the lowly, strengthened the weak, ate with publicans, and made the captives free." See Carson et al., eds., *Papers*, 1:111. King reported that "the New Testament was a great influence in my life in the philosophical, from a moral, from a spiritual point of view." See King, "Doubts and Certainties Link," 4.

64. King, "Speech Made in Savannah," 21; Carson et al., eds., *Papers*, 3:230, 273, and 276; Carson et al., eds., *Papers*, 4:131 and 136; and Martin Luther King Jr., "Levels of Love," unpublished version of a sermon, Ebenezer Baptist Church, Atlanta, Georgia (21 May 1967), KCLA, 9.

65. King, *Strength to Love*, 36–46; King, "Nonviolence: The Christian Way," 12; Martin Luther King Jr., "Out of Segregation's Long Night: An Interpretation of a Racial Crisis," *Churchman* 172 (February 1958): 7; Martin Luther King Jr., "An Analysis of the Ethical Demands of Integration," unpublished version of an address, Nashville Consultation, Nashville, Tennessee (27 December 1962), KCLA, 1; and Baldwin, *Voice of Conscience*, 98.

of spirit, are the weapons we must depend upon"[66] in the struggle, he wrote. King labeled "every true Christian" a "fighting pacifist," "involved in a spiritual war"—a believer who struggles with "Christian methods and Christian weapons."[67]

King insisted that the spiritual dimensions of nonviolence were really about "a power" that comes from "within." Convinced that nonviolence "does something to the hearts and souls of those committed to it," he also asserted that "for a person to really believe in nonviolence as a way of life, he must have some religious orientation."[68] He further noted that "the tactics of nonviolence without the spirit of nonviolence may indeed become a new kind of violence."[69] Evidently, King shared Gandhi's belief that "Nonviolence is impossible without self-purification," and this is why the "Commitment Card" King and his followers carried in Birmingham in 1963 pledged "person and body to the nonviolent movement," while specifically vowing, aside from the singing of Negro spirituals and anthems, to "meditate daily on the teachings and life of Jesus," "to pray daily to be used by God in order that all men might be free," to "walk and talk in the manner of love," to "sacrifice personal wishes" for the freedom and welfare of others, to "refrain from the violence of fist, tongue, or heart," and to "strive to be in good spiritual and bodily health."[70] King was particularly emphatic about avoiding not only "external physical violence" but also "corroding hatred," which he equated with an "internal violence of spirit." Such a posture, he argued, was inconsistent with what he variously termed "the Christian spirit,"

66. Washington, ed., *Testament of Hope,* 91–92; Carson et al., eds., *Papers,* 3:393; Carson et al., eds., *Papers,* 5:427; and Carson et al., eds., *Papers,* 4:190 and 502.

67. Carson et al., eds., *Papers,* 3:208; Carson and Holloran, eds., *Knock at Midnight,* 32; and Martin Luther King Jr., "When Peace Becomes Obnoxious," *Louisville Defender* (29 March 1956). King's associate Wyatt Tee Walker noted that "King's spiritually grounded *nonviolence* conscientized the Western world to the pervasive presence" of social evil. See Walker, "Spirituality as an Instrument of Social Change," 2–3.

68. King conceded that "it is possible for a nonreligious person to believe in nonviolence as a technique and as a passing strategy," but not "as a way of life." See Carson et al., eds., *Papers,* 7:406 and 410; and King, *Strength to Love,* 152. King's sense of "the spiritual dimensions of nonviolence" equated well with that of Mohandas K. Gandhi. See Thomas Merton, ed., *Gandhi on Nonviolence: Selected Texts from Mohandas K. Gandhi's Nonviolence in Peace and War* (New York: New Directions, 1965), 43–50.

69. Carson et al., eds., *Papers,* 5:427.

70. "Self-Purification" was the third of the "four basic steps" that both Gandhi and King felt characterized nonviolent campaigns. The other three are (1) "collection of facts to determine whether injustices exist"; (2) attempts at "negotiation"; and (3) "direct" or "*satyagraha*" action. See King, *Why We Can't Wait,* 63–64 and 78; Merton, ed., *Gandhi on Nonviolence,* 23–76; Martin Luther King Jr., "Commitment Card," unpublished, prepared by the Alabama Christian Movement for Human Rights, Birmingham Affiliate of SCLC (1963), KCLA, 1; and Washington, ed., *Testament of Hope,* 537–38.

"the forgiving spirit," "the basic spiritual doctrine of Christianity," or "the spiritual and moral doctrine of Christianity."[71] Needless to say, the violent spirit also ran counter to King's sense of personal ethics and to his "sacred vocation of liberating his people" from social evil.[72]

King felt that "suffering is infinitely more powerful" than violence, or "the law of the jungle," when it came to "converting" the oppressor and "opening his ears" to "the voice of reason." Put another way, undeserved suffering is redemptive—it "has tremendous educational and transforming possibilities."[73] King obviously brought a sense of the *spiritual* to his analysis of civil rights campaigns at this point. Thus, he could speak of going to jail, as he and his followers did so often, as having not only "educational value" and "psychological value," but, above all, "great spiritual value." This is why he described the deaths of those four little black girls in Birmingham as "a crucifixion," noting that they were "martyrs" in a "Holy Crusade" to free their people.[74] [75] This, King declared, was what Jesus's command to "Turn the other cheek" demanded; that the determined crusader for justice and righteousness will "get scarred up" and at times even face death. "But Jesus would say to you in substance," King added, "that it is better to go through life with a scarred up body than a scarred up soul."[76] King never wavered in his conviction "that physical death may be more desirable than a permanent death of the spirit." This explained his love for the Negro spiritual, "Oh Freedom!," which contained those powerful and haunting lyrics: "before I'll be a slave, I'll be buried in my grave, and go home to my Lord and be free."[77]

Nothing was more revealing as far as King's own religious self-understanding was concerned. While he often referred to himself as "a

71. King, *Stride toward Freedom*, 103–4 and 212; Carson et al., eds., *Papers*, 3:230, 393, and 474; Carson et al., eds., *Papers,* 4:131, 232, 297, and 534; Carson et al., eds., *Papers*, 7:198; and Washington, ed., *Testament of Hope,* 46. Those closest to King were encouraged never to forget "the spiritual and emotional value of nonviolence." Here King was really about "a radical spirituality." See Carson and Holloran, eds., *Knock at Midnight,* 39; and Harry Belafonte, *My Song: A Memoir,* with Michael Shnayerson (New York: Alfred A. Knopf, 2011), 150.

72. Peter J. Paris, "The Theology and Ethics of Martin Luther King, Jr.: Contributions to Christian Thought and Practice," *The Princeton Theological Review* 40, no. 1 (Fall 2004): 5.

73. King, *Stride toward Freedom,* 103.

74. Martin Luther King Jr., "Transcript of a Radio Interview Regarding the Nobel Prize," unpublished, Oslo, Norway (9 December 1964), KCLA, 2; and King, "Eulogy for the Martyred Children," 2.

75. Carson et al., eds., *King Papers*, 5:531; Martin Luther King Jr., "A Challenge to the Church and Synagogues," in *Race: Challenge to Religion*, ed. Mathew Ahmann (Chicago: Henry Regnery, 1963), 168–69; Washington, *Testament of Hope*, 42; and David J. Garrow, "Evaluating King's Life and Legacy: Author's Response," *The Christian Century* 104 (29 April 1987): 411.

76. King, "Speech Made in Savannah," 19–20.

77. Carson et al., eds., *Papers,* 5:248–49, 269, 288, and 339; King, *Where Do We Go from Here?,* 123; and Carson et al., eds., *Papers*, 4:88.

Baptist preacher" and "a civil rights leader," he felt that these roles were indistinguishable and that both ultimately fell under the general rubric of his religious or spiritual leadership,[78] which was very much in the servant and sacrificial style of Jesus Christ. In conformity with the Jesus tradition, and his ongoing practice of self-purification, he brought clearly defined spiritual and devotional practices to his leadership, often setting aside a "quiet day" of prayer, of "reading and silence and meditation," thus "refreshing" himself "spiritually and intellectually."[79] The "spiritual lift" that came with such experiences always inspired a renewed commitment to press on, even as the cross King shouldered on behalf of others became larger and heavier. Imbued with a spirit of no surrender, and with the belief that "other preservation is the first law of life," he looked beyond self to serve others by offering new vistas of hope, and by sacrificing himself as a source of inspiration and healing for the bruised, brokenhearted, and outcast. "So like the Apostle Paul I can now humbly yet proudly say, 'I bear in my body the marks of the lord Jesus,'" he commented. "Recognizing the necessity for suffering I have tried to make of it a virtue" while also seeing it "as an opportunity to transform myself and heal the people involved in the tragic situation which now obtains."[80]

King brought certain characteristics to his spiritual leadership that established him as a towering figure in Christian spirituality. Drawing on L. W. Fry's "spiritual leadership theory," Andrea Pierce describes those characteristics as "vision, hope/faith, and altruistic love."[81] A fourth characteristic, prophetic witness and activism, might also be included.[82]

78. Bryan Massingale is right in suggesting that King's spiritual leadership accounted for his civil rights leadership—that "The praying King made the activist King possible." See Martin Luther King Jr., "Statement at a Press Conference on the Chicago Movement," unpublished, Chicago, Illinois (7 July 1965), KCLA, 3; King, "Doubts and Certainties Link," 3; Washington, ed., *Testament of Hope,* 408; and Massingale, "Book Explores King's Living Faith," 18.

79. "I subject myself to self-purification and to endless self-analysis," said King in an interview in January 1965. "I question and soul search constantly into myself to be as certain as I can that I am fulfilling the true meaning of my work, that I am maintaining my sense of purpose, that I am holding fast to my ideals, that I am guiding my people in the right direction." See Washington, ed., *Testament of Hope*, 372 and 376; and Baldwin, *Never to Leave Us Alone,* vii, 68–69, 78, and 123n5.

80. The Jewish rabbi Abraham J. Heschel occasionally called King "this great spiritual leader" in the 1960s, but scholars have largely failed to sufficiently treat King in this capacity. See Washington, ed., *Testament of Hope,* 41–42; Carson et al., eds., *Papers*, 4:529; and King, *Where Do We Go from Here?,* 180.

81. Andrea Pierce, "Dr. Martin Luther King, Jr. as Spiritual Leader: Abstract," *International Journal of Business* 3, no. 8 (2013), 1–3; and L. W. Fry, "Toward a Theory of Spiritual Leadership," *The Leadership Quarterly* 14 (2003): 693–727.

82. King occasionally mentioned his "prophetic role," in which "I must constantly speak to the moral issues of our day far beyond civil rights." See Martin Luther King Jr., "Transcript of an Interview," unpublished, "Newsmakers," Channel 2, KNXT-TV, Los Angeles, California

King the prophetic-spiritual leader believed that the God of history was involved in the movement he led. Like the ancient Hebrew prophets, he was also convinced that the promises of God would come to pass, that God would not long endure the cruelty and destructiveness of people against people, that God would not continue to allow the faithful not to practice daily what they affirmed in creeds and doctrine on Sunday mornings. This is why King could continuously speak in terms of "spiritual progress," of "the spiritual growth and the democratization of our nation," even as he saw his "dream turn into a nightmare."[83] He had that amazing ability to appeal to the deepest recesses of the American spirit, and most certainly the human spirit.

FROM "SPIRITUAL MEANS" TO "SPIRITUAL ENDS": HUMANITY'S ENDURING CHALLENGE

Martin Luther King Jr.'s sense of the *spiritual* must ultimately be studied and understood in a global context, for it was rooted in his conception of the interrelatedness of all life, or "the interrelated structure of all reality." In the final year of his life, he made the point in graphic terms, taking into account not only the spiritual bond that existed between humans across generations but also those rhythms of reality that explained why all "inhabitants of the globe" had become "neighbors":

> All men are interdependent. Every nation is an heir of a vast treasury of ideas and labor to which both the living and the dead of all nations have contributed. Whether we realize it or not, each of us lives eternally "in the red." We are everlasting debtors to known and unknown men and women. When we rise in the morning, we go into the bathroom where we reach for a sponge which is provided for us by a Pacific Islander. We reach for soap that is created for us by a European. Then at the table we drink coffee which is provided for us by a South American, or tea by a Chinese or cocoa

(10 July 1965), KCLA, 2. Barbara Holmes describes King as "this great spiritual leader"—"as a great contemplative, one who used the spiritual essence of nonviolence as a tool for liberating the social order and the spiritual authority of a denigrated people." See Barbara A. Holmes, *Joy Unspeakable: Contemplative Practices of the Black Church* (Minneapolis: Fortress, 2004), 27, 138–40, and 157–61.

83. Carson et al., eds., *Papers,* 6:338; Martin Luther King Jr., "Statement to the Press," unpublished (13 June 1957), 2; Baldwin, *There Is a Balm in Gilead*, 326–30; and Martin Luther King Jr., "Civil Rights in Its Second Phase: An Interview," unpublished, NBC, Arlene Francis Show, New York (19 June 1967), KCLA, 6. Also see Jonathan Wilson-Hartgrove, "The Spiritual Legacy of Martin Luther King, Jr.," *Relevant Magazine*, January 16, 2017, https://tinyurl.com/y9qs3wyw; Marty Jezer, "The Spiritual Politics of Martin Luther King," *Alternet*, January 15, 2003, https://tinyurl.com/yclrddkp; and Tony Alessandra, "Martin Luther King, Jr.: Spiritual Genius," Dr. T's Timely Tips, https://tinyurl.com/y786hhko.

> by a West African. Before we leave for our jobs we are already beholden to more than half of the world. . . . In a real sense, all life is interrelated.[84]

To further elaborate the point, King went on to note that "equality with whites" in America would "not solve the problems of either whites or Negroes if it" meant "equality in a world society stricken by poverty and in a universe doomed to extinction by war." In other words, the realization of the American dream ultimately depended on the actualization of that "larger dream of a world of brotherhood and peace and good will."[85] To be sure, this perspective took on added significance as King considered the more complicated question of the coherence of "spiritual means" and "spiritual ends" in an international context.

King often said that the spiritual maturation of humankind worldwide during his time left much to be desired. "Our spiritual progress," he lamented, has not "been commensurate" with our "scientific progress." "Through our scientific genius" and "technological ingenuity," we "have made the world a neighborhood," he conceded, "but we have failed to employ our moral and spiritual genius to make it a brotherhood." "The great problem facing modern man," he maintained, "is that the material means *by* which we live have outdistanced the spiritual ends *for* which we live. So we find ourselves caught in a messed-up world. The problem is with man himself and man's soul. We haven't learned how to be just and honest and kind and true and loving." King advanced his analysis of the human condition to another level, insisting that "our moral and spiritual 'lag' must be redeemed." Said he: "The world in which we live is a world of geographical oneness and we are challenged to make it spiritually one."[86]

King reasoned that "the great problems" of humanity could only be resolved through a spiritually charged commitment to peaceful coexistence. This invariably entailed using peaceful means to eliminate the internal barriers (i.e., fear, ignorance, greed, hatred) and external barriers (i.e., racism, poverty, militarism) to the full realization of a truly integrated society and world based on "mutual acceptance of individuals and groups," "genuine inter-group, interpersonal living," and "the shar-

84. In King's thinking, the terms "all life is interrelated" and "the interrelated structure of all reality" meant essentially the same thing; namely, that humanity is essentially one "spiritually," despite differences in race, nationality, religion, culture, and interests. See King, *Where Do We Go from Here?,* 181; and King, *Trumpet of Conscience,* 69–70.

85. King, *Where Do We Go from Here?,* 167; and Washington, ed., *Testament of Hope,* 209.

86. Carson et al., eds., *Papers,* 6:87 and 338; King, "America's Chief Moral Dilemma," 2; Ayres, ed., *Wisdom of Martin Luther King, Jr.,* 10; Washington, ed., *Testament of Hope,* 209; Carson et al., eds., *Papers,* 2:248–49; Carson and Holloran, eds., *Knock at Midnight,* 6 and 26–27; and King, *Where Do We Go from Here?,* 171–72.

ing of power," thus blazing a path toward the most authentic expression of "the great world house" or "a global beloved community." Although King stated repeatedly that those internal barriers could be largely eroded through religion and education, he seemingly had far more to say in his later years about how those external barriers might be dismantled. Convinced that racism was "a treacherous foundation for a world house," King argued that "that corrosive evil" could "bring down the curtain on Western civilization" while ultimately leading to total human destruction.[87] Here again he recommended passionate and persistent appeals to the hearts and minds of those afflicted with racism. He longed for a human spirit that knew no racial nor ethnic boundaries.

King was equally perceptive when addressing world poverty, much of which was grounded in systems and structures of economic injustice and inequality. The fact that "two-thirds of the peoples of the world" were "undernourished, ill-housed, and shabbily-clad" was for him a sad commentary on the spiritual state of the human family, and particularly on those who had earned much wealth at the expense of the sweat and suffering of the less-fortunate. With a glance toward those who lived in luxury in wealthy nations while so many languished in poverty and neglect, King declared: "Our moral values and our spiritual confidence sink, even as our material wealth ascends." "The richer we have become materially," he remarked on another occasion, "the poorer we have become morally and spiritually." "Western civilization is particularly vulnerable at this moment," he asserted, "for our material abundance has brought us neither peace of mind nor serenity of spirit." King concluded that "Our only hope today lies in our ability to recapture the revolutionary spirit" that demands persistent and "eternal opposition to poverty."[88] He was especially critical of his own country, which claimed to be the wealthiest and most powerful nation on earth. The "United States has the material resources and technical competence to deal with these problems positively," he said. "The question confronting us now is whether we have the moral, spiritual, and intellectual resources."[89] Mindful that his country possessed the technology and the resources to end poverty, King noted that "there is no deficit in human resources; the

87. King, *Where Do We Go from Here?,* 167–91; Washington, ed., *Testament of Hope,* 118, 209–10, 317, and 555–653; Martin Luther King Jr., "After Desegregation—What?," unpublished version of a speech (n.d.), KCLA, 3; and Lewis V. Baldwin, *To Make the Wounded Whole: The Cultural Legacy of Martin Luther King, Jr.* (Minneapolis: Fortress, 1992), 163–313.

88. King, *Where Do We Go from Here?,* 171–72, 177–78, and 190; Washington, ed., *Testament of Hope,* 315; and King, "Doubts and Certainties Link," 1–8.

89. Martin Luther King Jr., "A Christian Movement in a Revolutionary Age," unpublished version of a speech (Fall 1966), KCLA, 5.

deficit is in human will."[90] In other words, the deficit was essentially spiritual in nature.

The problem of war, the proliferation of nuclear weapons, and human destruction were also uppermost in King's consciousness when he raised the necessity for "a revolution of values." He suggested that "When scientific power outruns moral power" and "spiritual power," "we end up with guided missiles and misguided men." He denied that "military genius" was the answer in the twentieth-century world, the most violent in human history, and he called for "a peace race" to replace "the arms race." The "most powerful forces in the universe are not those of military might but those forces of spiritual might," he declared. Again, King aimed his fiercest attack at the United States, "the greatest purveyor of violence in the world today." "Our nation is sick with militarism," he argued, as he considered the United States misadventure in Vietnam. "Any nation that spends some seventy or eighty billion dollars on military pursuits is headed toward its spiritual doom." Thus, he admonished all peoples of the world, and especially "non-governmental persons," to "champion the cause of peace from the perspectives of moral, religious and spiritual orientations." This, King conceded in 1966, was the "challenge confronting the world citizen even in this latter half of the twentieth century"; namely, "to break down the dividing walls of hostility," and to "free men of all nations" so "they may face one another without protective devices and defense mechanisms in confidence that men can live together in love and that the family of man can encompass many nations," extending "beyond oceans" and overcoming "the historic, racial, political and economic factors which have perennially plunged man into the depths of dissension and divided him into warring factions." King obviously had a spiritually rooted devotion to saving humanity from what he termed "the quagmire of tragic self-destruction," and he gave poignant and unwavering expression to this in his call for an absolute end to war, and as he marched with peace or anti-war activists in the late 1960s.[91]

King advocated employing the spiritual means of nonviolence to achieve the spiritual ends of "the Kingdom of God on earth," which he viewed as the theological equivalent of the ethical ideal of the beloved

90. King, *Where Do We Go from Here?*, 177.

91. King, *Where Do We Go from Here?,* 172, 186, and 188; Carson et al., eds., *Papers,* 5:145 and 365; Washington, ed., *Testament of Hope,* 233; King, "Meaning of Hope," 5; Martin Luther King Jr., "An Address at the Synagogue Council of America," unpublished version (5 December 1965), KCLA, 11; Martin Luther King Jr., "Statement: For Immediate Release," unpublished (5 October 1965), KCLA, 2; and Martin Luther King Jr., "Speech on European Tour," unpublished (March, 1966), KCLA, 2.

community.[92] As far back as his seminary years, he had written about the "common Christian view that history is moving toward the kingdom of God," which is in some sense both present and future, and he spoke to that with an even greater sense of urgency in the 1960s.[93] While acknowledging that "the Kingdom of God is not yet as a universal phenomenon," he explained nonetheless that the "promise of the Kingdom of God has not been lost to mankind."[94] The kingdom would indeed come, he thought, not as a political structure or materialistic outlook, but as a global society of "ideal humanity" in which the length (i.e., achieving personal ends and ambitions), breadth (i.e., concern for others), and height (i.e., love of God) of life are lived in completeness.[95]

The idea of committed human beings becoming coworkers with God in bringing about God's kingdom on earth was central to both King's spirituality and his religious-social ethic. He urged people of goodwill everywhere to apply the spirit of Jesus, Gandhi, Thoreau, and other great souls "to domestic and international problems."[96] This challenge was particularly important for white people, King declared, whose "doctrine of white supremacy" had long accounted for "the exploitation of the colored peoples of the world." He felt that all too many white people had become victims of "mental" and "spiritual slavery" through their own enslaving and oppressive routines. Hence, the path to a world of "ideal humanity," as King envisioned it, depended on "the spirit and the

92. Kenneth Smith suggests that democratic socialism was for King the political-economic equivalent of the ethical ideal of the beloved community and the theological ideal of the kingdom of God on earth. All three were seemingly rooted in a "scriptural view of the millennial hope," and expressed a certain optimism about society's future and historical progress. See Kenneth L. Smith, "The Radicalization of Martin Luther King, Jr.: The Last Three Years," *Journal of Ecumenical Studies* 26, no. 2 (Spring 1989): 270–88; and Kenneth L. Smith and Ira G. Zepp Jr., *Search for the Beloved Community: The Thinking of Martin Luther King, Jr.* (Valley Forge, PA: Judson, 1974), 43–45 and 128–29.

93. While a student at Crozer Theological Seminary, King associated "social justice" with "the possibility for realizing the kingdom of God on earth." See Carson et al., eds., *Papers*, 1:250 and 280.

94. King, "Meaning of Hope," 11; and King, "Address at the Synagogue Council of America," 9.

95. It is difficult to avoid the conclusion that King used terms like the "kingdom of God," the "New Jerusalem," and the "promised land" interchangeably to refer to essentially the same kind of ideal society and world. King says at some points that this "will be a kingdom of the spirit." See Carson et al., eds., *Papers*, 6:198; Carson et al., eds., *Papers*, 5:579; King, *Measure of a Man*, 35–56; and King, "Christian Movement in a Revolutionary Age," 2.

96. Interestingly enough, King had argued as early as his seminary years that figures like Jesus, Schweitzer, Gandhi, and others revealed the "working of the spirit of God in bringing about moral transformation." See Carson et al., eds., *Papers*, 1:248–49; Carson et al., eds., *Papers*, 5:135, 146, 148–49, 504, and 510–11; Carson et al., eds., *Papers*, 4:115n2 and 332; Carson et al., eds., *Papers*, 3:268–69; Carson et al., eds., *Papers*, 7: 156 and 163; and King, "Doubts and Certainties Link," 4.

readjusting qualities of the white peoples of the world." In King's estimation, so much of the burden fell primarily on the shoulders of whites in America, especially since they took so much pride in the United States as the moral leader of nations and the greatest force for good in the world.[97]

Of particular significance was the special, vanguard role King assigned to his own people, the American Negroes, in the quest for a higher human and ethical ideal. He often said that "the American Negro has in his nature the spiritual" and "moral fortitude," "forged by centuries of oppression," not only to "win his own struggle for justice and freedom," but also to constructively impact the global human quest. As early as the 1950s, King, quoting from Arnold Toynbee's *A Study of History*, predicted that "it may be the Negro who will give the new spiritual dynamic" that "Western civilization" so "desperately needs to survive." "The spiritual power that the Negro can radiate," he added, "comes from love, understanding, good will, and nonviolence."[98] King was convinced, as he pointed out in 1964, that "the Negro is now in a position to lead the world." "As the Negro goes," he asserted, "so goes the world." He knew that through their folklore, art, and spiritual values, and the civil rights movement itself, American Negroes were already having perhaps a greater impact on the world than any other single group of people in Western society. The image of the "the 'new Negro' as heralding 'a new world order' to replace the 'old order' of colonialism, exploitation, and segregation"[99] was endlessly fascinating for King—and quite reassuring as he struggled and sacrificed life daily for the true realization of the ideal of the kingdom of God on earth.

But King also knew that any successful struggle to enlarge the human reach or endeavor ultimately had to involve human cooperation and a mingling of the highest human values of peoples from every part of the globe.[100] This is why he endlessly sought to build coalitions across the boundaries of race, ethnicity, nationality, politics, culture, and religion. Clearly, he was driven by a spirit of freedom that was, by any reasonable standard, not only genuine and indomitable but inclusive as well. James W. Fowler rightly regards King as representative of what he calls "universalizing faith,"[101] or what might also be termed "universalizing spir-

97. King, "Doubts and Certainties Link," 1–8; and Carson et al., eds., *Papers,* 6:168.

98. Washington, ed., *Testament of Hope*, 316; and King, *Stride toward Freedom*, 224. Here King was echoing W. E. B. Dubois's idea, repeatedly stated throughout his writings, that "Negro blood has a message for the world." See Franklin, ed., *Souls of Black Folk*, 215.

99. Washington, ed., *Testament of Hope*, 318–19; King, *Where Do We Go from Here?,* 57; and Lewis V. Baldwin and Paul R. Dekar, eds., *"In an Inescapable Network of Mutuality": Martin Luther King, Jr. and the Globalization of an Ethical Ideal* (Eugene, OR: Cascade, 2013), 49–50.

100. See Baldwin, *To Make the Wounded Whole*, 286.

101. Fowler developed the theory of a developmental process in faith or spirituality that

ituality."[102] This stage of faith, according to Fowler, embraces humans as part of a universal community while advocating the application of universal principles of love and justice in the treatment of other selves. In conformity with this stage of faith, King transcended selfishness and self-centeredness, displayed a genuine compassion in his dealings with others, lived his life in service to humanity, translated spirituality into action by challenging the status quo and struggling to bring about justice, peace, and equality of opportunity in the world, and lived as if the kingdom of God was already a reality on earth.[103] Ultimately, it was King's sense and experience of the spiritual realm that make his life so unique, powerful, profound, and influential.

begins with childhood. He outlined several stages of faith, among which were "primal faith," "intuitive-projective faith," "mythic-literal faith," "synthetic-conventional faith," "conjunctive faith," "individuative-reflective faith," "universalizing faith," and "transpersonal and nondual commonwealth faith." Fowler also concluded that few in human life reached the stage of "universalizing faith." Aside from King, he mentioned Mohandas K. Gandhi, Thomas Merton, Mother Teresa of Calcutta, Dag Hammarskjöld, Dietrich Bonhoeffer, and Abraham Herschel. See Fowler, *Stages of Faith*, 1–332; and Rollie Stanich and Ken Wilber, "Stairway to Heaven: Honoring Dr. James Fowler, April 8, 2009, https://tinyurl.com/y968rrnv.

102. The term "universalizing spirituality" seems more appropriate for this chapter and this entire volume, but it clearly draws heavily on the insights of James W. Fowler. See Fowler, *Stages of Faith*, 113, 199–211, 292–93, 295, and 302.

103. Fowler, *Stages of Faith*, 1–3.

4.

The Manifestation of an Immanent God: The Holy Spirit in the Theology of Martin Luther King Jr.

AARON J. HOWARD

> The Spirit of the Lord is upon me, because he hath anointed me to preach the gospel to the poor; he hath sent me to heal the brokenhearted, to preach deliverance to the captives, and recovering of sight to the blind, to set at liberty them that are bruised, to preach the acceptable year of the Lord.
>
> —Luke 4:18–19

> It is a common tendency today to be skeptical concerning the presence of the Holy Spirit in the world. Even Christians have fallen victims to this notion.
>
> —Martin Luther King Jr.[1]

Within the last twenty-five years, scholars have devoted considerable attention to analyzing various aspects of Martin Luther King Jr.'s theological methods and framework.[2] However, the paucity of scholarship devoted to specifically examining the role of the Holy Spirit in his life and thought remains. Perhaps this is because King's speeches and writ-

1. Clayborne Carson et al., eds., *The Papers of Martin Luther King, Jr.: Called to Serve, January 1929–June 1951* (Berkeley: University of California Press, 1992), 1:248.

2. Rufus Burrow Jr., *Martin Luther King, Jr. and the Theology of Resistance* (Jefferson, NC: McFarland, 2015); Richard Wayne Wills Sr., *Martin Luther King, Jr. and the Image of God* (New York: Oxford University Press, 2009); Johnny Bernard Hill, *The Theology of Martin Luther King, Jr. and Desmond Mpilo Tutu* (New York: Palgrave MacMillan, 2007); Luther D. Ivory, *Toward a Theology of Radical Involvement: The Theological Legacy of Martin Luther King, Jr.* (Nashville: Abingdon, 1997); and Noel Leo Erskine, *King among the Theologians* (Cleveland: Pilgrim, 1995).

ings seem largely bereft of overt allusions to the Holy Spirit and its influence upon his life and ministry. For example, in the book, *Bonhoeffer and King: Speaking Truth to Power,* J. Deotis Roberts derides King for disregarding the Holy Spirit within his theological worldview. Referring to King and Bonhoeffer, Roberts opines, "In my judgment, neither theologian lifted up the importance of the Christian belief . . . in the guidance and power of the Holy Spirit in their theological perspectives. To effectively witness against the powers of evil, Christians need all the 'resources of grace' in their struggle."[3] In his review of Robert's book, Rufus Burrow Jr. challenges this criticism of King's theological framework by recalling King's "kitchen experience" in Montgomery.[4]

The religious experience invoked by Burrow happened early in King's career, following a series of death threats. On the night of January 27, 1956, after his wife and baby had gone to sleep, King received a phone call. The voice on the other end said, "Listen nigger, we've taken all we want from you; before next week you'll be sorry you ever came to Montgomery."[5] King, at his wits end, sat down with a cup of coffee at his kitchen table, and prayed to God. He told God, "I am at the end of my powers. I have nothing left. I've come to the point where I can't face it alone."[6] King states, "At that moment I experienced the presence of the Divine as I had never experienced Him before. It seemed as though I could hear the quiet assurance of an inner voice saying: 'Stand up for righteousness, stand up for truth; and God will be at your side forever.'"[7] King discovered that his fears began to immediately subside, and he found himself ready to face impending challenges with strength and determination. Burrow notes that King recounted this vision many times in his speeches and sermons throughout his career, and it remained a constant source of strength and encouragement as he weathered continual storms of opposition. Burrow also suggests that the 'inner voice' to which King referred could be equated with the Holy Spirit, and he

3. J. Deotis Roberts, *Bonhoeffer and King: Speaking Truth to Power* (Louisville: Westminster John Knox, 2005), 128.

4. Rufus Burrow Jr., "Review of J. Deotis Roberts, *Bonhoeffer and King: Speaking Truth to Power,*" *Encounter* 67, no. 3 (Summer, 2006): 329–30.

5. Clayborne Carson and Peter Holloran, eds., *A Knock at Midnight: Inspiration from the Great sermons of Reverend Martin Luther King, Jr.* (New York: Warner, 1998), 160–62; Martin Luther King Jr., *Stride toward Freedom: The Montgomery Story* (Boston: Harper & Row, 1958), 134–35; and Clayborne Carson et al., eds., *The Papers of Martin Luther King, Jr.: Advocate of the Social Gospel, September 1948–March 1963* (Berkeley: University of California Press, 2007), 6:533–34.

6. King, *Stride toward Freedom,* 134.

7. King, *Stride toward Freedom,* 134–35.

thereby concludes that the Holy Spirit was more important to King than Roberts recognizes.[8]

In this chapter, I will provide evidence for the richness and depth of King's pneumatological thought in order to thoroughly support Burrow's claim. The Holy Spirit, in King's perspective, was not an inconsequential Christian doctrine that fostered over-emotionalism and an escapist stance toward sociopolitical involvement. In King's theological analysis and personal experiences, the existence of the Holy Spirit provided persuasive validation of God's immanence, and King considered it fundamental to his conception of a personal, compassionate, and loving God. While it is true that King's writings have few unambiguous references to the Holy Spirit per se, this is in part due to his theological and temporal context. Amongst black churches, a renewed focus on pneumatology occurred in the latter twentieth century, and scholars' discovery of global Pentecostalism and the neo-Pentecostalism of black churches as fertile sites for theological inquiry reintroduced terminology that now pervades both ecclesial and academic circles.[9] To expect to find often this language within King's work is anachronistic and offers an inadequate appraisal of his mid-twentieth-century academic theological milieu. Therefore, properly understanding King's pneumatological methodology means that we must first inhabit the academic world that contributed to his theological formation. By doing so, we will discover the tools needed to decode allusions to the Holy Spirit that are masked by language and concepts appropriate to the mid-century theological scholarship from which King drew heavily.

We must be careful, however, to avoid portraying King's theology of the Holy Spirit as merely academic or intellectualist in nature. King was a dialectical thinker, and he usually avoided extremism in philosophical and theological arguments, preferring to moderate extremes by extracting elements of truth from competing ideologies, thereby reconciling them into a carefully nuanced and balanced synthesis.[10] The same can be said of King's thinking regarding the Holy Spirit. In this chapter, I

8. Burrow, "Review," 330.

9. This introduction from an edited volume on Afro-Pentecostalism underscores this point: "Until recently the idea of a 'Pentecostal theology' would have been considered an oxymoron, given the Pentecostal emphasis on the emotions, affections, and ecstatic worship. However, over the last generation there has emerged a growing consideration of how Pentecostal spirituality and piety harbors within itself a unique set of theological intuitions and sensibilities, and Pentecostal theologians have been working to articulate these in their own tongues. The result has been, at least in part, a distinctive Pentecostal contribution to the recent renaissance of interest in the doctrine of the Holy Spirit in the wider academy." See Amos Yong and Estrelda Y. Alexander, eds., *Afro-Pentecostalism: Black Pentecostal and Charismatic Christianity in History and Culture* (New York: New York University Press, 2011), 167.

10. For a comprehensive view of King as a dialectical thinker, see George Russell Seay Jr.,

endeavor to show that King's thought regarding the Holy Spirit bears the indelible imprint of the convergence of his black church spirituality and his liberal theological training in the Western academy. We will see, however, that attempting to pin King down as an orthodox or liberal thinker concerning his conception of the Holy Spirit presents considerable difficulties. King's terminology and allusions to the Holy Spirit often differ depending on his audience, immediate context, and objective. Thus, we will find instances when he leans toward a black evangelical position, others where he seems to embrace theological liberalism, and still others in which we can discern the influences of both of these traditions.[11]

King's spiritual sensibilities and identity were cultivated in the black church, and he considered it a vital place of nurture and support.[12] He remembers, "The church has always been a second home for me. As far back as I can remember I was in church every Sunday. I guess this was inevitable since my father was the pastor of my church, but I never regretted going to church until I passed through a state of skepticism in my second year of college."[13] King here admits that his later theological training chastened his commitment to some of the beliefs inculcated within him by his family and Ebenezer Baptist Church in Atlanta,

"Theologian of Synthesis: The Dialectical Method of Martin Luther King, Jr. as Revealed in His Critical Thinking on Theology, History, and Ethics," PhD diss., Vanderbilt University (2008).

11. In speaking of the black evangelical tradition, I am not referring to the mid-twentieth century movement constituted by black religious leaders educated within white conservative seminaries who were often affiliated with white evangelical denominations. Such exemplars include Howard O. Jones, Tom Skinner, William H. Bentley, John Perkins, and William E. Pannell. I have in mind a specific belief system emphasized by the black church tradition that scholars trace back to slave religion. This tradition arose out of the Great Awakening and structures black church beliefs until the present. It emphasizes the experience of the Almighty Sovereign God culminating in conversion as the definitive event that distinguishes one as a Christian. Black evangelicalism also considers the Bible an authoritative revelation from God for deciphering God's will for humanity and for cultivating a relationship with God. For more on black evangelicalism as a twentieth century movement, see James Earl Massey, "African Americans and Evangelicalism," Fuller Seminary, https://tinyurl.com/y8kkupnl. For more on the belief system of black evangelicalism that emerged from slave religion, see Cecil W. Cone, *Identity Crisis in Black Theology* (Nashville: AMEC, 1975) and Albert J. Raboteau, *Slave Religion: The "Invisible Institution" in the Antebellum South* (New York: Oxford University Press, 1978).

12. Lewis V. Baldwin has argued most persuasively and extensively for the primary role of black cultural institutions and practices in influencing King's life and thought. His conclusions are now widely accepted and assumed within King scholarship. He carefully researches and investigates the influence of King's family and the black church upon King's spiritual development. See Lewis V. Baldwin, *The Voice of Conscience: The Church in the Mind of Martin Luther King, Jr.* (New York: Oxford University Press, 2010), 13–50 and 101–40; and Lewis V. Baldwin, *There Is a Balm in Gilead: The Cultural Roots of Martin Luther King, Jr.* (Minneapolis: Fortress, 1991), 1–339.

13. Martin Luther King Jr., "An Autobiography of Religious Development," in Carson et al., eds., *Papers*, 1:361.

Georgia. As Lewis V. Baldwin observes, "Though he was introduced as a child to a church culture that was decisively fundamentalist or evangelical in terms of its faith, doctrine, and practice, there was much tangible in King Jr.'s boyhood to indicate that he would become . . . an uncompromising critic of the church."[14]

For instance, instead of joining the church due to a conversion experience, which was widely considered the prerequisite for becoming a part of the church, King merely joined as a child to compete with his sister Willie Christine, who had joined first.[15] King diverges from the dramatic "call experience" expected of preachers within the black church tradition, stating, "My call to the ministry was not a miraculous or supernatural something, on the contrary it was an inner urge calling me to serve humanity."[16] It is telling that due to his father's influence, he was ordained at eighteen years of age even though he denied the veracity of the virgin birth.[17] In another revealing self-description, King writes,

> The lessons which I was taught in Sunday school were quite in the fundamentalist line. None of my teachers ever doubted the infallibility of the Scriptures. Most of them were unlettered and had never heard of biblical criticism. Naturally, I accepted the teachings as they were being given to me. I never felt any need to doubt them—at least at that time I didn't. I guess I accepted biblical studies uncritically until I was about twelve years old. But this uncritical attitude could not last long, for it was contrary to the very nature of my being. I had always been the questioning and precocious type. At the age of thirteen, I shocked my Sunday school class by denying the bodily resurrection of Jesus. Doubts began to spring forth unrelentingly.[18]

King, by age thirteen, was already questioning the core tenets of his Christian upbringing. He also later embraced theological liberalism's attempts at harmonizing science with Christianity through rational explications of Christianity's core beliefs, a process that factored into his emerging concept of the Holy Spirit. His doubts regarding fundamentalism's ability to adequately account for differences between scientific discovery and Christian narratives crested during his first two years at Morehouse. He writes, "It was then that the shackles of fundamentalism were removed from my body. . . . My studies had made me skeptical, and I could not see how many of the facts of science could be squared

14. Baldwin, *Voice of Conscience,* 16.
15. Carson et al., eds., *Papers,* 1:361.
16. Carson et al., eds., *Papers,* 1:363.
17. Baldwin, *Voice of Conscience,* 46.
18. Martin Luther King Jr., *The Autobiography of Martin Luther King, Jr.,* ed. Clayborne Carson (New York: Warner, 1998), 6.

with religion."[19] King's exposure to ministers who were also well educated, namely, Benjamin E. Mays and George D. Kelsey, helped him to see that "religion could be intellectually respectable as well as emotionally satisfying."[20]

King enrolled at Crozer Theological Seminary following his graduation from Morehouse College. Crozer was a small liberal Baptist seminary in Chester, Pennsylvania, a town southwest of Philadelphia, and King quickly aligned himself with the historical and critical approaches that the seminary favored. For example, in James Bennett Pritchard's Old Testament course, in which King enrolled during his first semester, King demonstrated an acceptance of Pritchard's scientific methodology, which was based upon historical and archaeological research. Undoubtedly with the Bible and much more in mind, King stated, "No logical thinker can doubt the fact that . . . archaeological findings are now indispensable to all concrete study of Hebrew-Christian religion."[21] Be that as it may, such exposure most certainly informed King's emerging view of the Holy Spirit.

Of all his professors at Crozer, perhaps George Washington Davis was most influential in demonstrating the persuasiveness of theological liberalism for King. Davis, a Baptist who received his doctorate from Yale, had attended Colgate-Rochester Divinity School, and was heavily influenced by the Social Gospel of Walter Rauschenbusch. King took seven courses from Davis, and through Davis he was exposed to the American Ritschlianism of William Adams Brown[22] and the evangelical liberalism of William Newton Clarke.[23] King's essays for Davis exhibit the hallmarks of American liberal Protestantism. In an essay titled, "A View of the Cross Possessing Biblical and Spiritual Justification," King, like Rauschenbusch, subscribes to the moral influence theory regarding the atonement and rejects the ransom and substitution models and even goes so far as to refer to the ideas of ethical and penal substitution, in which

19. King, *Autobiography*, 15.

20. King, *Autobiography*, 15–16.

21. Carson et al., eds., *Papers*, 1:163.

22. In an essay called, "The Humanity and Divinity of Jesus," King referred extensively to Williams Adams Brown's *How to Think of Christ* (1948). King also had to write six outlines for brief lectures based upon Brown's *Beliefs That Matter: A Theology for Laymen* (1928). Both of these were standard textbooks in early to mid-twentieth-century liberal Protestant thought. See Carson et al., *Papers*, 1:257 and 1:280.

23. In Davis's class, called, "Christian Theology for Today," King had to submit six outlines for six brief lectures based upon William Newton Clarke's *An Outline of Christian Theology* (1898), which was a standard text of American Christian liberal theology. See Carson et al., eds., *Papers*, 1:242.

Christ bears the guilt and punishment of sinners, as immoral.[24] In defining this theory, King states, "According to this theory, the atoning work of Christ was revelation of the heart of God, not intended to remove obstacle to forgiveness on God's side . . . but designed to bring sinful men to repentance and win their love to himself."[25]

Although King wrestled with the evangelical doctrines taken for granted by Ebenezer Baptist Church, he unwaveringly maintained his belief in a personal, compassionate God, whom he had come to view strictly in spiritual terms. The God of his childhood, introduced to him in the prayers, songs, and sermons at Ebenezer, resonated deeply with the basic philosophical position he adopted while earning his PhD in systematic theology at Boston University.[26] This philosophical position, called personalism, provided academic language and texture for King's belief in a loving and personal God, which would be quite relevant as he thought through his view of the Holy Spirit. He writes regarding personalism, "It gave me metaphysical and philosophical grounding for the idea of a personal God, and it gave me a metaphysical basis for the dignity and worth of all human personality."[27] Under personalism, the universe is categorized as "a society of interacting and intercommunicating selves and persons, united by the will of God, who is the creator and sustainer of all things."[28] While the material world exists around us, this world is still an expression of personality, which is the "deepest and only substantial fact."[29] King's openness to personalism also underscored his dialectical approach to theological thinking, as it allowed him to sidestep the naturalism and impersonalism favored by prominent liberal theologians while also circumventing the fundamentalism of his childhood.[30]

The black church, in no small measure, bears responsibility for helping

24. Carson et al., eds., *Papers*, 1:265.

25. Carson et al., eds., *Papers*, 1:264.

26. King, *Autobiography*, 31. King's black church upbringing had already instilled within him a "homespun" personalism that made it easy for him to adopt personalism at Boston University. For more on "homespun" personalism, see Rufus Burrow Jr., *God and Human Dignity: The Personalism, Theology, and Ethics of Martin Luther King, Jr.* (Notre Dame: University of Notre Dame Press, 2006).

27. King, *Autobiography*, 31–32.

28. Rufus Burrow Jr., *Personalism: A Critical Introduction* (St. Louis: Chalice, 1999), 12.

29. Gary Dorrien, *The Making of American Liberal Theology: Imagining Progressive Religion, 1805–1900* (Louisville: Westminster John Knox, 2001), 377.

30. King's dissertation compared the conceptions of God in the thought of Paul Tillich and Henry Nelson Wieman. He concludes that Weiman's naturalism and Tillich's impersonal idea of God as Being are inadequate since they deny God the category of personality. This, too, had major implications for the fashioning of King's concept of the Holy Spirit. See Clayborne Carson et al., eds., *The Papers of Martin Luther King, Jr.: Rediscovering Precious Values, July 1951–November 1955* (Berkeley: University of California Press, 1994), 2:339–548.

King to maintain his theological equilibrium and his unshakeable faith in the idea of a personal, compassionate, and good God while he completed his studies at Crozer Seminary and Boston University. Throughout his academic journey, he maintained a deep and abiding connection to the black church, remaining active as a preacher and vibrant contributor to the life of that institution. During his tenure at Crozer Seminary, he attended Calvary Baptist Church in Chester, Pennsylvania. The church was pastored by J. Pius Barbour, a friend of the King family, and the members considered King one of the "sons of Calvary."[31] The communal culture of the church provided King with a family away from home, and "explains why King, Jr., who was only nineteen when he went to Crozer, escaped the spiritual pain that would have otherwise characterized his transition from Morehouse and the larger black culture in Atlanta to life on an essentially white seminary campus."[32] After arriving in Boston in late 1951 to begin his graduate studies, King attended another church pastored by a friend of his father. Like Barbour, Rev. William H. Hester, the pastor of Twelfth Baptist Church, was supportive of King, and his church, like Calvary, provided King with a comforting familiarity in worship, preaching, and communal fellowship that kept the young man firmly in touch with the religion of his childhood.

Perhaps it was the steadying influence of the black church that ensured the Holy Spirit's continual prominence in the mind of King. In the spring of 1951, King wrote a sermon outline at Crozer titled, "The Relevance of the Holy Spirit." He wrote, "Most people have either forgotten that there is such a concept or they have a misconception of it. It remains true, however, that this is one of the most important doctrines in the Christian religion."[33] He gave three points in arguing for the Holy Spirit's relevance: (1) It shows that God is still revealing himself now; (2) it stresses the immanence of God, a concept that King finds useful for refuting the concept of the "otherness" of God that pervaded modern theology; and (3) it underscores the fact that God is still working in history.[34]

Approximately one year later, on May 18, 1952, King preached a sermon titled "The Relevance of the Holy Spirit" at Ebenezer Baptist Church in Atlanta, Georgia, his home church.[35] No extant text of this sermon remains. However, King wrote another outline in 1953, titled "The Relevance of the Holy Spirit." This means that we have three sepa-

31. Baldwin, *Voice of Conscience,* 41.
32. Baldwin, *Voice of Conscience,* 42.
33. Carson et al., eds., *Papers,* 6:118.
34. Carson et al., eds., *Papers,* 6:118
35. Carson et al., eds., *Papers,* 6:46.

rate instances where King either preached or planned to preach a sermon on the relevance of the Holy Spirit. In his last outline, he delineated no outline points underneath the title but instead wrote, "For central points, see DeWolf, TLC, 272 F," apparently a reference to L. Harold DeWolf's book, *A Theology of the Living Church.*[36] DeWolf became King's major professor at Boston University. King planned to appropriate headings from DeWolf's book, *A Theology of the Living Church,* to the extent that he did not initially need to list the main points to be covered in the sermon.[37] Although DeWolf's text was presumably not published until 1953, each of King's points recorded in his 1952 outline corresponds to one of the subsections in DeWolf's text, which demonstrates that King exhibited intimate knowledge of DeWolf's theological ideas concerning the Holy Spirit even before DeWolf's book was issued in published form.

In planning his three main points for the sermon in 1953, King drew from a section of a chapter called, "Significance of Belief in the Holy Spirit," which is further divided into three subsections. DeWolf titles the first section "Warning against Mere Historicism." DeWolf writes, "The church's doctrine of the Holy Spirit . . . teaches that . . . God is . . . our Supreme Contemporary. In the present and in every present He lives, speaks and acts on behalf of His children."[38] In the second section, "Affirmation of a Growing Revelation," DeWolf argues that the doctrine of the Holy Spirit enables the right of believers to look beyond tradition to new truths that emerge from unexpected sources. He comments, "In such a time our hope is that the Holy Spirit will guide humble, truth-seeking men into new understanding and into new realization of the divine purpose," because there is always a new truth that will break forth "from the God in whom is all truth and who speaks anew in every age."[39] The third section, titled "Affirmation of the Divine Presence with Us," affirms the Holy Spirit's work in the life of humanity. DeWolf describes Paul as knowing from experience "that God could and did speak and act presently in and through the freely responsive souls of men."[40] Throughout this section, DeWolf leans toward a modal understanding of the Trinity that interprets the word person according to a Latin usage that could refer to a mask being worn by an actor during a dramatic role, such that contemporary, psychological interpretations of "personhood" are rendered inadequate. According to this perspective, the Holy Spirit

36. Carson et al., eds., *Papers*, 6:567.

37. L. Harold DeWolf, *A Theology of the Living Church* (New York: Harper & Brothers, 1953).

38. DeWolf, *Theology of the Living Church*, 272.

39. DeWolf, *Theology of the Living Church*, 273.

40. DeWolf, *Theology of the Living Church*, 273.

is conceived as either a manifestation of God, or as a force or power sent by God.[41]

King was exposed earlier to a similar understanding of the Holy Spirit in a text written by William Newton Clarke called *An Outline of Christian Theology*.[42] While enrolled at Crozer Theological Seminary, King's professor, George W. Davis, required students to submit outlines for six talks from this treatise. At the beginning of chapter 5, titled "The Holy Spirit and the Divine Life in Man," Clarke presents a section titled, "What Is Meant by the Holy Spirit." In response, Clarke answers, "The practical definition is, the Holy Spirit is God in man; God working in the spirit of man, and accomplishing the results that are sought in the mission and work of Christ."[43] Clarke, noting that it is common to refer to the Holy Spirit as the third person in the Trinity, reminds the reader that the early church understood God as acting in the world *via* three manifestations or operations. The first operation concerns God's relation to the world and humanity. The second refers to God's manifestation in the mission, person, and work of Christ. In this third operation, "God approaches as a Spirit to the spirit of man for the purpose of holy communication and influence; most appropriately therefore was he named the Holy Spirit."[44] Clarke continues, "This Spirit . . . is not a mere influence, but is rather God himself as a Spirit, in contact with human spirits."[45] Clarke's conception of the Holy Spirit echoes DeWolf's in that he also denies personhood central importance, and instead highlights the meaning of the Holy Spirit as representing God's spiritual agency and activity within the world.

Clarke's conception of the Holy Spirit also resembles DeWolf's in that he conceives of and narrates the early church's sense of the Holy Spirit as "a present force." In explicating the relationship of the early church to the Holy Spirit, Clarke declares, "It was glorious to live with such a sense of present divine energy, a consciousness that God dwelt graciously within and was moving omnipotently without."[46] Thus, in both Clarke's systematic theology and in DeWolf's, the Holy Spirit inhabits two forms of existence. The first is as God himself, working in the world and in humanity through his spirit. This first form can be described as

41. DeWolf, *Theology of the Living Church*, 279.

42. William Newton Clarke, *An Outline of Christian Theology* (New York: Charles Scribner's Sons, 1899).

43. Clarke, *Outline of Christian Theology*, 369.

44. Clarke, *Outline of Christian Theology*, 369.

45. Clarke, *Outline of Christian Theology*, 369.

46. Clarke, *Outline of Christian Theology*, 370, 372.

"God in action." The second form is as a sense of "energy," or as a "force" that works to carry out the purposes of God.

In his outline for Davis's class, titled "How God Works Today through His Spirit," King adumbrates Clarke's pneumatology. He wrote:

> Many suppose it irreverent to believe that the Holy Spirit is as great in the world now as it was in the days of the apostles. But by such thoughts we do injustice to God and render our faith ineffective. We must believe that the living Spirit—*that is, the present living God*—is working through history.[47]

In another outline titled, "The Character of the Christian God," King defines the nature of God as "the personal spirit," or "a personal spirit."[48] He later expounds upon the nature of God, writing, "The early Christians conceived of spirit as meaning that man could have spiritual fellowship with God. It meant that spirit could meet spirit. This was a practical view."[49] King's understanding of God's practical nature as represented by spiritual activity rehearses Clarke's delineation of the Holy Spirit as the spiritual manifestation of God's agency and activity within the world in relationship with humanity. We can be reasonably certain that at this early stage in his theological journey, King rejected orthodox views of the Holy Spirit as a distinct person within the Trinity, and instead viewed the Holy Spirit as a mode of God himself in action.[50] Accounting for the influence of DeWolf and Clarke allows for the construction of a hermeneutical apparatus that identifies the implicit pneumatology within King's idea of a personal God. When viewed through this lens, King's discourse regarding God's activity in the world, his governance of history, and his fellowship with humanity can often be interpreted as pneumatological in nature. Second, DeWolf and Clarke's description of the Holy Spirit as "energy," or as a "force," sheds light on King's own usage of these terms. Based upon his familiarity with their conclusions, his own deployment of these terms suggests strongly that he used them to describe manifestations of the Holy Spirit. In the rest of this chapter, I will show that King predominantly thought and spoke pneumatologi-

47. Carson et al., eds., *Papers,* 1:248, emphasis mine.

48. Carson et al., eds., *Papers,* 1:243.

49. Carson et al., eds., *Papers,* 1:243.

50. In a paper, "The Sources of Fundamentalism and Liberalism Considered Historically and Psychologically," written at Crozer in the fall of 1949, King states: "Other doctrines such as a supernatural plan of salvation, the Trinity, the substitutionary theory of the atonement, and the second coming of Christ are all quite prominent in fundamentalist thinking. Such are the views of the fundamentalist and they reveal that he is opposed to theological adaptation to social and cultural change. He sees a progressive scientific age as a retrogressive spiritual age. Amid change all around he is willing to preserve certain ancient ideas even though they are contrary to science." See Carson et al., eds., *Papers,* 1:236, 242.

cally in regard to two of the three points from his sermonic outline. First, he envisioned the Holy Spirit as operative in superintending and miraculously intervening in history. Second, he viewed the Holy Spirit as the immanent presence of God acting to induce moral transformation and to comfort humanity.

GOD IS STILL WORKING IN HISTORY

Following DeWolf's "Warning against Mere Historicism," King envisioned the Holy Spirit as a divine entity presently at work in directing and creating history, such that history becomes "ecstatic" or imbued with miraculous instances of God's activity toward the creation of the beloved community. In this sense, the Holy Spirit acts upon and within history, superintending its events, and even miraculously altering its outcome. The most glaring evidence for this claim arises from King's memoir of the Montgomery bus boycott, *Stride toward Freedom*. This entire work can best be interpreted as a pneumatological narrative wherein King comes to terms with a newfound relationship with the Holy Spirit and experiences the concomitant realization that this same Spirit quickens history through ecstatic intervention.

The pneumatological narrative conveyed by King begins with his return to the South in 1954 to preach a trial sermon at Dexter Avenue Baptist Church in Montgomery, Alabama. King, who was being considered for the pastorate of Dexter, questioned what homiletical approach he should employ in order to make a good first impression. He even considered using his vast theological knowledge to impress the congregation. He finally resolved that he would "preach just as I had always done, depending finally on the inspiration of the spirit of God."[51] In this instance, King articulated a pneumatological understanding of his preaching that attributes its source and motivation to the Holy Spirit. King's reiterated this theological assessment of his preaching as buttressed and anointed by the Holy Spirit during his first sermon, after being hired as the pastor of Dexter. During this sermon, King exclaimed,

> I come with a feeling that I have been called to preach and to lead God's people. I have felt like Jeremiah, "The word of God is in my heart like burning fire shut up in my bones." I have felt with Amos that when God speaks who can but prophesy? *I have felt with Jesus that the spirit of the Lord is upon me,* because he hath anointed me to preach the gospel to the poor, to heal the

51. King, *Stride toward Freedom,* 17.

> brokenhearted, to preach deliverance to the captive and set at liberty those that are bruised.[52]

The attribution of his arrival in Montgomery to the providence and plan of God in the quote above exemplifies King's black evangelical understanding of his call. Furthermore, the idea of "inspiration," which refers to the belief that the Holy Spirit empowers the preacher to effectively fulfill his or her call, also emerges from King's identification with the black church preaching tradition.

King's pneumatological understanding of his call deepened during the early stages of the Montgomery bus boycott. Whereas he previously assumed pneumatological foundations for his arrival at Dexter, these foundations soon broadened to encompass the entire movement he was now tasked with leading. King recalls the day in 1955 when he was elected president of the Montgomery Improvement Association (MIA). After remaining in meetings all day, he arrived home at six-thirty in the evening with only twenty minutes to prepare for his main address at the first mass meeting in support of the boycott. Gripped by anxiety and fear, King felt overcome by a feeling of overwhelming inadequacy. He recalled: "With nothing left but faith in a power whose matchless strength stands over against the frailties and inadequacies of human nature, I turned to God in prayer."[53] King's reliance on "a power" can be interpreted pneumatologically. At this moment, King needed God's spirit to meet his spirit in a synergistic moment of communication and empowerment that would enable him to move and inspire the crowd in attendance. While King does not explicitly use the term "Holy Spirit," based upon his theological exposure to the conceptions of DeWolf and Clarke and his pneumatological understanding of inspiration, we can assume that the source of inspiration he sought in a power of matchless strength referred to the spirit of God. King's Holt Street Baptist Church speech, delivered December 5, 1955, catapulted him to national fame, esteem, and leadership. The speech, "virtually unprepared" and written without a manuscript or notes, was the first time King had experienced the type of divine inspiration that the older generations of black preach-

52. Martin Luther King Jr., "Address to the Dexter Avenue Baptist Church Congregation," Montgomery, Alabama unpublished version (2 May 1954), Coretta Scott King Collection (CSKC), Library and Archives of the Martin Luther King Jr. Center for Nonviolent Social Change, Inc. (KCLA), Atlanta, Georgia; Martin Luther King Jr., "The Three Dimensions of a Complete Life," unpublished version of a sermon, Dexter Avenue Baptist Church, Montgomery, Alabama (24 January 1954), CSKC, KCLA; Martin Luther King Jr., "Looking beyond Your Circumstances," unpublished version of a sermon, Dexter Avenue Baptist Church, Montgomery, Alabama (18 September 1955), CSKC, KCLA; and King, *Autobiography,* 46.

53. King, *Stride toward Freedom,* 59.

ers promised and had long proclaimed. Like had never happened before, he opened his mouth, and God filled it with words.[54]

The inclusion of these seemingly personal events, in a section in which we investigate King's pneumatological understanding of history, seems misplaced unless we also understand that King's reflections on his experiences with the Holy Spirit at the beginning of his Dexter pastorate and throughout the Montgomery Bus Boycott elucidated the interrelated nature of the Holy Spirit's activity in his own life and in the life of the burgeoning civil rights movement. Notwithstanding King's personal understanding of inspiration engendered by his black evangelical upbringing, he fused this personal understanding with a broad conception of the Holy Spirit's activity within history and society. King saw himself as a servant of his community, and therefore, what the Holy Spirit did for him occurred ultimately on behalf of the constituency he was called to serve. For example, King interpreted Rosa Park's refusal to give up her bus seat as more than an individual gesture of protest or resistance. For King, her refusal to relinquish occurred because "she had been tracked down by the *zeitgeist*—the spirit of the time."[55] Moreover, in his famous "Letter from Birmingham City Jail," King also interpreted the American Negro's struggle for freedom as orchestrated by the *Zeitgeist.*

King derives the term *Zeitgeist* from G. W. F. Hegel's *Philosophy of History* (1837), which he had read at Boston University during his spare time.[56] Hegel envisions history as a teleological process by which the World Spirit comes to actualize itself through successive stages of ever-increasing human freedom. This metaphysics of history places spirit at the center of reality, and material reality is a mere expression of this deeper underlying spiritual reality. King endorsed Hegel's liberalist conception of history, but his dialectical theological thinking led him to Christianize it. We can discern this dialecticism in King's rejection of communism's materialism and atheism. King comments, "for as a Christian I believe that there is a creative personal power in this universe who is the ground and essence of all reality—a power that cannot be explained in materialistic terms. History is ultimately guided by spirit, not matter."[57] King synthesizes the Hegelian understanding of history with his Christian belief in a personal God and claims that the creative personal power of God is the "spirit" that guides history. Based upon King's interpretation of God's spiritual manifestation in history as synonymous with

54. King, *Stride toward Freedom,* 63.
55. King, *Stride toward Freedom,* 43–44.
56. King, *Stride toward Freedom,* 100–101.
57. King, *Stride toward Freedom,* 92.

the Holy Spirit, King is undoubtedly speaking of the Holy Spirit here also.

King advances this pneumatological understanding of historical events even further in stating that "the Holy Spirit is the continuing community creating reality that moves through history."[58] Reflecting on the meaning of *agape* as he explained his pilgrimage to nonviolence, King ascribes a social role to the Holy Spirit. This idea of the Holy Spirit as a force moving through history to unify people in love toward the ideal of beloved community is not intrinsic to black evangelical church traditions. In fact, Rev. James Forbes, renowned Pentecostal minister and former pastor of Riverside Church, developed a new and different understanding of the Holy Spirit due to King's insights. He states, "Dr. King introduced a new perspective for me when he linked the social mandates of the Christian faith to the Holy Spirit."[59] Forbes, accustomed to the Spirit's work in converting, renewing, and sanctifying individual souls, enlarged his conception of the Holy Spirit to include this community-creating aspect after reading King's quote in *Stride toward Freedom.*

Equipped with King's dialectic pneumatological understanding of history, we can better discern where this understanding of the Holy Spirit emerges within the text. For instance, in one portion of the boycott narrative, King remembers the influx of contributions that helped the MIA meet its monthly operating expenses. He quotes a letter from an elderly Pennsylvanian woman who contributed one hundred dollars. She wrote, "Your work . . . is outstanding and unprecedented in the history of our country. Indeed, it is epoch-making and it should have a far-reaching effect. . . . 'Not by might, nor by power, but by my spirit, saith the Lord'—this might well be the motto of the Montgomery Improvement Association."[60] King quotes *this* letter from the innumerable letters and contributions that deluged the MIA headquarters because the writer's emphasis on the spirit of God as the divine reality invading history resonated with King's own theological understanding of the Montgomery bus boycott. For King, the spirit of the Lord had inaugurated a historical cataclysm that worked to engender freedom for the oppressed and also instigated the ensuing rapid societal transformations.

King asks the question of the Montgomery bus boycott: "Why did this event take place in Montgomery, Alabama, in 1955?"[61] After giving sev-

58. King, *Stride toward Freedom,* 105–6.

59. James A. Forbes Jr., *Whose Gospel? A Concise Guide to Progressive Protestantism* (New York: The New Press, 2010), 8.

60. King, *Stride toward Freedom,* 81.

61. King, *Stride toward Freedom,* 64.

eral probable causes, King rejects each of these in turn as insufficient to fully explain the momentous occurrence. He writes,

> So every rational explanation breaks down at some point. There is something about the protest that is suprarational; it cannot be explained without a divine dimension . . . , some extra-human force labors to create a harmony out of the discords of the universe. There is a creative power that works to pull down mountains of evil and level hilltops of injustice. God still works through history His wonders to perform.[62]

King uses the term "force" to explicate his pneumatological-historical understanding of the bus boycott. While several factors contributed to its development and success, ultimately King considers the boycott to be a "wonder" wrought by the hand of God. If, as I have tried to show, King leans toward a modalist understanding of the Trinity, in which the Holy Spirit names the manifestation of God's action in the earth, then King's seemingly theistic language encourages a more pneumatological interpretation. Therefore, King conclusively demonstrates an understanding of the Holy Spirit that encompasses the Holy Spirit's provenance over the entire sweep of history, as well as periodic miraculous interventions within it.

THE HOLY SPIRIT AS REPRESENTATION OF GOD'S IMMANENCE

King considered the doctrine of the Holy Spirit to be a decisive representation of God's immanence. He valued the doctrine of the Holy Spirit for the same reason that he also believed in the possibility of miracles. First, both doctrines assume that there is a living and active God. Second, both doctrines disclose God's ability to do "new and unpredictable things." Third, both doctrines evoke belief in a God who answers prayer. Last, both doctrines support the view of God's immanence. As King asserts, "Miracle is important, finally, because it holds to an immanent God. God is not a deity who stands outside of the world and does nothing, but he is a deity immanent in the process of history."[63] While King seemed to limit his view of miracles to the confines of natural law, his overall explication of their salience bolsters the central importance that the conception of a loving, personal, compassionate God held within his theological worldview. This conception, which formed the bedrock of King's the-

62. King, *Stride toward Freedom,* 69–70.
63. Carson et al., eds., *Papers,* 1:294.

ological framework, also gives plausible explanation for King's consistent interest in preaching and writing about "The Relevance of the Holy Spirit" during his years at Crozer Seminary and Boston University.

Clearly, King was keenly aware that the spirit of God was present as an infinite resource upon which he and the movement could continually depend for grace, strength, and comfort, especially during periods of extreme turbulence and crisis. King declares, "In many instances I have felt the power of God transforming the fatigue of despair into the buoyancy of hope. I am convinced that the universe is under the control of a loving purpose and that in the struggle for righteousness man has cosmic companionship."[64] This reflection on cosmic companionship is thoroughly pneumatological in that God is present to the human spirit through His Spirit as a source of strength, comfort, and guidance.

King believed that one of the ways that the Holy Spirit prominently manifests God's immanence is by affecting moral transformation. In his outline for George W. Davis's class, titled, "How God Works Today through His Spirit," King included a subheading titled, "The working of the spirit of God in bringing about moral transformation within the individual."[65] One instance where King attributed moral influence to the Holy Spirit occurred during the Montgomery bus boycott. Following the bombing of his home, hundreds of angry supporters gathered at King's home. The policemen could not disperse the crowd, and the atmosphere was quite tense. King admonished the crowd to go home with the assurance of God's blessing upon the movement. He cautioned the crowd to avoid violence, and he declared, "Jesus still cries out in words that echo across the centuries: 'Love your enemies; bless them that curse you; pray for them that despitefully use you.'"[66] Even after King's remonstrations, the atmosphere remained tense and violence threatened to erupt at any moment. Eventually the crowd dispersed without incident. King explains what prevented violence that evening: "This could well have been the darkest night in Montgomery's history. But something happened to avert it: *the spirit of God was in our hearts*; and a night that seemed destined to end in unleashed chaos came to a close in a majestic group demonstration of nonviolence (emphasis mine)."[67] According to King, God's immanent presence, manifested in the Holy Spirit, restrained boycott supporters from seeking vengeance. The Holy

64. Martin Luther King Jr., "Pilgrimage to Nonviolence," in James M. Washington, ed., *A Testament of Hope: The Essential Writings and Speeches of Martin Luther King, Jr.* (New York: HarperCollins, 1991; originally published in 1986), 40.

65. Carson et al., eds., *Papers,* 1:248–49.

66. King, *Stride toward Freedom,* 137–38.

67. King, *Stride toward Freedom,* 138.

Spirit provided interior strength enabling them to pursue peace through obedience to Christ's commands.

As James Forbes discerns, however, King envisions pneumatological moral transformation as societal, and not merely individual. In his sermon, "The Man Who Was a Fool," King denounces the materialism and humanism of Western civilization. He correlated the formidable scientific and technological accomplishments of modern society with the rich man's wealth in the parable narrated by Jesus in the twelfth chapter of Luke. The rich man enjoyed extravagant wealth, and instead of exhibiting gratitude or generosity, he built larger structures to accommodate his growing prosperity. Similarly, for King, the revolutions of modern science had caused humanity to pursue greater and more frequent technological discoveries while lessening dependence on God. Science, in King's estimation, was limited in its potential, especially if humanity did not invite the Holy Spirit to enjoin its proper usage. In reflecting on the atomic bombs of Nagasaki and Hiroshima, King remarked: "Now we have come to see that science can give us only physical power, which, if not controlled by spiritual power, will lead inevitably to cosmic doom."[68] King seeks to place science under the moral influence of the Holy Spirit, thus ascribing to the Holy Spirit a role in the overall transformation of modern society. Regarding science he states, "It is an instrument which, under the power of God's spirit, may lead man to greater heights of physical security, but apart from God's spirit, science is a deadly weapon that will lead only to deeper chaos."[69] King exhorted his audience to return to dependence on God to ensure that their technological efforts enhance human flourishing instead of destroying it. In speaking directly to an apostate Western civilization, whose "scientific power has outrun our spiritual power," King concluded by adjuring his listeners to seek a "spiritual and moral reawakening."[70]

Once again, King's dialectical thinking is on display. While the idea of the Holy Spirit restraining churchgoers from engaging in violence would resonate with members of the black church, his view of the Holy Spirit as a restraining influence upon humanity's scientific violence evokes traces of the liberal theological strands of thought that also influenced him. In this sermon, "The Man Who Was a Fool," the moral reawakening that King sought was not the personal salvation associated with revivals and camp meetings, but the spiritual awakening of an entire civilization in pursuit of justice for the poor through the utiliza-

68. Martin Luther King Jr., *Strength to Love* (Philadelphia: Fortress, 1981; originally published in 1963), 72–73.

69. King, *Strength to Love*, 73.

70. King, *Strength to Love*, 74–75.

tion of science and technology for the good of all of God's children across the globe.

In the last example of the Holy Spirit's exemplification of God's immanence, I turn to King's sermon, "Antidotes for Fear." In this sermon, he recalls being emotionally drained after a week of several threatening phone calls and other stress-inducing events during the Montgomery bus boycott. Although he outwardly attempted to project an aura of courage, inwardly he was besieged by fear. King offered his depiction of the event:

> At the end of the meeting, Mother Pollard came to the front of the church and said, "Come here son. . . . Something is wrong with you," she said. "You didn't talk strong tonight." Seeking further to disguise my fears, I retorted, "Oh no, Mother Pollard, nothing is wrong. I am feeling as fine as ever." But her insight was discerning. "Now you can't fool me," she said. "I knows something is wrong . . . ' Before I could respond, she looked directly into my eyes and said, "I don told you we is with you all the way." Then her face became radiant and she said in words of quiet certainty, "But even if we ain't with you, God's gonna take care of you." As she spoke these consoling words, everything in me quivered and quickened with the pulsing tremor of raw energy.[71]

While King never attributes his experience of "raw energy" to the Holy Spirit, the concept of the Holy Spirit as divine energy is one with which he was familiar from William Newton Clarke's discourse on the Holy Spirit. Jürgen Moltmann also provides a pneumatological framework for understanding "energy" as an expression of the Holy Spirit's power and vitality. He oberves that "things begin to dance when we sense that God surrounds us from every side. We experience ourselves and our relationships to other people in the vibrancies of the divine field of force which penetrates us through and through."[72] Moltmann believes that God is felt within experiences of the Spirit as a primal and all-embracing presence that leads to intimacy as one reflects upon the Holy Spirit as the origin of this "the torrent of energy."[73]

Moltmann's vivid imagery peels back the layers of King's account to reveal the Holy Spirit as the fount and source of the raw energy that quickened King's body. Mary MacLeod Bethune, the renowned Christian educator and activist, uses descriptive terminology nearly identical to King's in her exposition of the moment when she was baptized with

71. King, *Strength to Love*, 125–26.

72. Jürgen Moltmann, *The Source of Life: The Holy Spirit and the Theology of Life* (Minneapolis: Fortress, 1997), 68.

73. Moltmann, *Source of Life*, 69.

the Holy Spirit. During her training at Moody Bible Institute, Bethune responded to Dwight L. Moody, who asked who wanted to be baptized in the Holy Spirit. After kneeling down, Bethune recalled, "I realized a quickening and awakening that I had not words to express from that day to the present. During all the years in my dealings with many I have drawn up this source for effective service."[74]

In both of these accounts, the narrators reporting their pneumatological experiences encountered the Holy Spirit in the early and initial stages of what would become profoundly influential careers as public figures. Each of them returned to the experience through memory to relive and be comforted by the divine presence whose reassurance left an indelible imprint upon their total being. Just as Bethune frequently relied upon her memory of this event for success, King found himself often "tortured without and tormented within by the raging fires of tribulation," and King said that "the eloquently simple words of Mother Pollard have come back again and again to give light and peace and guidance to my troubled soul."[75]

CONCLUSION

In this chapter, I have argued, in agreement with Rufus Burrow Jr., that the Holy Spirit plays a pivotal and decisive role in King's experiences and his theological framework, specifically bolstering and enriching his belief in a personal, compassionate, immanent, loving God. I have also argued that King approached his belief in the Holy Spirit dialectically, neither wholly embracing the categories of orthodoxy—including Trinitarian personhood taken for granted within the black church community—nor gravitating fully toward the philosophical idealism of scholars who endorsed the concept of "spirit" but denied personality to God. From analyzing King's writings and speeches, we can conclude that the Holy Spirit inhabits two major roles: first, the Holy Spirit governs history, ensuring that it moves toward the *telos* of beloved community and the unity of all people. This view of history is decidedly liberal in its optimism, yet orthodox in ascribing agency and will to the Holy Spirit. Second, King believed that the Holy Spirit manifested the immanent presence of God within individual humans and within society to foster moral transformation. The two examples I provided demonstrate King's dialectical thinking. The sanctifying ability of the Holy Spirit

74. Anthea D. Butler, *Women in the Church of God in Christ: Making a Sanctified World* (Chapel Hill: University of North Carolina Press, 2007), 110.

75. King, *Strength to Love,* 126.

restrained individuals from retaliating against city officials who had created a climate of hatred that led to King's home being bombed. Individual sanctification, which delineates the process of the Christian's moral transformation into the image of Christ, has long been a pillar of black evangelical doctrine. King, however, also grants the Holy Spirit a sanctifying influence over entire societies and civilizations, expanding his view of the Holy Spirit's sanctifying power so that even humanity's use of science and technology must be governed by the Holy Spirit in order to secure justice for the oppressed and peace for all humanity.

I conclude this chapter with one of King's final pneumatological reflections, taken from a sermon delivered at Mount Pisgah Baptist Church in Chicago on August 27, 1967. King again preached the sermon, "The Man Who Was a Fool," and he vigorously exhorted the congregation to recognize their dependence upon God. In doing so, he recounted his kitchen experience. Of that night, he recalls, "I discovered then that religion had to become real to me and I had to know God for myself."[76] As the congregation engaged with King in the dialogical interplay characterizing the black preaching tradition, he sonorously recited the prayer he prayed that memorable night. Again he vividly described an inner voice encouraging him to stand up for righteousness, justice, and truth. King identifies the inner voice he heard at the kitchen table as the voice of Jesus telling him to fight on, and promising to never leave him alone. King admonishes the congregation, "You'd better know him, and know his name, and know how to call his name." King ends the sermon by quoting the hymn, "Balm in Gilead." He told the congregation that he sometimes gets discouraged, but like his slave foreparents, he could sing, "Yes, sometimes I feel discouraged and feel my work's in vain. But then the Holy Spirit revives my soul again."[77]

76. Carson and Holloran, eds., *Knock at Midnight*, 162.

77. Carson and Holloran, eds., *Knock at Midnight*, 163–64.

5.

Cosmic Companionship: Martin Luther King Jr.'s Lived Theology

STEWART BURNS

> I am convinced that the universe is under the control of a loving purpose, and that in the struggle for righteousness man has cosmic companionship.
>
> —Martin Luther King Jr.[1]

> For our purposes, however, what is most characteristic of the God of the Bible is that he is *the God who takes sides.* He is not indifferent, he is not aloof, he is not uncaring. What happens to people matters to him. And if there is anything that is clear in the Biblical drama as a whole, it is that when God takes sides, he sides with the oppressed.
>
> —Robert McAfee Brown[2]

Was the greatness of Martin Luther King Jr. not just his civil rights and human rights leadership but being the most important theologian in American history, which James Cone claimed long ago?[3]

Exhausted, depressed, and swallowed up by the black movement, King in his later years never had the chance to articulate his evolving theology about how shared suffering inspired souls and connected them to form the beloved community, leading toward the union of humanity and divinity. Over the last half century, several religion scholars have extrapolated from his work to compose elements of a Kingian theology, though generally relying too much on King's seminary and graduate

1. Alex Ayres, ed., *The Wisdom of Martin Luther King, Jr.: An A-to-Z Guide to the Ideas and Ideals of the Great Civil Rights Leader* (New York: Penguin, 1993), 95.

2. Robert McAfee Brown, *Religion and Violence: A Primer for White Americans* (Philadelphia: Westminster, 1976), 95.

3. James H. Cone, "The Theology of Martin Luther King Jr.," *Union Seminary Quarterly Review* 40, no. 4 (1986): 35–36.

school writings and the influence of white theologians like Paul Tillich and Reinhold Niebuhr—and not enough on his mature life experience.[4]

Early on, Professor Cone, architect of black liberation theology, took a different tack, grounding King's unformed theology in slave religion, the black church, and the black Social Gospel. "A theologian of action," Cone explained, King was "actively seeking to transform the structures of oppression." His theology was "dynamic, constantly emerging from the historical circumstances in which he was engaged."[5] Cone stressed how MLK's incipient theology changed from the Montgomery bus boycott to the fateful Memphis strike, centering first on justice, then more on love (*agape*), and finally on hope and faith, as the black movement faced implosion and peril.[6]

During the past decade, religious historian Charles Marsh and colleagues at the University of Virginia have articulated the concept of "lived theology" to affirm theological expressions that are human-centered, drawn from personal or communal experience, often from laity—and conveyed not in the abstract, formal diction of Western white theology, but more down to earth, sometimes coming from stories, poetry, music, drama, dance, or direct action, that is, more attuned to action or performance than to words alone.[7]

Though King lived out aspects of his theology, starting with the Montgomery bus boycott, he did not always walk his talk, until dire personal crisis compelled him: Birmingham Sunday, the horrific church bombing of September 1963. From that *kairos* moment, his lived theology started to take shape, culminating in his great prophetic Memphis sermon on April 3, 1968, the night before he died. For five years, this modern-day "suffering servant" struggled with his depression of shifting depth and intensity that was set off and sustained by guilt, introjected anger, and empathy, but gave birth to a profound revelation on the potential interdependence of humanity and the divine.

4. See John Colin Harris, "The Theology of Martin Luther King, Jr.," (PhD diss., Duke University 1974); Luther D. Ivory, *Toward a Theology of Radical Involvement: The Theological Legacy of Martin Luther King, Jr.* (Nashville: Abingdon, 1997); and Richard W. Wills Sr., *Martin Luther King Jr. and the Image of God* (New York: Oxford University Press, 2009), esp. chap. 4, 87–89.

5. Cone, "Theology of Martin Luther King Jr.," 21.

6. Cone, "Theology of Martin Luther King Jr.," 29–35.

7. See Charles Marsh et al., eds., *Lived Theology* (New York: Oxford University Press, 2017); and Project on Lived Theology (University of Virginia), www.livedtheology.org.

BIRMINGHAM SUNDAY

Sunday morning, September 15, 1963. People heard the explosion all over downtown Birmingham. Four Ku Klux Klan terrorists had stashed a powerful bomb outside the Sixteenth Street Baptist Church, headquarters of the spring 1963 crusade to desegregate the most segregated city in the South. During worship, the bomb blasted through the basement's thick wall. Four girls dressing for the youth day service were killed: Denise McNair, eleven; and Cynthia Wesley, Carole Robertson, and Addie Mae Collins, all fourteen. The horrendous bombing was one of the most heinous crimes during the civil rights movement and the whole long struggle for black freedom in America.

"I had never seen him so depressed," King's oldest child Yolanda remembered. For several hours he seemed "almost catatonic, sitting alone in his office, head in his hands, brooding in silence."[8] Until that day, remarkably, no one had died in any of his campaigns. As he not only had led but *personified* the Birmingham movement, which was ongoing, and having four kids of his own, he was emotionally devastated unlike ever before.[9] Finally, he forced himself to the Atlanta airport.

King landed that Sunday night in a city about to implode.

"We feel that Birmingham is now in a state of civil disorder, an emergency situation," he told reporters. He called for the Army to take over the city, warning President John F. Kennedy that without drastic action, "We shall see the worst racial holocaust this nation has ever seen."[10] The White House did nothing. Black forbearance kept the city from blowing up.

In his eulogy for the slain girls in Birmingham, King sought to do what Abraham Lincoln had done a hundred years before at the gory Gettysburg battlefield: transform suffering and dying into redemptive rebirth.

"They are the martyred heroines," he said, "of a holy crusade for freedom and human dignity. . . . They say to each of us, black and white alike"—surely speaking to himself—"that we must substitute courage for caution." King continued:

8. Yolanda King, quoted in Frye Gaillard, foreword to Lewis V. Baldwin, *Behind the Public Veil: The Humanness of Martin Luther King, Jr.* (Minneapolis: Fortress, 2016), xi.

9. NAACP leader Medgar Evers in Jackson, Mississippi, and Herbert Lee, a local organizer working with Bob Moses and SNCC in southern Mississippi, had been killed by white supremacists in 1963 and 1961, respectively.

10. Quoted in David J. Garrow, *Bearing the Cross: Martin Luther King, Jr., and the Southern Christian Leadership Conference* (New York: William Morrow, 1986), 292.

> God still has a way of wringing good out of evil. History has proven over and over again that unmerited suffering is redemptive. The innocent blood of these little girls may well serve as a redemptive force that will bring new light to this dark city. . . . The spilt blood of these innocent girls may cause the whole citizenry of Birmingham to transform the negative extremes of a dark past into the positive extremes of a bright future.[11]

King opened his soul a week later at the convention of his Southern Christian Leadership Conference (SCLC); his presidential address, always before upbeat, was contrite, even despairing: "Today we are faced with the midnight of oppression which we had believed to be the dawn of redemption." He confessed that his leadership was "standing still, doing nothing, going nowhere."[12]

Three weeks after delivering his great dream in Washington, he had fallen from the loftiest peak to the lowest valley. He felt that his fame and glory were hiding his failures and sins—he was achingly aware of two selves at war within, his exalted self that felt fake and his sin-sick self all too real. His dream shattering into a nightmare, he sank into an acute depression that battered him for the rest of his life. His nightmare only grew darker as he struggled through the difficult years ahead.

SUFFERING SERVANTHOOD

The slave religion of North America that fused African traditions with Christian and Hebrew scriptures was born in and driven by the most extreme suffering, physical, emotional, and spiritual—the most brutal, exploitative slavery ever known. Slaves and their homegrown preachers, known as "exhorters," shaped their religious practices, their lived theology, to meet pressing needs and to foster their survival and salvation. Because their spirituality enabled them to live simultaneously in both sacred and profane worlds, they prayed for deliverance in this world and in a hoped-for afterlife. Black "slaves were in fact carving out a new style of earthly freedom," Professor Cone noted. "Slave religion was permeated with the affirmation of freedom from bondage and freedom-in-bondage. Sometimes black religious gatherings were the occasions for planning overt resistance."[13]

11. Quoted in James M. Washingon, ed., *A Testament of Hope: The Essential Writings and Speeches of Martin Luther King, Jr.* (San Francisco: HarperSanFrancisco, 1991), 221–22.

12. Martin Luther King Jr., quoted in Stewart Burns, *To the Mountaintop: Martin Luther King, Jr.'s Sacred Mission to Save America, 1955–1968* (San Francisco: HarperSanFrancisco, 2004), 217.

13. James H. Cone, *The Spirituals and the Blues: An Interpretation* (Westport, CT: Greenwood, 1980; originally published in 1972), 30.

When after the Civil War the black church reconstituted itself largely into black Baptists and black Methodists (AME, AMEZ, and CME), North and South, a majority of ministers strove for white acceptance, but a critical mass carried forward the heritage of monumental suffering into a distinct Social Gospel that paralleled its influential white counterpart associated with Walter Rauschenbusch, Washington Gladden, and others. Black Social Gospel's second generation included Howard Thurman (1900–1981) and Benjamin Mays (1894–1984), president of Morehouse College when King attended in the mid to late 1940s.[14]

Thurman, King's spiritual mentor, became dean of Marsh Chapel at Boston University when King was completing his PhD at that institution. He wrote a piece on the meaning of suffering that King surely read. Thurman saw suffering as a universal force: "It humiliates and violates the person and often the very dignity of the human spirit. . . . The more developed the sense of self and the more acute the self-awareness, the more definite is the potential for suffering." But in one of Christianity's great paradoxes, emotional and psychological pain—which might lead to psychic death if the pain numbs and congeals into hard-heartedness—can if faced and accepted strengthen people's characters "till they become like tempered steel"; suffering as the vital means of "generating energy in the spirit."[15]

This great theologian, whom some called a mystic and others a philosopher of religion, believed that the self-conscious, enlightened experience of suffering can alter one deeply, giving one "a subtle radiance and a settled serenity," and giving relationships a "vital generosity" and openheartedness. If one brings to bear upon suffering "all the powers of his mind and spirit," they can rise above their isolated pain to join "a fellowship of suffering as well as a community of sufferers." The sense of togetherness tends to lessen the pain or make it more endurable. Thurman seemed to be saying that mindful suffering opened the door to human solidarity.[16] King, his mentee, would lift this insight to a higher level.

King came to believe that suffering born of adversity can fortify, enlighten, encourage, ennoble, transform, and even "divinize" the sufferer. It can open up space for healing and to reconcile with one's

14. See Gary Dorrien, *Breaking White Supremacy: Martin Luther King, Jr. and the Black Social Gospel* (New Haven: Yale University Press, 2018), 96–97, 109–20.

15. Howard Thurman, *Disciplines of the Spirit* (Richmond, IN: Friends United, 1977), 65–66, 75–76.

16. Thurman, *Disciplines of the Spirit*, 64–85. Reprinted in Walter E. Fluker and Catherine Tumber, eds., *A Strange Freedom: The Best of Howard Thurman on Religious Experience and Public Life* (Boston: Beacon, 1998), 35–54.

adversary, even to forgiveness. What made suffering *unearned* for King was one's experience of *adversity*. The greater the adversity, the more unearned was suffering—a supreme example being the four Birmingham girls who perished—then presumably greater was the redemption.[17] King grounded his arising theology in the extreme suffering of African American slaves and all victims of white supremacy.

More than three years before Birmingham Sunday, in a *Christian Century* article titled, "Suffering and Faith," King testified about his own personal suffering. Acknowledging the danger of a martyr complex and being "self-centered in his self-denial and self-righteous in his self-sacrifice," he wrote that he had been arrested and jailed five times, his home bombed twice (actually once, the second time foiled), he and his family had gotten endless death threats, and he survived a nearly fatal stabbing. As King's troubles mounted, he saw that he could either "react with bitterness or seek to transform the suffering into a creative force." Then a familiar refrain: "I have lived these last few years with the conviction that unearned suffering is redemptive."[18]

But this self-portrait told only one side of the story—more about King's literary persona than his authentic self. Unearned or not, suffering had not really characterized his own lived experience until his mid-thirties. He knew, notwithstanding segregation, that he had been privileged from birth, his life "wrapped up like a Christmas package." Until December 1955, when the bus boycott began, he had been sheltered from racial discord. His life for the next several years was highly stressful with many moments of fear and terror. But one cannot call this a life of suffering—nothing like that of most black people he served. He and his family were healthy and lived in middle-class comfort. No one close to him had died; nor had he faced serious hardship or real sacrifice except too much time away from his family.[19]

Now, in fall of 1963, the cold-blooded destruction of Denise, Cynthia, Carole, and Addie Mae made his privilege and elevation unbearable. The darkness he had always held off, even in the darkest days of the bus boycott, was now engulfing him.

What was the nature of the black religiosity he inherited and then

17. See Washington, ed., *Testament of Hope*, 41–42.

18. Washington, ed., *Testament of Hope*, 41–42, and Martin Luther King Jr., "Why Jesus Called a Man a Fool" (27 August 1967), in Clayborne Carson and Peter Holloran, eds., *A Knock at Midnight: Inspiration from the Great Sermons of Reverend Martin Luther King, Jr.* (New York: Warner, 1998), 159–64.

19. I make these claims despite King's own testimony in his memoir, *Stride toward Freedom: The Montgomery Story* (1958), and comments in various sermons and writings, in which he sought to create the persona of a "suffering servant."

combined with the personalist philosophy he absorbed at Boston University?

Though not unique, African Americans' gift to Christianity was their magic of intimate interplay with the divine. Just as their West African forebears had conversed directly with their nature gods and ancestral spirits, so did enslaved African Americans commune with their divinities. For the slaves and many generations of descendants, their all-pervasive spirit world transmuted into the experience of what Christians called the Holy Spirit. If God was the transcendent supreme being and Jesus the incarnate personality who sacralized the cosmos, the Word become flesh—the Spirit showed up as the divine force manifested on earth, the "inner light" that glorified each creature who acknowledged and embraced it. For these believers, religious historian Mircea Eliade explained, "life is lived on a twofold plane; it takes its course as human existence and, at the same time, shares in a trans-human life, that of the cosmos or the gods."[20]

Drawn more from the Old Testament than the New Testament, the black Social Gospel taught that every person, though created in God's image, was cleaved by jagged fault lines internally between good and evil. God was commanding humankind, especially black people, to pursue a messianic mission to fight the devil within and without.

King learned both from the black Social Gospel (especially Howard Thurman) and from Gandhians (especially Bayard Rustin and Glenn Smiley) that this divinely authorized moral force must be tempered by compassion, understanding, and humility, qualities compressed in what King called goodwill—"the love of God working in the lives of men" (an inherently ambiguous phrase, a two-edged sword)—which rendered righteousness a power that could be wielded safely.[21] It also deepened this power by making it simultaneously a force for personal transformation, expunging one's inner evil, realizing one's higher self. The complex alchemy of justice and love (or agape) was the only way to avert psychological legacies of hatred and bitterness.

At first blush, sedate New England personalism appeared to inhabit a different world from the dynamism of the black Social Gospel. Nevertheless King sought to synthesize elements of both in his emerging theology, at first intellectually and later existentially. He encountered personalism at Crozer Theological Seminary outside Philadelphia, then

20. Mircea Eliade quoted in Burns, *To the Mountaintop*, 51. The Quakers' immanent "inner light" goes back to mid-seventeenth-century England, then migrating to the American colonies and taking hold after the revolution in the new nation.

21. Ayres, ed., *Wisdom of Martin Luther King, Jr.*, 140–42; and Martin Luther King Jr., *Strength to Love* (Philadelphia: Fortress, 1981; originally published in 1963), 36–55.

fully at Boston University School of Theology, its wellspring. A term Walt Whitman coined after the Civil War (1871), personalism entered the twentieth century as a school of thought holding that all reality is of a tender, loving, personal nature; that God is the ultimate personality—which in fact resonated with the divine intimacy of slave spirituality. In the human realm, "personality" in this sense manifested as the divine inner light sacralizing each person.[22]

Whether divine or human, personality meant innate worth and dignity, the aspiration that King and the freedom movement made as vital as freedom. Personality on any scale was characterized by self-consciousness, self-direction, and self-determination. True to masculinist theology, the Boston personalists, unlike Whitman, left out the realm of emotions, of feeling, a far cry from the black religion that worshipped a "God of emotion" (Cone's term) and of empathy. It seems common sense, though, that self-consciousness cannot segregate or deny the sphere of feelings.

I interpret personalism as a rationalization of the immanent divine in human life, which Catholic and Protestant hierarchies sought to banish or sideline for centuries, in part because of enmity toward Gnosticism and its mystical descendants—though divine immanence reemerged among Catholic and Protestant nonconformists, notably Quakers and Shakers and black Christianity. It may not be too much of a stretch to suggest that the personalism coming out of Boston University constituted a philosophical and theological representation of German, English, and American romanticism, articulating in philosophical language the ethos or sensibilities that blended human experience, nature, and divinity in such romantic writers as Johann Wolfgang von Goethe, Samuel Taylor Coleridge, William Wordsworth, Ralph Waldo Emerson, Henry David Thoreau, Emily Elizabeth Dickinson, and Walt Whitman, whose prose and poetry bridged the sacred and secular realms.

In my view, the philosophy of personalism redefined divine immanence to mean a beneficent spiritual force dwelling within (call it holy spirit, inner light, divine spark, atman, or what have you), not only symbolic or metaphorical but actual, immanent not only in persons but embedded in the times (*zeitgeist*) and human history, a notion stressed by Boston's Borden Parker Bowne in *The Immanence of God*.[23]

Boston personalism may have disregarded emotions in its quest for a rational interpretation of personal spirituality, but in the final analysis,

22. Walt Whitman, *Democratic Vistas* (1871).

23. Borden P. Bowne, *The Immanence of God* (Boston: Houghton, Mifflin, 1905). Though Bowne is considered the founder of Boston personalism, he rarely used the term.

feelings and relationships define personality more than does rational thought. In any event, King's conception of personality was pure immanence. It lived and breathed on the micro-level of personal soul and on the macro-levels of the historical past, the lived present, and the future through prophesy.

King demonstrated his comprehension of personality when he told his Ebenezer congregation one day that they didn't really see him standing at the pulpit, the "real" person—his invisible personality, but only the shadow that appeared on the surface concealing the light within, also an allusion to Plato's parable of the cave in *The Republic*.[24] "The real me, you can never see . . . ," he declared. "Everything that we see is a shadow cast by that which we do not see. The visible is a shadow cast by the invisible."[25]

DARK NIGHT OF THE SOUL

For a full year after Birmingham Sunday, absorbed in building the movement, fighting for the civil rights bill, battling vicious white supremacists in Saint Augustine, and barnstorming for Lyndon Johnson's election, King was able to keep his depression under wraps. But winning the Nobel Peace Prize in fall 1964 forced it in the open among his inner circle. As the Nobel glory lifted his public persona into the stratosphere, he felt overwhelmed by guilt and unworthiness. More than ever he felt himself an imposter. Four angels blown to kingdom come, yet he would be celebrated as a messiah by world leaders. Flying to Oslo with his princely entourage of family and friends, King's inner self was as despondent as his public face projected exaltation. "Only Martin's family and close staff members knew how depressed he was during the entire Nobel trip," Coretta King later disclosed. "We had to work with him and help him out of his depression. Somehow he managed all the official functions, the speeches, the whole trip and the public never knew what he was going through."[26]

More famous than ever around the globe, he was welcomed home as a national hero, outside his homeland, the deep South. President Johnson feted him at the White House. He now reigned as moral leader of the

24. When toward the end of his life King was asked what one book he would want with him if marooned on a desert island (besides the Bible), it was Plato's *Republic*. See Martin Luther King Jr., "Playboy Interview," in Washington, ed., *Testament of Hope*, 372. Also see Clayborne Carson et al., eds., *The Papers of Martin Luther King, Jr.: Advocate of the Social Gospel, September 1948–March 1963* (Berkeley: University of California Press, 2007), 6:402–3.

25. Carson et al., eds., *Papers*, 6:402–3.

26. Quoted in Garrow, *Bearing the Cross*, 366.

planet, in his mind anointed by God's will, a responsibility and burden he could not push away.

Vanquishing Bull Connor in Birmingham, King forced President Kennedy to condemn segregation and push the civil rights bill, electrified the nation with his prophetic dream, pressured Kennedy's successor to bulldoze the bill through Congress, and achieved fame as a world leader for peace and justice. King, as a good Hegelian, must have seen himself as a singular, world historic figure, riding the *zeitgeist* that he first recognized during the bus boycott in Montgomery. But he did not know what his global leadership would demand of him, the cost of his discipleship.[27]

Birmingham Sunday had thrust King into the dark night of his soul, which enclosed the wrenching events he faced in the last four years of his life; notably the Nobel Prize tailspin, four deaths in the Selma movement, Watts and the blood-soaked summers to follow, the Vietnam crucible, and the desperation of the urban (Chicago) and rural poor (Mississippi).

For half a millennium, many devout Christians, especially Catholics, have resonated with the writing of Spanish Carmelite monk John of the Cross (1542–1591) on the trials, tribulations, and veiled blessings of the soul's dark night. Embattled with the church hierarchy and imprisoned for his nonconforming views, John told about his acute emotional and spiritual suffering. The suffering, doubt, and loss of faith of Christian believers have compelled many to journey through their dark night, each in their own way, to cleanse themselves of their sins and suffering and rejuvenate their faith. During the dark night of the soul (days, months, years), one strived to subdue one's ego and empty oneself of selfishness, especially of spiritual sins like pride. The metaphorical darkness, both conscious and unconscious, was a zone of torment for the soul but also the forcing house of re-creation. From the darkness of this psychic womb a believer prayed for new life, new selves, new worlds, to be born. We know how passionately King prayed. The premise of King's maturing theology, which he sought to apply to himself, was an individual's commitment to remake their character (i.e., their personality) in the image of divinity.

Rev. Harry Emerson Fosdick (1878–1969), Baptist founding pastor of interdenominational Riverside Church in New York, influenced King more than any other white preacher . Fosdick placed character re-

27. The term "cost of discipleship" comes from Dietrich Bonhoeffer (1906–1945), German Lutheran pastor, theologian, and Nazi resister whose well-known work, *The Cost of Discipleship*, was published in 1937. His involvement in a plot to assassinate Hitler led to his imprisonment and execution in May 1945, like King at age thirty-nine.

formation at the center of his faith. One can forge moral character, courage, and passion only out of adversity and suffering. "Character grows on struggle," Fosdick wrote in *The Meaning of Faith* (1917). "Without the overcoming of obstacles, great quality in character is unthinkable. Whoever has handled well any calamitous event possesses resources, insights, wise attitudes, qualities of sympathy, power," patience, fortitude, and courage, "that by no other road could have come to him."[28]

Bearing the cross, which King evoked more often in his later years, with courage, mindfulness, and humility, was the most promising route to enlightenment and self-actualization, he believed. Fulfilling and maximizing oneself meant integrating one's personality with one's indwelling Holy Spirit; thus by each specific spirit's "concrete universality" connecting to all people, fashioning over the long haul the beloved community. But it was not until King engaged with a prominent Jewish rabbi/theologian, Abraham J. Heschel, that he grasped the crucial element to make his theology work.

King saw the world in a different light after the massacre of the four innocent girls in Birmingham, unearned suffering in the extreme. He could not rest on his laurels, which felt oppressive to him, like a crown of thorns, and take for granted his leadership as anointed by his personal God. He had to prepare himself for the dark days ahead, for his own coming desolation and ultimate crucifixion. He knew his days were numbered. He knew that when he burst out of his agonizing silence on the Vietnam War, he would have to put on the whole armor of God.

For years King had preached about nurturing certain qualities of character, which were necessary for African Americans in the South to stand their ground, to sustain themselves, to survive, and to fend off psychological and spiritual death. Chief among these qualities were courage, fortitude, humility, and patient persistence—one's inner equilibrium.

By summer and fall of 1965, despite the voting rights triumph in Alabama, King's depression, guilt, and fear signaled to him that he was not ready for the cruel days ahead, the foreboding climate dominated by the Vietnam War and black militants' war at home.

Starting that year he employed a series of sermons to instruct himself and his followers on how to prepare for the coming apocalypse, confident that God would give the faithful "interior resources" if he and his followers were willing to suffer and sacrifice, even unto death. These

28. Harry Emerson Fosdick, *The Meaning of Faith* (1917; republished by Memphis: General Books, 2012), 55. From a secular standpoint, psychiatrist Viktor E. Frankl showed how he and others survived Nazi concentration camps by finding meaning and purpose in suffering. Frankl, *Man's Search for Meaning* (Boston: Beacon, 2006).

change agents, along with himself, must "undergo a mental and spiritual reevaluation," he told a gathering of rabbis in December 1965, who gave him their Judaism and World Peace award, in order "to enter in to the new world which is now possible."[29]

King hoped the virtues he sought to embody might serve as a model for many, morphing into new marrow and muscles among the multitude. To begin with, heeding the Apostle Paul, one should strive to resist conformism; not living as a nonconformist, pure and simple, but as a "transformed nonconformist," not letting one's ego or pride take over, neither self-righteous nor exhibitionist. Each person needs to discover "what they are made for" and to pursue this particular passion regardless of how "maladjusted" they might appear or be. Indeed creative maladjustment served King as a prime virtue—though he rarely practiced it till late in his life—as long as kept within responsible bounds.[30]

Following his dialectical approach, King urged creative maladjustment and responsible nonconformity while holding "antitheses strongly marked," understanding if not embracing opposing positions that might resolve into a synthesis, or remain in productive tension.[31] Seeking to see things from the standpoint of the "whole," not just the particulars, which if done mindfully allows one to stay anchored in oneself, adhering to one's principles while striving to make *principled* compromises that respect both one's tribe and the higher common good. One might at once be conservative—as critics accused him, conserving traditions and familiar ways (e.g., biblical virtues)—and radical, nurturing healthy roots while replacing the rotten ones with new shoots.

With eyes on the long haul, even on ultimate human destiny,[32] King advised, one must learn the art of recasting perceived negatives into positives, failure into advantage, breakdowns into breakthroughs, while sensing when to act and when to hold back, the time and place for listening guided by humility; for action guided by humility; when to let events and others' actions move on their own, setting aside one's ego investment. King quoted James Russell Lowell, Langston Hughes, and

29. Martin Luther King Jr., "Address to Rabbinical Council," unpublished version (December 5, 1965), Library and Archives of the Martin Luther King Center for Nonviolent Social Change (KCLA), Atlanta, Georgia.

30. Martin Luther King Jr., "Transformed Nonconformist," unpublished version of a sermon, Ebenezer Baptist, Atlanta, Georgia (16 January 1966), KCLA; and King, *Strength to Love*, 17–25.

31. King, *Strength to Love*, 17–25.

32. Pierre Teilhard de Chardin (1881–1955), controversial French Jesuit paleontologist, philosopher, and mystic, argued that humankind was continuing to evolve toward an end point ("omega") when humans will be essentially divine beings and achieve union with Christ. King was undoubtedly familiar with Teilhard's evolutionary Christology and his thinking probably influenced by it.

other prophetic poets, stressing that present defeats, including personal ones, can plant the seeds, set the stage, for future victories with staying power.[33]

By his mid-thirties, King got in his gut the meaning of unearned suffering produced by adversity, and how it might redeem. To strengthen himself to face mounting adversity, especially what he saw as his inevitable violent death, he now, at least rhetorically, pushed himself and his followers to rebirth, along with all of America and eventually the whole "world house." He saw his indwelling spirit mediating between his personality and the Ultimate, comforting and guiding each person he reached, each one adhering to the world spirit advancing humanity. King likely learned how his guilt-driven depression powered his own imagined rebirth, as well as connecting him with others, with what Ralph Waldo Emerson called the "oversoul," Martin Buber's "I and Thou," the Buddhists' "interbeing," and riffing on philosopher Josiah Royce's conception of the beloved community.

During the turbulent time in the mid-1960s, when King's depression intensified, he came to identify ever more with the Hebrew prophets who were social outcasts like himself—distraught, creatively maladjusted, transformed nonconformists, paying the price. Prophets were wounded healers, not inherently divine but divine agents, the power of their words amplified by their pain. Ever since the Montgomery bus boycott, prominent elder pastors such as his father and his father's friends, whom he had known since childhood, had proclaimed King a prophet for the times, like eighth-century Amos (name meaning "burden bearer") from near Jerusalem, or Second Isaiah's suffering servant (Isaiah 49–55).

To my knowledge, King did not publicly call himself a prophet until he gave his antiwar sermon at Ebenezer Baptist in April 1967. By then he had grown close to Rabbi Abraham Joshua Heschel (1907–1972), the Jewish theologian and mystic who had studied the Hebrew prophets intimately and who had encouraged him to oppose the Vietnam War in prophetic fashion.[34]

Toward the end of his life, King's new close friend, Rabbi Heschel, a Polish immigrant, the greatest living Jewish theologian who marched with him in Selma and Washington ("my legs were praying," he said), publicly *anointed* King as both prophet and saint to influential Jewish audiences. King told his friend Dorothy Cotton that the great rabbi calling him a saint distressed him because he was a sinner (confidant Andrew

33. Prophetic poet and abolitionist James Russell Lowell (1819–1891), "The Present Crisis," 1845, concluding Martin Luther King Jr.'s address, "Time to Break Silence," Riverside Church, New York (April 4, 1967), in Washington, ed., *Testament of Hope*, 233–34, 243–44.

34. Burns, *To the Mountaintop*, 280, 345, 393–94, and 453.

Young reassured him that saints did sin).[35] But King did not complain about being anointed a prophet by a Jewish spiritual leader, the most respected interpreter of the Hebrew prophets.

King almost certainly had read Heschel's masterpiece, *The Prophets* (1962). This definitive text taught that divine pathos was shared and shouted back and forth by God and the prophets, *felt intensely* by both; that these dialogues (*not* monologues) about suffering, divine and mortal—this *relationship* of suffering ("I and Thou") broadcast the deity's profound concern for human beings. The prophet was not merely God's mouthpiece but a mortal partner.

Heschel's implicit message was about the ambiguity or veiled meaning of pathos, which he never explicitly defined. Unlike ordinary pain, pathos meant that its bearer, divine or mortal, cannot feel pain without it *compelling* empathy and compassion for others feeling pain. The pain of pathos cannot be self-centered; it must be de-centered as if by centrifugal force, experienced as if outside one's self, connected to others from deep within (even subconsciously, like Carl Jung's collective unconscious). One can only feel authentic empathy when one truly feels the suffering of another, of many others, ultimately of all others, as role modeled by the divine. Pathos means pain that has been sacralized in the sense of inter-being and wholeness—pain that has been shared and spread. The greater and more intense one's own pain (physical, emotional, or spiritual), the greater may be one's *potential*, one's *potency*, to share others' pain, to make others' pain their own and be energized by it.

Besides its power to activate empathy, change hearts, and galvanize the multitude to act, King discovered from his inner searching that his own suffering tied him inescapably to all others' suffering ("inescapable network of mutuality"), no matter their faith or lack of, in the past, present, and future. Like Heschel, he came to see collective *pathos* as the fundamental condition of both humanity and deity—potentially linking all humans with each other and with their divinity.[36]

If more and more people can be empowered to feel not only personal pain but interrelational pathos, they, like King, might push themselves to confront and transform the shared pain, building up power to overcome widespread suffering, even transforming the structural or systemic

35. Quoted in Susannah Heschel, "Theological Affinities in the Writings of Abraham Joshua Heschel and Martin Luther King Jr.," in Yvonne Chireau and Nathaniel Deutsch, eds., *Black Zion: African American Religious Encounters with Judaism* (New York: Oxford University Press, 2000), 175 and 177; personal conversation with Dorothy F. Cotton (January 2009); and Burns, *To the Mountaintop*, 280.

36. Heschel, "Theological Affinities," 168–83. Also appears in *Conservative Judaism* 50, nos. 2–3 (1998): 126–43.

sources of suffering. This may be another way to say that unearned suffering, widely shared, jointly felt as pathos by humans and the divine, universalized as Thurman suggested, can in the rightful circumstances redeem humankind.

We shall never know the whole story of King's depression and its consequences. Still, we have enough circumstantial evidence, comments by his wife Coretta and close associates, and his own anguished words in conversations and sermons, especially at his home church Ebenezer Baptist, to gather the essentials of his inner struggle and how they interacted with his spiritual convictions, each influencing the other.

His depression ebbed and flowed during these years (age thirty-four to thirty-nine), its depth and intensity shifting but worsening overall, reaching such an extreme in his last few months that his friend, New York psychiatrist Arthur Logan, urged him to get medical treatment, which he refused. Instead, he continued to self-medicate with compulsive orating—often three or four gigs a day, traveling three weeks out of four—and addictive behavior such as drinking, partying, and sex.[37]

For King, as for many Americans, the Vietnam War altered his life, maybe even led to its end. The last thing he and fellow citizenry needed was a massive US invasion in Southeast Asia to nullify America's one chance to become a social democracy like its European allies (King called his goal a "socially conscious democracy"): advancing racial justice, alleviating poverty, providing health care and other necessaries for elderly and poor Americans, and funding public education. King dared not protest the war vigorously until movement forces had pushed his close ally Lyndon B. Johnson to steamroll passage of the Voting Rights Act. Right after Johnson signed it, King secured the president's backing (so he thought) for an unofficial peace mission with the combatants, only to be humiliated when Johnson pulled the rug out. Meanwhile, the Watts rebellion convinced King to refocus SCLC's resources on black ghettos in the big cities, starting with Chicago.[38]

Having failed at freelance Vietnam peacemaking, King then endured eighteen months of public silence about the war, a wilderness time trapped by guilt and cowardice, as he admitted to his advisers. During this dark time, ardent prayer and agonizing introspection helped him rebirth his soul.

37. Burns, *To the Mountaintop*, 260–61, 280, 287, 345–47, 355, 377–78, 394, 403, 406–7, 421–22, 427, and 429–30.

38. Burns, *To the Mountaintop*, 288, 297–307, 309–10, 314–15, and 327–28.

CRUCIBLE

Like other great men and women of history, Martin Luther King Jr. has drawn biographers and historians of great skill and insight. But none have been able to portray the true greatness and supreme pathos of his final year, when he led the fracturing black movement through one of the most tumultuous turnings in United States history. The ubiquity and ferocity of the forces out to get him were almost literally beyond description. He faced foes from all sides, not just usual suspects but ex-allies, moderate and militant African Americans in his own broadening movement, and within himself, struggling to contain his inner civil war while giving his all to stem a second American civil war.

What kept King from breaking down when it felt like the whole nation was breaking down while seeking to defeat him, from the time of his Vietnam sermon at Riverside Church to his death exactly one year later? As the stakes got higher, he grew increasingly certain that he was doing God's will.[39] His constant praying, days of quiet reflection, and chats with divinity fortified his resolve to fight till the end.

In the winter of 1967, rising death tolls on all sides, thousands of body bags flown home, and Vietnamese kids in flames, propelled King to act. His seasons of silence had prepared him with courage and equilibrium to make the ultimate sacrifice, feeling in his bones that America's doom might be forestalled only by his own. But the cost of his discipleship was not only that he would lose his physical life, but that his out-of-bounds grandiosity would magnify his guilt and the pain it inflicted.

Sharp angles of his guilt tore at him for presuming that he could stop the war and for personifying the black movement, the antiwar multitude, the nation as a whole, and the American creed. He even transcended the American nation, taking responsibility for the "world house" by lacerating the war and the American empire (also the Soviet's) in the name of humanity. He must have believed that his grandiosity, his cosmic self unchained, was carrying out God's will—the rightful end seeming to justify his self-aggrandizing means that violated his values and worsened his guilt and depression. How could he carry out the divine will in good faith if his hubris burst all human bounds, his spiritual pride unbridled by humility? Still, he knew he had promises to keep, and miles to go before he slept. "I come to this magnificent house of worship tonight because my conscience leaves me no other choice," he proclaimed to the overflowing audience at New York's Riverside Church

39. Martin Luther King Jr., "I See the Promised Land" (3 April 1968), in Washington, ed., *Testament of Hope*, 286.

on April 4, 1967. "Some of us who have already begun to break the silence of the night have found that the calling to speak is often a vocation of agony. But we must speak."[40] Beyond ending the Vietnam War, he called for Americans to prioritize persons over things (commodities), and to calm nationalist fervor, giving overriding loyalty to the oneness of humanity. He hoped that a new spirit was "rising among us," that "our own inner being would be sensitive to its guidance, for we are deeply in need of a new way beyond the darkness that seems to close around us." Transcending tribalism and nationalism required "that force which all of the great religions have seen as the supreme unifying principle of life." He quoted from the biblical John's first epistle about the ultimate intimate reality that all faiths share: "Let us love one another; for love is God and everyone that loveth is born of God and knoweth God. . . . If we love one another God dwelleth in us, and his love is perfected in us" (1 John 4:7–8).[41]

Learning of his "Vietnam Sermon," the principalities and powers cared little about King's spiritual ranting or even his charge to Americans to fight on the right side of the world revolution; all they heard was his treason on Vietnam. He expected to get raked over the coals by the White House, establishment liberals, and media. But not that the White House would orchestrate attacks by prominent African Americans and unleash Hoover's FBI to target him as public enemy number one. Nor be slammed by close friends like baseball hero Jackie Robinson whose public denunciation made him cry. The soul crisis King suffered engendered in him the full-blown prophet whom Rabbi Heschel would soon sanctify.[42] "I answered a call," he preached soon after at Ebenezer, "and when God speaks, who can but prophesy?" He called Americans to repent, for "the kingdom of God is at hand." He heard God saying to America, and to himself, you are way too arrogant and self-righteous. "And if you don't change your ways, I will rise up and break the backbone of your

40. Washington, ed., *Testament of Hope*, 231.

41. MLK address, "Time to Break Silence" (4 April 1967), Riverside Church, in Washington, ed., *Testament of Hope*, 231 and 242–43; and Martin Luther King Jr., *Where Do We Go from Here: Chaos or Community?* (Boston: Beacon, 1968; originally published in 1967), 190–91.

42. Ten days before his death, Dr. King spoke at the 68th annual convention of the Rabbinical Assembly (US), introduced by Rabbi Heschel: "Where in America today do we hear a voice like the voice of the prophets of Israel? Martin Luther King is a sign that God has not forsaken the United States of America. God has sent him to us. His presence is the hope of America. His mission is sacred. . . . Martin Luther King is a voice, a vision, and a way. I call upon every Jew to harken to his voice, to share his vision, to follow in his way. The whole future of America will depend upon the impact and influence of Dr. King. May everyone present give of his strength to this great spiritual leader." See "Conversation with Martin Luther King," in Washington, ed., *Testament of Hope,* 657–58.

power."[43] "America is a great nation," he preached again at his home church in early July 1967, but if America doesn't deal with its racism, "I'm convinced that God will bring down the curtains on this nation, the curtains of doom." "There are times that you reap what you sow in history. . . . Be not deceived. God is not mocked. Whatsoever a man soweth, that shall he also reap. America must resolve this race problem, or this race problem will doom America."[44]

King might well have felt that doom had come when most of the nation's cities exploded in rioting that July 1967. The most catastrophic urban rebellion in American history erupted in Detroit, where black residents and white cops had been warring for years. A thousand buildings gutted by spreading windswept fires, fire fighters kept away by gunfire. From above, it looked like half the city had been bombed out, several square miles in flames. About one hundred were killed, mainly poor blacks.

Coretta King had endured her husband's worsening depression for four years. Having seen him through many black moods, she worried more than ever during the July riots. He fell into a state of depression "greater than I had ever seen," she recalled.[45]

Now when King proclaimed "midnight in our world today," he meant it. "We are experiencing a darkness so deep," he told a Los Angeles congregation, "that we can hardly see which way to turn."[46] In his soul's relentless tug of war between hope and despair, he usually had managed to give hope the edge, in his public words at least. But now the dark chambers of pessimism were closing in on him like claustrophobic jail cells.

Fighting for hope, he clung to his faith that divine force was buried in the deepest darkness and could be retrieved. Doubt and hopelessness seemed to have defeated him when in late August 1967 he preached at Mount Pisgah Missionary Baptist Church, in the West Side Chicago ghetto where he had lived during the SCLC-led Chicago Freedom Movement. He was still shaken by the riots and wreckage that he felt responsible for (victimized by his own grandiosity), not only as the leader but the embodiment of the broadening black movement. As he

43. Martin Luther King Jr., "Why I Am Opposed to the War in Vietnam," unpublished version of a sermon, Ebenezer Baptist Church, Atlanta, Georgia (11 April 1967), KCLA; and Washington, ed., *A Testament of Hope*, 233–34.

44. Martin Luther King Jr., "Great, but . . . ," audiotape of a sermon, Ebenezer Baptist Church, Atlanta, Georgia (2 July 1967), KCLA.

45. Burns, *To the Mountaintop*, 345–47.

46. Martin Luther King Jr., "A Knock at Midnight," unpublished version of a sermon, Los Angeles, California (25 June 1967), KCLA; and Carson and Holloran, eds., *Knock at Midnight*, 65–78.

did often with black Baptist congregations, he upbraided himself while admonishing his working-class followers to fortify their faith as the only way out of no way. He had let his ego and hubris glorify his leadership, neglecting that the means, including humility, would determine the ends. He chastised himself, saying that he had "allowed the means by which he lived to outdistance the ends for which he lived," allowing his ego to "outrun his morality."[47]

Fostering the myth that it was "Dr. King's movement," which he did as much as others, had in fact enervated many of his followers, freeing them to sit back and pass the buck, rather than empowering them. We still live with this negative aspect of his legacy. He admitted to this working-class black congregation that he had failed to realize his dependence on his followers and supporters, and worse, his dependence upon God. King also told of the fellow in Luke's parable who was a fool because "he said 'I' and 'my' so much until he lost the capacity to say 'we' and 'our.'" The man was foolish because "he ended up acting like he was the Creator. . . . So many people have come to feel that on their own efforts they can bring in a new world."[48] Of course he was fingering himself. He confessed that he had been more caught up in his quest for praise, adulation, and earthly power, even addicted to it, than to the sacred aim, many generations to come, of actualizing the kingdom of God for everyone, building toward it day by day.[49]

King told how in the Montgomery bus boycott, despairing over an avalanche of death threats, he heard in his midnight kitchen an inner voice, his indwelling Holy Spirit, fortifying him to fight on by promising never to leave him alone. Now eleven years later he had to remind himself of his utter dependence on the divine, and on his followers who reflected and even embodied the divine, whose inner spirits, like his own, potentially manifested divine power. King had to remind himself that not only did his followers invoke divinity, a divine spark at least, but that what was truly sacred was their *interdependence* with each other and with God, "I and Thou," aimed at realizing the beloved community that was "already, but not yet." He sensed that this ultimately inescapable network of interdependence, once activated and mobilized, could transform history for the good of all. People and God co-acting, cooperating, and

47. King frequently spoke in these terms in many of his sermons. See Carson and Holloran, eds., *Knock at Midnight*, 149–50; and King, *Strength to Love*, 68–69.

48. King, *Strength to Love*, 69–70; and Martin Luther King Jr., "Why Jesus Called a Man a Fool" (27 August 1967), in Carson and Holloran, eds., *Knock at Midnight*, 150–51, 155–56, and 158.

49. King, "Why Jesus Called a Man a Fool," in Carson and Holloran, eds., *Knock at Midnight*, 150–51, 155–56, and 158.

covenanting as a "single garment of destiny." King believed that the differentiated wholeness of this web of interdependence would continue to grow and evolve, from inside out.[50] He boldly proclaimed in a Chicago sermon:

> And so I'm not worried about tomorrow. I get weary every now and then. The future looks difficult and dim, but I'm not worried about it ultimately because I have faith in God. . . . I don't mind telling you this morning that sometimes I feel discouraged. . . . Living every day under the threat of death, I feel discouraged sometimes. Living every day under extensive criticisms, even from Negroes, I feel discouraged sometimes. Yes, sometimes I feel discouraged and feel my work's in vain. But then the Holy Spirit revives my soul again.[51]

King was struggling to sustain his hope, along with his faith, during the remaining seven months of his life.

CONCLUSION: GREATER READINESS

Martin Luther King Jr. constructed his lived theology out of his religious training, black Social Gospel and personalism, out of his own enlightened suffering, and from his lived experience in the black freedom movement, especially as times grew more desperate. He manifested his lived theology in action, emotion, and prayer as much as in oratory, none of which conveyed the elements of his theology in a coherent, much less systematic fashion. So the quest for us to comprehend and apply his lived theology, embodied and spoken, has called for interpretation, extrapolation, and a measure of conjecture.

Though I have not addressed it until now, surely we cannot grasp the meaning of King's theology without seeing it as the spiritual foundation for his nonviolent methodology, which he preferred to call "soul force." King's soul force derived from Gandhi's "satyagraha." In fact, King's picture of the human soul resonated with the Hindu Self, or "atman."[52] From his mature perspective, the empowering of one's soul came from

50. As theologian Rufus Burrow has noted concerning Dr. King's personalist philosophy, "The universe is a society of interacting and intercommunicating selves and persons with God at the center." Rufus Burrow Jr., "Personalism, the Objective Moral Order, and Moral Law in the Work of Martin Luther King Jr.," in Lewis V. Baldwin et al., *The Legacy of Martin Luther King Jr.: The Boundaries of Law, Politics, and Religion* (Notre Dame: University of Notre Dame Press, 2002), 216.

51. King, "Why Jesus Called a Man a Fool," in Carson and Holloran, eds., *Knock at Midnight*, 163–64.

52. Martin Luther King Jr., *Stride toward Freedom: The Montgomery Story* (New York: Harper & Row, 1958), 96–97.

shared suffering and empathic power more than from religious conviction or willful self-sacrifice. This meant that pluralist soul force can be embraced by persons of any faith or none, thus less likely to provoke religious extremism such as the Hindu fanaticism that slew Gandhi, or like violent religious extremists of our time.

Implicit in King's theology was the commission to train practitioners of soul force to be capable of fighting not just familiar battles but extraordinary ones in times of peril and existential danger, where the survival of humanity and *humanness* against de-personalization and barbarism was at stake. King dichotimized this as coexistence or co-annihilation, nonviolence or nonexistence. More than training but *remaking*, as King himself may have accomplished part way while struggling through his dark night of the soul. His mission armed him to keep moving upward during his last year, when all seemed lost, all that he had been fighting for a dozen years. Because of his disciplined preparation since Birmingham Sunday, his lonely leadership soared even as he fell, reaching new heights of moral vision and righteous action.

King's legacy would be to inspire his followers, then and generations hence, to learn the lessons he had learned so precariously. More important than honing skills will be the re-formation of temperament and character, spiritual healing, and living the revolution of values inside and out—shifting from psychic death to psychological, emotional, and spiritual regeneration.

Thus, King's message in his final sermon at Pentecostal Mason Temple on the eve of his home going: for the first time in history, people were capable of truly uniting together, transcending their differences, creating a global neighborhood. They *must* unite, thus they can. They *can* unite, thus they must. Just as he had come to accept that his own redemption would occur only after he hit bottom, so he believed that this nation would be regenerated when doom in fact thundered across the sky. Humanity and divinity were making a new covenant. People the world over had no choice now but to confront the planetary crises boiling up. "Let us rise up tonight with a greater readiness," he spoke that stormy night. "Let us move on in these powerful days, these days of challenge, to make America what it ought to be."[53]

We who are his heirs face in these times such powerful days, such fierce urgency. When King asked if our fate would be chaos or community, he was prophesying the extreme chaos of the world's undoing, which he had not yet lived but that we are now confronting. He called not only for mobilization of soul force worldwide but for its harvest,

53. King, "To See the Promised Land," in Washington, ed., *Testament of Hope*, 285–86.

the beloved community, as the ideal in the making, one brave step after another—the only way out of no way, already but not yet.[54]

54. King, *Where Do We Go from Here?*, 167–202.

6.

The Attuning of the Spirit: Martin Luther King Jr. and the Circle of Prayer

LEWIS V. BALDWIN

> After the afternoon services three prayer meetings were begun, in which the brethren took part with vigor and animation. . . . Gathered together in a small circle, stirring prayers were made in the sing-song manner peculiar to the race.
>
> —*Every Evening*, Wilmington, Delaware (27 August 1888)[1]

> Prayer is the attuning of the spirit, and is besides its own high discipline.
>
> —George A. Buttrick, 1941[2]

Recent scholarship on Martin Luther King Jr.'s spirituality is leading to a new understanding and appreciation of the role of prayer in both his private devotional life and his public ministry. Prayer was a vital part of that spirituality that nurtured, renewed, and sustained King throughout his years, and, aside from preaching, was perhaps one the most distinguishing features of his activities as a person of faith, spiritual leader, and social change agent. In short, King's devotion to, habit of, and experi-

1. The August Quarterly was a religious festival inaugurated in Wilmington, Delaware in August 1813 by Peter Spencer in connection with an independent church movement that resulted in the Union Church of Africans in that same year, and the festival was sustained throughout the nineteenth century by slaves and free Africans and their descendants. Occurring annually on the last weekend of August, it still takes place today, and is the oldest continuously celebrated African American religious festival in America. See *The Every Evening*, Wilmington, Delaware (30 August 1886): 4; *The Morning News*, Wilmington, Delaware (26 August 1889): 1, 8; and Lewis V. Baldwin, *"Invisible" Strands in African Methodism: A History of the African Union Methodist Protestant and Union American Methodist Episcopal Churches, 1805–1980* (Metuchen, NJ: Scarecrow, 1983), 140.

2. George A. Buttrick, *Prayer* (New York: Abingdon, 1941), 73.

ences with prayer over the course of his life revealed the very essence of *who* and *what* he actually was as a human being and servant of God.[3]

This chapter treats prayer as a window into the heart, soul, mind, and activities of King. It highlights the ways in which King approached the sacred art and practice of prayer over time, with particular attention to his earliest experiences with prayer, to his emerging sense of the meaning, purpose, and transformative power of prayer, to prayer as a built-in, spiritually constructed dimension of his private and public life, to the openness he brought to his sense of the disciplined prayer life, and to his role in making the time-honored tradition of the prayer circle and other creative uses of prayer relevant to the movement for freedom, social justice, equal rights, and peace.[4] Two main points drive the discussion around these topics. First, that there was a real connection between King's rootedness in a southern sense of place and the shaping of his prayer habits.[5] Second, that prayer was part of King's effort to develop not only a mature, vital, engaging, and contagious spirituality, but also "a balanced spirituality,"[6] or a spirituality that was consistent with his understanding of the well-ordered, active, productive, and complete life.[7]

3. See Lewis V. Baldwin, "Prayer and Testimony: The Spirituality of Martin Luther King, Jr.," *National Baptist Union-Review* 93, no. 2 (January 1989): 7; Lewis V. Baldwin, *Never to Leave Us Alone: The Prayer Life of Martin Luther King, Jr.* (Minneapolis: Fortress, 2010), 1–101; Martin Luther King Jr., *"Thou, Dear God": Prayers That Open Hearts and Spirits—The Reverend Dr. Martin Luther King, Jr.*, ed. Lewis V. Baldwin (Boston: Beacon, 2012), 3–233; Stewart Burns, *To the Mountaintop: Martin Luther King, Jr.'s Sacred Mission to Save America: 1955–1968* (New York: HarperCollins, 2004), 12–482; and Stewart Burns, ed., *Cosmic Companionship: Spirit Stories of Martin Luther King, Jr.* (Kindle Edition, 2013), 1–144.

4. This chapter draws heavily on Baldwin, *Never to Leave Us Alone*, 1–101; and King, *"Thou, Dear God,"* ix–233.

5. The importance of the phenomenon of *place*, which grounded King's identity, sense of mission, and vision of the beloved community, was first explored at length in Lewis V. Baldwin, *There Is a Balm in Gilead: The Cultural Roots of Martin Luther King, Jr.* (Minneapolis: Fortress, 1991), 30–44. This chapter also benefitted from a reading of Philip Sheldrake's more recent study, which contends that "a sense of place" is critical in "the construction of our personal and religious identities," and that it has "the greatest impact on the way we see the world." "The concept of place," writes Sheldrake, "refers not simply to geographical location but to a dialectical relationship between environment and human narrative." He continues: "Place is space that has the capacity to be remembered and to evoke what is most precious." See Philip Sheldrake, *Spaces for the Sacred: Place, Memory, and Identity* (Baltimore: The Johns Hopkins University Press, 2001), 1–32.

6. This idea of "a balanced spirituality" came from Donal Dorr, *Spirituality and Justice* (Maryknoll, NY: Orbis, 1984), 8–18.

7. In his sermon, "The Dimensions of a Complete Life," King equated "The length of life" with the achievement of "personal ends and ambitions," "The breadth of life" with "the outward concern for the welfare of others," and "The height of life" with "the upward reach for God." His reflections on "the height of life" are perennially relevant to any clear sense of how

"MY CHILDHOOD EXPERIENCES": INTRODUCTION TO THE DISCIPLINE AND PRACTICE OF PRAYER

Reflecting on his early years, Martin Luther King Jr. once declared that it "was quite easy" for him to believe in "a God of Love," in the basic friendliness of the universe, and in the essential goodness of humanity "because of my childhood experiences" and "my uplifting hereditary and environmental circumstances." He felt similarly regarding his faith in the power and potentiality of prayer, which anchored his life from his earliest childhood.[8] The son, grandson, and great-grandson of preachers and pious and God-fearing women, who were deeply rooted in southern black Baptist Protestantism, and exposed to generations of church deacons, church mothers, and other powerful spiritual symbols at Ebenezer Baptist Church in Atlanta, Georgia, King came to know great pray-ers before he actually understood what prayer really meant. He was introduced very early to family prayer around the dining table at the King home at 501 Auburn Avenue Northeast in Atlanta, and to the prayer circle that routinely occurred around the altar at Ebenezer, the congregation located less than a block away and pastored by his father, Martin Luther King Sr. Memorized and recited prayers in various forms and settings were part of a well-worn family and church tradition. The vitality of these traditions in King's family and church extended across generations, for his own maternal grandfather, Adam D. Williams, had pastored Ebenezer Church earlier while also living at the Auburn Avenue residence.[9]

Before reaching the required age to enroll in elementary school, King had become acquainted with prayer as a daily practice in his home and throughout much of his neighborhood in Atlanta. This would have been expected since, as King himself once put it, "most of our neighbors were deeply religious" and "all of my childhood playmates were Sunday School goers." King and his siblings, Willie Christine and Alfred D.,

he perceived the life of prayer. See Martin Luther King Jr., *The Measure of a Man* (Philadelphia: Fortress, 1988; originally published in 1959), 35–56.

8. Clayborne Carson et al., eds., *The Papers of Martin Luther King, Jr.: Called to Serve, January 1929–June 1951* (Berkeley: University of California Press, 1992), 1:103, 105, and 360.

9. Martin Luther King Sr., *Daddy King: An Autobiography*, with Clayton Riley (New York: William Morrow, 1980), 10, 14, 25, 47, 51, 62, 82–83, 91, and 128; Christine King Farris, *Through It All: Reflections on My Life, My Family, and My Faith* (New York: Atria, 2009), xi and 16–18; Clayborne Carson and Peter Holloran, eds., *A Knock at Midnight: Inspiration from the Great Sermons of Reverend Martin Luther King, Jr.* (New York: Warner, 1998), 162; and Alberta King, "Dr. Martin Luther King, Jr.: Birth to Twelve Years Old by His Mother," a recording, Ebenezer Baptist Church, Atlanta, Georgia (18 January 1973), Library and Archives of the Martin Luther King Jr. Center for Nonviolent Social Change (KCLA), Atlanta, Georgia.

were always required by their parents, King Sr. and Alberta Williams King, to be thankful and to offer blessings over their food at mealtime, and to pray in the morning before school and at night prior to bedtime.[10] Unquestionably, this was part of the family's binding credo. While King was a student at the David T. Howard Elementary–Junior High School in Atlanta in the late 1930s, the chanting of the Lord's prayer was a well-established practice, and its Faculty Choral Club's presentation of William Harold Neidlinger's cantata, "Prayer, Promise, and Praise," which was based on Psalms 106:6–7 and carried "with it the idea of praise and thanksgiving," frequently occurred as part of the Thanksgiving celebration.[11] Some of King's childhood letters offer a glimpse into his own thinking about prayer during those times. In two of those letters, written by the eleven-year-old King to his mother when his parents were out of town on church business, the youngster asserted that "I am praying that you and daddy" have "a safe" and "successful trip back home."[12] As young King moved along the sacred path of prayer, he almost certainly found guidance not only in what he learned from his teachers at Atlanta University Laboratory High School and Booker T. Washington High School,[13] but also in what he got from his parents, his maternal grandmother, Jennie C. Parks Williams,[14] his great aunt, Ida Worthem, and others in the Ebenezer Church family, in which deacons commonly recited informal, extemporaneous, and highly emotional prayers while on bended knees. There was also the abiding influence of that larger black church culture in the South, in which the prayer

10. King, *Daddy King*, 127–28; King, "Dr. Martin Luther King, Jr." (18 January 1973); Carson and Holloran, eds., *Knock at Midnight*, 162; Carson et al., eds., *Papers*, 1:360; and Baldwin, *Never to Leave Us Alone*, 20.

11. "Hundreds to Receive Certificates in City Schools: Mid-Term Graduation Holds Keen Interest in Atlanta Schools," *The Atlanta Daily World* (26 January 1936): 6; "D. T. Howard Cantata Set for Sunday," *The Atlanta Daily World* (20 November 1936): 1; and "Howard Faculty in Cantata this Afternoon," *The Atlanta Daily World* (22 November 1936): 3.

12. Carson et al., eds., *Papers*, 1:103 and 105.

13. The discussion of spiritual matters, including prayer, commonly occurred in these public high schools, and the Lord's Prayer was occasionally recited in French. In May 1942, while King was attending Atlanta University Laboratory High School, a number of students there spoke at a religious service on "Spiritual Defense against the Shock of War," undoubtedly with some references to prayer. King's father, Martin Luther King Sr., occasionally offered the invocation at his son's high school events. See "Lab High Religious Service to Be at Ten this Morning," *The Atlanta Daily World* (24 May 1942): 6; Mrs. W. A. Scott Sr., "School and PTA Notes," *The Atlanta Daily World* (8 March 1942): 3; S. Grace Bradley, "Be Alert, Dr. King Advises 400 Seniors," *The Atlanta Daily World* (7 June 1943): 1; and William A. Fowlkes, "Teachers to Hear Fed'l Officials Today: Rev. Borders Will Address Body Tonight," *The Atlanta Daily World* (16 April 1943): 1.

14. King's reference to his "saintly grandmother" should not be seriously considered here. See Carson et al., eds., *Papers*, 1:359. Also see Farris, *Through It All*, 11–12.

circle was an important ritual in congregations of virtually every denominational identity.

King's Morehouse College years, 1944–1948, evidently constituted a pivotal point in terms of the development of his prayer life. At this historically black, all-male institution in Atlanta, at which King's father and maternal grandfather had also matriculated, students were encouraged to combine exceptional work in the classroom with a disciplined devotional life. There were a number of black preacher-intellectuals serving administratively and on the faculty at Morehouse, and some of them, such as Benjamin E. Mays, the president, and George D. Kelsey, the professor of ethics, became important spiritual resources for King, who was only fifteen when he enrolled at the institution. King called Mays "my spiritual and intellectual father,"[15] and it is not difficult to imagine the impact of Mays's weekly talks at the Morehouse Tuesday morning chapel services, which routinely began and ended with prayer, on King's understanding and practice of prayer. Kelsey's influence on young King was equally significant in this regard, for Kelsey had long cautioned Morehouse students, through his preaching and writings, against any scale of values and habits that created a spiritual void in life.[16] During King's last year at Morehouse, he was actually ordained by a committee of ministers that included his father, Mays, Samuel W. Williams, and others from both the college and the State Baptist Convention of Georgia,[17] and, in the course of that process, he was most certainly questioned and challenged repeatedly around the question of his prayer habits, concerning the need to always be prayerful and prayer-minded, and about the state of his devotional life as a whole. This was standard practice among black Baptists in the South in those days, especially for very young men who felt the call to ministry. King was only nineteen at the time.

Apparently, King's public prayers from those Morehouse years have not survived in written nor recorded form. The earliest prayer discovered so far is dated August 1948, some two months after King graduated from Morehouse. This is a "Wedding Prayer," recited at the ceremony for Samuel P. Long and Ruth Bussey at the Thankful Baptist Church in

15. Martin Luther King Jr., "Statement Regarding the Retirement of Benjamin E. Mays" (1967), unpublished, KCLA, 1.

16. See "Friendship Bap't Church Observes 79th Anniversary," *The Atlanta Daily World* (27 October 1941): 1; "Kelsey Spelman Vesper Speak," *The Atlanta Daily World* (2 March 1947): 3; and "Morehouse Alumni Contribute to New Religious Volume," *The Atlanta Daily World* (13 February 1948): 3.

17. *Set for the Defence of the Gospel: Ordination Certificate for Martin Luther King, Jr.*, Ebenezer Baptist Church, Atlanta, Georgia (25 February 1948), KCLA, 1; Carson et al., eds., *Papers*, 1:153; and Keith D. Miller, *Voice of Deliverance: The Language of Martin Luther King, Jr. and Its Sources* (New York: The Free Press, 1992), 40.

Decatur, Georgia, and it is reasonable to think that it provides clues into what must have been King's attitude toward prayer and his manner of praying as a college student. That particular prayer pulsated with poetic language and with lyrics of praise, gratitude, joy, wonder, and petition. King praised God as "the originator of all life," and he asked God to help the couple "to see the primacy of love" and to develop "a deep awareness of the sacredness of this venture."[18] Clearly, King had come to understand prayer as something more than merely inspired speech or religiously informed rhetoric. From all indications, he had also learned the importance of carefully crafting his prayers to fit specific occasions, and he made sure that they were delivered in ways that appealed to the mind as well as the heart and soul. His sense of how to pray, what to pray for, and what he might expect of prayer were evidently sharpened as he moved from Morehouse to study at Crozer Theological Seminary in Chester, Pennsylvania, in the period from September 1948 to June 1951, for it was during this time that he made references to "the experience of prayer" as a "valid religious experience."[19]

King's increasing spiritual growth around these concerns are also apparent when his prayers from the early 1950s, when he was pursuing a PhD in systematic theology at Boston University, are read and analyzed. During this time, King frequently returned to his home church in Atlanta, where the "mid-week prayer services" offered "spiritual uplift for all who" came and spent "an hour on Wednesday evenings at 8 p.m."[20] On such occasions, the entire Ebenezer membership "and friends" were "expected to be present and on time." Spirited and heartfelt prayers were commonly offered, often in a circle, and these experiences, along with his seminary training and King Sr.'s occasional sermons on prayer, came together in King Jr.'s consciousness as he brought to his prayers an intriguing blend of spiritual insight, down-to-earth wisdom, and a keen sense of a vital cycle of daily, real-life experiences.[21] From July

18. Clayborne Carson et al., eds., *The Papers of Martin Luther King, Jr.: Advocate of the Social Gospel, September 1948–March 1963* (Berkeley: University of California Press, 2007), 6:570–71.

19. King extended this definition of "a religious experience" to also include "experiences such as sacraments, conversion, worship," and "mystical moments." See Carson et al., eds., *Papers*, 1:413.

20. See "'Communism's Challenge to Christianity,' King, Jr.'s Topic, Ebenezer," *The Atlanta Daily World* (9 August 1952): 2. Weekly prayer meetings on Wednesday nights at Ebenezer were a longstanding tradition, extending through King's childhood and beyond. See "Church News: Ebenezer Baptist Church," *The Atlanta Daily World* (25 May 1940): 6; and "Rev. M. L. King, Jr. Preaches Farewell at Ebenezer Sunday," *The Atlanta Daily World* (1 September, 1951): 4.

21. Some of King Sr.'s sermons, which attracted attention from print media, were titled, "Prayer," "Prayer without Doubt," "The Effects of Prayer," and "True Religion Is the Religion of Prayer," some of which the younger King most certainly heard at one time or another. Visit-

to September 1953, King prepared an interesting collection of prayers and recited them as part of a radio broadcast from Atlanta's Ebenezer Baptist Church, and these prayers revealed a devotional and spiritual life that was maturing quite well. The prayers vary in length and basically conform to the traditional trajectories of Christian prayer, especially the elements of adoration, confession, contrition, thanksgiving, intercession, and petition.[22] Interestingly enough, King was preaching more at Ebenezer and also at churches throughout parts of the South and northeast during these years, and the prayers he routinely uttered were in tandem with his growing ability to prepare and deliver well-organized and moving sermons. King Sr., or Daddy King, was an abiding influence, always reminding his son to pray fervently and unceasingly, especially since, in his own way of thinking, Satan was always there to tempt and destroy the faithful.[23]

It is also conceivable that much of King's maturation, spiritually and intellectually, resulted from his exposure to the kind of culture that the seminaries at Crozer and Boston provided—a highly academic culture in which the language and the life-filling richness and power of prayer must have come up occasionally in discussions in classrooms, during chapel services, and even in the rooms of the most theologically minded and liturgically conscious students, all of whom were preparing for an engagement with the parish or some other form of ministry.[24]

ing preachers at Ebenezer also occasionally addressed prayer in their sermons when King Jr. was growing up there, often during revivals. Also, "the singing of the Lord's Prayer at Ebenezer," under the choir director Alberta King, King Jr.'s mother, was a common practice on Sunday mornings. See "Rev. King to Fill Pulpit Twice at Ebenezer Sunday," *The Atlanta Daily World* (19 June, 1948): 5; "Ebenezer to Hear Dr. King Sunday," *The Atlanta Daily World* (16 April 1949): 4; "King Fills Pulpit at Ebenezer this Sunday," *The Atlanta Daily World* (17 September 1949): 2; "Ebenezer Church Services Slated," *The Atlanta Daily World* (8 November 1947): 2; Taschereau Arnold, "Says Hot Prayers Would Move Hitler: Rev. Bivins in Warning Sermon; Ebenezer Celebration Continues," *The Atlanta Daily World* (12 March 1942): 2; "Too Little Prayer Makes Church Cold, Asserts Rev. Ford," *The Atlanta Daily World* (6 March 1944): 2; and L. P. Reynolds, "What Sam of Auburn Avenue Says: Just Dots and Dots," *The Atlanta Daily World* (7 July 1943): 6.

22. Carson et al., eds., *Papers*, 1:137–39; Baldwin, *Never to Leave Us Alone*, x, 11, and 54–55; and King, *"Thou, Dear God,"* 3, 33, 54, 69, 105, and 139.

23. Clayborne Carson et al., eds., *The Papers of Martin Luther King, Jr.: Rediscovering Precious Values, July 1951–November 1955* (Berkeley: University of California Press, 1994), 2:320; Coretta Scott King, *My Life with Martin Luther King, Jr.* (New York: Henry Holt, 1993; originally published in 1969), 4, 50, 62–64, 72, and 89; and King, *Daddy King*, 147.

24. This point is based largely on the fact that King mentioned prayer in a number of his academic papers, and he indicated that his "religion" was "closely knitted to life"—that it was indeed "life" for him in this period. With this in mind, one might conclude that King took his personal faith seriously, which would have included experiences of prayer and meditation. See Carson et al., eds., *Papers*, 1:190–93, 204, 226, 232, 248, and 363; and Carson et al., eds., *Papers*, 6:137–39 and 590–95.

"A THROBBING DESIRE OF THE HUMAN HEART": ON THE MEANING, NECESSITY, AND POWER OF PRAYER

When Martin Luther King Jr. left Morehouse to study at Crozer Theological Seminary in Chester, Pennsylvania, in the fall of 1948, he already knew enough about prayer to write and speak intelligently on the subject. In a paper for a philosophy of religion course at Crozer, he noted that "all religious ceremonials are explained as consisting chiefly in elaborations of prayer and sacrifice," and he insisted that prayer "is seen as the endeavor to secure the conservation of socially recognized values through 'an imaginative social process' or conversation between the ordinary ego of the individual and the agency invoked." He had a special interest in what the Bible had to say about prayer and praying. In another paper on "The Significant Contributions of Jeremiah to Religious Thought," written for an Old Testament course during his first semester at Crozer, King called the prophet "the father of true prayer, in which the wretched soul expresses both its subhuman misery and its superhuman confidence." Focusing primarily on Jeremiah's "piety" or "personal religion," King went on to note that the prophet prayed "for healing" (Jer 17:14) and "for help against his adversaries" (17:18), and that he embodied the concept of prayer as "communion with God." "But to Jeremiah," King wrote, "prayer was more than petition. It was no escape from the harsh realities of life. It was an 'intimate converse with God, in which his inner life is laid bare, with its perplexities and struggles and temptations.'" "It is such a prayer," King added, "that contains the assurance of an answer."[25] Although King delighted in quoting prayer lines from the psalmist (Ps 139:12), Isaiah (45:15), and Habakkuk (1:2), in which there are questions about the divine presence and cries for divine help, he was convinced that Jeremiah, who was "original in his exercise of prayer," had actually modeled the meaning, necessity, and purpose of prayer in the Old Testament. Even so, King wondered about the extent to which the Hebrew prophets were "men of prayer,"[26] a topic that was, in his estimation, insufficiently treated in that part of the Scriptures.

The New Testament was no less important when it came to King's search for a biblically anchored understanding of prayer. Here he focused with telling insight on the historical Jesus, whom he believed epitomized the spirit of prayer while providing the blueprint for the ideal prayer life. According to King, prayer was "not at all uncommon in the life of Jesus,"

25. Carson et al., eds., *Papers,* 1:190–93, 255, 387–88, and 413; Carson et al., eds., *Papers,* 2:87–88; Baldwin, *Never to Leave Us Alone*, 1–2; and King, *"Thou, Dear God,"* 193.

26. Carson et al., eds., *Papers*, 1:191 and 192n24.

and the images of the man from Nazareth praying actually exposed "his genuine humanity." "We see him agonizing in prayer" in the Garden of Gethsemane before embracing and suffering on the cross "with Joy and faith," King wrote, in a paper titled, "The Humanity and Divinity of Jesus." In other papers, also written for courses at Crozer, King made references to the Lord's Prayer as recorded in Matthew 6:9–13, the prayer that Jesus taught his disciples.[27] In King's mind, this became the prayer for every disciple of Jesus in every age, irrespective of the person's background or station in life. King would declare years later, in a draft of a sermon titled, "On Being a Good Neighbor," that when Jesus "addressed God in the Lord's Prayer, he said 'Our Father,' which immediately lifted God above the category of a tribal deity concerned only about one race of people."[28] When it came to the content, discipline, and activity of prayer, Jesus became perhaps more paradigmatic for King than any other biblical, spiritual, or historical figure.[29] Be that as it may, King discovered in both Jesus and the Hebrew prophets powerful prophetic voices that were less concerned about the ritualistic and ceremonial aspects of prayer and related it more specifically to the ethical and social concerns of human life.

Also during that period from 1948 to 1954, while King was completing his seminary and graduate school education, he wrote a brief but provocative piece titled, "The Misuse of Prayer."[30] Here King dealt with prayer on several levels, taking into account its historical significance, its native-ness to the spirit of persons, and how it should be approached by believers. "Men always have prayed and men always will pray," he declared. King went on to variously refer to prayer as "a native tendency," as "indigenous to the human spirit," as representing "a throbbing desire of the human heart," and "as natural to the human organism as the rising of the sun is to the cosmic order." Moving deeper into his analysis, King insisted that prayer is never "irrational," and nor is it "absurd and presumptuous":

> But a yearning so age-long and deep-rooted cannot be slain by a couple of adjectives. Men have often tried to dismiss it by affirming that pressing rigidity of natural law makes it impossible. But such a declaration is unconvincing; for there is something deep down within us that makes us know

27. Carson et al., eds., *Papers*, 205, 226–27, 255, and 259; and Baldwin, *Never to Leave Us Alone*, 2.

28. Carson et al., eds., *Papers*, 6:486; and Baldwin, *Never to Leave Us Alone*, 2 and 104n8.

29. Baldwin, *Never to Leave Us Alone*, 2.

30. It is not possible to give the precise date for this short statement and outline, but it is rather clear that these were committed to paper while King was still a student. See Carson et al., eds., *Papers*, 6:590–91.

> that God works in a paradox of unpredictable newness and trustworthy faithfulness. And so even the most devout atheist will at times cry out for the God that his theory denies.[31]

King focused at some length in this paper on what he occasionally termed "a callous misuse of prayer," during which "God becomes little more than a 'cosmic bellhop'" or "a universal errand boy" who "is summoned for every trivial need." "Although prayer is native to man," and "is a natural outpouring of his spirit," he wrote, "there is the danger that he will use it in an unnatural way." The believer should "never make prayer a substitute for work and intelligence," King continued, for it "must be a supplement and not a substitute." Quoting from Exodus 14:10–15, King asserted that when Moses and his followers were en route to the promised land, they confronted many hardships, and most notably the Egyptian armies and Red Sea, but God commanded that they "Go forward"—"that He would not do for them what they could do for themselves." Noting that there were numerous ways to misuse prayer, King maintained that one should "Never pray for anything which if done would injure somebody else." "Never pray," he added, "For God to help you get even with your enemy," "that your country will win the war," or "for God to change the fixed laws of the universe." Clearly, these were the reflections of a youngster who had become quite pragmatic when it came to the question of the power and potentiality of prayer. Convinced that prayer was perhaps the most under-studied and misunderstood dimension of human spirituality, King, in later years, would repeatedly write and speak about the human tendency to misuse, abuse, and think in exaggerated and unrealistic terms about this sacred phenomenon, especially after he became a pastor and civil rights leader.[32]

Drawing on a range of influences, among which were the Bible, the religious and spiritual resources of the black church, and insights from that larger Christian tradition, King thought of prayer as a sacred obligation, as communicating, conversing, or talking to God, as crying out to God, as the human response to God, as bowing before the God of the universe, as facilitating an intimate relationship with a living and comforting spirit, and as a gift from God that has infinite dimensions

31. Carson et al., eds., *Papers*, 6:590.

32. Carson et al., eds., *Papers*, 6:85, 351, and 590–91; Martin Luther King Jr., *Strength to Love* (Philadelphia: Fortress, 1981; originally published in 1963), 131–32; Martin Luther King Jr., "Answer to a Perplexing Question," unpublished version of a sermon, Ebenezer Baptist Church, Atlanta, Georgia (3 March 1963), KCLA, 9–11; Clayborne Carson et al., eds., *The Papers of Martin Luther King, Jr.: Threshold of a New Decade, January 1959–December 1960* (Berkeley: University of California Press, 2005), 5:215; and O. Richard Bowyer, et al., *Prayer in the Black Tradition* (Nashville: Upper Room, 1986), 64–65.

for exploration.[33] Here King was actually blending his voice not only with the voices of the ancient Hebrew prophets, Jesus, and the apostles, but also with the voices of generations of his black forebears, who spoke in their testimonies and songs about "talking to the Lord," "ringing up heaven," "bowing or kneeling before the throne of grace," and "taking their burdens to the Lord and leaving them there." King's parents, grandparents, and great-grandparents were familiar with, and undoubtedly employed, this kind of prayer language. Furthermore, they knew of lyrics in Negro spirituals and gospel songs that spoke to the believers' close communion and personal dialogue with God, such as "Walk with Me Lord," "Precious Lord, Taking My Hand," "Nobody but You, Lord," "Couldn't Hear Nobody Pray," and "Jesus Is on the Mainline, Tell Him What You Want," and King's reflections on the meaning, necessity, and power of prayer owed much to these folk sources,[34] some of which were rooted in the slave quarters of the old South. Clearly, any discussion of King's thinking concerning prayer and praying should begin with these sources, which were also inspired by a certain reading of Scripture. His training in the academy simply aided him in expressing in more sophisticated terms what had already been passed down to him from the well-springs of his familial and church traditions.[35]

One of King's greatest debts to these traditions was evident in his conviction that God answers prayer, and that prayer has the potential to change people and conditions. The idea of a biblical God who listens, speaks to, and responds to the cries of the faithful was never really seriously doubted nor questioned, and testimonies shared and heard in black churches nationwide during King's lifetime are a treasure chest pulsating with the belief that God hears and is moved to act by the prayers of the righteous. The assertion that "He may not come when you want Him, but He's always on time," saturated the language of not only prayers, but folk testimonies, songs, stories, and sermons as well. King obviously had some assurance of this when he referred, on at least one occasion, to an inner voice urging him to "call on that something" or "that person that you daddy used to tell you about"—"That power that can make a

33. Carson et al., eds., *Papers*, 1:162–63, 192–93, and 200; Carson and Holloran, eds., *Knock at Midnight*, 162; Baldwin, *Never to Leave Us Alone*, 10; and King, *"Thou, Dear God,"* xii.

34. Mindful of the sheer vibrancy of this folk tradition, King once said that "sometimes Aunt Jane on her knees can get more truth than the philosopher on his tiptoes." See Carson and Holloran, eds., *Knock at Midnight*, 94.

35. See Coretta Scott King, foreword to *Standing in the Need of Prayer: A Celebration of Black Prayer* (New York: The Free Press, 2003), ix–xiii; Baldwin, *Never to Leave Us Alone*, 9–24; and Harold A. Carter, *The Prayer Tradition of Black People* (Valley Forge, PA: Judson, 1976), 65–67, 94, 106–13, and 129–30.

way out of no way."[36] This concept of God as "a way maker," or a God who "evokes and answers prayers," figured prominently in King's consciousness. He had this and much more in mind when he reflected on the "great spiritual lift" that comes with praying, or on the "great resources of power in prayer and worship."[37]

There was always that larger Christian tradition to which King also turned for probing insights into prayer as a sacred obligation, as a gift from God with infinite possibilities, and as a spiritual quality that must be continuously cultivated, and this too informed much of what he wrote and said about praying and the prayer life. Beginning with the church fathers, he found great models of prayer in the history and traditions of the Christian church. From the *Confessions* of Saint Augustine (354–430 CE), the most influential of the fathers of the Western church, King found in the following prayer lines support for his view that humanity's very essence lies in a communicative relationship with God: "Thou awakest us to delight in Thy praise; for Thou madest us for Thyself, and our heart is restless, until it repose in Thee." King also noted that there is something in humanity's yearning spirit, in its deepest longing for wholeness, "that causes us to cry out loudly and continuously with Augustine," "Lord, make me pure but not yet." For King, Augustine's eloquent and seemingly desperate prayerful utterances acknowledged the enduring and matchless power of God, underscored humanity's dependence upon God, captured the emptiness, irrationality, and futility of the prayer-less life, and spoke emphatically to the need for humans to "shake the lethargy from our souls."[38]

The following prayer from Saint Francis of Assisi (1182–1226), the founder of the Franciscan Order in Catholicism, figured prominently among King's most cherished resources from the Christian tradition, for it echoed the core of his spiritual and ethical values as they related to peace, love, faith, hope, joy, understanding, compassion, and forgiveness:

36. The image of God as "a way maker" is commonly projected in black church life and culture. See Carson and Holloran, eds., *Knock at Midnight*, 161–62; and James M. Washington, ed., *A Testament of Hope: The Essential Writings and Speeches of Martin Luther King, Jr.* (San Francisco: HarperSanFrancisco, 1991), 343 and 509.

37. Washington, ed., *Testament of Hope*, 343 and 509; Carson et al., eds., *Papers*, 5:425; Clayborne Carson et al., eds., *The Papers of Martin Luther King, Jr.: Symbol of the Movement, January 1957–December 1958* (Berkeley: University of California Press, 2000), 4:504–5 and 529; and Carson et al., eds., *Papers*, 6:293–94.

38. Carson et al., eds., *Papers*, 6:156n26, 190, and 335; Carson et al., eds., *Papers*, 5:579; Baldwin, *Never to Leave Us Alone*, 2–3; and King, *"Thou, Dear God,"* 220–23.

> Lord, make me an instrument of Thy peace;
> Where there is hatred, let me sow love;
> where there is injury, pardon;
> where there is doubt, faith;
> where there is despair, hope;
> where there is darkness, light;
> and where there is sadness, joy.
> O Divine Master, grant that I may not
> so much seek to be consoled, as to console;
> to be understood, as to understand;
> to be loved, as to love;
> for it is in giving that we receive;
> it is in pardoning that we are pardoned;
> and it is in dying that we are born to eternal life.[39]

King would have noticed that Saint Francis's prayer, much like those he frequently quoted from Saint Augustine, offered rich insight into how the poor in spirit might discover in their own daily, personal experiences the capacity for true life transformation, tranquility within, and genuine feelings of happiness or delight. Also, King was evidently inspired by Saint Francis's enduring spiritual search, and especially his imitation of the life of Jesus, which also involved an unwavering commitment to the sacred art and discipline of prayer. Nothing could have been more important for King, who was himself a spiritual seeker for most of his life.

King found in the prayerful declarations of the Protestant reformer Martin Luther (1483–1546), the English Puritan preacher John Bunyan (1628–1688), the Methodist founder John Wesley (1703–1791), and the great revivalist George Whitefield (1714–1770) support for his belief that the person of faith must always act on the basis of conscience. In these sources, and in the lyrics of classics by the great song writer Isaac Watts (1674–1748), such as "Our God, Our Help in Ages Past," King also

39. This prayer was found among King's unpublished papers in the library and archives at the Martin Luther King Jr. Center for Nonviolent Social Change, Inc., Atlanta, Georgia. In 1963, King was the recipient of the Saint Francis Peace Medal, given by the North American Federation of the Third Order of Saint Francis, "In recognition of his truly Christian and Franciscan approach to the civil rights problem through his program of nonviolence." This prayer was also among the valued spiritual sources of Mohandas K. Gandhi and Howard Thurman, both of whom impacted King's life, spiritually, ethically, and otherwise. See "A Prayer a Fellow Like Martin Luther King, Junior Would Say," A Promotional Flyer, Public Relations Promotions, Ajaye Clarke Associates, San Francisco, California (3 April 1961), KCLA, 1; "Dr. King's Acceptance Speech," The North American Federation of the Third Order of Saint Francis (9 November 1963), KCLA, 1–6; King, *"Thou, Dear God,"* 224–25; Baldwin, *Never to Leave Us Alone*, 3 and 105n10; and Martin Luther King Jr., "On Accepting the St. Francis Peace Medal," *Peace* 1 (March 1964): 11–15.

detected what he considered calls to a deep, personal union with God in the face of life's continuous and seemingly insurmountable challenges. These sources significantly enriched his thinking about prayer and the prayer life, especially as he combined what he got here with the practical side of what he experienced in the liturgical life of black churches, and with what he learned about spirituality as a whole in his reading of Karl Barth, Walter Rauschenbusch, Paul Tillich, Reinhold Niebuhr, Edgar S. Brightman, L. Harold DeWolf, Harry Emerson Fosdick, and other theologians and pastors he studied.[40]

King's sense of the prayer experience as a whole probably benefitted more from Harry Emerson Fosdick's classic work, *The Meaning of Prayer* (1915), than any other single written source. King apparently read and drew heavily on this book, and he found in Fosdick, whom he once called "the greatest preacher of this century" and "a Christian Saint," perhaps the foremost authority on the subject in his time. Fosdick, the voice of Protestant liberalism and pastor of New York's historic Riverside Church in the 1920s and '30s, had much to say in his book about "the naturalness of prayer," "prayer as a communication with God," "the reasonableness of prayer," "prayer as the soul of religion," "prayer and the goodness of God," "prayer and the reign of law," "unanswered prayer," "prayer as dominant desire," "prayer as a battlefield," and "unselfishness in prayer,"[41] and King employed language from Fosdick in describing his own view of prayer and the prayer life, as much of the foregoing discussion shows.[42] For King, Fosdick's *The Meaning of Prayer* was an indispensable resource for accessing the spiritual depths of the Christian tradition, particularly in reference to the basics of prayer.

But King chose not to limit himself to Fosdick, the Bible, and what he called Judeo-Christian sources when arguing that prayer, and indeed the totality of the worship experience, is part of the fundamental necessities of living. In other words, he associated prayer and the larger core of spir-

40. Carson et al., eds., *Papers*, 6:86 and 476; Carson et al., eds., *Papers*, 1:340; King, *"Thou, Dear God,"* 226–233; and Baldwin, *Never to Leave Us Alone*, 3–4.

41. Harry Emerson Fosdick, *The Meaning of Prayer* (New York: Cosimo, 2005; originally published by Association Press in 1915), 1–38, 55–70, and 92–194. Fosdick called this work, which addressed to some extent the larger issue of Christian devotion, "my most influential book." See Robert Moats Miller, *Harry Emerson Fosdick: Preacher, Pastor, Prophet* (New York: Oxford University Press, 1985), 69–71, 235–39, and 335. Also see Carson et al., eds., *Papers*, 6: 590–91.

42. Carson et al., eds., *Papers,* 6:3, 43, 207, 376, 411, 545, and 590–91; and Carson et al., eds., *Papers*, 5: 532. It is also highly possible that King read the book on prayer by George Buttrick, another great New York pastor who was also a resource for many of his sermons. Buttrick's book was called "The timeliest, greatest book on prayer since" Fosdick's. See Buttrick, *Prayer* (1941).

ituality with values embraced by all of the world's great religions. King found in Mohandas K. Gandhi, the Hindu and leader of India's quest for independence, a model of the disciplined prayer life, especially since Gandhi combined prayer with an intense practice of fasting.[43] Referring to what he had observed while he and his wife Coretta were vacationing in Nigeria in March 1957, King mentioned Muslim "men and women praying five times a day," an experience that reinforced his belief that "this quest and this desire to somehow be attached to something beyond self" appears "to be the elemental function, or rather the elemental longing, of human nature." Convinced that "dependence" on God has always been a hallmark of religion, King went on to conclude that "that basic drive and that basic urge that cries out for the eternal and something beyond self" means that "man is innately religious; man worships unconsciously."[44] Some of King's prayers are suffused with this sense of the inevitability of prayer, and with the conviction that no single religion has a monopoly on the habit and power of the prayer experience. Note, for example, the following:

> O God, our gracious Heavenly Father, we thank Thee for the fact that you have inspired men and women in all nations and in all cultures. We call you different names: some call Thee Allah; some call you Elohim; some call you Jehovah; some call you Brahma; and some call you the Unmoved Mover; some call you the Archetectonic . . . Good. But we know that these are all names for one and the same God, and we know you are one.[45]

The words voiced here are most revealing on several levels, and especially so when King's attitude toward the universality of prayer is seriously entertained. First, they are consistent with King's claim that the great faith traditions worldwide were essentially one in terms of their beliefs about "ultimate reality," and in what he labeled their conception of "the supreme unifying principle of life."[46] Second, they raise the possibility that King's own prayer life was enriched by his encounter with other faiths. Finally, they reveal something of his sense of and contribution to the direction of ecumenical thought and practice in that period.

43. This was probably much of what King had in mind when he said that Gandhi "caught the spirit of Jesus Christ and lived it more completely in his life." See Carson et al., eds., *Papers*, 5:146, 148 and 154–55; and King, *My Life with Martin Luther King, Jr.*, 159 and 161–65.

44. Carson et al., eds., *Papers*, 6:293–94; and Carson et al., eds., *Papers*, 4:256.

45. Carson et al., eds., *Papers*, 5:157; and King, *"Thou, Dear God,"* 44–45.

46. Martin Luther King Jr., *Where Do We Go from Here: Chaos or Community?* (Boston: Beacon, 1968; originally published in 1967), 190–91.

"I HAVE DIVINE COMPANIONSHIP": PRAYER IN THE LIFE OF A PASTOR, PRIEST, AND PROPHET

Referring to the "inner sense of assurance" and "security" that came whenever he confronted the possibility of "moments of real fear," Martin Luther King Jr. declared in 1961: "I have always felt a sense of cosmic companionship." This feeling of having "cosmic companionship"[47] carried over from his early life as a preacher to shape and inform his prayer life as a pastor, priest, and prophet. In these capacities, King cultivated personal prayer habits while also serving as a prayer teacher and prayer leader for his parishioners and others who came under his spiritual leadership. His emphasis was always, first and foremost, on prayer as both the sacred heart of the Christian faith and the key to a spiritually rich and fulfilled life.

The decision to become the pastor of "a large black church in the South" was considered prayerfully by King, and once the opportunity arose, with his call to the Dexter Avenue Baptist Church in Montgomery, Alabama, in April 1954, he embraced a personal prayer life that was grounded in the fundamental virtues of obedience and a willingness to serve and sacrifice. From the beginning, cultivating his own vital and meaningful prayer life was uppermost in King's mind. He consciously developed more of a habit of praying daily, usually beginning at 6:00 or 7:00 a.m. with prayer and meditation in his den. He habitually prayed with his wife and others in his family, with individual church members, before preparing his sermons, when opening worship and other congregational activities, with the sick and shut-in, before bed at night, and in silence when he was alone at home, in his pastor's study, in his hotel rooms, or in some other private setting.[48] To "further strengthen the spiritual life" of the Dexter Church family as a whole, King "rejuvenated" the "regular mid-week prayer services," and insisted that "some organization from the church" be "called on" to "lead" or take charge

47. King was saying, in other words, that there was "something in the very structure of the cosmos working with us." See "Face to Face: Dr. Martin Luther King, Jr. and John Freeman," London, unpublished interview, recorded from transmission and aired (29 October 1961), KCLA, 9; Martin Luther King Jr., "Address at a Valedictory Service, University of the West Indies, Mona, Jamaica (20 June 1965), unpublished version of a speech, KCLA, 10–11; and "King's Plan for Selma: Transcript of an Interview," Selma, Alabama (19 January 1965), unpublished statement, KCLA, 2.

48. Lawrence D. Reddick, *Crusader without Violence: A Biography of Martin Luther King, Jr.* (New York: Harper & Brothers, 1959), 9–10; and Mervyn A. Warren, *King Came Preaching: The Pulpit Power of Dr. Martin Luther King, Jr.* (Downers Grove, IL: InterVarsity Press, 2001), 136–37 and 158.

each week.[49] It is not difficult to imagine that what took place in the circle of pray-ers on Wednesday nights and Sunday mornings was not merely formality, for what the worshipers saw, heard, and experienced undoubtedly helped make it possible for them to function each day without losing their sanity and a sense of themselves as shaped in the divine image.

King's pastoral role, which for him was "divinely sanctioned" and "humanly conferred," cast him in the image of *religious leader*, which entailed, aside from administrative tasks and other functions, teaching people about prayer, how to pray, and the need to discover the efficacy and the special rewards of praying daily. For King, this was not simply a matter of giving instructions, and he never prepared a guide to or a primer on prayer. He gave lessons in prayer by words and example, frequently demanding that Dexter become a praying congregation with a praying pastor. King took the same approach as co-pastor of Ebenezer in Atlanta, often echoing the words of his father and brother, who shared the pulpit with him from 1960 until his death in 1968. Prayer, King maintained, was not to be taken lightly or casually because it represents Christ's call to both holiness and service, and it always yields new possibilities for envisioning and experiencing a closer walk with God, or a more satisfying and fulfilling relationship to the realm of the divine.[50] King's own pastoral prayers covered needs that were not only personal, spiritual, psychological, and material, but social and political as well, and this proved enormously beneficial to people who had learned to live and respond to oppression liturgically.[51] Something of the flavor and spark of his praying ability and style are exposed in the following excerpts from a prayer he repeatedly recited with slight variations in language during the years he served as a pastor at Dexter and co-pastor at Ebenezer:

> Most gracious and all wise God, before whose face the generations rise and fall; Thou in whom we live, and move, and have our being. We thank thee for all thy good and gracious gifts; for life and for health; for food and for raiment; for the beauties of nature and the love of human nature. We come before thee painfully aware of our shortcomings. . . . Break the spell of that

49. Carson et al., eds., *Papers*, 2:582.

50. Carson et al., eds., *Papers*, 2:287; Wally G. Vaughn and Richard W. Wills, eds., *Reflections on Our Pastor: Dr. Martin Luther King, Jr., at Dexter Avenue Baptist Church, 1954–1960* (Dover, MA: Majority Press, 1999), 42, 55, 62, 80, and 118; and a telephone interview with Nelson Malden (23 May 2014). Interestingly enough, King, while serving as co-pastor of Ebenezer in 1963, preached a sermon on "The Problem of Unanswered Prayer." See "'Problem of Unanswered Prayer,' Ebenezer Topic; Dr. King, Jr. at Ebenezer Sunday," *The Atlanta Daily World* (2 February 1963): 3.

51. Vaughn and Wills, eds., *Reflections on Our Pastor*, 42, 55, 62, 80, and 118; and a telephone interview with Nelson Malden (23 May 2014).

> which blinds our minds. Purify our hearts that we may see thee. O God in these turbulent days when fear and doubt are mounting high give us broad visions, penetrating eyes, and the power of endurance.[52]

This typifies the ways in which King approached the pastoral prayer—with words of praise, confession, petition, intercession, gratitude, wonder, and joy. All of these key elements, in addition to a righteous anger at times, came together in King's thinking as he designed the content and delivery of his pastoral prayers to not only remind his church folk that they should "go out and work as though the very answer to their prayers depended on us and not upon thee,"[53] but also to invoke responses of "Amen," "hallelujah," and "thank God" from them. Here the dialogical character of King's pastoral prayers, or their participative nature, came through, as was also the case when he gave the invocation, the benediction, funeral prayers, or other forms of prayer.[54] Here King stood squarely in what Harold Carter calls "the prayer tradition of black people."[55]

King's influence as a pastor or "spiritual shepherd"[56] ultimately extended beyond his work at Dexter and later at Ebenezer Baptist Church, for many in Montgomery and Atlanta regarded him as "the community pastor," and some later came to view him as "an American pastor" as well. Such images were quite fitting for King since he embodied a spirituality that was not only personal but communal as well. As "a community pastor," he was interested in not only redeeming "the souls" of his people, thereby uniting "them with God," but also in changing "the environmental conditions" so their souls would "have a chance" after they were changed. As "an American pastor," he "cared deeply about the soul of his nation," and sought to save it from an impending "spiritual death."[57] King believed deeply in life-changing prayer, and he

52. See King, *"Thou, Dear God,"* 145; Carson et al., eds., *Papers*, 6:138; and Clayborne Carson et al., eds., *The Papers of Martin Luther King, Jr.: To Save the Soul of America, January 1961–August 1962* (Berkeley: University of California Press, 2014), 7:453.

53. See James M. Washington, ed., *Conversations with God: Two Centuries of Prayers by African Americans* (New York: HarperCollins, 1994), 190; and J. Alfred Smith Sr., ed., *No Other Help I Know: Sermons on Prayer and Spirituality* (Valley Forge, PA: Judson, 1996), 11.

54. Baldwin, *Never to Leave Us Alone*, 45–46.

55. The dialogical character or participative quality that marked prayers in this tradition was also typical of black folk sermons. See Carter, *Prayer Tradition of Black People*, 57–59; and Baldwin, *Never to Leave Us Alone*, 45–47.

56. Another term King used to describe a pastor. See Carson et al., eds., *Papers*, 5:474–75.

57. Vaughn and Wills, eds., *Reflections on Our Pastor*, 141–47; a telephone interview with Nelson Malden (15 March 2014); a telephone interview with Nelson Malden (23 May 2014); Earl E. Shelp and Ronald H. Sunderland, eds., *The Pastor as Prophet* (New York: Pilgrim, 1985), 15; Martin Luther King Jr., *Stride toward Freedom: The Montgomery Story* (New York: Harper &

knew that changing individual souls meant essentially nothing if his own country's soul was lost. Thus, prayer was part of the course he charted for the redemption of the nation's soul. "To redeem the soul of America" became the motto of his Southern Christian Leadership Conference (SCLC), the organization he and other clergy founded "to serve as a channel through which local protest organizations in the South could coordinate their protest activities," and to "give the total struggle a sense of Christian and disciplined direction."[58] Under the banner of the SCLC, King consistently prayed for the salvation of a nation that was, strangely enough, ill-prepared to understand, let alone accept, the kind of pastoral leadership and guidance he sought to provide.

Praying, meditation, and occasional fasting were, aside from preaching, what made King's spirituality so alive, genuine, dynamic, and contagious for the people he served as pastor. In other words, this is what grounded his amazing appeal and effectiveness as a church pastor. The sheer power and poignancy of his prayers, and the depths of their striking imagery and poetic wisdom, moved hearts, stirred souls, and enlightened minds.[59] When it came to King's pastoral prayers, he, as was the case with his sermons, combined the heart, soul, and caring function of a good shepherd with the imagination of a poet, the rational faculties and inquisitive mind of a philosopher, and the learning and discerning spirit of a theologian.[60]

King occasionally acknowledged that his pastoral role also involved what he called "a priestly function,"[61] and this, too, became significant in terms of his adventures in prayer. Here he took on the mantle of

Row, 1958), 36; King, *Where Do We Go from Here?,* 188; Baldwin, *Never to Leave Us Alone*, 53; and Martin Luther King Jr., "Address to a Joint Convention of the Two Houses of the General Court of Massachusetts, Boston, Massachusetts" (22 April 1965), unpublished version, KCLA, 13.

58. Baldwin, *There Is a Balm in Gilead*, 192–93; Adam Fairclough, "The Southern Christian Leadership Conference and the Second Reconstruction, 1957–1973," *The Southern Atlantic Quarterly* 8, no. 2 (Spring 1981): 178; and Martin Luther King Jr. to Dr. P. J. Ellis, unpublished letter (6 February 1960), KCLA, 1.

59. King, *My Life with Martin Luther King, Jr.,* 58, 91, 95, 151, and 211; King, *Stride toward Freedom*, 21, 26, 59, 67, 81, 88, 134–35, 137–38, and 178; Carson et al., eds., *Papers*, 2:287, 292, and 582; Clayborne Carson et al., eds., *The Papers of Martin Luther King, Jr.: Birth of a New Age, December 1955–December 1956* (Berkeley: University of California Press, 1997), 3:74, 110, 231, 240, 279–80, 346, and 488; Vaughn and Wills, eds., *Reflections on Our Pastor*, 42, 55, 62, 80, and 118; Warren, *King Came Preaching*, 136–37 and 158; and Reddick, *Crusader without Violence*, 9–10.

60. King, *"Thou, Dear God,"* 3–173.

61. Martin Luther King Jr., "Transcript of an Interview with Local Newscasters," KNXT TV, Los Angeles (10 July 1965), KCLA, 2; and Martin Luther King Jr., "Transcript of an Interview on 'Face the Nation,'" Broadcast of CBS Television Network (29 August 1965), KCLA, 3.

ritual leader and functioned more consciously as a *prayer leader*. In this role, King constantly established and reestablished his people's relationship with each other and with God through prayer and in other ways (i.e., interpretation of the Word, administration of sacraments, etc.), so that they could vividly perceive themselves as the people of God. Put another way, King became a mediator between God and his church folk—one who pointed out where, when, and how the divine was present for them not only in the prayer circle and other prayer rituals, but also in the total experience of worship, Scripture, the black experience, the freedom movement, society, and the world. King related this world to the other world, mediating between the living and the dead in order to lessen the hardships for his congregants in this life, and prayer was central to that effort as well. Furthermore, King demonstrated the divine presence and will in his praying, and he allowed his people to participate with him in this communion with God.[62] Sunday after Sunday at Dexter, and to some extent as co-pastor with his father and brother at Ebenezer years later, he lifted before God the prayers of the worshippers, while also commending to them and modeling for them the practice of praying daily for themselves and others. Thus, what W. E. B. DuBois wrote about the slave preacher as priest—as "the interpreter of the unknown, the comforter of the sorrowing, and the supernatural avenger of wrong"—applies in some measure to King as well.[63]

In his role as priest, King led his parishioners to a fuller understanding that prayer avails the faithful to the bountifulness of God's blessings, including infinite possibilities for healing. Prayer opened him to healing, transformation, and new life, and he sought the same kind of blessings and spiritual renewal for his flock. King's stress on the therapeutic, transformative, and restorative power of prayer took on layers of special significance since he was, as part of an oppressed and suffering community himself, always willing to expose his own wounds as a source of comfort and healing for others. "Recognizing the necessity for suffering, I have tried to make of it a virtue," King maintained. "If only to save myself from bitterness, I have attempted to see my personal ordeals as an opportunity to transform myself and heal the people involved in the

62. King's ritual role was very much in the tradition of that ascribed to the slave priest by scholars like W. E. B. DuBois, James Weldon Johnson, and Sterling Stuckey. See John Hope Franklin, ed., *The Souls of Black Folk in Three Negro Classics* (New York: Avon, 1965; originally published in 1903), 342; James Weldon Johnson, *God's Trombones: Seven Negro Sermons in Verse* (New York: Viking, 1969; originally published in 1927), 2–3; Sterling Stuckey, *Slave Culture: Nationalist Theory and the Foundation of Black America* (New York: Oxford University Press, 1987), 255 and 257; and Baldwin, *There Is a Balm in Gilead*, 318 and 320.

63. Baldwin, *Never to Leave Us Alone*, 55–56; Baldwin, *There Is a Balm in Gilead*, 317–21; and Franklin, ed., *The Souls of Black Folk in Three Negro Classics*, 342.

tragic situation which now obtains." "I bear in my body the marks of the Lord Jesus," he further asserted as he, in a typically priestly fashion, reminded worshippers, who constantly endured abuse, sorrow, sickness, and even death at the hands of an evil system, that their own reaffirmation, renewal, and revitalization were always possible under the healing and redemptive qualities of prayer. This message echoed through King's eulogy for those four little girls in Birmingham in 1963, and also at other times when tragedy and disappointment struck and people needed to be consoled, reinforced, fed "the bread of hope," and graced with the will to, as King himself put it at times, "keep on keeping on."[64] King's goal as priest was always to comfort, restore, re-energize, and give new hope to the afflicted, as the lines from the following prayer suggest:

> Oh God, our gracious Heavenly Father, we come on this Easter morning, thanking Thee for revealing to us the ultimate meaning and the ultimate rationality of the universe. We thank you, this morning, for your Son, Jesus, who came by to let us know that love is the most durable power in the world, who came by to let us know that death can't defeat us, to take the sting out of the grave and make it possible for all of us to have eternal life.[65]

Interestingly enough, the image of King as a priest at prayer was most evident in the prayers he delivered during the Lenten season, and especially on Palm Sunday, Good Friday, and Easter Sunday, when reflections on the meaning of Jesus's suffering, death, and resurrection evoked powerful emotions in many church circles, and when many Christians themselves were observing a period of sacrifice involving fasting, moderation, self-discipline, self-denial, or, as in King and his followers' case, social change efforts rooted in a sense of the redemptive power of love and suffering. During such occasions, the sense of sharing in the sacrifice of Jesus Christ must have weighed heavily on the minds and hearts of King and so many others who risked life and limb for freedom.[66]

When King spoke of his "prophetic role," he had in mind the need to "bring the great principles of our Judeo-Christian heritage to bear on the social evils of our day," or to "constantly speak to the moral issues of our day far beyond civil rights."[67] Here he took on the obligations of a *moral*

64. Washington, ed., *Testament of Hope*, 41–42; Carson and Holloran, eds., *Knock at Midnight*, 69–78; Martin Luther King Jr., "A Knock at Midnight," unpublished version of a sermon, All Saints Community Church, Los Angeles (25 June 1967), KCLA, 13 ; Baldwin, *There Is a Balm in Gilead*, 317–22; and Baldwin, *Never to Leave Us Alone*, 13, 55–56, 59, and 63.

65. Carson et al., eds., *Papers*, 6:292–93.

66. King, *"Thou, Dear God,"* 36–43.

67. King, "Transcript of an Interview with Local Newscasters," 2; and King, "Transcript of an Interview on 'Face the Nation,'" 3.

leader. He became a mouthpiece for God, called and commissioned to speak clearly and boldly about racism, arrogance, greed, economic injustice, war, and other individual and collective sins and evils that kept people alienated from themselves, each other, and God. King became a transgressor, a disturber of the status quo, a transformed nonconformist, a maladjusted personality, and he felt compelled to consistently combine fervent prayer with powerful proclamations that God's judgment and wrath were upon those who failed to practice what they affirmed in creeds and in worship, and that God would not long endure the cruelty and destructiveness of people against people.[68]

There were many points in King's public life when he epitomized the portrait of the prophet at prayer, but the focus here is essentially limited to the prayer he recited in his study in his home at 309 South Jackson Street in Montgomery in December, 1955, at the beginning of his true leadership in the bus boycott there; to the talk he had with God at midnight in his kitchen at that residence on January 27, 1956, after receiving an obscene and threatening telephone call from a white bigot; to an emotional prayer experience he had during a mass meeting in Montgomery on January 14, 1957, after his home, the homes of other leaders, and several black churches had been bombed; and to the personal prayer retreats that had become a part of his weekly routine by the time of the Birmingham campaign in 1963. An explanation of the context for each of these experiences with prayer is in order here.

The events that led to the prayer in King's study actually unfolded on December 5, 1955, when King, the newly selected president of the Montgomery Improvement Association (MIA), the organization formed to spearhead the boycott, learned that he had little time to ready himself to speak at a mass meeting hastily called to propel the boycott. Pacing back and forth in his study, with "only twenty minutes to prepare the most decisive speech of my life," King recalled, "I became possessed by fear" and "obsessed by a feeling of inadequacy." For perhaps the first time in his life, King was deeply conscious of a prophetic responsibility being imposed upon him, and he "turned to God in prayer." "My words were brief and simple," he wrote, "asking God to restore my balance and to be with me in a time when I needed His guidance more than ever."[69]

68. Baldwin, *There Is a Balm in Gilead*, 322–23 and 328.

69. King, *Stride toward Freedom*, 58–59; and Baldwin, *Never to Leave Us Alone*, 68–69. This prayer falls into the category of what Martha Rowlett calls "the 'spur-of-the moment' prayer," which "reflects a consciousness that all of life is lived in God's presence." See Martha Graybeal Rowlett, *Responding to God: A Guide to Daily Prayer* (Nashville: Upper Room, 1996), 8. Many have said that the civil rights movement began with a song, but King's true leadership in that movement actually started with a prayer. See Baldwin, *Never to Leave Us Alone*, 68.

This prayer was evidently in the best tradition of the ancient Hebrew prophets, Jesus, and the apostles, and it is possible that King's first real sense of himself as both a prophet and a priest began here, for he was praying for the ability to deliver the kind of speech "that would be militant enough to keep my people aroused to positive action and yet moderate enough to keep this fervor within controllable and Christian bounds." Also, this equated with King's sense of the true prophet as one who blends "opposites" or "bears within his character antitheses strongly marked"—as one who is wise and tough enough to speak and act boldly while motivating others to act, and yet tender hearted and harmless enough to pray while modeling for them passion, fervor, and the sacrificial life without bitterness and violence.[70] King discovered in the biblical prophets—who had recognized the problems of social dislocation, of the mistreatment of the poor and humble by the privileged, and of idolatry, and who had consistently urged the people to seek God and not evil in the face of the coming judgment—echoes of the same concerns he had as he spoke against America's racism, her idolatry, her militarism, and her mistreatment of the destitute and victimized, and he, also like the prophets, relied on prayer for direction in courageously proclaiming God's righteousness, justice, and wrath even under the threat of verbal abuse, physical attack, and death. With this prophetic role in mind, King once remarked: "My great prayer is always for God to save me from the paralysis of crippling fear, because I think when a person lives with the fears of the consequences for his personal life he can never do anything in terms of lifting the whole of humanity and solving many of the social problems which we confront in every age and every generation."[71]

King's "vision in the kitchen," shared with Dexter Church in January 1957, a year after it actually happened, is equally significant for highlighting his practice of prayer as a prophet and the prophetic quality that marked many of his prayers. Here he gave a searing personal account of what was essentially a spiritual crisis. On a Friday night, January 27, King arrived at home late after an MIA meeting to discover his wife Coretta and infant daughter Yolanda asleep, and, as he was about to retire himself, his telephone rang. "On the other end," King recounted,

70. King would most likely have made this claim in some fashion regarding the pastor and priest as well, for he argued categorically that "the strong man holds in a living blend strongly marked opposites." See King, *Strength to Love*, 9–16.

71. Many of King's friends, clergy and lay, felt much like Kelly Miller Smith Sr., who declared, in a letter to King, that "the mantle of the prophets rests well upon your shoulders." See Carson et al., eds., *Papers*, 3:129–30, 143, 181, 183, 202–3, and 398; and Vaughn and Wills, eds., *Reflections on Our Pastor*, 39.

"was an ugly voice" which referred to him as "a nigger" and threatened to kill him and bomb his home if he did not leave Montgomery "in three days." Restless and overcome with fear, King went to his kitchen, made coffee, sat at his table, and "started thinking about many things," including what could possibly happen to his wife and child. In search of "a little relief," King "pulled back on the theology and philosophy that" he "had just studied in the universities, trying to find philosophical and theological reasons for the existence and the reality of sin and evil, but," he said, "the answer didn't quite come there." Then came that inner voice, telling King to "call on" the God about whom he had been told as a child. Bowing over "that cup of coffee," he "prayed aloud" a heart and soul-stirring prayer, and, indeed, the prophet's prayer: "Lord, I'm down here trying to do what's right. I think I'm right; I think the cause that we represent is right. But Lord, I must confess that I'm weak now; I'm faltering; I'm losing my courage. And I can't let the people see me like this because if they see me weak and losing my courage, they will begin to get weak."[72]

"At that moment," King reported, "I experienced the presence of the Divine as I had never experienced Him before." He heard "an inner voice saying" to him, "Martin Luther, stand up for righteousness, stand up for justice, stand up for truth. And lo, I will be with you even until the end of the world." Undoubtedly, this was only one of the many such episodes of spiritual crisis King endured over the course of his public life. Be that as it may, in that kind of existential appropriation of black faith, King learned something that the world of academia at its best could never have taught him. From that point and throughout his public life, he continued to hear that "inner voice" which gave him "an inner calm" in "the midst of outer dangers" and the "lonely days and dreary nights."[73]

Phenomenologically speaking, the kitchen prayer and vision constituted for King a living encounter with the living God in the serenity

72. This is a striking example of how King's prayers and prayer life arose out of his life experiences and his social and cultural contexts. See Carson and Holloran, eds., *Knock at Midnight,* 160–62; King, *Stride toward Freedom*, 134–35; and Carson et al., eds., *Papers*, 6:533–34. Mervyn Warren calls that Kitchen prayer King's "prayer of relinquishment." See Warren, *King Came Preaching*, 40; and Baldwin, *Never to Leave Us Alone*, 69 and 140n10.

73. Apparently, King never admitted to having "a crisis" nor an instantaneous or momentary conversion, and one could argue that this was in fact what this was. But it is better to say that King's conversion resulted from many years of spiritual, emotional, and intellectual struggle in the church, the academy, and that broader public sphere. In any event, King clearly embraced, in this case, what Diana Hayes would call "a liberating spirituality," and never doubted that any encounter with the *holy* can be life-transforming, or can bring healing, transformation, and new life. See King, *Stride toward Freedom*, 134–35; Carson and Holloran, eds., *Knock at Midnight*, 162; King, *Strength to Love*, 154; Baldwin, *There Is a Balm in Gilead*, 187–90; and Diana L. Hayes, *Forged in the Fiery Furnace: African American Spirituality* (Maryknoll, NY: Orbis, 2012), 5.

of King's own solitary and sacred space, and this was really part of his journey of spiritual self-discovery. It deepened his prayer life, his personal prayer practice, and also his capacity for spiritual discernment. It was a decisive moment, a watershed moment, a sort of *Kairos* moment in King's spiritual life when he relied not on his own strength, but entrusted himself entirely to God.[74] It was a special call to a deeper, personal relationship with God in the face of the increasing possibility of the specter of death, and King opened himself to the peace of God, to God's responses, to a closer walk with God, and to the vital necessity of living with God at the center of his life. He became even more convinced that prayer could be a refuge and a guide in times of fear, disillusionment, uncertainty, and mingled hope and despair, and he found in the experience an individual relationship with God that would sustain him for the rest of his days.[75]

King's complete immersion in that sacred kitchen moment not only calmed his soul and provided other personal spiritual benefits, it also, in a more general sense, signaled a decisive shift in his life, thought, and activities. He came to see more clearly that spirituality and the struggle for justice were indeed one and the same. He developed a new and more mature sense of the virtuous life, which involves living in response to God's grace. Moreover, King saw how he could be a blessing to his people, the nation, and the world, and was more willing and able to embrace his true identity as a prophet along with the depths of his prophetic calling. In other words, that life-affirming and transforming encounter with his divine companion in his kitchen influenced the course of his spiritual leadership, for he was empowered in new ways and renewed and reinforced in his determination to fulfill God's will, plan, and purpose for his life. Perhaps more importantly, King's kitchen experience largely defined the role that spirituality would play not only in his own life but also in the life of the movement he led. He then had the discipline of a prophetic imagination along with the inner spiritual resources to provide strong, proactive leadership in the struggle for equal rights, social justice, and peace.[76]

Interestingly enough, proof of this growth on King's part came in mid-January 1957, almost a year after the kitchen vision, with a prayer experience he had after his home and the homes of Ralph Abernathy and Robert Graetz, and also four Baptist churches in Montgomery—First Baptist, Bell Street, Hutchinson Street, and Mt. Olive—had been either

74. Baldwin, *Never to Leave Us Alone*, 69–70.

75. King, *Strength to Love*, 154–55; and Carson et al., eds., *Papers*, 6:534.

76. Carson et al., eds., *Papers*, 6:534; Carson and Holloran, eds., *Knock at Midnight*, 162–64; King, *Strength to Love*, 154; and Reddick, *Crusader without Violence*, 9–10.

damaged or destroyed by explosions. King graphically described his feelings and actions on that occasion as he, in the true manner of a prophet standing before the people, bowed in the presence of that "living reality" that he had come to know also as "a personal God":

> Discouraged, and still revolted by the bombings, for some strange reason I began to feel a personal sense of guilt for everything that was happening. . . . In this mood I went to the mass meeting on Monday night. There for the first time, I broke down in public. I had invited the audience to join me in prayer, and had begun by asking God's guidance and direction in all our activities. Then, in the grip of an emotion I could not control, I said, "Lord, I hope no one will have to die as a result of our struggle for freedom in Montgomery. Certainly I don't want to die. But if anyone has to die, let it be me." The audience was in an uproar. Shouts and cries of "no, no" came from all sides. So intense was the reaction, that I could not go on with my prayer. Two of my fellow ministers came to the pulpit and suggested that I take a seat. For a few minutes I stood with their arms around me, unable to move. Finally, with the help of my friends, I sat down.[77]

Here was an occasion when the traditional prayer meeting served to solidify a prophetic leader and a prophetic community around a common vision, faith, hope, purpose, and strategy for change. Though seemingly trapped in a web of guilt and emotion, King did not stand alone, for that sense of being a prophetic people, a suffering community, and a divinely ordained instrument for much-needed social change proved overwhelming for all involved. The emotive qualities of black church life powerfully surfaced, as prayer rose to sermon, the crying out gave way to song, tears turned into rejoicing, and King's calm manner surrendered to an infectious frenzy. Hence, King's connection to the ecstatic side of the black prayer tradition and to the African American worship experience as a whole was amazingly revealed.[78]

King's personal prayer retreats revealed essentially as much about his spirit as a prophet as any other category of his religious experiences. Here King developed the habit of stepping into the tranquility of his prayer closet or other private sacred spaces to re-center, nurture, refresh, and revitalize his spiritual life. These prayer retreats, which began during

77. King and Abernathy were in Atlanta for "a meeting of Negro leaders" when they heard about the bombings, and from that moment, "in the early morning hours," King reported, "we prayed to God together, asking for the power of endurance, the strength to carry on." See King, *Stride toward Freedom*, 175–79; Martin Luther King Jr., *The Autobiography of Martin Luther King, Jr.*, ed. Clayborne Carson (New York: Warner, 1998), 102; Carson et al., eds., *Papers*, 4:109 and 113; and Baldwin, *Never to Leave Us Alone*, 72 and 141–42n19.

78. King, *Stride toward Freedom*, 177–78; Baldwin, *There Is a Balm in Gilead*, 191–92; and Baldwin, *Never to Leave Us Alone*, 72.

King's time in Montgomery and carried over into his later years, included silent and sanctified moments at night in his bedroom or office at home. Wyatt T. Walker, a close associate of King, often spoke of King's "self-imposed 'Day of Silence,'" during which he would retreat to his den, his church study, a hotel room, or some other venue that provided quiet sacred space where he, without telephone, television, radio, and other potential distractions, spent time sitting or reading in silence, praying out loud or silently, fasting, meditating, or engaging in a "rigorous discipline of think time." At such times, King was most conscious of being a prophet in the presence of a higher power, and his experiences of silent prayer allowed him to speak out of his soul while also listening to God.[79] This concept of prayer as listening to and responding to God, and not simply talking to God, was vital to King's sense of his own prophetic role. This was part of his gift of spiritual discernment.

Unquestionably, these prayer retreats were central to King's pilgrimage toward spiritual awareness and a healthy sense of what he termed "divine companionship." They were consistent with his idea of both sacred time and self-purification time because King made space for the God who accompanied him through the daily events of his life and shared with that God the depths of his doubts, fears, insecurities, sorrow, and pain. In this regard, he was true to his inner self, to his thirst for a deep-seated, God-centered faith, because what mattered most was finding his inner purpose, or that which endowed life with creative energy and true meaning. Thus, King, largely through prayers voiced and unvoiced,[80] was able to put into proper perspective his study of "the idea of a personal God," which had previously been "little more than a metaphysical category that" he "found theologically and philosophically satisfying," and to better entertain the concept of God as "a living reality" that "was validated in the experiences of everyday life."[81]

But there was also a more practical side to King's prayer retreats. He found here opportunities to escape for a time the daily chaos, demands,

79. King, *Stride toward Freedom*, 59 and 134–35; and King, *Autobiography*, 43, 58–59, and 77–78. Aside from the letters we exchanged, Wyatt Walker and I had a few conversations in 2009, in person and via telephone, in which King's personal prayer retreats were mentioned. See also A Letter from Wyatt Tee Walker to Lewis V. Baldwin (30 April 2009); Carson et al., eds., *Papers*, 4:256; Baldwin, *Never to Leave Us Alone*, vii and 123n5; and Washington, ed., *Testament of Hope*, 372 and 376.

80. So many of King's prayers were apparently silent or unvoiced, or what Jane Vennard calls "arrow prayers." "Arrow prayers are informal prayers spoken aloud or silently in our hearts in the midst of our daily life," and "they are so named because it has been said that these fervent prayers fly straight to the heart of God." See Jane E. Vennard, *A Praying Congregation: The Art of Teaching Spiritual Practice* (Herndon, VA: Alban Institute, 2005), 120.

81. King, *Strength to Love*, 154–55.

and pressures of the movement, and to open himself to much-needed moments of relaxation, solitude, self-examination, and self-reflection. His days were always so busy, demanding, and hectic, and he routinely confronted extremist forces determined to literally destroy him and to consolidate and maintain white power. This took a heavy emotional and psychological toll on King, and he needed time to himself to reexamine himself,[82] even as he pondered future moves and directions his movement might take. The prayer retreats strengthened him physically, emotionally, and psychologically. They were, in essence, a critical aspect of his journey of self-discovery and survival not simply as a prophet, but as a human being. Consequently, King was able to absorb all of the blistering criticism and to survive those bitter experiences of personal struggle and suffering without succumbing to fear, anger, recrimination, and violence. Put another way, he experienced defeats but was not ultimately defeated.

"THIS IS A SPIRITUAL MOVEMENT": UNITING THE PRAYER CIRCLE AND THE PICKET LINE

Martin Luther King Jr. frequently said that the civil rights cause was at its core "a spiritual movement" that depended "on moral and spiritual forces," and that he was "just a symbol of that movement."[83] Here King was saying, in essence, that the movement he led was not only rooted in spiritual and moral values, but was also a real-life, practical expression of "the spiritual power" he and his people were radiating to the nation and the world through an adherence to the principles of love, understanding good will, and nonviolence.[84] King made this claim, knowing that spirituality had always been a force in the human impulse toward freedom, and also with the understanding of spirituality as a life of service to both God and humanity. This is why he had no problem translating his own spirituality into a sustained and effective commitment to liberating and empowering people socially, politically, and economically, a cause in which he sacrificially believed.

King's portrayal of the civil rights movement as "a spiritual move-

82. This is not to suggest that King was the incredibly self-absorbed personality that his enemies persistently projected. It should be noted that much of his physical, emotional, and psychological relief came not only through prayer, but through play and his amazing gift of humor and laughter as well. See Lewis V. Baldwin, *Behind the Public Veil: The Humanness of Martin Luther King, Jr.* (Minneapolis: Fortress, 2016), 223–324.

83. Carson et al., eds., *Papers*, 3:113, 151, 200, 280, 428, and 430; Washington, ed., *Testament of Hope*, 84 and 357; King, *Autobiography*, 105; and Carson et al., eds., *Papers,* 7:576.

84. King, *Stride toward Freedom*, 224.

ment" had much to do with prayer and praying. Movement time for him also meant prayer time, or "self-purification" time,[85] and it is evident that he understood the movement as essentially "a prayer movement" or "a prayerful event."[86] King's own extraordinary spiritual odyssey, and particularly the transformative power of that "vision in the kitchen" back in 1956, helped solidify his thinking regarding the essentiality of prayer in the civil rights movement. He harked back on that kitchen experience at times to clarify the point that prayer was never "a substitute for direct action campaigns for justice" but a crucial part of those campaigns.[87] King knew that the discipline of daily devotion through moving prayers was part of the holy habits of so many of the good church people who marched and went to jail with him. They saw that the prayer life and the life of service were inseparable, because both mirrored the life of Jesus.

Convinced that the civil rights program and activities were as much the fruit of prayer as anything else in his people's lives, King routinely urged his followers and supporters to offer not simply physical and financial support, but also spiritual support through prayer,[88] because the movement was always in need of God's creative and sustaining presence and activity. King believed that prayer, like the wise employment of disciplined nonviolent action, could be liberating and empowering in and of itself, and he regularly led movement activists in prayer at mass meetings, at his home, in the streets, inside jail cells, and in other contexts, always calling on the divine presence to manifest itself in their lives and efforts. All movement business, King felt, had to be given "serious and prayerful consideration." His prayers saturated his own ethical choices and activities, reflected his deep awareness of the world of human need, revealed his keen sense of where his people were spiritually, socially,

85. King listed "four basic steps" in "any nonviolent campaign": collection of the facts to determine whether injustices exist, negotiation, self-purification, and direct action. "Self-purification" had to do with the inward experience of piety, prayer, fasting, and meditation, which preceded forms of nonviolent direct action (i.e., boycotts, marches, demonstrations, sit-ins, voter registration, etc.). See Martin Luther King Jr., *Why We Can't Wait* (New York: The New American Library, 1963), 78.

86. Michael G. Long, "A Review of Lewis V. Baldwin, *Never to Leave Us Alone: The Prayer Life of Martin Luther King, Jr.* (2010)," in *Interpretation: A Journal of Bible and Theology* 66, no. 1 (January 2012): 110.

87. King often spoke of the "spiritual lift" he got from the prayers of those who stood for and with him. See Long, "Review," 110; Martin Luther King Jr., *The Trumpet of Conscience* (San Francisco: Harper & Row, 1987; originally published in 1967), 59; Carson et al., eds., *Papers*, 5:215; Carson et al., eds., *Papers*, 6:85, and 590–91; Carson et al., eds., *Papers*, 4:505; and King, *Strength to Love,* 131–33.

88. Washington, ed., *Testament of Hope*, 84; Carson et al., eds., *Papers*, 4:90, 113, and 239; Carson et al., eds., *Papers*, 3:153, 231, 279–80, 353, 361, and 373; and Carson et al., eds., *Papers*, 5:282, 351–52, and 355.

psychologically, and otherwise, and also increased and sharpened their social sensitivity. Prayer in such instances was not merely a call to deep, personal relationship with God but a call to action and an extension of their work for the common good. Furthermore, King's prayers wrought a decisively religious tone to the movement, and they, as a critical aspect of his moral leadership, were essentially as instrumental as his preaching, nonviolent activism, and eventual martyrdom in inspiring a renewal of the Christian faith.[89]

In highlighting the need for prayer, King was not merely thinking in terms of a movement but a holy crusade, imbued with the spirit of Christ. He had in mind moving from faith to service, from prayer to altruistic behavior and action. He convinced many of the movement's foot soldiers that God was not dead, as some theologians posited; that "God is with us"; that "the God of the universe marches with us"; that God could be found whenever and wherever people of goodwill combined prayer with determined struggle for human freedom and welfare. Clearly, King's gifts as a preacher, pastor, priest, and prophet were brought together in this venture, especially as he sought to instill the conviction that prayer constituted not only a form of "self-purification," but also "creative energy" that "can move the immovable, give rest to the weary, and at last, draw" the faithful "ever closer to the one who will never leave us alone."[90]

Evidently, King-led civil rights campaigns provided the vehicle through which folk praying and the black prayer tradition could live and find expression. King gave voice to the essentials of that tradition while remaining true to its genius and vitality. He reclaimed the language of freedom and deliverance in the prayers of his enslaved ancestors, as he prayed for the strength and wisdom needed for the continuing struggle through the Egypt of slavery, the wilderness of segregation, toward the promised land of freedom, justice, and equal opportunity. King also remained true to that tradition by stressing the idea of prayer as "talking with God," by blending this-worldly and otherworldly concerns in his prayers, by highlighting the necessity of prayer, by extolling the wonders and possibilities of prayer, and by embracing the scriptural

89. Carson et al., eds., *Papers*, 7:395; Baldwin, *Never to Leave Us Alone*, 67–89; Long, "Review," 110; Carter, *Prayer Tradition of Black People*, 65–67, 94, 106–13, and 129–30; and C. Eric Lincoln, "The Black Church and a Decade of Change," part 2, *Tuesday at Home* (March 1976): 7; Baldwin, *There Is a Balm in Gilead*, 227–28; King, *Autobiography*, 361; and King, *"Thou, Dear God,"* 139–73.

90. Carson et al., eds., *Papers*, 3:113; King, *Strength to Love*, 154–55; Carson et al., eds., *Papers*, 6:253–55; Carson and Holloran, eds., *Knock at Midnight*, 15, 17–19, 156–57, and 200; and "King's Plan for Selma," 2. This idea of prayer as "creative energy" is defined and developed in Baldwin, *Never to Leave Us Alone*.

view that God answers prayer. But he, at the same time, challenged certain preconceived notions about prayer among all too many otherwise well-meaning and dedicated black churchpersons, the most common among which were that God should be petitioned for every trivial need, that prayer can often be a substitute for intelligence and action, and that prayer alone could eliminate structures of social evil. Knowing that prayer was a symbol with which he could appeal not only to ordinary church folk, but even many of the unchurched in the movement, King repeatedly questioned such misconceptions, equating them with "superstition," while also modeling the concept of prayer as "a marvelous and necessary supplement" to sustained and tireless human initiative and efforts.[91] "As a minister," King asserted, "I take prayer too seriously to use it as an excuse for avoiding work and responsibility."[92] "But if you end up doing nothing but praying," he declared in a sermon one Sunday morning, "we will be living in segregation two or three hundred years from now."[93] This type of instruction proved beneficial not only in the struggle, but in how his people went about pursuing their liturgical choices and practices in those challenging and tension-packed days.

The creativity that marked the various forms and uses of prayer in the movement owed much to King's thinking and leadership. He inspired those who marched and went to jail with him to consider new ways of praying or prayer expression outside the church setting. Influenced by the Sermon on the Mount in the New Testament, he made Jesus's admonition to "pray for those who persecute" and "despitefully use you" (Matt 5:44) a recurring theme in many of the prayers and statements he delivered at mass meetings, and was a spiritual source for others who did likewise. King also frequently called for and was the keynote speaker at celebrations of "a Day of Prayer," "an Annual Week of Prayer," and "prayer pilgrimages," and occasionally led "prayer vigils," "prayer marches," "prayer campaigns," "prayer rallies," and "kneel-ins," mostly across parts of the South.[94] Moreover, King figured prominently

91. King, *Strength to Love,* 131–33; Carson et al., eds., *Papers,* 5:215; Carson et al., eds., *Papers,* 6:85 and 590–91; and Baldwin, *Never to Leave Us Alone,* 87.

92. Here King's comments were aimed at the great evangelist Billy Graham, who called on President Lyndon B. Johnson "to declare a national day of prayer" in response to racially charged riots in 1965. Apparently, King could see that the abuse and misuse of prayer or using prayer as an escape from social and ethical responsibility were far more pervasive in white churches than in black churches. See King, *Trumpet of Conscience,* 59; and Long, "Review," 110.

93. King, "Answer to a Perplexing Question," 9–11; and Baldwin, *Never to Leave Us Alone,* 149n78.

94. Carson et al., eds., *Papers,* 6:50; Carson et al., eds., *Papers,* 3:291 and 353; Harry Belafonte, *My Song: A Memoir* (New York: Alfred A. Knopf, 2011), 243; "Why Our Prayer Vigil?," Group Statement of the Negotiating Committee of the Albany Movement and Its Chief Consultants, Dr. Martin Luther King Jr. and Dr. Ralph D. Abernathy, unpublished document,

in reclaiming and making the prayer circle, a longstanding practice in the history and traditions of black churches, dating back to slavery,[95] perhaps the most important ritual of the civil rights movement. This was a period during which experimentation with prayer, song, sermon, and other art forms was in vogue, and the union of the prayer circle and the picket line actually epitomized the merging of the spiritual and political in King's consciousness and in King-led freedom campaigns. King often reminded his followers that the power was ultimately in the prayer circle,[96] in which the faithful combined song with reverent petitions to God, and not in police clubs, attack dogs, cattle prods, water hoses, or dingy jail cells. Here the notion of prayer as creative energy took on yet another layer of meaning.

King was instrumental in enlarging the black prayer tradition. On the one hand, he made that tradition relevant to a mass movement of nonviolent direct action. Although prayer had always been a central ingredient for blacks involved in movements for social change, King and his followers were the first to make such a disciplined and creative use of prayer in a church-centered, nonviolent crusade for freedom, justice, peace, and equality. King saw the movement as an outpouring of God's spirit upon the nation, and prayer went hand in hand with his spirited call for peaceful resistance to systemic social evil in all forms. Both the discipline of prayer and the discipline of nonviolence became for him a daily activity and a total way of life. By infusing prayer into civil rights campaigns, King and his followers became the very embodiment of prayer as cre-

Albany, Georgia (1962), KCLA, 1–2; "Transcript of the WINS-News Conference: An Interview with Martin Luther King, Jr.," WINS RADIO 1010, New York (31 May 1964), unpublished version, KCLA, 4; King, *Stride toward Freedom*, 137–38; and Baldwin, *Never to Leave Us Alone*, 21–22 and 115n63. As the NBA superstar Lebron James has suggested, the kneel-ins at professional football games, started by Colin Kaepernick in 2016, are very much in the tradition of King's civil rights campaigns. See Adam K. Raymond, "Lebron James Compares 'Blackballed' Colin Kaepernick to Martin Luther King and Muhammad Ali," *Maxim* (20 November 2017), https://tinyurl.com/ycjgt8dz.

95. The prayer circle was part of that larger phenomenon that Sterling Stuckey, in his treatment of the culture of African American slaves and their descendants, calls "the circle of culture." Stuckey's primary focus is on the ring shout, which also included prayer and song as well. See Stuckey, *Slave Culture*, viii–ix and 3–97; Carter, *Prayer Tradition of Black People*, 28–29; Baldwin, *Never to Leave Us Alone*, 15; *Every Evening*, Wilmington, Delaware (28 August 1882): 1; *The Delaware State Journal*, Wilmington, Delaware (30 August 1883): 1; *The Evening Journal*, Wilmington, Delaware (27 August 1888): 4; and Baldwin, *"Invisible" Strands in African Methodism*, 137–40, 218, and 224–25.

96. Some clue as to how this sense of the spiritual and the political came together for King is apparent in this statement from him: "For to deny a person the right to exercise his political freedom at the polls is no less a dastardly act as to deny a Christian the right to petition God in prayer." See Martin Luther King Jr., "Let My People Vote," unpublished statement, prepared for *New York Amsterdam News*, New York (19 June 1965), KCLA, 1.

ative energy while also lending credence to the image of black people as "a creative minority."[97]

On the other hand, King was largely responsible for bringing the resources of the black prayer tradition to life for people outside of the ranks of the black church. In other words, many white people of different faith traditions—Protestants, Catholics, and Jews—had their first real exposure to the traditions associated with folk praying through their involvement in King-led civil rights campaigns. These whites seemingly shared King's view of prayer as an essential ingredient of both spiritual devotion and social activism. Images of King and other black preachers praying in Albany, Selma, and other places, while encircled by black and white clergy and laity, are etched in the memories of movement activists and documented in some of the photo-biographies, photographic histories, and other collections of pictures from that era. The power of the black worship experience was made accessible to white Protestants, Catholics, and Jews through the prayer circle. By word and example, King actually pioneered in making prayer an engaging factor in advancing the spirit of interreligious dialogue and cooperation in the interest of human freedom, a contribution unprecedented for preachers and pastors in both the black church and the larger American church traditions. Obviously, King felt that reviving the prayerful experience and making it relevant to social movements for justice stood as the perpetual responsibility of people of all faiths everywhere.[98]

The content of this chapter shows that King approached life in a prayerful mood and attitude. Clearly, prayer grounded every aspect of his personal and public life, and was a critical component of that which linked him, in matters of spirit, to other humans, across the boundaries of race, religion, and nationality. In one sense, prayer was the voice of his soul—the entry point into the nature of his own inner self, of his spirituality and/or religious experience. In another sense, it was his way of witnessing on behalf of others, for he was fully convinced that spirituality in terms of personal and communal prayer and spirituality in the form of social outreach and activism could never be antithetical but intrinsically related to and dependent upon each other.

97. Here King was heavily influenced by Henry David Thoreau, the nineteenth century social critic and advocate for civil disobedience, who "believed in the effectiveness of a creative minority who serve the state by resisting it with the intention of improving it." For King, blacks in America constituted that "creative minority." See John J. Ansbro, *Martin Luther King, Jr.: The Making of a Mind* (Maryknoll, NY: Orbis, 1982), 111; Baldwin, *Never to Leave Us Alone*, 21 and 67–68; and Lewis V. Baldwin, *The Voice of Conscience: The Church in the Mind of Martin Luther King, Jr.* (New York: Oxford University Press, 2010), 7 and 112.

98. Baldwin, *Never to Leave Us Alone*, 22.

7.

To Tell the Truth: Martin Luther King Jr.'s Preaching and Spirituality

MERVYN A. WARREN

> No pleasure is comparable to the standing upon the vantage-ground of truth.
>
> —Francis Bacon[1]

> He who lives with untruth lives in spiritual slavery. Freedom is still the bonus we receive for knowing the truth.
>
> —Martin Luther King Jr.[2]

Steamy hot Chicago. August 31, 1966. Motoring down the Dan Ryan Expressway. Crosscurrents of racial tension testing the "Windy City." Attitudes as torrid as the weather imperil the civil rights crusade led by Martin Luther King Jr. Truth to tell, I am nervous. Being in the car with him has to be nothing short of a distraction to him, so I'm thinking. But he has a broader vision and grasp of the moment. Allowing me to shadow him for academic purposes hints of potential value to the struggle for human rights and social justice. With his assistant Andrew Young at the wheel, Dr. King and I are talking about my doctoral research at Michigan State University, focusing on him as pastor and preacher more than a civil rights activist. My interview list is long, and time is of the essence. A speaking engagement awaits King that evening. Nevertheless,

1. John Bartlett, *The Shorter Bartlett's Familiar Quotations: A Collection of Passages, Phrases, and Proverbs Traced to Their Sources in Ancient and Modern Literature*, ed. Christopher Morley and Louella D. Everett (New York: Pocket Books, 1964), 15.

2. Martin Luther King Jr., *Where Do We Go from Here: Chaos or Community?* (New York: Harper & Row, 1967), 67.

I am invited to his motel should I need more time. My mind wonders. Am I dreaming?

How did all this happen? Am I really in an uninterrupted, private, face-to-face conversation with *Time* magazine's "Man of the Year" (January 3, 1964)? Is not he the Nobel Peace Prize recipient of 1964, the twelfth American to receive the award and, as a thirty-five-year-old, the youngest ever to be so honored? This privileged moment to interview Dr. King was no happenstance, for it resulted from the efforts and courtesy of Dr. Robert Green, Professor of Education at Michigan State University and an African American who had marched with King in Selma, and of Dora McDonald, personal secretary to Dr. King and his Southern Christian Leadership Conference (SCLC). Of course, King himself had to approve.

Among the myriad of questions I planned to ask King, one in particular stands out in the context of his *preaching* and *spirituality*. My research had traced his steps through his earliest theological fundamentalism while growing up in his home community of faith, the Ebenezer Baptist Church in Atlanta, pastored by his father, Martin Luther King Sr. Possessing a growing appetite for intellectual growth, however, young King turned to liberalism and neo-orthodoxy, both of which provided tones to that "Social Gospel" that some felt limited societal solutions only to secular means. One of my questions to Dr. King elicited his response to those critics who were labeling him un-Christian and non-biblical because of what they saw as his acceptance of an extreme liberal Social Gospel that embraced a this-worldly mindset, and also his reliance on what some regarded as secular means to accomplish spiritual ends. To some of his critics, King wore two masks—one religious to appeal to the psyche of "one nation under God, indivisible, with liberty and justice for all," and the other a secular-philosophical core that, according to others, really defined his central self. So I had to put to him this question: "Dr. King, are you aware that your all-consuming dedication for social justice on this present earth leads some critics to conclude that you believe in an extreme social gospel which views this world as the ultimate goal of all humanity?" Without hesitation, he responded: "I do not claim to know all the details about the furniture of heaven or the temperature of hell, but I definitely believe in an afterlife prepared by God for His people."[3]

This ready response from King would not have answered all queries from critics about his quasi-liberalism and neo-orthodoxy, theological positions that offered solutions for human tragedy in a this-worldly

3. Mervyn A. Warren, *King Came Preaching: The Pulpit Power of Dr. Martin Luther King, Jr.* (Downers Grove, IL: InterVarsity Press, 2001), 123.

"Kingdom of God" that preclude any afterlife, and yet King's faith expressions in God's eternity beyond this earthly sojourn spoke volumes for his personal faith and spiritual landscape. I propose that the same devoted focus undergirded also his pulpit and podium proclamations.

PROFILES OF SPIRITUALITY

If we take seriously the idea that the content of the preacher influences the content of the sermon, then we understand and hear a distinct homiletic overtone emanating from the words of Jesus Christ as he commissions the apostle Peter: "When you are converted, strengthen thy brethren" (Luke 22:32 KJV). Perhaps even more clearly, this preacher-spirituality relationship discloses itself during a second conversation between Jesus and Peter, when Jesus took Peter on a tripartite love tour. Following a confession by the loquacious apostle; "Lord, you know all things; you know that I love you," Peter receives ratification when Jesus commissions him: "Feed my sheep" (John 21:17 NIV). I would say that Quintilian, a contemporary of New Testament apostles and a classical rhetorician who lived and taught in the first century CE, was on to something when he inextricably linked speaker and ethical appeals. One of his quotes profiling the perfect public speaker maintains that: "Since an orator, then, is a good man, and a good man cannot be conceived to exist without virtuous inclinations . . . , the orator must above all things study morality, and must obtain a thorough knowledge of all that is just and honorable, without which no one can either be a *good* man or an *able* speaker."[4]

You may have seen a recurring condensation of this description by Quintilian as: "Speaking is a good man speaking well." By the second, third, and fourth centuries CE, the post–New Testament church included converted practitioners and teachers of public discourse like Origen (ca. 185–ca. 254), John Chrysostom (ca. 347–407), and Augustine (ca. 354–430), who applied rhetorical principles to the preaching of the Christian gospel where expected *spirituality* in the pulpit was not unconventional. For a definition, spirituality in the Biblical context would refer to *a regenerate person, one who is enlightened by the Holy Spirit in contrast to someone given over to carnality or worldliness* (1 Cor 2:13, 15; 3:1). In the context of our present discussion, the spiritual minister receives preaching, leadership, organization, and other gifts from the Holy Spirit for the edification and equipping of the church (Rom 12:6–8;

4. Lester Thonssen and A. Craig Baird, *Speech Criticism: The Development of Standards for Rhetorical Appraisal* (New York: Ronald, 1948), 92, emphasis mine.

1 Cor 12:4–11, 28–31; Eph 4:11–13). The called and chosen then go forth credentialed both as *prophet* and *priest* seeking love, justice, equality, hope, and ultimate salvation for all humankind and for the advancement of the kingdom of God in this world and for the world to come.

How did the spirituality of Martin Luther King Jr. the preacher come into play to further his summons for equality and human rights? In what ways did his spirituality profile itself? King himself understood the inevitable interrelation between spiritual substance and the person and voiced it powerfully on August 28, 1963, in his immemorial speech at the March on Washington. Who does not remember his run of anaphora: "I have a dream . . . I have a dream . . . I have a dream . . . I have a dream"? The specific "dream" he envisioned that forever lingers tenderly yet forcefully with us is that someday his four little children would be "judged not by the color of their skin but by the content of their character." Out of the fertile soil of one's essential being, spirituality profiles itself first through *character* recognition. The preacher is perceived and without words registers himself up front in the public eye as a minister of the gospel of Jesus Christ. His integral Christ affiliation generates high expectations and even credibility probably beyond that afforded some social activists, politicians, or community activists who, for whatever reason, tend to steer clear of pronounced religious affinity except for relying on the church for a captive audience and on pastors for necessary support. Unquestionably, the strong perception of King's character and spirituality breeds high credibility.

Another profile of King's spirituality was reflected in his *ethics,* which allowed people to believe that he would do the right thing, because he in fact "sat where they sat." Having been born and raised in the South, where he, too, tasted harsh racism himself, King was perceived as a genuine person of like passion and persecution and, therefore, one who really felt the hurts and knew the hopes of his followers and supporters. Consequently, his preaching and leadership were generally persuasive without serious or impeding dissonance between what he said and what he did. *Time* noted that King "has an indescribable capacity for empathy that is the touchstone of leadership."[5] We may identify this profile as *ethics* or *ethical* appeal, which King himself esteemed when he said: "One must not only preach a sermon with his voice, he must preach it with his life." With this in mind, Ernest Dunbar, senior editor of *Look*, added that "King does just that."[6]

Not infrequently, one's prideful position of privilege reacts negatively

5. "Man of the Year: Never Again Where He Was," *Time*, 83, no. 1 (3 January 1964): 14.
6. Ernest Dunbar, "A Visit with Martin Luther King," *Look* (12 February 1963): 96.

to personal attacks by retaliating with rejoinders like "Do you not know who I am?," or "Your scummy level is below my dignity and not worthy of my response." Fully aware of his elevated reputation as a national leader for justice with numberless accolades to his credit, and steeped in a spirituality that encouraged peaceful resistance in the face of evil, King absorbed beatings, repeated jailings (more than twenty times), a stabbing, bombings of his home, and a variety of other attacks on his person and property. Nevertheless, he consistently took the high road and "turned the other cheek" (Matt 5:39). In other words, he evinced the profiles of *humility* and *love,* the former of which reflects the quality of living devoid of haughtiness, arrogance, or hubris; while the latter at its best reveals agape—the quality of bestowing unconditional favor. King's sermon, "Paul's Letter to American Christians," carries an affirmation that challenges us all to the core: "Even if physical death is the price that some must pay to free their children from psychological death, then nothing could be more Christian."[7] I find the two profiles of *humility* and *love* operating in such intimate relational functionality on King's spiritual landscape until I merged them together here while fully aware that each can easily stand alone and doubtless deserves more attention than afforded here. On the one hand, I would not claim that humility and love have a Siamese twins relatedness; on the other hand, however, I do perceive an extraordinarily close connection between them that is akin to that of sister and brother. Take a look at their interaction in the kenotic experience of Jesus Christ in Philippians 2. There the apostle to the gentiles declares, "If you have any encouragement from being united with Christ, if any comfort from his *love*, if any fellowship with the Spirit, if any tenderness and compassion, then make my joy complete by being like-minded, having the same *love*, being one in spirit and purpose. Do nothing out of selfish ambition or vain conceit, but in *humility* consider others better than yourselves. . . . Your attitude should be the same as that of Jesus Christ: Who, being in very nature God, did not consider equality with God something to be grasped, but made himself nothing" (Phil 2:1–7, emphasis mine).

Yet another component of the spirituality of Dr. King is observed in his *competence* as a spiritual gift honed and informed by education and experience. He was known to possess essential qualifications and abilities to deliver what his preaching promised and to attain that which was expected of him. King's success in reaching a high level of competence, spiritually and in terms of his resistance to social evil, is attested

7. Martin Luther King Jr., *Strength to Love* (Philadelphia: Fortress, 1981; originally published in 1963), 144.

to by a statement from a leading theologian, L. Harold DeWolf, who had been King's teacher at Boston University: "Martin Luther King, Jr. is an able religious thinker, as well as a man of action."[8] As a scholar, the young minister from Atlanta appealed to both African Americans and Caucasians of the middle and upper classes. The fact that King was not a "jack-leg" preacher but, rather, one who had undergone academic study at the college, seminary, and graduate school levels, tended to enhance people's confidence in his competence to carry out the responsibilities and expectations of the ministerial office.

King's competence should not be considered a product of accident or chance. Even as a youth, he wanted to possess rather than merely simulate proficiency; and while his Christian parents taught him to believe the "church was the path to morality and immortality," he was also taught that "education was . . . the path to competence."[9] By differentiating between King and W. E. B. DuBois, Carl T. Rowan, successor to Edward R. Murrow and former director of the US Information Agency, contrasted the two different roads that competence, with or without spirituality, might lead the influential spokesperson when stakes are exceedingly high for all humankind:

> [Du Bois and King] personify the colored man's quandary: whether to fight hate with hate or with love. Du Bois is an old man whose cup of racial bitterness runneth over—a nonagenarian brooding out his last days in a desperate admiration of things Russian and an irreconcilable hatred of things white American. King, a mere thirty, is a bright new intellectual general in America's racial wars, unique in that he offers the refuge of love to those who might follow Du Bois down that forlorn trail of bitterness. . . . Martin Luther King brings to his mission a belief in the power of religion to move men; Du Bois never did . . . . And one cannot escape the concomitant hope that love can—indeed, will—be the powerful, saving force that the young man from Montgomery thinks it is.[10]

Looking back over the years since 1959, when Rowan first penned these words in the context of race and equality in America, there might be a consensus that love accompanying competence has indeed accomplished more than hate. At its best in human relations, love, as King understood it and gave voice to it in his sermons, exerts itself through nonviolent

8. L. Harold DeWolf, *Present Trends in Christian Thought* (New York: Association, 1960), 18.

9. Lawrence D. Reddick, *Crusader without Violence: A Biography of Martin Luther King, Jr.* (New York: Harper & Brothers, 1959), 51.

10. Carl T. Rowan, "Heart of a Passionate Dilemma," *The Saturday Review* 42 (August 1, 1959): 20–21.

direct action and speaking truth to power in various ways and on varied levels.

Finally, I submit *goodwill* as a spiritual profile revealing itself in the life and labor of Dr. King as preacher. Goodwill may be defined accordingly: a personal quality of friendliness, congeniality, likeableness, rapport, concern, interest, and a desire to reach out and help others. Although in some sense the King mystique was almost inexplicable and tinged with pensiveness, he remained a clear, living, practical, helping hand for humanity, albeit a disturbing reality to some. A *Time* writer summed it up quite succinctly: "By deed and by preachment, he stirred in his people a Christian forbearance that nourishes hope and smothers injustice."[11] King's close friend and fellow churchman Ralph D. Abernathy has been quoted as saying: "He is a humble man, down to earth, honest. He has proved his commitment to Judaeo-Christian ideals. He seeks to save the nation and its soul, not just the Negro." But let us not "gild the lily." Were there challenges to the ethos of Dr. King? Of course. He faced such accusations as (1) leading civil rights activities that were communist inspired and controlled; (2) being a prevaricator; (3) offending and rendering other African Americans helpless with his doctrine of nonviolence; (4) misusing the pulpit for sociopolitical activities; (5) employing nonbiblical sources to support Bible concepts, a practice some condemned as un-Christian; (6) plagiarism; and (7) adultery.[12] Truth is its own best defense and always wins out ultimately. Furthermore, truth can never be more powerful and effective than when corroborated by a truthful life. Meanwhile, one truth is undeniable: our social, political, economic, and religious world experiences are immeasurably better due largely to the spiritual resources that nurtured the ministry, preaching, and leadership of Dr. Martin Luther King Jr.

THAT TRUTH BE TOLD

Remember the Dan Ryan Freeway car ride and interview with Dr. King in Chicago, which I referenced at the beginning of this chapter? King's response to my particular inquiry mentioned there pertained to his theology. Another question that our conversation addressed sheds light on his understanding of preaching, which he shared with me: "A good, solid sermon has to have three elements which I call 'three p's': it proves an appeal to the intellect, it paints an appeal to the imagination, and it per-

11. "Man of the Year," 14.

12. For a discussion of each of these challenges, see Warren, *King Came Preaching*, 80–86.

suades an appeal to the heart."[13] Wisely, in my opinion, King described a balanced tripartite preaching appeal directed to the listener's mind (or volition), creativity, and emotions, thus allowing three avenues for truth to reach and influence decision-making. By truth, I submit here a two-dimensional determination operative in the Christian worldview. First, truth intellectually is that which coheres with reality, exists, and includes a moral and spiritual dimension with the Bible serving as the principal written source. Second, truth finds its embodiment in Jesus Christ, who says: "I am the Way, the Truth, and the Life" (John 14:6).

King endeavored to "tell the truth" by accomplishing generally two things; namely, calling attention to the unjust suffering of African Americans in America as the most ostracized, marginalized, and forgotten citizenry, and declaring that the Judeo-Christian God is available and willing to participate in solving the problem. Truth would demand, however, that while the main focus of King was principally the conditions of black people, reality widened the circle appropriately to include others among the "poor," "neglected," and "homeless," irrespective of race, class, national origin, or religion. Revisiting some of King's sermons will expose us to the content of truth that King brilliantly applied to human rights issues of American life and life as a whole. And we see again his genius for clothing prophetic content with word symbols without sounding pedantic, without "dumbing down" his message, and in ways appreciated by the educated and understood even by the uneducated.

TELLING THE TRUTH: THE VOICE OF SPIRITUALITY

Clearly, King began ministering more in the prophetic than the priestly function the moment he heard the voice of God in his kitchen in Montgomery in January 1957, confirming his call to lead in that city's bus boycott. While continuing his pastoral (priestly, mediator) role in terms of nurturing the church members, increasingly King led them prophetically into new and appropriate spheres of witness in their social and cultural environment. He quite pointedly said during our Chicago conversation in 1966: "As a minister of the Gospel, I have a priestly function and a prophetic function."[14] Reinforcing this perspective, Dr. Walter G. Muelder, Dean of the School of Theology at Boston University, the alma mater of King, couched it pungently when he remarked: "King took the gospel from behind stained-glass windows and placed it on courthouse

13. See Warren, *King Came Preaching*, 90–91.
14. Personal interview with Martin Luther King Jr., Chicago, Illinois (3 August 1966).

steps."[15] There and everywhere else he struggled, King, when given a hearing, told the truth with a consciousness of being grounded and fortified by "his prophetic demands in the holiness . . . [and] . . . righteousness of God."[16] Such a divine grounding surely afforded the King ethos and persona a credible and authentic spirituality that facilitated situational expectations, enhanced the preaching moment, and persuaded hearers to gird up their faith and hope because a better day was coming. The following excerpts will allow brief snapshots from sermons by King that both summarize the particular truth conveyed while also providing another glance into his spiritual values and commitment.

TRUTH THROUGH "GOD"

The most explicit expression of King's doctrine of God is found in his sermon, "The Death of Evil upon the Seashore," where God is described as a supernatural being or spirit who possesses the quality of omnipotence, that is, unlimited power: "Above all, we must be reminded anew that God is at work in his universe. He is not outside the world looking on with a sort of cold indifference. Here on all the roads of life, he is striving in our striving. Like an ever-loving Father, he is working through history for the salvation of his children. As we struggle to defeat the forces of evil, the God of the universe struggles with us."[17] Here King discredits what are essentially deistic and Aristotelian notions of God, while also associating divine truth with the omnipotent God who struggles with and for his people in the triumph over evil.

TRUTH THROUGH "JESUS CHRIST"

Divinity clothed in humanity summarizes the biblical Jesus Christ as understood and proclaimed by Dr. King. According to King, Christ came to humankind for the purpose of revealing God in spirit and in truth: "Where do we find this God? In a test tube? No. Where else but in Jesus Christ, the Lord of our lives? By knowing Christ we know God. Christ is not only God-like but God is Christ-like. Christ is the word made flesh. He is the language of eternity translated in the words of time.

15. Personal interview with Walter G. Muelder, Boston, Massachusetts (4 March 1966).

16. Richard Lischer, "Anointed with Fire: The Structure of Prophecy in the Sermons of Martin Luther, Jr.," in Timothy George et al., eds., *Our Sufficiency Is of God: Essays on Preaching in Honor of Gardner C. Taylor* (Macon, GA: Mercer University Press, 2010), 229–33, 240.

17. This and all sermons by Dr. King referenced by title in this essay are from either books authored by King or collections of his sermons in books by certain King scholars. See King, *Strength to Love*, 83.

If we are to know what God is like, and understand his purposes for humankind, we must turn to Christ. By committing ourselves absolutely to Christ and his way, we will be participating in that marvelous act of faith that will bring us to the true knowledge of God." These ideas are repeatedly echoed throughout King's sermon, "The Three Dimensions of a Complete Life," in which Christ is imaged as one in spirit with God the Father.[18] They reveal a concept of God that is largely Christocentric.

TRUTH THROUGH THE "HOLY SPIRIT"

Admittedly, I have been less than absolutely successful to my satisfaction in identifying among the published sermons of King explicit references to the "Holy Spirit." Although his sermons are replete with such expressions as "spirit," "spiritual," "spiritually," "being of spirit [man]," "his spirit [God]," "spirit of Christ," "Jesus's spirit," and "your Spirit" (the latter in Ps 139:7; note capital "S" in some Bible versions, probably interpreted as "Holy Spirit," but lower case "s" in King James Version), this is not so much the case with "Holy Spirit." I do recall, however, a recording of King preaching a sermon, at the close of which he offers the benediction with the traditional conclusion: "in the name of the Father, the Son, and the Holy Spirit." If my recollection, which I will not push too fervently, is reliable about the benediction, then I can claim that King believed in the Trinity without necessarily making frequent mention of the third member of the Godhead. Furthermore, I submit the following from his sermon, "Shattered Dreams," which I firmly believe is more than just an implicit allusion to the Holy Spirit: "Our capacity to deal creatively with shattered dreams is ultimately determined by our faith in God. Genuine faith imbues us with the conviction that beyond time is a *divine Spirit* and beyond life is Life."[19]

TRUTH THROUGH THE "CHURCH"

When calling the church the body of Christ in his sermon, "Paul's Letter to American Christians," King depicts a mystical relation between the church and its spiritual leader, Jesus Christ. The sermon, "Love in Action," declares that the church is the chief moral guardian of the community and, thereby, is charged to implore humanity to be "good" and

18. Martin Luther King Jr., *The Measure of a Man* (Philadelphia: Fortress, 1988; originally published in 1959), 9–56; and Warren, *King Came Preaching*, 126.

19. Quoted in Warren, *King Came Preaching*, 126; and King, *Strength to Love*, 95, emphasis added.

"well-intentioned" and must extol "conscientiousness" as well as "kind-heartedness." Not only does humanity look to the church, as the body of Christ, for moral guidance, but the church, as King proclaimed, should disconnect itself from the status quo, or society's tendency to be apathetic about appropriate change, and unequivocally address economic deprivation and corrupt political and social systems. This is also the message coursing through other King sermons, such as "A Knock at Midnight." The question becomes: How must the church relate to the state? The same sermon asserts that "The church must be reminded once again that it is not to be the master or the servant of the state, but the conscience of the state. It must be the guide and the critic of the state—never its tool. As long as the church is a tool of the state it will be unable to provide even a modicum of bread for men at midnight." The fact of a "white" church and "black" church disturbs King to the core and wrings from his soul the painful admission that "eleven o'clock on Sunday morning, when we stand to sing 'In Christ There Is No East or West,' is the most segregated hour of America."[20] In his indictment of the Christian church in general, King does not fail, in "A Knock at Midnight," to chide the so-called Negro church in particular for breeding within its ranks two ineffective extremes that too often stifle genuine spirituality, from pulpit to pew:

> Two types of Negro churches have failed to provide bread. One burns with emotionalism, and the other freezes with classism. The former, reducing worship to entertainment, places more emphasis on volume than on content, and confuses spirituality with muscularity. The danger in such a church is that the members may have more religion in their hands and feet than in their hearts and souls. At midnight this type of church has neither the vitality nor the relevant gospel to feed hungry souls. The other type of Negro church that feeds no midnight traveler has developed a class system and boasts of its dignity, its membership of professional people, and its exclusiveness. In such a church the worship service is cold and meaningless, the music dull and uninspiring, and the sermon little more than a homily on current events. If the pastor says too much about Jesus Christ, the members feel that he is robbing the pulpit of dignity. If the choir sings a Negro spiritual, the members claim an affront to their class status. This type of church tragically fails to recognize that worship at its best is a social experience in which people from all levels of life come together to affirm their oneness and unity under God.[21]

20. See King, *Strength to Love*, 62; and Martin Luther King Jr., "An Address before the National Press Club" (19 July 1962), in James M. Washington, ed., *A Testament of Hope: The Essential Writings and Speeches of Martin Luther King, Jr.* (San Francisco: Harper & Row, 1986), 101.

21. Washington, ed., *Testament of Hope*, 501–2; and King, *Strength to Love*, 62–63.

Undoubtedly, the church as the custodian of spirituality and the nurturer of the sustained spiritual life stood at the center of Dr. King's sermonic proclamations. This was how he defined the church not only in relation to humanity, but also in connection to the Trinity.

TRUTH THROUGH THE "PREACHER"

References in King's sermons to the state of the ministerial profession reveal a dissatisfaction similar to that he directed at some churches. He never ceased to target those preachers who too often conform when they should transform, frequently preaching sermons irrelevant to the real needs of their hearers. Such preachers, King held, apparently feel safe when functioning within the physical and philosophical walls of the church building itself. In versions of his sermon on "Transformed Nonconformist," King voiced dissatisfaction with preachers who "often joined the enticing cult of conformity." He conceded:

> We, too, have often yielded to the success symbols of the world, feeling that the size of our ministry must be measured by the size of our automobiles. Too often we turn into showmen, distorting the real meaning of the gospel, in an attempt to appeal to the whims and caprices of the crowd. We preach soothing sermons that bypass the weightier matters of Christianity. We dare not say anything . . . that will question the respectable views of the comfortable members of our congregations. If you want to get ahead in the ministry, conform! Stay within the secure walls of the sanctuary. Play it safe. How many ministers of Jesus Christ have sacrificed truth on the altar of their self-interest, and, like Pilate, yielded their convictions to the demands of the crowd?[22]

Preaching was one mode through which King criticized preachers and called them to the true task and cost of discipleship, but he never stopped here. Commendations to ministers are made in King's contrasting the "pastor" from the "prophet." The major and/or primary role and calling he embraced for himself was defined in the latter:

> Any discussion of the role of the Christian minister today must ultimately emphasize the need for prophecy. Not every minister can be a prophet, but some must be prepared for the ordeals of this high calling and be willing

22. See Clayborne Carson et al., eds., *The Papers of Martin Luther King, Jr.: Advocate of the Social Gospel, September 1948–March 1963* (Berkeley: University of California Press, 2007), 6:196–97 and 472–73; and Martin Luther King Jr., "Transformed Nonconformist," unpublished version of a sermon, Ebenezer Baptist Church, Atlanta, Georgia (16 January 1966), Library and Archives of the Martin Luther King Jr. Center for Nonviolent Social Change (KCLA), Atlanta, Georgia.

to suffer courageously for righteousness. May the problem of race in America soon make hearts burn so that prophets will rise up, saying, "Thus saith the Lord," and cry out as Amos did, ". . . let justice roll down like waters, and righteousness like an ever-flowing stream." Fortunately, a few in the South have already been willing to follow the prophetic way. I have nothing but praise for these ministers of the gospel of Jesus Christ and rabbis of the Jewish faith who have stood unflinchingly before threats and intimidations, inconvenience and unpopularity, even at times in physical danger, to declare the doctrine of the Fatherhood of God and the brotherhood of man. For such noble servants of God there is the consolation of the words of Jesus: "Blessed are ye, when men shall revile you, and persecute you, and shall say all manner of evil against you falsely, for my sake. Rejoice, and be exceedingly glad: for great is your reward in heaven: for so persecuted they the prophets, which were before you."[23]

TRUTH THROUGH "PRAYER"

King strongly believed, consistently practiced, and urgently advocated the experience of prayer as confirmed by all his biographies and personal papers in the M. L. King Collection at the Boston University Library.[24] His habit of beginning and ending his sermons with prayer, and of reciting short prayer lines while delivering sermons, reveals as much or more about the relationship between his preaching and his spirituality than anything else. King's preaching and his nonviolent direct action organizational meetings and activities were consistently reinforced by special days of prayer and fasting. Remember the Prayer Pilgrimage to the Lincoln Memorial, May 17, 1957? This occasion of united and consolidated prayer proved pivotal and moved King beyond being a nationally and internationally known preacher to becoming the number-one spokesman for African Americans.[25] The fervent desire of King was that people would place prayer in a practical perspective, as stated in his sermon, "The Answer to a Perplexing Question":

> The idea that man must wait on God to do everything has led to a tragic misuse of prayer. He who feels that God must do everything will end up asking him for anything. Some people see God as little more than "a cosmic bellhop" that they will call on for every trivial need. Others see God as so omnipotent and man so powerless that they end up making prayer a substitute for work and intelligence. A man said to me the other day: "I believe in

23. Martin Luther King Jr., *Stride toward Freedom: The Montgomery Story* (New York: Harper & Row, 1958), 210.

24. See Martin Luther King Jr., *"Thou, Dear God": Prayers That Open Hearts and Spirits—The Reverend Dr. Martin Luther King, Jr.*, ed. Lewis V. Baldwin (Boston: Beacon, 2012), 3–173.

25. Warren, *King Came Preaching*, 41, 136, and 158.

> integration, but I know it will not come until God gets ready for it to come. You Negroes should stop protesting and start praying." Well, I'm sure we all need to pray for God's help and guidance in this integration struggle. But we will be gravely misled if we think it will come by prayer alone. God will never allow prayer to become a substitute for work and intelligence. God gave us minds to think and breath and body to work, and he would be defeating his own purpose if he allowed us to obtain through prayer what can come through work and intelligence. No, it is not either prayer *or* human effort; it is both prayer *and* human effort. Prayer is a marvelous and necessary supplement of our feeble efforts but it is a dangerous and callous substitute. Moses discovered this as he struggled to lead the Israelites to the Promised Land. God made it clear that he would not do for them what they could do for themselves. In the book of Exodus we read: "And the Lord said unto Moses, Wherefore criest thou unto me? Speak to the children of Israel, that they go forward."[26]

In references to prayer in his sermons, speeches, and interviews, King often associated prayer without deliberate, sustained, and concrete action with an empty, meaningless, and misguided spirituality. It was the kind of spirituality he associated with all too many black and white churches.

TRUTH THROUGH "FAITH"

Along with one's candid self-analysis, courage, love, and faith provide a remedy for fear in King's sermon, "Antidotes for Fear." Effectively contrasting the efficacy of human beings' religious faith with human trust in psychiatry and utopian hopes, King expounds:

> Abnormal fears and phobias that are expressed in neurotic anxiety may be cured by psychiatry; but the fear of death, non-being, and nothingness, expressed in existential anxiety, may be cured only by a positive religious faith. A positive religious faith does not offer an illusion that we shall be exempt from pain and suffering, nor does it imbue us with the idea that life is a drama of unalloyed comfort and untroubled ease. Rather, it instills us with the inner equilibrium needed to face strains, burdens, and fears that inevitably come, and assures us that the universe is trustworthy and that God is concerned.[27]

A serious analysis of this statement suggests some equivalency between faith and spirituality for King. The two carried overlapping meanings for

26. Martin Luther King Jr., "Answer to a Perplexing Question," unpublished version of a sermon, Ebenezer Baptist Church, Atlanta, Georgia (3 March 1963), KCLA, 9–11; King, *Strength to Love*, 131–32; and Carson et al., eds., *Papers*, 6:590–91.

27. Carson et al., eds., *Papers*, 6:317–21; and King, *Strength to Love,* 123.

him, and the words "religious experience," "faith," and "spirituality" were used interchangeably in some of his sermons to make the same point about the committed life—or the life devoted to the service of both God and humanity.

TRUTH THROUGH "GOOD AND EVIL"

The notion of dualistic forces in the universe, personalized in Scripture as God and Satan contending for supremacy, is quite prevalent in the sermons of King. These forces are irreconcilable opposites, and were known to King as "good" and "evil." "Good" eventually emerges as victor over "evil" in his sermon, "The Death of Evil upon the Seashore." The nature of humanity is dichotomized by these forces inasmuch as we are at once creatures formed in God's image (good) and also sinners (evil). King insists, in "The Answer to a Perplexing Question" and other sermons, that we must strive to cast out evil in all of its societal and personal forms, which "will not be [done] . . . by man alone nor by a dictatorial God who invades. It will be removed when we open the door and allow God through Jesus Christ to enter. 'Behold, I stand at the door and knock,' saith the Lord; 'if any man will open the door I will come in to him and sup with him and he with me.'"[28] Ultimately, humans must become co-workers or co-laborers with God in transforming the human condition for the better and in creating the climate for the full realization of the kingdom of God on earth.

TRUTH THROUGH "LOVE"

As queen of the virtues and attributes of God, love easily becomes the most recurring theological theme found in the messages of King. He proclaimed over and over again that love is the most powerful force in the universe, and that it must always be foundational to cries and causes for justice. In his sermon, "Love in Action," forgiveness is elevated as an active expression of love. The sermon, "Loving Your Enemies," presents essentially the identical treatment of love but emphasizes forgiveness as its empirical manifestation. The same pulpit proclamation goes beyond what King calls the "practical *how*" of loving enemies to the "theoretical *why*."[29]

28. King, "Answer to a Perplexing Question," 7–8; and King, *Strength to Love*, 136–37.

29. Martin Luther King Jr., *A Time to Break Silence: The Essential Works of Martin Luther King, Jr., for Students* (Boston: Beacon, 2013), 21; Clayborne Carson and Peter Holloran, eds., *A Knock*

I confess having a favorite among the quotes from the King love exhortations. It comes from "Loving Your Enemies":

> To our most bitter opponents we say: "We shall match your capacity to inflict suffering by our capacity to endure suffering. We shall meet your physical force with soul force. Do to us what you will, and we shall continue to love you. We cannot in all good conscience obey your unjust laws, because non-cooperation with evil is as much a moral obligation as is cooperation with good. Throw us in jail, and we shall still love you. Bomb our homes and threaten our children, and we shall still love you. Send your hooded perpetrators of violence into our community at the midnight hour and beat us and leave us half dead, and we shall still love you. But be ye assured that we will wear you down by our capacity to suffer. One day we shall win freedom, but not only for ourselves. We shall so appeal to your heart and conscience that we shall win *you* in the process, and our victory will be a double victory." Love is the most durable power in the world. This creative force, so beautifully exemplified in the life of our Christ, is the most potent instrument available in mankind's quest for peace and security.[30]

This quote is not simply about truth finding expression through the power of *agape* love. It is not merely about the spiritual resources of love, or love as a redemptive, transforming, and reconciling force. Clearly, it captures Dr. King's sense of being involved in a spiritual movement that was grounded in the best of spiritual and moral values, but it is, perhaps more importantly, a stirring affirmation that when love is organized into a social movement, it, much like truth, cannot be conquered. Redemptive suffering, redemptive victory, redemptive love! Truth nurtured in spirituality! In the summing up of things, what more shall we say but "Amen."

at Midnight: Inspiration from the Great Sermons of Reverend Martin Luther King, Jr. (New York: Warner, 1998), 41–60; and King, *Strength to Love*, 36–55.

30. Carson et al., eds., *Papers*, 6:428; and King, *Strength to Love*, 54–55.

8.

A "Spirituality of Improvisation": Martin Luther King Jr.'s "I Have a Dream" in Rearticulating American National Identity

NICHOLE R. PHILLIPS

> So I say to you, my friends, that even though we must face the difficulties of today and tomorrow, I still have a dream. It is a dream deeply rooted in the American dream. I have a dream that one day this nation will rise up and live out the true meaning of its creed: "We hold these truths to be self-evident, that all men are created equal. . . ." I have a dream that my four little children will one day live in a nation where they will not be judged by the color of their skin but by the content of their character. I have a dream today.
>
> —Martin Luther King Jr.[1]

> King's "I Have a Dream Speech" was a powerful and prophetic exposition of his civic vision of a flourishing and integrated future for the nation. However, King's "dream" speech was not the quintessential summary of his lifework.
>
> —Barbara A. Holmes and Susan Holmes Winfield[2]

Martin Luther King Jr.'s original manuscript did not contain the now famous "I Have a Dream" peroration. While speaking to a national audi-

1. Martin Luther King Jr., "I Have a Dream," in James M. Washington, ed., *A Testament of Hope: The Essential Writings and Speeches of Martin Luther King, Jr.* (New York: HarperCollins, 1991; originally published in 1986), 219; Martin Luther King, Jr., *The Autobiography of Martin Luther King, Jr.,* ed. by Clayborne Carson (New York: Warner, 1998), 226; and James M. Washington, ed., *I Have a Dream: Writings and Speeches That Changed the World* (New York: HarperCollins, 1992; originally published in 1986), 104.

2. Quoted in Lewis V. Baldwin, et al., *The Legacy of Martin Luther King, Jr.: The Boundaries of Law, Politics, and Religion* (Notre Dame: University of Notre Dame Press, 2002), 175.

ence on the Washington Mall on August 28, 1963, King inserts the "Dream" peroration at the prodding of gospel singer turned civil rights activist, Mahalia Jackson.[3] It comes at a critical juncture as he addresses post–World War II social and political conditions, primarily concerning race and civil rights in America. In this essay, I attribute the insertion of the peroration to what I name a "spirituality of improvisation," where King harnesses the creative nature of spirit and soul[4] illustrative of rhetoric that draws upon history, myth, and ritual to rearticulate American national identity. Philip Gorski argues for an American civil religion that describes the history and identity of the nation more so through collective symbols and beliefs than specific rituals as outward expressions of American political creeds.[5] However, King's "spirituality of improvisation" combines both ritual and creed, for he placed a demand on the civil religious[6] myth of America as a "city upon a hill,"[7] pushing him to risk

3. For other accounts, see Michael Eric Dyson, *I May Not Get There with You: The True Martin Luther King, Jr.* (New York: The Free Press, 2000), 143 and 280; and W. Jason Miller, *Origins of the Dream: Hughes's Poetry and King's Rhetoric* (Gainesville: University Press of Florida, 2015), 1-216; and Lewis V. Baldwin, "The Dream Language of Martin Luther King, Jr.," author's files, unpublished paper, 1-5.

4. Émile Durkheim, *The Elementary Forms of Religious Life*, trans. Carol Cosman (New York: Oxford University Press, 2008), 183–84, 187. Durkheim describes the soul as the "animating principle of life that continues, outlives the death of the body, and that reincarnates itself."

5. Philip S. Gorski, "Barack Obama and Civil Religion," *Political Power and Social Theory*, 22 (2011): 181–97.

6. Robert N. Bellah, "Civil Religion in America," *Journal of the American Academy of Arts and Sciences* 96, no. 1 (Winter 1967): 3. Bellah coined the term and described *American civil religion* as "certain common elements of religious orientation that the great majority of Americans share [and] that have played a crucial role in the development of American institutions . . . , including the political sphere. This public religious dimension is expressed in a set of beliefs, symbols, and rituals." *Civil religion* also expresses the deep-seated values, commitments, and ethical principles of a people, not articulated in everyday life. Throughout his academic career, Bellah wrote numerous articles, further developing and refining the definition of *civil religion* to include "the religious dimension of a people through which it interprets its historical experience in light of transcendent reality," and to reflect moral discourse based on civil religion being involved with the moral, religious, and political crises in America during times of trial. See Robert N. Bellah, *The Broken Covenant: American Civil Religion in Time of Trial* (Chicago: University of Chicago Press, 1992), 3; and Robert N. Bellah, "Civil Religion in America," in Russell E. Richey and Donald G. Jones, eds., *American Civil Religion* (New York: Harper & Row, 1974), 33.

7. Philip S. Gorski, "Barack Obama and Civil Religion," *Political Power and Social Theory* 22 (2011), 186 and 201. In this article, Gorski attempts to revive interest in the study of American civil religion, a concept initially presented by Robert Bellah. In his writing, he weighs three traditions demonstrating the relationship between religion and politics in America. Arguing along [Max] Weberian lines and in support of Bellah's Durkheimian approach, Gorski suggests that the civil religion tradition outperforms the other two competing traditions of religious nationalism and liberal secularism. To showcase this and to prove the strength of civil religion, he conducts a historical survey of leading civil theologians, from John Winthrop to Barack Obama. In the case of John Winthrop's metaphor, which compares America to a "city upon a hill" in Winthrop's now famous sermon, "Christian Charity," presented to the Puritan community, Gorski contends the church and civil society carry covenantal obligations and responsibilities

delivery in a public, institutional space by ritualizing and reframing the "Dream" that ultimately offered Americans a new collective social identity and embraced a racially and culturally plural nation.

RHETORICAL STRATEGY, SYMBOLISM, AND SOCIAL MOVEMENTS

Martin Luther King Jr. was a foremost thinker and leader of the 1950s–1960s multiracial but mostly black-led, grass-roots civil rights social movement in America. The Lincoln Memorial stood in the shadows as a cultural signifier of rights and freedom as well as religious and political liberty, both reinforcing and stimulating King's soaring oratory and social commentary on that hot August day. A movement "preacher and intellectual," King "infused his activism with a well-known set of symbols and rhetorical tools"[8] that sociologists of race, Michael Omi and Howard Winant, suggest such leaders need to grant social movements the ability to

> create collective identity by offering their adherents a different view of themselves and their world; different, that is, from the worldview and self-concepts offered by the established social order. Movements take elements and themes of existing cultures and traditions and infuse them with new meaning. This process of *rearticulation* produces new subjectivity by making use of information and knowledge already present in a subject's mind. Drawing on the insights of Antonio Gramsci, we [Omi and Winant] define *rearticulation* as a *practice of discursive reorganization or reinterpretation of ideo-*

to actualize the common good. Actualization happens when a citizenry is indebted to a sovereign God able to rise above the human affairs of the nation-state. He describes the "city upon a hill" metaphor as representing an early version of the American Dream. Later, he contrasts Winthrop's historical version of the American Dream to Martin Luther King Jr.'s more modern version, stating: "Two years earlier [King] had redefined [Winthrop's] dream as 'a dream yet unfulfilled'" (201). King's dream, writes Gorski, "[was] a modern version of Winthrop's dream [of] a land where men of all races, of all nationalities and of all creeds, can live together as brothers," best expressed in the words of the Preamble of the Declaration, which he cited in full.

8. Michael Omi and Howard Winant, *Racial Formation in the United States*, 3rd ed. (New York: Routledge, 2015), 165. Omi and Winant updates their classical text on a sociology of race, which views race through the lenses of US political life, from enslavement to present times. They also unfold a "theory of racial formation" situated at the intersection of social structure and cultural representation. Upon examining post–World War II racial politics, both sociologists argue that the 1960s black social movement inspired America's Great Transformation, as evidenced by the development of many other and *new social movements* in America and around the globe: anti-imperial, student, feminist, and gay (162), and *paradigm shifts* with respect to descriptions of race and ethnicity (161). These social movements, with the black movement at the helm organized around race, eventually broadened the interpretation and understanding of race in America while *rearticulating* group racial identities.

> *logical themes and interests already present in the subjects' consciousness, such that these elements obtain new meaning or coherence.* In Gramsci's account, this practice is ordinarily the work of "intellectuals," those whose role is to interpret the social world for given subjects—religious leaders, entertainers, school teachers.[9]

When King approached the podium to deliver a speech in the form of what would decidedly be a "topical sermon" engaging a "provocative topic, usually an existential and/or contemporary issue that can be related to the biblical text,"[10] freedom was on his mind and his focus on this most pressing subject culminated in the apogee of a dream advocating for the full equality and racial justice of black Americans.

In the process of delivering his rendition of the "dream," and with the force of a creative spirituality infusing him and by extension his national audience, King reconstrued the social world of all Americans, attaching new meaning to American collective identity in the presence of his listeners, many of whom had already a long-held and dogged grasp of the conception of "peoplehood" as the white nation.[11] In the United States, race and nation have historically been linked to the notion of "peoplehood."[12] However, "We the People" from the nation's founding had been equated with whiteness, and, consequently, this identification of white identity with America developed into an "anglo-conformity" that has influenced and shaped the national image and culture even up to the present time.[13]

Omi and Winant further explain that one of the components of a *nation-based paradigm of race* is observing that *race as peoplehood* implies the use of racial categories to distinguish oppressors from the oppressed, colonizers and the colonized, and the "free" from the enslaved.[14] Additionally, they purport that the trope of America as a white nation is paradoxical, for it represents both nation-building and the zeal of the pioneering spirit to open up new frontiers and borders, contributing to social cohesion and national unity; but it is also the site of racial division that persistently dismisses, disregards, violates, and negates "other" races and ethnicities.[15] King more than tinkers, he disrupts that trope, by enlisting civil religious imagery to give new expression and meaning to

9. See Omi and Winant, *Racial Formation*, 165.

10. John S. McClure, *The Four Codes of Preaching: Rhetorical Strategies* (Louisville: Westminster John Knox, 2003), 2.

11. Omi and Winant, *Racial Formation*, 75–79.

12. Omi and Winant, *Racial Formation*, 78.

13. Omi and Winant, *Racial Formation*, 75–77.

14. Omi and Winant, *Racial Formation*, 83.

15. Omi and Winant, *Racial Formation*, 76.

the "Dream." By drawing on provocative national symbols such as the Emancipation Proclamation and the Declaration of Independence; scriptures from the Jewish-Christian Bible, such as Isaiah 40:4–5 and Amos 5:24; metaphorical language; mythical associations related to the standard American Dream; as well as to the luminary historical figure and civil theologian Abraham Lincoln; King drives home the point that one hundred years after Lincoln's signing of the Emancipation Proclamation, equal treatment continued to elude black America. Therefore, the nation was still in need of redemption.

RHETORIC AS BODILY WAYS OF KNOWING

As a preeminent spokesperson for the civil rights movement, Martin Luther King Jr. would come to embody the ideals of freedom and justice to his largely black movement audience and predominantly white viewing audience. Sociologist Philip Gorski, in fact, asserts that King is "arguably the greatest homilist of civil theology and the best known to contemporary Americans."[16] By virtue of his race, through strength of his spirit and faith, with vigor of soul, and by dint of his masterful delivery, King transcended social reality and mere mortality to embody, up until that moment, unreachable aspirations. He *was* the Dream. In theorizing about speech criticism, Thonssen, Baird, and Braden characterize the distinctive features of the mediums wherein rhetoric functions. They describe two characteristics of speech situations as

> involv[ing] direct social interaction among a plurality of persons. Every public speech is an experience in audience adjustment. The speech situation provides a give-and-take between the speaker and the hearer. The interaction, properly achieved, makes for spirited, effective discourse. The speaker stimulates his hearers who in turn respond with visible or audible symbols or both. To these responses the speaker then makes the necessary adjustments as may be proper and necessary. . . . Whereas a writer can only offer *more words* to command attention at a point where words themselves are already discouraging a reader, a speaker can couple words with vocal and bodily action and ethical appeal to keep the theme of his discourse in the field of interest.[17]

King's ability to rearticulate the dream can be attributed to how he interacted with his audience: his embodiment, sermonic delivery, and messaging translated into forms of bodily knowing that remade him

16. Gorski, "Barack Obama and Civil Religion," 201.
17. Lester Thonssen et al., *Speech Criticism*, 2nd ed. (New York: Ronald, 1970), 9.

into the cultural representation of the Dream. In no way static, but rather dynamic—a stamp of black American church preaching and theatrics—this master orator was in touch with the cognitive, emotional, bodily expressions, and existential hopes and angst of his black audience. Inspiring the moment, he intones the peroration, "I have a dream," with creativity; and that instant reciprocally suffuses his bodily creativity.

Anthropologist Thomas Csordas "treats the body as the cognitive ground of culture."[18] "The term 'body,'" for philosopher Mark H. Johnson, "is used as a generic term for the embodied origins of imaginative structures of our understanding."[19] And anthropologist Kathryn Linn Geurts surmises: "Our embodiment is essential to who we are, to what meaning is, and to our ability to draw rational inferences to be creative."[20] Exemplary of the black preaching tradition, King worked the crowd—engaging in the call-and-response dialectic; alternating his vocal tone from hushed to fevered pitches to suit the energy of the people; and at times moving with the audience. Having experienced the heat and turbulence of political struggle through protests, sit-ins, and other forms of direct action, the legislative campaigns and nonviolent resistance, while enacting *ahimsa*/soul force, served to prime King for the final moments of his speech. Part highbrow oration and part performance during those last seven minutes were a display of embodied ways of knowing that "transformed the racial identity"[21] of American blacks and the social reality of the rest of the hearers and the world.

REIMAGINING SOCIAL REALITY

Old Testament scholar and theologian Walter Brueggemann writes that in the preaching situation "reality is scripted, that is, shaped and authorized by a text." Brueggemann continues:

> Paul Ricoeur has done the most to show us that reality lives by text . . . that text may be recognized or invisible. It may be a great religious "classic," a powerful philosophical tradition, or a long-standing tribal conviction.[22] It is an account of reality that the community comes to trust and to

18. Kathryn Linn Geurts, *Culture and the Senses: Bodily Ways of Knowing in an African Community* (Berkeley: University of California Press, 2002), 73.

19. Mark Johnson, *The Body in the Mind: The Bodily Basis of Meaning, Imagination, and Reason* (Chicago: University of Chicago Press, 1987), xv, xxxvii–xxxviii.

20. Johnson, *Body in the Mind*, xxxviii.

21. Omi and Winant, *Racial Formation*, 167.

22. On the "classic," see David Tracy, *The Analogical Imagination: Christian Theology and the Culture of Pluralism* (New York, Crossroad, 1981), quoted in Walter Brueggemann, *Cadences of Home: Preaching among Exiles* (Louisville: Westminster John Knox, 1997), 26.

> take for granted as a "given" that tends to be beyond reexamination. This text "describes" reality in a certain way and shape. In a world where there is more than one text, that is, a world of plurality, one text may describe, but if another text intrudes, it is possible for the second text to "redescribe" reality.[23]

The long-standing "text" that King was describing *and* disputing in his public address, which simulated the preaching of the black religious tradition, was the Emancipation Proclamation. It was signed by that great American—Abraham Lincoln—whom he contended had envisioned, as stated in the Gettysburg Address, not only the end to the Civil War, thereby a restoration of the Union, but also true equality for all citizens in the United States: "a government of the people, for the people, by the people shall not perish from the earth." The Emancipation Proclamation was actualized on January 1, 1863, to end slavery in parts of the South. However, that did not happen, leaving a conflict between the "text" and what was "realized." Feeling that the United States had defaulted on its obligations toward its black citizens, as guaranteed by this document, King declares: "But one hundred years later, the Negro is still not free; one hundred years later, the life of the Negro is still sadly crippled by the manacles of segregation and the chains of discrimination; one hundred years later, the Negro lives on a lonely island of poverty in the midst of a vast ocean of material prosperity; one hundred years later, the Negro is still languished in the corners of American society and finds himself in exile in his own land."[24]

King called for a reinvestigation of this "text," which he himself then conducts by appearing on the Washington Mall to "dramatize the shameful condition" of all black Americans.[25] In the midst of public discourse, he introduces his own text—the intruding text was *his* "Dream," not only meant to address the country's dismal treatment of Negro Americans but also to re-describe American social reality via a "spirituality of improvisation."

As a further matter, Brueggemann considers the work of preaching to be *imagination.* Preaching offers an image through which perception, experience, and finally faith can be reorganized in alternative ways.

23. See the concept of "construal" and re-construal in David H. Kelsey, *The Uses of Scripture in Recent Theology* (Philadelphia: Fortress, 1975). This notion also influences Brueggemann's "reimagination" concept introduced in Brueggemann, *Cadences of Home,* 26.

24. Clayborne Carson and Kris Shepard, eds., *A Call to Conscience: The Landmark Speeches of Dr. Martin Luther King, Jr.* (New York: Warner, 2001), 81; and Martin Luther King Jr., *A Time to Break Silence: The Essential Works of Martin Luther King, Jr., for Students* (Boston: Beacon, 2013), 186.

25. Washington, ed., *Testament of Hope*, 217.

Through skilled oration that rose to the level of preaching, King points out the disjuncture between the life of black Americans in the 1950s and 1960s and the past promises of the Emancipation Proclamation. He then "reimagines" reality by reinterpreting the deeply anchored and long established American Dream as the ways in which America can be transformed into a more racially inclusive "city on a hill." Imagination requires a reconstrual of time and place, according to Brueggemann. King exemplified this by moving between history and what was then his present moment to reimagine his own future and that of all American social actors.

Then in 1974, American religious historian Martin Marty writes about "Two Kinds of Civil Religion," identifying one as "priestly" and the other as "prophetic."[26] While Robert Bellah describes American civil religion as often signaling and involved with moral, religious, political crises, Marty explains "civil religion" as mainly functioning as "what Peter Berger and Thomas Luckmann call a 'social construction of reality.'"[27] As such, the "priestly" version of civil religion is "celebrative, affirmative, and culture building,"[28] while the "prophetic" version possesses "dialectical-judgmental" potential.[29] Both focus on what it means to belong to the American nation, even if each does so in a divergent way. In "dreaming," King exercised what it meant to be a civil religious prophet by fulfilling the role of a "dialectician." He addresses the Negro problem of racial injustice by elevating a God who transcends the limits of "peoplehood" and nation; yet a God that is no less judgmental about "the American people's" infractions against democratic principles laid out in the country's most sacred documents and aimed at paving the path to a more social justice oriented and ethnically diverse nation, thus adding to the "Is-ness" of America.

THE "IS"-NESS OF AMERICA, A CULTURAL CANOPY: "A NATION WITH THE SOUL OF A CHURCH"

"Metaphor," said Aristotle, "is a 'strange' word. It is *and* it is not." Along the same lines, "I Have a Dream" is replete with "is and is nots." King uses *metaphorical* language effortlessly; he also employs it, creatively and strategically. For instance, the following metaphors send specific mes-

26. Martin Marty, "Two Kinds of Civil Religion," in Richey and Jones, eds., *American Civil Religion*, 145–51.
27. Marty, "Two Kinds of Civil Religion," 141.
28. Marty, "Two Kinds of Civil Religion," 145.
29. Marty, "Two Kinds of Civil Religion," 145.

sages about justice and injustice: (1) justice rolls down like waters/righteousness like a mighty stream (Amos 5:24);[30] (2) a state sweltering with the heat of injustice is like [a state] sweltering with the heat of oppression; (3) [a state can be] transformed into an oasis of freedom and justice.[31] In the first, justice is like mighty rushing waters. In the second, injustice and oppression are like sweltering heat, and in the third, freedom and justice are like an oasis.

Metonymies are also in abundance. "A metonymy is a predictable metaphor . . . ; the relationship between the image and the idea is logical."[32] Take, for example, the following: (1) "a lonely island of poverty" is unlike a "vast ocean of prosperity"; (2) the "dark and desolate valley of segregation" is unlike "the sunlit path of racial justice"; (3) the "quick sands of racial injustice" is unlike "the solid rock of brotherhood"; and (4) this "sweltering summer of the Negro's discontent" is unlike "an invigorating autumn of freedom and equality."[33] From these analogies we gather, for example, that poverty is lonely, prosperity is like a vast ocean, segregation is like a dark and desolate valley, and racial justice is like a sunlit path.

While King employs metaphors and metonymies to explain the "dialectics" of America—its contradictions, we can locate his resolution, that is—*the "Is"-ness of America*—in the form of a nation-based paradigm and analysis of race [which] is

> an important component of our understanding of race: in highlighting "peoplehood," collective identity, it "invents tradition" and "imagines community." Nation-based understandings of race provide affective identification: They promise a sense of ineffable connection within racially identified groups; they engage in "collective representation." The tropes of "soul," of "folk," of *hermanos/hermanas unidos/unidas* uphold Duboisian themes. They channel Marti's hemispheric consciousness; and Vasconcelos's ideas of *la raza cosmica*. In communities and movements, in the arts and popular media, as well as universities and colleges (especially in ethnic studies), these frameworks of peoplehood play a vital part in maintaining a sense of racial solidarity, however uneven or partial.[34]

Returning to Aristotelian thought, I believe King's prolific use of metaphors and metonymies was meant to communicate to America

30. Washington, ed., *Testament of Hope,* 218–19.

31. Washington, ed., *Testament of Hope,* 219.

32. Richard Lischer, *The Preacher King: Martin Luther King, Jr. and The Word That Moved America* (New York: Oxford University Press, 1995), 123.

33. Washington, ed., *Testament of Hope*, 217–18.

34. Omi and Winant, *Racial Formation*, 95.

what she *was* and *was not*. "I Have a Dream" was a "dialectic" seeking synthesis. Likewise, King viewed America as dialectical and in need of synthesis. A nation-based paradigm of race carries the potential to furnish such synthesis. I offer that King's prophetic civil religious imagery based in a nation-centered paradigm of race allowed him to express new ideas about American collective identity, to reimagine community and peoplehood, and to add new definition to what he considered the merits of the "soul"—that is, the "Is"-ness of America.

"What is America?," asked early twentieth century famous writer and Catholic theologian, G. K. Chesterton.[35] Chesterton observed that America became unique because it became a "home for the homeless"—a place for exiles and spiritual refugees who had arrived to America realizing "the pure classic conception that no man must aspire to be anything more than a citizen, and that no man shall endure anything less."[36] In short, America was peculiar because it possessed the personality of "a nation with the soul of a church."[37] Almost thirty years after Chesterton's death, King characterized the "soul" of America in terms of "We the People," persuasively arguing that the term includes the then dispossessed and disenfranchised of our nation; namely, blacks. And consequently, a 1960s black social movement, with King as one of its most ardent advocates, led the way to enfold many other folks into America's cultural canopy. Precisely because of this, and because of spiritual perspicuity as confirmation of an active spiritual life, King was able to introduce and present an alternative to what he thought America actually *was* and yet could *strive* to be.

RHETORICAL PLEASURE, SOCIAL INTEGRATION, AND THE CONTOURS OF COMMUNITY

In King's strivings, he rewrites and reimagines American social reality while simultaneously crafting the national situation in such a way that rhetorical pleasure moves "resistant people to unreasonable and destabilizing behavior."[38] "It can exalt the spirit and create hope where none has a right to exist."[39] Ergo, King couples spirit and soul-force, *satyagraha*—at the March on Washington to propel the campaign for freedom

35. Sidney E. Mead, "The Nation with the Soul of a Church," in Richey and Jones, eds., *American Civil Religion*, 45.

36. Quoted in Richey and Jones, eds., *American Civil Religion*, 46.

37. Mead, "Nation with the Soul of a Church," 45.

38. Lischer, *Preacher King*, 120.

39. Lischer, *Preacher King*, 120.

and jobs forward. As part of his strategy, he used metaphor and myth to capture the plight of black Americans and to compel the rest of the nation to reconsider the truths and value of certain cultural creeds and ideals, like the Declaration of Independence and the American Dream. How and where, diachronically, cultural ideals emerge is based on language. Language is important because it is a *social fact*, and it determines how we identify ourselves and what cultural ideals materialize to support these identities. Ferdinand de Saussure reinforces this notion, telling us that in order to have a language, there must be "a community of speakers."[40] In other words, language is merely linguistic structure if not tied to social reality. But this is not a complete definition of language. Ferdinand de Saussure continues: "Contrary to what might appear to be the case, a language never exists for a moment except as a social fact, for it is a semiological phenomenon. Its social nature is one of its inner characteristics."[41] Yet, de Saussure's most comprehensive definition of language includes "what is brought about by the passage of time, as well as what is brought about by the forces of social integration. Without taking into account the contribution of time, our grasp of linguistic reality remains incomplete."[42]

Language is a social fact—happening in a community of speakers—and affected by time. These components are essential to understanding the debut of the American Dream onto the national scene at the moment in time it was initiated by King's creative spirituality. Language as a social fact also increases understanding of the ways in which King engages mythic language to move his agenda forward for the purposes of social integration.

RELIGIOUS MYTH, NATIONAL IDENTITY, AND DESTINY

In *Chosen People: The Big Idea That Shaped England and America*, Clifford Longley delves into American religious history to provide a basis for understanding American national identity. He concludes that American national identity has been shaped and reformulated according to a religious analogy established by the first American settlers—the Puritans. Strongly disagreeing with a traditional and authoritative Catholic

40. Ferdinand de Saussure, *Course in General Linguistics,* ed. Charles Bally and Albert Sechehaye in collaboration with Albert Riedlinger, trans. Roy Harris (Chicago: Open Court, 1983), 77.

41. de Saussure, *Course in General Linguistics*, 77.

42. de Saussure, *Course in General Linguistics*, 78.

Church, and fleeing the persecution of an English monarchy and reformed Anglican Church, the Puritans traveled across the Atlantic Ocean into unchartered territory—America—to begin life anew. Although uprooted from country, extended family, and friends, this new place afforded them a greater opportunity to practice what they considered an ancient Christian faith.

Yet, a new land left the Puritans isolated, lonely, and sensing that they stood against the world. Only God was on their side. They perceived their situation as similar to the Old Testament Jews who, with God's help, fled from the Egyptian pharaoh, crossed the Red Sea, and were delivered into a promised land—Canaan. God journeyed alongside and guided this group of British settlers who were also spiritual refugees wanting to worship their Creator without restriction; that is, freely. Considering this story alongside their own, Puritans subsequently reimagined and recast themselves as the new Israel: "England became Egypt, the Atlantic Ocean became the Red Sea, and the American wilderness became their own land of Canaan."[43]

A covenantal obligation to God became the basis of a new identity.[44] It became quite clear that language, specifically metaphorical language, was seminal to how Puritans understood themselves as the "new Israel." This metaphor framed their conception of "chosenness," the notion of being selected by God for a special mission in the world. The enduring influence of this myth is reflected in the remarks of Albert Beveridge, a senator from Indiana from 1899 to 1911, almost three centuries later. He declared:

> God has not been preparing the English-speaking and Teutonic peoples for a thousand years for nothing but vain and idle self-contemplation and self-admiration. No. He made us master organizers of the world to establish system where chaos reigned. . . . He made us adept in government that we may administer government among savage and senile peoples. Were it not for such a force as this the world would relapse into barbarism and night. And of all our race, He has marked the American people as His chosen nation to finally lead in the redemption of the world.[45]

Mythical language, particularly religious mythical language, endures.

43. Richard T. Hughes, *Myths America Lives By* (Urbana: University of Illinois Press, 2003), 30.

44. Eddie S. Glaude, "Myth and African American Self-Identity," in *Religion and the Creation of Race and Ethnicity: An Introduction*, ed. Craig R. Prentiss (New York: New York University Press, 2003) 31.

45. *Congressional Record* 33 (Washington, DC: Government Printing Office, 1900), 17; quoted in Hughes, *Myths America Lives By*, 37.

This is obvious from Beveridge's comments. Yet, on a grander scale, American national identity finds its footing on religious myth because, as historian William McLoughlin, quoting anthropologist Clifford Geertz, says: "Sacred symbols function to synthesize a people's ethos—the tone, character, and quality of their life, its moral and aesthetic mood—and their worldview—the picture they have of the ways things in sheer actuality are, and their most comprehensive ideas of order."[46] Geertz's speculations serve as a rationale for why religious myths have an abiding quality and why the "myths Americans live by" are deeply seated in religious conceptions of the self.

One set of myths can comfortably become the seedbed for another set. This is the case with the American Dream, or what McLoughlin renames "the Success myth." Derived from the myth of the chosen nation, the Dream recognizes America as a select place where God rewards courageous, determined, and diligent workers with social and financial prosperity. Inherent to the Dream are two ideas—identity and destiny. This is why the Dream was so relevant to King; and donned the mantle of the "unalienable rights of life, liberty, and the pursuit of happiness"—anchoring national identity and destiny.

"How does King's 'I Have a Dream' rhetorically assume the feat of 'convincing white America that his vision is consistent with their heritage and in their best interest?,'" asks homiletician Richard Lischer. Martin Luther King Jr. lucidly expressed universal and sacred truths to communicate that the dream includes both blacks and whites. He critically draws on Abraham Lincoln's role in the Emancipation Proclamation as a way of connecting Lincoln, thereby whites in general, to the black community, and vice versa, as a way for black Americans to lay claim to Lincoln as a mythical figure who stood tall at both ends of American society.

Moreover, King introduces the Constitution and the Declaration of Independence into his speaking, even if arguably incontestable public documents. They held "certain truths to be self-evident, that all men are created equal, that they are endowed by their Creator." King further argued, persuasively, that to dispute the global and inviolable truths of these documents that define nationhood would ultimately be taken as a challenge to the core of what it means to be American. Accordingly,

> Rhetoric functions only where uncertainty prevails. If there were no doubt about the wisdom of certain courses of action or about the measures of right and wrong—if decisions could be arrived at with reasonable finality and cer-

46. William G. McLoughlin, ed., *Revivals, Awakenings, and Reform: An Essay on Religion and Social Change in America, 1607–1977* (Chicago: University of Chicago Press, 1978), 102.

> tainty—there would be no need for the art of persuasion. It would serve no useful purpose. Demonstrations would suffice. Machines could settle the problems; words would be superfluous. But the milieu of social and political life is not of that sort. It subsists on doubt, on the unsure. And persuasion goes to work when man must make decisions on admittedly inadequate, imprecise data.[47]

The speech situation in which King found himself, at the March on Washington, was unsure; yet, the spirituality of this visionary was such that he was able to catch hold of a "new" American Dream—a myth that continued to "theologize" the history of Americans, provoking unconscious notions of their relationship to God as a covenantal people who continue to have a special mission in the world.[48] Except that King uses the art of persuasion to highlight the differences between the America of the 1960s and the American colonies of the 1600s. Redemption of the world in the 1960s involved redeeming the American self. King hints that this can happen once the country realizes that America's destiny is bound to both races. Precisely because of the impact of prophetic *and* priestly civil religions on this nation, King adroitly makes his point about his "Dream," inclusive of whites, blacks, and other racial groups.

MYTHIC STORY AND HISTORICAL MEMORY IN SACRED TIME

Scheduled as the last speaker of the day, Martin had only a few moments to convince white America that the Dream included everyone. He did this by raising the Dream to mythic status and iconic proportions. In surveying the "narrative function of preaching," John McClure remarks: "Mythic narration serves the same function as myth in a community. . . . It creates a feeling of centeredness in time and space by generating communal identity rooted in a sacred story that transcends the vicissitudes of daily experience."[49] Here, myth is a "popular belief or story that has become associated with a person, institution, or occurrence considered to illustrate a cultural ideal."[50] At the instant King intones, "I have a dream," the American Dream becomes associated with King who then

47. Thonssen, et al., *Speech Criticism*, 8.

48. "Theologizing" history is a concept I borrowed from Glaude, "Myth and African American Self-Identity," 36.

49. John McClure, "The Narrative Function of Preaching: Myth or Parable," *Liturgy* 8, no. 2 (Fall 1989): 47–51.

50. Elizabeth J. Jewell and Frank R. Abate, eds., *New Oxford American Dictionary* (New York: Oxford University Press, 2001), 1132.

performs the task of dramatically elevating the Dream to an iconic but accessible cultural ideal for all Americans by connecting it to "history" and, by default, "time."

History is a process that happens synchronically—in time—as well as diachronically—over time. Historian Hayden White argues that "'history' is essentially a rhetorical activity in which past memory is 'told' and 'retold' in alternative ways, ways that may be intentional but that also take into account the vested interest of the narrating community."[51] In this political speech, "I Have a Dream," King continuously retells American history on behalf of and from the perspective of the black community. He does so by relating the Dream to two historical documents—the Constitution and the Declaration of Independence—and one historical event—the signing of the Emancipation Proclamation. By using this mode of thinking, he raises the Dream to the level of a cultural ideal.

Furthermore, by comfortably connecting the Dream to "mythical" documents and a heroic figure, King reminded white Americans of all they had already invested into maintaining the promise of liberty. This hopefully would compel them to act on behalf of those disenfranchised from the Dream—blacks. King's "dreaming" signaled his wish that their actions would encourage them to rectify a trail of broken promises tearing at the fabric of the nation. A true democracy had to extend freedom to all citizens.

Myths are ancient stories involving supernatural beings, heroes, and ancestors. The American Dream is a myth of exceptionalism, rooted in the founding values and ideals of this nation. Behind it is the story of a group of New Englanders seminal to the development of the United States. Yet, myths as ancient narratives are also caches for history. They are "sacred" histories.[52] Mircea Eliade, historian of religion, reminds us about the three functions of reactualizing myth in "sacred" history: *"By* reactualizing myths, religious man approaches his gods and participates in sanctity; *through* reactualizing myths, he attempts to approach the gods and to participate in *being; for each* reactualization, he again has the opportunity to transfigure his existence, to make it a divine model."[53]

By developing his speech around an exceptional myth—the American Dream, King recalls the story of America by introducing a "sacred" his-

51. Hayden White, "The Politics of Historical Interpretation: Discipline and De-Sublimation," in *The Politics of Interpretation*, ed. W. J. T. Mitchell (Chicago: University of Chicago Press, 1983), 119–43, quoted in Brueggemann, *Cadences of Home*, 34.

52. Mircea Eliade, *The Sacred and the Profane: The Nature of Religion*, trans. Willard R. Trask (San Diego: Harcourt, 1987), 95.

53. Eliade, *Sacred and the Profane*, 106, emphases added.

torical memory which raises this myth to the level of a civic aspiration and standard.

There the Dream transforms into an enduring symbol of "history" *and* "time." Eliade remarks: "*By* its very nature *sacred time is reversible* in the sense that, properly speaking, it is *a primordial mythical time* made present . . . ; sacred time is indefinitely recoverable, indefinitely repeatable."[54] King recognized the March on Washington as a sacred event both because of his spiritual development and because his public address invoked the sacred. His sense of transcendence moved beyond biblical Scripture and language to include: (1) a "sacred" figure—Abraham Lincoln; (2) a "sacred" anthem—America ("My Country 'tis of Thee"); and (3) a "sacred" myth—the American Dream.

As each one of these associations with the sacred were invoked, King's "spirituality of improvisation" was placed on display, as was his reframing of America. By doing so, he was obliged to insert himself into primordial time in order to create a new world and new social order. Because mythical "sacred" time always signals the beginning of existence, King's introduction of a new association to the Dream "returned [his audience] to original time . . . the abolition of profane past time . . . , thus [motivating them to participate in] a symbolic rebirth" of the American nation.[55]

RITUAL PROCESS AS PASTORAL COMMUNICATION

J. Randall Nichols proposes that pastoral communicators are leaders who "reimagine" and, to that extent, "reframe" particular social circumstances and conditions. Pastoral communication is all the more distinguished by three movements: it (1) gives individuals permission to experience a range of inner feelings and emotions by drawing them into the "sanctuary" and away from a chaotic world; (2) it should furnish a milieu for "re-framing" issues; and (3) it should teach new ways of communicating. Nichols parallels the *ritual process* to the *therapeutic process* with the following result: both processes entail orientation-disorientation-reorientation phases.[56] His style of speech criticism relates pastoral and prophetic communication to the ritual process while stressing the "re-framing" function. In the same way, King's spirited and visionary pastoral communication of the "dream" drew him into a ritual process,

54. Eliade, *Sacred and the Profane*, 68–69.

55. Eliade, *Sacred and the Profane*, 78 and 82.

56. J. Randall Nichols, *Restoring Word: Preaching as Pastoral Communication* (New York: Harper & Row, 1987), 69.

though fraught with social dramas, that aided in transitioning the nation into the realm of more racially diverse and culturally inclusive.

SOCIAL DRAMA ON AMERICA'S PUBLIC STAGE

"Social dramas" only happen where there are already established relationships and one party comes into conflict with another.[57] Although blacks and whites in America had an unequal relationship before and during the 1950s and 1960s, both groups still were, in one form or another, related and relating to each other. That is where the "social drama" entered; it found its footing in a historically conflicted relationship. However, a common history also tied both groups together, what King exemplifies in his articulation of the American Dream.

The four stages of a social drama are the breach, crisis, redress, and reconciliation, that is "the reintegration of the disturbed social group."[58] Black Americans were the distressed social group who had experienced a breach of principles in two cultural documents—the Constitution and the Declaration of Independence—which are meant to ensure the human dignity and rights of all American citizens. King articulated the breach in the following way: "America has defaulted on this promissory note insofar as her citizens of color are concerned. Instead of honoring this sacred obligation, America has given the Negro people a bad check; a check which has come back marked 'insufficient funds.'"[59]

57. Symbolic and cultural anthropologist Victor Turner intended his doctoral dissertation turned book, *Schism and Continuity in an African Society: A Study of Ndembu Life* (Manchester: Manchester University Press, 1957), to be "a study of social conflict and the mechanisms introduced to reduce, exclude and resolve conflict" (3). It is also an exploration into the social life of Zambian Ndembu villagers and their community social processes. Developing the term *social drama,* Turner was able to peer under the surface of the Ndembu social structure to view the hidden paradoxes and disruptions causing inter-family and inter-village conflict in family and communal life. He concluded that social dramas are processual. Along with that, Turner identified the four phases of *social dramas* as: (1) a violation of the standards that govern social relationships between persons or groups of a social unit; (2) formation of a crisis or extension of the breach (i.e., violation), unless the conflict can be interrupted and quickly closed off; (3) leadership of a social group by applying methods and instruments to solve the problem; (4) either reincorporation of the social group once the problem has been addressed or social recognition that the breach or schism is irreparable. Rituals functioned to keep the groups involved in the social conflict connected to one another because ritualistic activity performed by certain segments of the population cut across boundaries reinforced by family lineages and village rules. Rituals operate to widen the circle of individuals involved in the social conflict and thus broaden networks of association to close off the breach (89–91); Mathieu Deflem, "Ritual, Anti-Structure and Religion: A Discussion of Victor Turner's Processual Symbolic Analysis," *Journal for the Scientific Study of Religion* 30, no. 1 (1991): 2–4.

58. Nichols, *Restoring Word,* 71.

59. Washington, ed., *Testament of Hope*, 217.

Because the breach was quite prominent and irrevocable, the public was propelled into a crisis. The true meaning of American democracy was being questioned with, What constitutes a true democracy? How will we move forward? Will it be inclusive of all Americans? King responded with the mandate—act now. "*Now is the time* to make real the promises of democracy . . . ; *now is the time* to make justice a reality for all God's children. It would be fatal for the nation to overlook the urgency of the moment."[60]

King's redressive mechanism was to remind white Americans that their destinies and freedoms were enmeshed with black Americans. Matt Ridley would likely consider this an argument for "groupishness": "If a creature puts the greater good ahead of its individual interests, it is because *its fate is inextricably tied to that of the group* [emphasis mine]: it shares the group fate."[61] Precisely because King believed in the inherent "brotherhood of man and the fatherhood of God," Ridley's deliberations are relevant.

King articulated his dream for reconciliation despite the obstacles and challenges that the American people had to overcome. As evidence, consider his words: "So I say to you, my friends, that even though we must face the difficulties of today and tomorrow, I still have a dream. It is a dream deeply rooted in the American Dream that one day this nation will rise up and live out the true meaning of its creed—we hold these truths to be self-evident, that all men are created equal."[62] At this final phase, Victor Turner proposes, the relationship will change—either for good or ill.

King's leadership in a public ritual, using the resources of prophetic "pastoral" preaching, set forth a new vision for the nation, making the Dream available to not just blacks and whites but others of varying backgrounds, ethnicities, and faith traditions. "The social drama," according to Turner, "is our native way of manifesting ourselves to ourselves and of declaring where power and meaning lie and how they are distributed."[63] It is where we engage in the process of self-understanding, identity formation, reformation, and transformation. The social dramas borne of racial and social injustices throughout American history had to be treated with an analgesic. The peroration, "I have a dream," a phrase developing out of King's own spirit and overflow, would be just that antidote.

60. Washington, ed., *Testament of Hope*, 218.

61. Matt Ridley, *The Origins of Virtue: Human Instincts and the Evolution of Cooperation* (New York: Penguin, 1996), 39.

62. Washington, ed., *Testament of Hope*, 219.

63. Victor Turner, *From Ritual to Theatre: The Human Seriousness of Play* (New York: PAJ Books, 2001), 78.

THE "NEW" DREAM IN AMERICA'S RITES OF PASSAGE

King's spirituality permeated the day's public rituals, metamorphosing into a social glue for the group gathered and listening. Van Gennep developed the term *rites of passage* from studying small-scale societies to describe rituals that "accompanied an individual's transitions from one situation to another and from one cosmic or social world to another."[64] Transitions are distinguished by three phases: separation, margin (*limen* meaning "threshold"), and aggregation (reincorporation). Victor Turner later tells us that "ritual could be best understood as a set of mechanisms for promoting group solidarity, in fact, [it] is a 'sort of all-purpose social glue,' . . . and its symbols are merely 'reflections of expressions of components of social structure.'"[65]

A "new" Dream was a sign that King and the American people had already entered into rites of passage through the portals of history, space, and time. Even if anachronistic, "dreaming" had placed King into the "imaginary" but pivotal position of being an "unofficial" signatory to the Emancipation Proclamation. King's speech signaled that the past had had relevance and bearing on the present. Thus, the *separation* phase of America's national rites of passage, although it had taken some time, started with the signing of the Emancipation Proclamation, eventually detaching southern whites and separating blacks and the rest of America living under the duress of physical segregation from the old social order. America's movement through the *liminal* phase was precipitated by Reconstruction, marked with race riots, and followed by the institutionalization of Jim Crow laws. These events showed a nation in social limbo, yet King was dreaming up and gradually developing a reconstituted American myth that was making its way to the horizon. During *reincorporation*, boycotts, sit-ins, freedom rides, and new civil rights legislation would lay the foundation and open the door to integration.

Here King launches a reimagined American dream and the rest of America seizes his vision. King's dream must be read in light of the three phases of a rites of passage experienced by an initiand. Turner writes, "In *preliminal* rites of separation the initiand is removed from the indicative quotidian social structure into the subjunctive antistructure of the *liminal* process and is then returned, transformed by liminal experiences by the rites of *reaggregation* to social structural participation in the indicative

64. Quoted in Turner, *From Ritual to Theatre*, 80.
65. Turner, *From Ritual to Theatre*, 82.

mood. The subjunctive, according to Webster's Dictionary, is always concerned with 'wish, desire, possibility, or hypothesis': it is a world of 'as if,' . . . ; it is 'if it *were* so,' not 'it *is* so.'"[66]

On that hot August day in 1963 at the Washington Mall, Martin Luther King Jr.'s ritual performance ended up mimicking what had all the while been happening in American history. He was able to generate a new myth because liminal space was where he stood, spoke, and conducted what seemed like a worship service, with all of the nation in attendance. "Ritual liminality contains the potentiality for cultural innovation, as well as the means for effecting structural transformations."[67] For the demonstrators present that day, for those watching from around the world, and for Martin himself, the liminal space became an "as if" space, an "if it *were* so" this is how it would be space. "'If it *were* so' my four little children would one day live in a nation where they would not be judged by the color of their skin but by the content of their character. 'If it *were* so' we would be able to transform the jangling discords of our nation into a beautiful symphony of brotherhood. Finally, 'if it *were* so' we would be able to work together, to pray together, to struggle together, to go to jail together, to stand up for freedom together, knowing that we will be free one day."[68]

This space gave Martin the freedom to make declarations about an envisioned yet unrealized future spurred by a creative spirituality that dreamed beyond measure.

KING'S SPIRITUALITY, AMERICAN NATIONAL IDENTITY, AND "E PLURIBUS UNUM"

The American Dream as both religious and ideological myth supported American black strivings toward inclusion into a new reality.[69] King's "social construction of reality" could be described as "switching worlds"; the almost entire transformation of an individual's or group's subjective reality.[70] Using rhetoric as his medium, King drew on religious myth,

66. Turner, *From Ritual to Theatre*, 82–83.

67. Turner, *From Ritual to Theatre*, 85.

68. Washington, ed., *Testament of Hope*, 219.

69. Ideology in this case means "the production of ideas, beliefs, and values that make up the entirety of a particular form of life, *and* it is within this whole complex of meanings and processes that various battles are waged as individuals and groups reflect on their conditions of living." This is how Eddie S. Glaude defines and uses the term. See Glaude, "Myth and African American Self-Identity," 30.

70. Peter L. Berger and Thomas Luckmann, *The Social Construction of Reality: A Treatise in the Sociology of Knowledge* (New York: Anchor, 1966) 156–57.

social and religious history, and public space as ritual space to offer a "reframed" American national identity.

A "prophet of revitalization," shorn from the best of oratory traditions, King offered the American public a rearticulated American dream, "sustain[ing] the reality of culture myths and reinterpret[ing] them to meet the needs of social change, while cloth[ing] them with an aura of reality that grew from his conviction that he was a messenger of God."[71] As a civil theologian, he harnessed the creativity, like a jazz musician of a "spirituality of improvisation," in order to rearticulate "peoplehood" and thereby a new definition of nationhood and what it means to be American—to be one who upholds the democratic principle "e pluribus unum": out of many, one nation.

71. McLoughlin, ed., *Revivals, Awakenings, and Reform,* 104.

9.

Transformed Nonconformity: Spirituality, Ethics, and Leadership in the Life and Work of Martin Luther King Jr.

WALTER EARL FLUKER

> The face of man is the medium through which the invisible in him becomes visible and enters into commerce with us.
>
> —Emmanuel Levinas[1]

> Lord guide me
> If you try me, send me out into the foggy night,
> So that I cannot see my way.
> Even if I stumble, this I beg,
> That I may look and smile serenely,
> Bearing witness that you are with me and I walk in peace.
> If you try me,
> Send me out into an atmosphere too thin for me to breathe
> And I cannot feel the earth beneath my feet,
> Let my behavior show men that they cannot part me forcibly from you
> In whom we breathe and move and are.
> If you let hate hamper and trap me,
> Twist my heart, disfigure me,
> Then give my eyes,
> His love and peace,
> My face the expression of your son.
>
> —Dom Helder Camara[2]

1. Emmanuel Levinas, *Difficult Freedom: Essays on Judaism*, trans. Sean Hand (Baltimore: John Hopkins University Press, 1997), 140.
2. Dom Helder Camara, *The Desert Is Fertile* (Eugene, OR: Wipf & Stock, 2005; previously published by Orbis in 1974), 26–27.

INTRODUCTION AND OVERVIEW

In the following discussion, I am using Martin Luther King Jr.'s language of "transformed nonconformity" as a critical resource to examine the relationship between spirituality, ethics, and leadership in African American churches.[3] I am also building on an argument begun in an earlier essay, titled, "Recognition, Respectability, and Loyalty: The Quest for Civility in African American Churches," where I contend that civility, as understood within the black church tradition, is both problematic and redemptive.[4] It is problematic because of its historical roots in what has been variously described as *the American dilemma*, that is, the problem of *doubleness* in African American history and culture. It is redemptive because black churches have dealt with the problematic in ways that have also produced three underlying social practices: recognition, respectability, and loyalty. These practices have informed a transformative praxis that has sought the best in American democratic idealism. My general inquiry is concerned, therefore, with black churches' socio-historical entrapment in race and ideology expressed most profoundly in the language of the *American dilemma* and the genealogy of civility in black churches as a *post-bellum* phenomenon.

In this continuing examination, I am interested in the question of African American church leadership and the ways in which Martin Luther King Jr.'s thematic of transformed nonconformity provides a conceptual and practical framework for rethinking leadership strategies for this new season of struggle and possibilities. I begin our discussion with operational definitions of spirituality, ethics, and leadership. I build upon the discussion of leadership literature that incorporates spirituality and ethics with a model of discourse that I refer to as "ethical leadership," which finds resonance with King's transformed nonconformity formulation. Second, I examine the ways in which King's dialectical appropriation of knowledge, faith, and practice informed his view of transformed nonconformity. Finally, I recommend a conceptual grid for black church leadership that captures the inherent tensions in the *doubleness* of black

3. In his sermon, "Transformed Nonconformist," one first notices King's improvisational play with great ideas, borrowed from the critiques of social conformity by Harry Emerson Fosdick, Eugene Austin, and other sources. See Martin Luther King Jr., *Strength to Love* (Philadelphia: Fortress, 1981; originally published in 1963), 17–25. See also Keith D. Miller, *Voice of Deliverance: The Language of Martin Luther King, Jr. and Its Sources* (New York: The Free Press, 1992), 105–8, 110–11, and 164.

4. See R. Drew Smith, ed., *New Day Begun: African American Churches and Civic Culture in Post-Civil Rights America* (Durham: Duke University Press, 2003), 113–41.

life and offers directions for new subversive possibilities utilizing the triune ethical constructs of character, civility, and community.

DEFINITIONS

SPIRITUALITY

Discussions of spirituality cover a broad and increasingly complex spectrum of beliefs, practices, and approaches within and beyond traditional religious circles. For our purposes, *spirituality refers to a way or ways of seeking or being in relationship with an Other, who is believed to be worthy of reverence and the highest devotion.* In this definition, I am concerned with the Other as inclusive of both individuality and community, or, in the language of Emmanuel Levinas, the Other has a face—and the face of the Other is the foundation of ethics and the origin of civil society.[5] I encounter the face of the Other, in its strangeness and transcendence, but also in its force of obligation and interdependence. The human face is also the face that is hidden and present for me in all its force and meaning. The face invites me to revel in memory—collective memory as diverse and beautiful as the world. If such a human face were to visit me, then I would understand that I am not alone, unrelated neither to history nor to memory.[6]

Spirituality is also a discipline that places emphasis on *practice*—spirituality is something that we *do*. Prior to any act of cognition, spirituality has to do with the practical, day-to-day encounter with the Other; the Other being both friend and stranger, comrade and oppose, individual

5. Emmanuel Levinas, *Totality and Infinity*, trans. Alfonso Lingis (Pittsburgh: Duquesne University Press, 1969), 201. The question, "Can things have a face?," is important for the definition above. Levinas suggests that art may be an appropriate lens through which to identify "Being" in the face of a thing. He asks, "Is not art an activity that lends faces to things? Does not the façade of a house regard us? . . . We ask ourselves all the same if the impersonal but fascinating and magical march of rhythm does not, in art, substitute itself for sociality, for the face, for speech." Emmanuel Levinas, "Is Ontology Fundamental?," in *Basic Philosophical Writings*, ed. Adriaan T. Peperzak et al. (Bloomington: Indiana University Press, 1996), 10.

6. Luther Smith's definitions of spirit and spirituality are helpful. He writes, "Spirit is the 'breath of God' in creation, providing value and meaning to existence. Realizing and expressing itself in the material world, the work of the spirit is historical and political. It is the source for the definition of the individual, and the individual in relationship to the collective. As it discerns itself, it discerns God and what it means to be a creature of God. . . . Spirituality is a way of life committed to understanding the nature and urgings of the spirit; the life organizes all its desires, energies, and resources so that they might be dominated by the spirit. Spirituality brings a harmony to living consistent with the peace and will of God." See Luther E. Smith, *Howard Thurman: The Mystic as Prophet* (Richmond, IN: Friends United, 1991; originally published in 1981), 18–19.

and collective, divine and demonic. In its active, dynamic expression, spirituality is *life generating* and *disfiguring*. Utilizing these indicators, I would like to talk about spirituality from three perspectives: (1) formal notions of spirituality that are related to established religions; (2) informal notions of spirituality that are "self-actualized" or self-defined by individuals or small groups not associated with an established religious institution; and (3) philosophical or ethical notions of spirituality related to values and perceived goods, for instance, truth, beauty, justice, and the like. Martin Luther King Jr.'s understanding of spirituality is located within the first category of established religions, and incorporates the third category as it pertains to faith-based notions of ethics that are philosophically justified. I also use these three categories as heuristic devices that provide lenses through which to look at the vast landscape of a developing literature that incorporates ideas, beliefs, and practices from an array of traditions and perspectives—health, science, technology, politics, business, and education.[7]

7. Examples of the first perspective on spirituality are those promoted within established religious institutions. Here there is a vast array of definitions and approaches to the subject. See, for instance, Cheslyn Jones et al., eds. *The Study of Spirituality* (New York: Oxford University Press, 1986), especially "Note on Spirituality," xiv–xvi. Emphasis is placed on traditions of contemplation, reflection, and mystical life practices within institutionalized religious forms. In recent years, there has been growing interest and awareness of ecumenical and interfaith practices of spiritualties that enhance understanding of respective religious traditions through common dialogue and sharing. See Thich Nhat Hanh, *Living Buddha, Living Christ* (New York: Riverhead, 1995); Dalai Lama, *Ethics for the New Milennium* (New York: Riverhead, 1999); and Walter Earl Fluker and Catherine Tumber, eds., *A Strange Freedom: Howard Thurman on Religious Experience and Public Life* (Boston: Beacon, 1998). African Americans tend not to place emphasis on "formalized structures" of spirituality. However, there is a significant presence and a growing literature that suggest that the place of liturgy, ritual, and inherited practices have long standing in the life of African American churches. In the third area refers to the broad-his perspective one finds the recent writings of Peter J. Paris, Cheryl Sanders, Carlyle Fielding Stewart III, Dwight Hopkins, and Renita Weems very helpful.

In respect to the second usage of spirituality, a stream of public conversations from Parker Palmer to Deepak Chopra, which incorporate therapeutic and self-actualization discourses, have found audiences beyond the traditional academic and ecclesiastical institutions that have long dominated the contest. African American women writers, theologians, preachers, clairvoyants, movements like the broadly defined New Age Spirituality, and Promise Keepers, are among the many sources that compete for voice and place on a quickly changing playing field. See Deepak Chopra, *How to Know God: The Soul's Journey into the Mystery of Mysteries* (New York: Harmony, 2000); Deepak Chopra, *The Seven Spiritual Laws of Success: A Practical Guide to the Fulfillment of Your Dreams* (San Rafael, CA: Amber-Allen, 1994); Herbert Benson, *Timeless Healing: The Power and Biology of Belief* (New York: Scribner's, 1996); Larry Dossey, *Healing Words: The Power of Prayer and the Practice of Medicine* (New York: HarperCollins, 1993); Larry Dossey, *Prayer Is Good Medicine: How to Reap the Healing Benefits of Prayer* (San Francisco: HarperCollins, 1996); Parker Palmer, *Let Your Life Speak: Listening for the Voice of Vocation* (San Francisco: Jossey-Bass, 2000).

The third area refers to the broader philosophical and ethical notions of *spirit*. Here spirituality is discussed as source of authority for private and public discourse that again are located

ETHICS AND LEADERSHIP

I have outlined my thoughts on ethics and leadership in an earlier publication, where I define *ethical leadership* as the critical appropriation and embodiment of moral traditions that have historically shaped the character and shared meanings of a people (an *ethos*). Ethical leadership does not emerge from a historical vacuum but arises from the *lifeworlds* of particular traditions and speaks authoritatively and acts responsibly with the aim of serving the collective good. Ethical leaders are leaders whose characters have been shaped by the wisdom, habits, and practices of particular traditions, often more than one, and yet they tend to be identified with a particular ethos and cultural narrative. Ethical leadership asks the question of values in reference to ultimate concern.[8]

Moreover, ethical leadership demands that we cultivate and nourish a *sense of self* that recognizes the interrelatedness of life or a *sense of community*. Spirituality plays a key role in this process. *A sense of community* refers to the larger extended ecological sphere made tangible by nature, defined as the universe and the cosmos, but in its final essence, it is *spirit*. This idea of spirituality finds resonance with Peter Paris's definition of spirituality in the African context, that is, spirituality is never individualistic, but is part of a larger sphere of unity that is diverse in its dynamics and character. "The 'spirituality' of a people," he writes, "refers to the animating and integrative power that constitutes the principle frame of meaning for individual and collective experiences."[9] For Robert M. Franklin, spirituality refers to "a person's sense of identity in relation to other people and that which is conceived as ultimate concern. Rooted in spiritual identity are a person's fundamental values, moral commitments,

across the spectrum of conservative, liberal, and progressive ideologies. William Bennett, ed., *The Moral Compass: Stories for a Life's Journey* (New York: Simon & Schuster, 1995); Marianne Williamson, *Healing the Soul of America: Reclaiming Our Voices as Spiritual Citizens* (New York: Simon & Schuster, 1997); and Michael Lerner, *Spirit Matters* (Charlottesville: Hampton Road, 2000) may well represent the broad social and cultural context for the language game of spirituality in this perspective. See also Sara Lawrence-Lightfoot, *Balm in Gilead: Journey of a Healer*, 2nd ed. (New York: Penguin, 1995); and James M. Washington, ed., *Conversations with God: Two Centuries of Prayers by African Americans* (San Francisco: HarperCollins, 1997). Michael Dash, Jonathan Jackson, Stephen Rasor, Peter J. Paris, Robert Franklin, and Stephen Carter are outstanding exemplars of theologians, ethicists, and educators who have done some significant work in the area of African American spirituality.

8. Walter Earl Fluker, ed., *The Stones That the Builders Rejected: The Development of Ethical Leadership from the Black Church Tradition* (Harrisburg, PA: Trinity, 1998).

9. Peter J. Paris, *The Spirituality of African Peoples: The Search for a Common Moral Discourse* (Minneapolis: Fortress, 1995), 22.

and ability to engage in ethical reasoning. Spiritual health is reflected in a person's ability to trust and care for others."[10]

Looming large in this perspective is the question of ethics. In respect to its ethical dimension, spirituality is *life generating* and *disfiguring*; and its primary ethical locus is the human face. James Hillman writes, "The Other's face calls upon my character. Rather than thinking my character shows in my face and that my face is my character exteriorized . . . character requires the face of the Other. Its piercing provocation pulls us from every possible ethical potential. In bad conscience we turn away from the face in the wheelchair, the face of the beggar; we hood the face of the executed, and we ignore the faces of the socially ostracized and hierarchically inferior so that they become 'invisible' even as we walk down the same street."[11]

Significantly, this vulnerable face is *disfigured* in encounter with the Other, especially the Other who presents itself as Diabolos—as threat, tempter, and destroyer. In the struggle for social transformation, the ethical leader experiences the transformation of self, which is a *disorienting*, *disfiguring*, and ultimately, a *dying* encounter with the Other. Dom Helder Camara's prayer, in *The Desert Is Fertile*, has much of the same force and import:

> If you let hate hamper and trap me,
> Twist my heart, disfigure me,
> Then give my eyes,
> His love and peace,
> My face the expression of your Son.[12]

In the experience of *disorienting*, *disfiguring*, and *dying*, the ethical leader also becomes aware of the transforming power of the encounter with the Other. For ethical leaders, as transformed nonconformists, this means that each encounter with the Other carries within itself the danger of *disfiguring*; of being tested and proven so that that which is hidden (and that which *calls* me) *discloses* itself in acts of compassion and justice. Ethical leaders, therefore, are *transfigured* and *transforming* actors who present themselves to the world as symbols and for instances of what is possible and hopeful. In the experience of encounter, one is readied or predis-

10. Robert Michael Franklin, *Another Day's Journey* (Minneapolis: Fortress, 1997), 86. See also Franklin's taxonomy in "The Spiritualities of the Black Church," where he places King in the social justice tradition (42).

11. James Hillman, *The Force of Character and the Lasting Life* (New York: Random House, 1999), 142.

12. Camara, *Desert Is Fertile*, 27.

posed to hope; hope being simultaneously the transformation of threat, temptation, danger, and death into a vision of the possible, a sense of values, a sense of the future, that is, having faith to move on in creative activity that aspires to goodness. The task of the ethical leader is to *inspire* and *guide* others in the process of transformation through spiritual acts of defiance and resistance against systems of injustice. At a personal level, this process involves reliving and recovering their cultural futures through life stories, rituals, and creative actions that give meaning to life; a focus is placed on reconciling acts of community with the primary theological and ethical question being, *"What can I hope for?"*

SPIRITUALITY, ETHICS, AND LEADERSHIP

Why is the relationship among spirituality, ethics, and leadership important? First, leaders in many public venues are increasingly turning to approaches that emphasize some form of spirituality as an authoritative source in making decisions that impact the lifestyles, attitudes, and behaviors of many people—especially in the areas of government, health, science, and business. Often these appeals to spirituality fail to address the larger ethical questions of justice, equity, and truth-telling that are raised in public life.

The second reason is the role that spirituality and ethics will increasingly play in the development of leadership for the future. A significant challenge for the next generation of leadership will be the promotion and advancement of science, technology, and business to serve the interests of human development and the environment. The changes produced by this triumvirate have already resulted in a significant upheaval in society, the meaning of life, intelligence, and work. For example, there is a growing movement within profit and not-for-profit sectors to incorporate ethical principles and practices pertaining to issues of transparency, diversity, transcultural dynamics, sustainability, the environment, and human development. Increasingly, large corporations, think-tanks, and political leaders are relying upon spirituality as a form of human resource development to address these larger structural issues.

Finally, in order for a just civil society to exist, persons in responsible leadership roles must make decisions based on ethical guides.[13] Some of

13. The question arises whether we must become ethical in order for society to exist or whether we are necessarily ethical insofar as we enter into the make-up of any actual society. The latter, of course, means that society is always, already directed by ethical—technically directive—principles and could not otherwise exist. But this forces us to distinguish between the ethical principles that happen to exist and competing ethical principles that are after. Hence ethical principles are always embedded in actual practice, which means that leadership principles are

these argue that the most significant problem besetting civil society in the United States of America is the *failure of ethical leadership*.

For historically marginalized peoples, the relationship of spirituality, ethics, and leadership is most urgent. With the long-range economic, political, and social costs of war, a troubled market economy, and rapid advances (crusades) in technology, science, and global democracy, if we believe analysts like Robert Kaplan, we now have the makings of a social anarchy that threatens the very foundations of our social purpose. The impending catastrophic fallout of the present situation will have far-reaching negative consequences for the least of these—those whom Samuel Proctor called "the lost, the left-out, and left behind." At a deeper level, however, there *is* a spiritual malaise, a nihilistic threat promoted by the predominance of a utilitarian individualism that appeals endlessly to therapeutic remedies that begin and end with *self*. Who will lead in the twenty-first century? Better yet, how shall they lead?[14] *Who will go for us, and whom shall we send?* What are the resources and methodologies at our disposal to train a new generation of leaders for this millennium?

MARTIN LUTHER KING JR. AS A CRITICAL RESOURCE

The leadership legacy of Martin Luther King Jr. provides a critical resource for answers to these questions as we enter a new century beset by ethical issues and challenges. More than any other American leader in the twentieth century, King challenged the nation to take seriously the role of spirituality and ethics in resolving what the authors of *Habits of the Heart* called the most important unresolved contradiction in our history, the tension between "self-reliant competitive enterprise and a

necessarily based on ethical guides. In this view, the problem cannot be to categorically intrude ethical guides, which did not previously exist, but rather first to disengage the guides we know must be there; and second, to confront these with alternates, which we seek to demonstrate to be better. This is another way of saying there is always room for argument and discovery in ethics as a science, and that we must press on with counter-arguments, and open ourselves to its inherent possibilities if we are to make spiritual progress. (Many thanks to Preston King for this observation.)

14. In determining or establishing how we ought to lead, we must clearly identify the sort of leadership that is vital to change—and why. In short, moral argument ought to clarify not just what it supports but also what it opposes. In the case of King, the question that arises is: Did he introduce new principles within the ethos of his *koinonia*? If so, what traditional principles was he opposing? If he was deploying merely traditional principles, how is it possible to explain their failures in the past and their triumph via King?

sense of public solidarity espoused by civic republicans."[15] It was King's spiritual genius that provided for him the essential assets and tools to lead a revolution of values that expanded the moral grammar of American history and culture from parochially applied democratic principles to concrete proposals for inclusiveness and action. This amazing feat, performed in a brief period of our history—from 1954 to 1968—was no doubt the nation's finest example of what Martin Buber called "turning." In doing so, King also changed the leadership equation: public leadership no longer belonged to the strict province of position, power, and privilege, but also to the marginalized moral minority—those whom King labeled "transformed nonconformists."

Much of the scholarship on Martin Luther King Jr. has centered on his role as a civil rights leader, his eclectic intellectual formation, and his distinctive place within the African American church tradition.[16] Little attention, however, has been given to the relationship between spirituality, ethics, and leadership in his thought and praxis.[17] This, of course,

15. Robert N. Bellah et al., *Habits of the Heart: Individualism and Commitment in American Life* (New York: Harper and Row, 1985), 256.

16. See Miller, *Voice of Deliverance*; James H. Cone, *Martin and Malcolm and America: A Dream or a Nightmare?* (Maryknoll, NY: Orbis, 1991); Clayborne Carson et al., eds., *The Papers of Martin Luther King, Jr.: Called to Serve, January 1929–June 1951* (Berkeley: University of California Press, 1992), 1:1–74; John Ansbro, *Martin Luther King, Jr.: The Making of a Mind* (Maryknoll, NY: Orbis, 1982); Kenneth L. Smith and Ira G. Zepp Jr., *Search for the Beloved Community: The Thinking of Martin Luther King, Jr.* (Valley Forge, PA: Judson, 1974); Adam Fairclough, *To Redeem the Soul of America: The Southern Leadership Conference and Martin Luther King, Jr.* (Athens: University of Georgia Press, 1987); David Garrow, *Bearing the Cross: Martin Luther King, Jr., and the Southern Christian Leadership Conference* (New York: William Morrow, 1986); David L. Lewis, *King: A Critical Biography*, 2nd ed. (Urbana: University of Illinois Press, 1978); Stephen Oates, *Let the Trumpet Sound: The Life of Martin Luther King, Jr.* (New York: New American Library, 1982); and Taylor Branch, *Parting the Waters: America in the King Years* (New York: Simon & Schuster, 1988). See especially Branch's treatment of Vernon Johns (1–26). William D. Watley, *Roots of Resistance: The Nonviolent Ethics of Martin Luther King, Jr.* (Valley Forge, PA: Judson, 1985). See especially chap. 1, "Formative Influences, Black Religious Experience, Evangelical Liberalism, and Personalism," 17–46. Walter E. Fluker, *They Looked for a City: A Comparative Analysis of the Ideal of Community in Howard Thurman and Martin Luther King Jr.* (Lanham, MD: University Press of America, 1989); Lewis V. Baldwin, *There Is a Balm in Gilead: The Cultural Roots of Martin Luther King, Jr.* (Minneapolis: Fortress, 1991); and Lewis V. Baldwin, *To Make the Wounded Whole: The Cultural Legacy of Martin Luther King, Jr.* (Minneapolis: Fortress, 1991). For examples of articles that address the impact of the African American church on King's intellectual and social development, see Cornel West, "Martin Luther King, Jr.: Prophetic Christian as Organic Intellectual," in *Prophetic Fragments* (Grand Rapids: Eerdmans, 1988), 3–12; James H. Cone, "Martin Luther King, Jr., Black Theology—Black Church," *Theology Today* (January 1984): 409–20; and Paul R. Garber, "King Was a Black Theologian," *Journal of Religious Thought* 31 (Fall–Winter 1974): 16–32.

17. With the notable exceptions of Peter J. Paris, Lewis V. Baldwin, Vincent Harding, and, to some extent, Michael Eric Dyson, very little scholarship has been devoted to the spiritual biography of Martin Luther King Jr. and the ways in which it shaped his role as a leader.

strikes one as surprising since the most casual observer of King's life and work cannot help but be struck by a deep-seated spirituality wedded to a strong sense of Christian character and vocation. It is not surprising, however, that with the noble heritage bequeathed to him by his family, the Ebenezer Baptist Church, Morehouse College, and the larger black Atlanta community, that King emerged as a luminous exemplar of the black church tradition of spirituality and social transformation. Equally revealing is his articulation of the thematic that characterizes the wedding of the notions of "spirituality" and "social transformation" in the language of "transformed nonconformity." Embedded in his formulation of "transformed nonconformity" are significant elements of King's biography and thinking regarding the place of spirituality, ethics, and leadership in his dream of human community.

I will examine King's contributions in respect to the three overarching dimensions of character, civility, and community. At stake in this discussion is not the claim to a metaphysical model or mandate for spirituality. Rather, we are looking at a developmental model that allows us to examine the ways in which spirituality, ethics, and leadership might be linked while providing a resource for training a new generation of leaders who are spiritually disciplined, morally anchored, and socially engaged. First, we will give attention to the ways in which King's dialectical appropriation of knowledge, faith, and practice informed his view of transformed nonconformity.

THE DIALECTIC OF TRANSFORMED NONCONFORMITY

TRUTH IS THE WHOLE: KING'S USE OF DIALECTICAL METHODOLOGY

An important element in King's thinking about spirituality, ethics, and leadership is the dialectical methodology that he employed as a critical and hermeneutical principle in his quest for truth-as-praxis. King acknowledged his indebtedness to Hegel for the philosophical method of rational coherence.[18] King rejected Hegel's "absolute idealism" because

18. Martin Luther King Jr., *Stride toward Freedom: The Montgomery Story* (New York: Harper and Row, 1958) 82; Ansbro, *Martin Luther King, Jr.,* 119–28. King's major philosophical and theological studies at Boston University were with Edgar Sheffield Brightman and L. Harold DeWolf. It was mainly under these thinkers that King studied personalism. Smith and Zepp suggest that there are four significant themes of personalism that shaped King's intellectual quest for the beloved community: (1) the inherent worth of personality; (2) the personal God of love and reason; (3) the moral law of the cosmos; and (4) the social nature of human existence.

he felt it tended to merge the One and the Many, yet he was deeply influenced by the Hegelian contention that "truth is the whole." This contention led King to a philosophical method of rational coherence, which is a key personalist doctrine.[19] The dialectic enabled King to develop a methodology for dealing with conflict and struggle, in both his personal and public life. More revealing, however, is the fact that dialectical thinking has long been a hallmark of black religious traditions. Cornel West claims,

> Black theologians have either consciously or unconsciously employed a dialectical methodology in approaching their subject matter. This methodology consists of a three-step procedure of negation, preservation, and transformation; their subject matter, of white interpretations of the Christian gospel and their own circumstances. Dialectical methodology is critical in character and hermeneutic in content. For black theologians, it is highly critical of dogmatic viewpoints of the gospel, questioning whether certain unjustifiable prejudgments are operative. It is hermeneutic in that it is concerned with unearthing assumptions of particular interpretations and presenting an understanding of the gospel that extends and expands its ever-unfolding truth.[20]

THE DIALECTIC OF SELF: FREEDOM AND FINITUDE

Transformation, for Martin Luther King Jr., is a dynamic process born of dialectical tensions between the freedom and finitude of persons and the corollary notions of individuality and democracy. A consistent theme in King's moral anthropology is his view of the dialectical nature of persons that is rooted in their spiritual and physical existences. While

See Smith and Zepp, *Search for the Beloved Community*, 118. King stated that personal idealism was his basic philosophical position. He credits personalism with two valuable contributions to his developing religious and ethical convictions—namely, the metaphysical and philosophical grounding of the idea of a personal God, and a metaphysical basis for the dignity and worth of all human personality. See King, *Stride toward Freedom,* 82. Under E. S. Brightman's tutelage, King began studying the philosophy of Hegel. Although he was primarily concerned with Hegel's *Phenomenology of Mind* (1807), he also read Hegel's *Philosophy of Right* (1820–21) and *Philosophy of History* (1822–30).

19. Brightman had written that rational coherence is a method of verification of truth. He maintained that a proposition was true if it met the following criteria: (1) it is self-consistent; (2) it is consistent with all known facts of experience; (3) it is consistent with all other propositions held as true by the mind that is applying this criterion; (4) it establishes explanatory and interpretative relations between various parts of experience; and (5) these relations include all known aspects of experience and all known problems about experience in its details and as a whole. See Edgar S. Brightman, *A Philosophy of Religion* (New York: Prentice Hall, 1940), 128.

20. Cornel West, *Prophesy Deliverance! An Afro-American Revolutionary Christianity* (Philadelphia: Westminster, 1982), 108–9.

we share our physical existence with other forms of nature, persons are also spiritual and rational beings. For King, this is our crucial link with God. Human beings are not only biological creatures; they are also spiritual beings with the capacity for reason and self-transcendence.[21] Persons are both children of nature and children of spirit; they live in two realms, the internal and external. "The internal is that realm of spiritual ends expressed in art, literature, morals, and religion. The external is that complex of devices, techniques, mechanisms, and instrumentalities by which we live."[22] The existential problem of persons, according to King, is the struggle to live a balanced existence in which the "means" by which we live do not outdistance the ends for which we live. This is the ongoing struggle for each person and whenever one allows the "means" to dominate the "ends," the occasion for sin is present.[23] This creates a "persistent civil war" within, "a tragic schizophrenic personality divided against ourselves."[24] This inner struggle, according to King, presents itself as a test—a test of character; character being the revelation of freedom over fate. (Later in our discussion, I will comment on how this inner tension is a sign of the disfiguring, nonconforming praxis of spirituality, ethics, and leadership.) The resolution of this inner conflict is brought about by the grace of God. The inherent potential for goodness within persons and the intervening grace of God were the basis for King's hope in respect to the actualization of the human community.[25]

21. Rationality, says King, distinguishes persons from the lower animals, for "somehow man is in nature, and yet he is above nature; he is in time, and yet he is above time; he is in space, and yet he is above space. This means that man can do things lower animals could never do. He can think a poem and write it; he can think a symphony and compose it; he can think up a great civilization and create it." See Martin Luther King Jr., *The Measure of a Man* (Philadelphia: Fortress, 1988; originally published in 1959), 14–18.

22. Martin Luther King Jr., *Where Do We Go from Here: Chaos or Community?* (Boston: Beacon, 1968; originally published in 1967), 171.

23. Martin Luther King Jr., "Unfulfilled Dreams," in Clayborne Carson and Peter Holloran, eds., *A Knock at Midnight: Inspiration from the Great Sermons of Reverend Martin Luther King, Jr.* (New York: Warner, 1998), 149–50. Also Martin Luther King Jr., "Thou Fool," unpublished version of a sermon, Mt. Pisgah Baptist Church, Chicago (27 August 1967), 4–5, Library and Archives of the Martin Luther King Jr. Center for Nonviolent Social Change (KCLA), Atlanta; and King, *Measure of a Man*, 10–55.

24. King, *Strength to Love,* 49.

25. See King, *Strength to Love,* 134–37; King's understanding of the moral life of persons is religious, i.e., faith precedes morality. While it is true that we all are created in the image of God, there is a tension at the heart of human nature "between good and evil" that tends to drag persons down to lower levels of existence. See King, *Strength to Love,* 134–37. Because of the dialectical nature of the self, there is an endless struggle between freedom and finitude, which wars against moral perfection. King affirmed with the Apostle Paul, "The good that I would, I do not; and the evil that I would not, I do." King, *Measure of a Man,* 12.

THE DIALECTIC OF SOCIETY: INDIVIDUALITY AND DEMOCRACY

As part of King's embrace of the dialectical interplay with thought and action, there is also the social corollary of individuality and democracy.[26] For King, because persons are decidedly communitarian, the logic of individuality is fulfilled in community and the best-suited political context for this realization is democracy. In his many statements about law and resisting unjust laws, the underlying assumption is that moral agency is best equipped to interact and respond to power in situations that are *rational* and *just*. But since the rational nature of human beings seeks conformity to law, people are inclined to make conformity the normative equation for truth and justice. Such conformity, according to King, yields to blindness of action and staleness of culture. Blind conformity makes us paranoid and distrustful of opinions that go against the majority; stale conformity quietly supports the status quo through inaction that leads to apathy and neglect of our duties as citizens. "Most people," he writes, "and Christians in particular are thermometers that record and register the temperature of majority opinion, not thermostats that transform and regulate the temperature of society."[27]

Nonconformity, on the other hand, is not a good in and of itself; rather it must be transformed through spiritual regeneration, which is an ongoing, disciplined and deliberate practice characterized by love for the neighbor. Untransformed nonconformity, for King, leads to unwarranted suspicion and calloused intolerance. Important for King, therefore, was the pragmatic thrust of law as an active, dynamic article that is renewed through conflict and struggle, through negation, preservation, and transformation. Democracy at its best, for King, is a squabble; a contentious exchange of ideas, opinions, values, and practices within the context of civil relations.

26. Cornel West aptly states this idea in his treatment of "prophetic Christianity": "For prophetic Christianity, the two inseparable notions of freedom are existential freedom and social freedom. Existential freedom is an effect of the divine gift of grace which promises to sustain persons through and finally deliver them from the bondage to death, disease, and despair. Social freedom is the aim of Christian political practice, a praxis that flows from the divine gift of grace; social freedom results from the promotion and actualization of the norms of individuality and democracy. Existential freedom empowers people to fight for social freedom, to realize its political dimension. Existential freedom anticipates history and is ultimately transhistorical, whereas social freedom is thoroughly a matter of this worldly human liberation." Cornel West, *Prophesy Deliverance!*, 18.

27. King, *Strength to Love*, 19.

THE DIALECTIC OF SPIRIT: LOVE AND JUSTICE

King's spiritual quest was rooted in his belief in a personal God of love and justice. Although King perceived the primary nature of God to be in the divine goodness expressed in *agape*, he made a critical distinction between the love of God and the justice of God. In his sermon titled, "A Tough Mind and a Tender Heart," he holds the two concepts in dialectical tension. God's relationship to persons is presented as a creative synthesis between the wrath and justice of God and God's love and grace. King claims, "God has two outstretched arms. One is strong enough to surround us with justice, and one is gentle enough to embrace us with grace."[28] The justice of God is manifested in the moral law of the cosmos, which is an imperative for persons to struggle against all forms of injustice working against the actualization of human community. The power of God furnishes those who struggle for justice with the inner resources to bring about creative change that leads to just and loving human relations.[29]

For King, transformation is possible because of the way in which the universe is structured. He believed that God "has placed within the very structure of the universe certain absolute moral laws. We can neither defy them nor break them. If we disobey them, they will break us."[30] King's belief in the moral law enabled him to maintain optimism in the ultimate victory of good over evil as persons choose to become coworkers with God in fulfilling divine purposes in human history. This belief in the moral law was the basis for his attack upon unjust structures and laws that desacralized human personality. Segregation statues and other unjust laws, he argued, should be abolished not only because they are against the principles of democracy, but also because they are ultimately against the moral law of the cosmos. An unjust law, according to King, is a human code that is not in harmony with the moral law. Therefore, it is the transformed nonconformist's moral responsibility to break unjust laws. Just laws, on the other hand, are laws that uplift human personality and should be obeyed because they are in harmony with the moral law.[31]

28. King, *Strength to Love*, 15.

29. King, *Strength to Love*, 14–16. Also see Martin Luther King Jr., *Why We Can't Wait* (New York: Signet, 1964), 82; and King, *Strength to Love*, 17–25.

30. King, *Strength to Love*, 110. King writes, "There is a law in the moral world—a silent, invisible imperative, akin to the laws of the physical world—which reminds us that life will only work in a certain way. The Hitlers and Mussolinis have their day, and for a period they may wield great power, spreading themselves like a green bay tree, but soon they are cut down like grass and wither as the green herb." See King, *Strength to Love*, 109.

31. King, *Why We Can't Wait*, 82.

The transformed nonconformist, according to King, is under obligation to the moral law. Christians, as a creative minority, must never conform to the prevailing laws and customs of a society when they are in conflict with human dignity and justice. Moreover, Christians are called upon to break the law as an expression of their respect for law itself. "The hope of a secure and livable world lies with the disciplined nonconformists, who are dedicated to justice, peace, and brotherhood."[32]

But more is at stake in his view of transformed nonconformity—the regenerated individual is a "transformed nonconformist" in society, and following the way of Christ, is willing to suffer redemptively for others.[33] The "transformed nonconformist" refuses to cooperate with evil systems that exploit and destroy human personality, and willingly suffers the penalty of law for nonconformity. For the person who suffers redemptively for the sake of others, life becomes a living sacrament of the presence of God in the world, working for universal wholeness.[34]

THE ETHICAL DIMENSIONS OF TRANSFORMED NONCONFORMITY: CHARACTER, CIVILITY, AND COMMUNITY CHARACTER

King's dialectical treatment of transformed nonconformity helps us to better understand the place of character in respect to leadership. For the most part, character is relegated to a type of abstract individualism in leadership literature where the emphasis is placed on certain principles or practices that the individual appropriates in order to become an effective leader. Character, in both King's biography and in his expressed opinions on the same, emphasizes the dimensions of freedom and finitude, individuality and democracy, and love and justice. Character, in this perspective, is the narrative script that defines individuality: the stories that name the individual's experience and the "inner experiences" or core philosophies espoused by the individual within the context of a given community. A significant variable that is often not emphasized or completely neglected in leadership studies is the role of systems (institutions, traditions, practices) and their impact on the moral development of leaders. Simply stated, individuals are socially constructed, yet by defin-

32. King, *Strength to Love*, 22.

33. King writes, "To be a Christian, one must take up his cross, with all its difficulties and agonizing and tragedy-packed content, and carry it until that very cross leaves its marks upon us and redeems us to that more excellent way which only comes through suffering." See King, *Strength to Love*, 25.

34. King, *Strength to Love*, 53–54.

ition, are responsible and accountable for moral choices within the context of their social histories and stories. Hence the pertinent questions for ethical leadership in this respect are: Of what story or stories is the individual a part and how does the story (or stories) inform moral practices and habits? What is the role of institutions in this narrative perspective, and how might the moral agent develop habits and practices that conspire against unjust institutional practices that promote unhealthy and self-destructive existence?

Most mark King's public career with his leadership of the Montgomery Improvement Association (MIA), but before Montgomery his was a story intertwined with other stories that produced the grandiloquent baritone, which proclaimed the message of transformed nonconformity to America and the world. We must ask, therefore, "What was the narrative script that King was reading when he arrived in Montgomery?" "How had history uniquely prepared him for this grand performance?" Some of the answers lie in his early formation, in the contexts of his family environment, the fellowship of the black church, and in the larger context of the black community of Atlanta, Georgia. In these interrelated environs one sees most clearly the genesis of his spiritual quest and the developing character that accompanied his vision.[35] In a revealing statement in his "Autobiography of Religious Development," written while he was a student at Crozer Theological Seminary, King reflects on his reasons for entering the ministry and his early childhood experiences with his family and church:

> At present I still feel the effects of the noble moral and ethical ideals that I grew up under. They have been real and precious to me, and even in moments of theological doubt I could never turn away from them. Even though I never had an abrupt conversion experience, religion has been real to me and closely knitted to life. In fact the two cannot be separated; religion for me is life.[36]

35. Fluker, *They Looked for a City*, 82–86.

36. King, "An Autobiography of Religious Development," in Carson et al., eds., *King Papers,* 1:363. See also King, "Statement to the American Baptist Convention" (7 August 1959) in Clayborne Carson et al., eds., *The Papers of Martin Luther King, Jr.: Advocate of the Social Gospel, September 1948–March 1963* (Berkeley: University of California Press, 2007), 6:367–68. Here King shares his call to ministry.

CHARACTER AND THE LARGER DRAMATIC REPOSITORY OF TRANSFORMED NONCONFORMITY

King's dialectical appropriation of knowledge only touches the surface of what was at stake in his inner struggles of spirit and his inherited historical burdens of recognition, respectability, and loyalty.[37] The dialectical formulation of the theme of transformed nonconformity is at once an expression of King's sermonizing and of his own existential struggle with personal freedom and social liberation.[38] Michael Eric Dyson and others have documented this internal struggle and have shown how this inner tension of opposites informs the social discourse of King. Dyson, commenting on the criticisms of King's promiscuity and plagiarism, suggests:

> Character cannot be understood through isolated incidents or a fixation on the flaws of a human being during a selected period in life. Assessment of character must take into account the long view, the wide angle. Character is truly glimpsed as we learn of human beings negotiating large and small problems that test moral vision, ethical creativity, and sound judgment. Character cannot be grasped in disjointed details or sporadic facts. Character can only be glimpsed in a sustained story that provides plausible accounts and credible explanations of human behavior.[39]

King firmly believed that inner transformation is essential to involvement in social transformation. Transformation, however, is not equated with moral perfectionism; rather it is understood as an inner quality of life that issues forth in deeds of goodwill and love for the neighbor. "In the final analysis," says King, "what God requires is that your heart is right. Salvation isn't reaching the destination of absolute morality, but it's being in the process and on the right road."[40] For him, the person

37. Fluker, "Recognition, Respectability and Loyalty," in Smith, ed., *New Day Begun*, 113–41.

38. A cursory reading of King's sermons reveals how he utilizes this methodology to analyze and reinterpret long-standing biblical truths in his quest for personal and social transformation. See "Tough Mind and a Tender Heart," 13–14; "Transformed Non-Conformist," 18–19; "On Being a Good Neighbor," 35–46; "Loving Your Enemies," 47–55; "How Should a Christian View Communism," 96–105; "Antidotes for Fear," 115–26; "The Answer to a Perplexing Question," 127–37, in *Strength to Love*. See also King's unpublished sermons: "Is the Universe Friendly," unpublished version of a sermon, Ebenezer Baptist Church, Atlanta, Georgia (12 December 1965), KCLA, 8–9; "Thou Fool," 2–4; and "Discerning the Signs of History," unpublished version of a sermon, Ebenezer Baptist Church, Atlanta, Georgia (15 November 1964), KCLA, 1–5.

39. Michael Eric Dyson, *I May Not Get There with You: The True Martin Luther King, Jr.* (New York: The Free Press, 2000), 166.

40. King, "Unfulfilled Dreams," in Carson and Holloran, eds., *Knock at Midnight*, 196.

who opens her life to God in Christ experiences a new birth and a reorientation of values that enables her to struggle for social transformation. "Only through an inner spiritual transformation do we gain the strength to fight vigorously the evils of the world in an humble and loving spirit," King writes.[41]

For the development of leaders for the church and society, King provides a helpful insight into the centrality of "the inner theater" in the formation and care of leaders. "The inner theater" represents those core themes that affect an individual's personality and leadership style. "For each of us, our unique mixture of motivational needs determine our character and creates the triangle of our mental life—a tightly interlocked triangle consisting of cognition, affect, and behavior. No one of these dimensions of the triangle can be seen as separate from the other."[42] The cultivation of the private life or one's "inner theater" is the basis for spirituality and ethical awareness. Leaders involved in acts of social transformation must begin by remembering, retelling, and reliving their own stories. Again and again, we must ask ourselves what and whom we are seeking to change. This is the first step in the realization of calling and character.

Character, in this sense, refers to "the morally-anchored self in the context of socio-historical narrative."[43] For our purposes, this means the person's life experiences in relation to larger historical and social narratives. Reclaiming the ethical center requires that the unfinished business of one's life story (the pain, the hurt, the unresolved contradictions) be addressed. It also means reattachment to historically grounded virtues, which have protected the community through ritualistic healing: integrity and self-esteem, trust and empathy, and courage and hope as both personal and political practices. One should not (or better, cannot) begin the work of creating a just and healthy civil society until one has explored the deepest regions of self-knowledge and the motivational content of agency that mark the core of individuality, personal morals, and practices.

While there are formidable social, political, and economic issues that must be confronted, I am convinced that a critical dimension of the battle must be waged from within. King teaches us that even though the contradictions of life may never be completely resolved, our inner tensions can become the creative sources for self-reflection, healing, and dynamically engaged social praxis—in other words, self-reflection and

41. King, *Strength to Love*, 23.

42. Manfred Kets De Vries, *Leadership Mystique*, 5.

43. Laurence Thomas, *Living Morally: A Psychology of Moral Character* (Philadelphia: Temple University Press, 1989), 17–26.

personal healing are inextricably tied to empathy and care for others. In King's language, the cross is the single interpretative paradigm for understanding the role of the transformed nonconformist in the quest for civility and community:

> My personal trials have also taught me the value of unmerited suffering . . . I have lived these past few years with the conviction that unearned suffering is redemptive. There are some who still find the cross a stumbling block, others consider it foolish, but I am more convinced than ever before that it is the power of God unto social and individual salvation. So like the Apostle Paul I can humbly say, "I bear in my body the marks of the Lord Jesus."[44]

SPIRITUALITY AND SOCIAL JUSTICE

King's character was intricately related to his spiritual life and his quest for social justice. The pre-Montgomery King or the faces of "Little Mike," "Tweed," and "The Philosopher King," do not readily lend themselves to the character that is disclosed in the moments of testing that follow his public ministry in Montgomery and thereafter.[45] It is rather in engagement with the struggle for social justice that one begins to see the deep, furrowed glance of the preacher becoming leader of the people. This understanding of spirituality is not the same as the market-stimulated self-help philosophies on spiritual growth that promote development and solipsistic narcissism as the means to attain spiritual awareness that crowd the shelves in mega-bookstores. Rather, King's brand of spirituality stands in direct contradiction to the conforming, anesthetizing cultural deluge that dominates the printed and audio-visual media on leadership.

THE KITCHEN VISION

I cite here two events in King's life where one sees clearly the relationship between spirituality and social transformation in his portraiture of character. One is the oft-cited "kitchen vision." David Garrow maintains that the "kitchen vision" of January 27, 1956, which took place in the

44. Washington, ed., *Testament of Hope*, 40–41; and King, *Strength to Love,* 154.

45. These "faces" refer, respectively, to the early stages of King's development. "Little Mike," refers to his early formation under the shadow of a powerful father figure; "Tweed" was the nickname of his teenage years at Morehouse College; and "The Philosopher King," as he was dubbed, is a reference to his university days in Boston. Levinas writes, "The face of the man is the medium through which the invisible in him becomes visible and enters into commerce with us." See Levinas, *Difficult Freedom*, 140.

early stages of the Montgomery boycott, was the paradigmatic moment in King's spirituality.[46] The experience captures for us an example of the way in which King understood spirituality to be part of a larger dynamic of ethics and leadership. It is also a revealing portrait of the testing of character that is integral to the spirituality of transformed nonconformity. Caught in the early phases of the Montgomery bus boycott, King received a chilling telephone call threatening his life and the life of his family: The voice on the other end of the phone, said, "Nigger, we are tired of you and your mess now. And if you are not out of town in three days, we're going to blow your brains out, and blow up your house." King says he "sat there and thought about his little daughter who had just been born" and his "devoted and loyal wife" who was asleep. He thought about how he might be taken from her or she from him. He thought about his father and mother who had always been the steadying influences for him in trying moments, but they were one hundred seventy-five miles away in Atlanta. He said to himself:

> You've got to call on that something and that person that your Daddy used to tell you about, that power that can make a way out of no way. . . . And I discovered then that religion had to become real to me, and I had to know God for myself. And I bowed down over that cup of coffee. I never will forget it. . . . I prayed a prayer, and I prayed out loud that night. I said, "Lord, I'm down here trying to do what's right. I think I'm right. I think the cause we represent is right. But Lord I must confess that I am weak now. I'm faltering. I'm losing my courage. And I can't let the people see me like this because if they see me weak and losing my courage, they will begin to get weak."

Then it happened:

> And it seemed at that moment that I could hear an inner voice saying to me, "Martin Luther, stand up for righteousness. Stand up for justice. Stand up for truth. And lo I will be with you, even until the end of the world." . . . I heard the voice of Jesus saying still to fight on. He promised never to

46. King, *Stride toward Freedom*, 134–35; see also, Garrow, *Bearing the Cross*, 57–58; David Garrow, "Martin Luther King Jr., and the Spirit of Leadership," in Peter J. Albert and Ronald Hoffman, eds., *We Shall Overcome: Martin Luther King, Jr., and the Black Freedom Struggle* (New York: Pantheon, 1990), 19–20. I agree with Lewis Baldwin and Preston Williams that this vision, while important, should not be considered as an isolated phenomenon, but should be understood as one among other experiences in King's spiritual odyssey and as an example of the black church's belief in the intimacy of the divine in struggles for justice. See Baldwin, *There Is a Balm in Gilead*, 188–90; and Preston N. Williams, "The Public and Private Burdens of Martin Luther King, Jr.," *Christian Century* (25 February 1987): 198–99.

leave me, never to leave me alone. No, never alone. No, never alone. He promised never to leave me, never to leave me alone.[47]

HOWARD THURMAN AND THE HARLEM STABBING INCIDENT

In a lesser-known incident, Howard Thurman made one of his famous pastoral visits to Martin Luther King Jr. Thurman states in his autobiography that on more than one occasion he felt a premonition to minister to leaders engaged in the thick of the struggle. His relationship with Martin Luther King Jr. is but one example.[48] After the stabbing of Martin Luther King Jr. in Harlem on September 20, 1958, Thurman felt the inner necessity to go to him. In reference to this movement of the Spirit upon him, he writes:

> Many times through the years I have had strange visitations in which there emerges at the center of my consciousness *a face*, a sense of urgency, a

47. Quoted in Garrow, *Bearing the Cross*, 57–58; King, *Stride toward Freedom*, 134–35; and Carson and Holloran, eds., *Knock at Midnight*, 162.

48. Several writers have made reference to the influence of Thurman on his younger visionary. See Lerone Bennett, *What Manner of Man: A Biography of Martin Luther King, Jr.*, 2nd ed. (Chicago: Johnson, 1976), 74–75; Ansbro, *Martin Luther King, Jr.*, 27–29 and 272; "Dr. King Mentor Remembered," *The Boston Globe* (15 January 1982): 13–14; Lewis V. Baldwin, "Understanding Martin Luther King, Jr. within the Context of Southern Black Religious History," *Journal of Religious Studies* 13, no. 2 (Fall 1987): 21–22; Lewis V. Baldwin, "Martin Luther King, the Black Church and the Black Messianic Vision," *The Journal of the Interdenominational Center* 12, nos. 1–2 (Fall 1984/Spring 1985): 100 and 102–4; and Larry Murphy, "Howard Thurman and Social Activism," in Henry J. Young, ed., *God and Human Freedom: A Festschrift in Honor of Howard Thurman* (Richmond, IN: Friends United, 1983), 154–55. Perhaps, Thurman's own accounting of his relationship with King is sufficient for our purposes: "I am one of a few and maybe the only person who was a member of the faculty of the Graduate School of Theology at Boston University when Dr. King took his doctorate degree who did not have him in the classroom. I think this is a mark of distinction. We had contacts, but our primary contact was sitting around my television watching the World Series . . . I've known him and his family, his mother and his father for many years. And Mrs. Thurman's and my relationship to those two young people (Martin and Coretta King) was a personal and primary one. It was not involved in the light and the drama. My concern was always about the state of his spiritual life all the time. And I felt it was my relationship with him that gave me the right to do it, while Mrs. Thurman's interest was always in the little things involving the children and the wife of a man who had to live his private life in public. And this is a great agony. I understand from one of his biographers that a book that I wrote in 1949 was very influential on his thinking: *Jesus and the Disinherited*. But I did not hear this from him and I do not make a claim of it; but lest someone may know that it is in this biographical statement you will think that I am trying to be falsely modest by not mentioning it; so I've done it and now I can go on with my work." Thurman, "Litany and Words in Memoriam for Martin Luther King Jr.," The Church for the Fellowship of All Peoples, San Francisco, California (7 April 1968), Howard Thurman Educational Trust, San Francisco, California.

> vibrant sensation, involving some particular person. On a certain Friday afternoon, Martin emerged in my awareness and would not leave. When I came home I said to Sue [Thurman's wife], "Tomorrow morning I am going down to New York to see Martin. I am not sure why, but I must talk with him personally if the doctors will permit."[49]

During his visit with the young civil rights leader, Thurman encouraged him to extend his convalescence four weeks beyond those recommended by his doctor in order "to reassess himself in relation to the cause, to rest his body and mind with healing detachment, and to take a long look that only solitary brooding can provide." Thurman suggested, "The movement had become an organism with a life of its own to which he [King] must relate in fresh and extraordinary ways or be swallowed up by it."[50] King's biographers indicate that he did indeed take an extended convalescence culminating in his trip to the land of Gandhi in February 1959. Taylor Branch writes: "Recovering at home, King settled into a period of relative stillness unique to his entire adult life. He delivered no speeches or sermons outside the Dexter pulpit for many weeks. Nor did he travel." Branch also reports that King turned down the pressing agenda within the movement during this period.[51] Stephen B. Oates reports that

> as he convalesced, King had time to do what he had longed for all these months: he read books and meditated. And he talked a good deal about the trial he was going through. He decided that God was teaching him a lesson here, and that was personal redemption through suffering. It seemed to him that the stabbing had been for a purpose, that it was part of God's plan to prepare him for some larger work in the bastion of segregation that was the American South.[52]

These two events point to ways in which King understood spirituality to be more than a matter of personal development. For him, the issues of justice and community and the place of suffering are integral parts of the ongoing spiritual process that the transformed nonconformist must endure in his or her quest for wholeness. Such a process is fraught with provocations, challenges, and hopes that are rooted in larger historical

49. Howard Thurman, *With Head and Heart: The Autobiography of Howard Thurman* (New York: Harcourt, Brace and Jovanovich, 1979), 254–55.

50. Thurman, *With Head and Heart,* 255. Thurman recommended an "additional four weeks to those that the doctor felt you [King] needed for complete recovery." "Howard Thurman to Martin Luther King, Jr.," unpublished letter (20 October 1958), The Papers of Martin Luther King Jr., Special Collections, Mugar Memorial Library, Boston University, Boston, Massachusetts.

51. Branch, *Parting the Waters*, 245.

52. Oates, *Let the Trumpet Sound*, 140. See also Garrow, *Bearing the Cross*, 111–13.

and social narratives than the popular, mass-produced therapeutic formulae for personal healing and virtue. Moreover, they are statements about the *disorienting, disfiguring, and dying* experience of transformed nonconformity. Unlike the popular discourse on spirituality, which isolates the individual from the traffic of lifeworlds and systemworlds, King's experience of the divine is at the dangerous intersection where these worlds collide. Spirituality, ethics, and leadership, in this view, complicate the rather naïve conjecture that the leader experiences the transforming power of the divine apart from engagement with the powers of this world. Far from the Pollyanna, wishful practices of leadership defined by corporate behemoths, here the emphasis is on the care of others who are impacted by the leader's ethical discernment, deliberation, and decisions. The ability to hear the voice of the divine is intricately interwoven with the care of the vulnerable other—the other, in the first case, being the black and poor people of Montgomery who entrusted young King with their future.

In the Harlem Hospital event, there is clearly a sense of self that is related to the larger spiritual community. Thurman sees King's *face*—a *face* that is tested—and in this *face,* the fulfillment of the possibility and hope of a larger community. Thurman's advice and counsel provides King with the opportunity to deepen his own channels and commitment to the struggle for social transformation in the American South. For Thurman, spiritual discipline exposes the individual to "the tutor" or the "unseen model" by which one structures the facts of his or her experience. For this reason, Thurman counseled: "[T]he person concerned about social change must not only understand the materials with which he has to do, the things which he is trying to manipulate, to reorder, to refashion but again and again he must expose the roots of his mind to the literal truth that is the tutor of the facts, the orderer and reorderer of the facts of his experience."[53]

This must be done, Thurman contended, so that in the quest for social justice, one's vision of society never conforms to some external pattern, but is "modeled and shaped in accordance to the innermost transformation that is going on in his spirit."[54] Therefore, it was his insistence that those who were engaged in acts of liberation continually examine the sources of their motivation and the ways in which the circling series of social processes that they seek to change are related to their spiritual pilgrimages. Always, the primary questions for the social activist are, *"What*

53. Howard Thurman, "He Looked for a City." Taped Sermon, Marsh Chapel, Boston University, 2 January 1955, Special Collections, Mugar Library, Boston University.

54. Thurman, "He Looked for a City."

are you trying to do with your life? What kind of person are you trying to become?"[55] It was Thurman's conviction that the individual in his or her actions "is trying to snare into the body of his facts, his conviction of those facts." He cautioned, however, that faith thusly understood always runs the risk of becoming idolatrous as in patriotic visions of "the American way."[56] Therefore, one must always examine the motivational content of action that involves a tutoring of the will by an unseen model, which for him was the truth that is resident within the individual. Here the issues of *identity, purpose,* and *method* are combined in relation to the social context in which the individual finds himself or herself.

CIVILITY

Civility is used in a variety of contexts often masking complex historical, sociological, and methodological issues. Civility in common usage refers to a set of manners, certain etiquette and social graces that are rooted in specific class orientations and moral sensibilities.[57] Civility, however, does not simply refer to etiquette, manners, and social graces; rather it is inclusive of *social capital* and the inherent benefits accrued by *networks of reciprocity*. Civility also has to do with the individual's social dignity within that system. In the following discussion, the term civility is used as a framework for discussing the role of *social capital* in the leaders' repository of skills and competencies essential for negotiation and working for transformation in public space.[58] I do not limit civility, however, to social capital, but refer more broadly to the concept as *the social-historical script or contract that the individual citizen negotiates within*

55. See Howard Thurman, *Disciplines of the Spirit* (New York: Harper and Row, 1963), 26–37, where he discusses three primary questions related to the discipline of commitment. They are respectively, "Who am I?," "What do I want?," and "How do I propose to get it?"

56. Thurman, "He Looked for a City."

57. Amitai Etzioni's definition of civility is helpful. "The term of civility has been used in different ways, most commonly it has referred to the need to deliberate in a civil manner about the issues society faces, and to sustain intermediary bodies that stand between the individual and the state." Amitai Etzioni, *The New Golden Rule* (New York: Basic Books, 1996), 95–96.

58. Robert D. Putnam's *Bowling Alone* is one example of the ongoing public debate on the significance of civil discourse and social networking that is part of a larger conversation about the need to recapture, re-appropriate, and sustain the habits and practices essential for the survival of an American ethos of generalized reciprocity and mutual obligation. Robert D. Putnam, *Bowling Alone: The Collapse and Revival of American Community* (New York: Simon & Schuster, 2000). See especially Putnam's discussion on the significance of "social capital" as both a bonding and bridging social phenomenon and its relationship to civic infrastructures that build community. Bonding refers to the ways in which social capital tends to reinforce exclusive identities and homogenous groups. Bridging refers to ways in which social capital tends to produce broader and more inclusive group behavior and to encourage reciprocity (22–24).

the context of the larger society. Civility is the psychosocial ecology of the individual; a certain understanding or self-referential index of the individual's place within a social system as it relates to character. For King, as we shall see, civility is used as a subversive instrument to exaggerate the creative tension between conformity and nonconformity in the quest for a higher synthesis of transformed nonconformity.

TRANSFORMED NONCONFORMITY AND SUBVERSIVE CIVILITY

In black life generally, civility as a social and political option is severely limited. In fact, some scholars even question its utility as a political good.[59] Nonetheless, in black churches, because of the ideological and cultural precedents of *doubleness* and racial uplift among black elites, civility has come to represent precisely that—a social and political good elevated to the level of *civic virtue*. In this respect, it has to do with "the rules of association of free members (of society) and so the basis of social dignity."[60] Evelyn Brooks Higginbotham's examination of the "politics of respectability" signals part of what is at stake in the usages of civility as a social and political strategy for citizenship rights among women of the Negro Club Movement.[61] Similarly, early architects of the modern civil rights movement utilized civility as a means of cultivating habits and practices that conspired toward engagement in democratic society. Most notable among these leaders in mid-twentieth century were black religious elites and pastors such as Reverdy C. Ransom, Mordecai Wyatt Johnson, Howard Thurman, Benjamin E. Mays, and William Stuart Nelson.[62]

59. James Schmidt, "Is Civility a Virtue?," in *Civility*, ed. Leroy S. Rouner (Notre Dame: University of Notre Dame Press, 2000), 17–19.

60. Lawrence Cahoone, "Civic Meetings, Cultural Meanings," in Rouner, ed., *Civility*, 46.

61. Higginbotham writes, "The politics of respectability assumed a fluid and shifting position along a continuum of African American resistance. Through the discourse of respectability, the Baptist women emphasized manners and morals while simultaneously asserting traditional forms of protest, such as petitions, boycotts, and verbal appeals to justice." See Evelyn Brooks Higginbotham, *Righteous Discontent: The Women's Movement in the Black Baptist Church 1880–1920* (Cambridge, MA: Harvard University Press, 1993), 187.

62. See Anthony Pinn, ed., *Making the Gospel Plain: The Writings of Bishop Reverdy C. Ransom* (Harrisburg, PA: Trinity, 1999); Ralph Luker, *The Social Gospel in Black and White: American Racial Reform, 1885–1912* (Chapel Hill: University of North Carolina Press, 1991); Mordecai Wyatt Johnson, "Faith of the American Negro," in *Cavalcade: Negro American Writing from 1760 to the Present*, ed. Arthur P. Davis and J. Saunders Redding (Boston: Houghton Mifflin, 1971); and Fluker and Tumber, eds., *Strange Freedom*. Mordecai Wyatt Johnson, in a memorable speech titled, "The Faith of the American Negro," declared: "Since their Emancipation

The leadership of Martin Luther King Jr. in the modern civil rights movement represents the most outstanding example of this legacy of civility. Perhaps better than any other leader of the twentieth century, King was able to forge civility into a subversive weapon in the struggle for equality and justice in American society. By subversive civility, what I have in mind is akin to Jeffery Goldfarb's observation that intellectuals "contribute to a democratic life when they civilize political contestation and when they subvert complacent consensus; when they provide enemies with the discursive possibility to become opponents and when they facilitate public deliberations about problems buried by the norms of civility."[63] King's distinctive contribution in this regard is the way in which he dialectically explores the options afforded by democratic life and forces existing tensions through nonviolent direct action. Stephen Carter makes a similar observation. According to Carter, King and other leaders in the Southern Leadership Conference (SCLC) were able "to spark a dialogue" through nonviolent acts of civility. The transformed nonconformist is primarily concerned with the disruption of "negative peace" as a way of bringing to surface hidden tensions that create the conditions for creative understanding and new discursive possibilities.[64]

from slavery the masses of American Negroes have lived by the strength of simple but deeply moving faith. They have believed in the love of and providence of a just and holy God; they have believed in the principles of democracy and in the righteous purpose of the Federal Government, and they have believed in the disposition of the American people as a whole and in the long run to be fair in all their dealings." Mordecai Wyatt Johnson in Fluker and Tumber, eds., *Strange Freedom*, 681.

63. See Jeffrey C. Goldfarb's excellent discussion in *Civility and Subversion: The Intellectual in Democratic Society* (Cambridge: Cambridge University Press, 1998), 1. Although the example he cites is the disruptive public speech of Malcolm X, the civility practiced by King and the modern civil rights movement represents the epitome of civility as disruptive speech and action. In this sense, King is rightly depicted as a *bricoleur*. See Jeffrey Stout, *Ethics after Babel: The Languages of Morals and Their Discontents* (Boston: Beacon, 1988), 74.

64. Martin Luther King Jr., "Love, Law and Disobedience," in James M. Washington, ed., *A Testament of Hope: The Essential Writings and Speeches of Martin Luther King, Jr.* (New York: Harper & Row, 1986), 51. See also, Martin Luther King Jr., "Letter from a Birmingham Jail," where he writes: "I had hoped that the white moderate would understand that law and order exist for the purpose of establishing justice and that when they fail in this purpose they become the dangerously structured dams that block the flow of social progress. I had hoped that the white moderate would understand that the present tension in the South is a necessary phase of the transition from an obnoxious negative peace, in which the Negro passively accepted his unjust plight, to a substantive and positive peace, in which all men will respect the dignity and worth of human personality. Actually, we who engage in nonviolent direct action are not the creators of tension. We merely bring to the surface the hidden tension that is already alive. We bring it out in the open, where it can be seen and dealt with. Like a boil that can never be cured so long as it is covered up but must be opened with all its ugliness to the natural medicines of air and light, injustice must be exposed, with all the tension its exposure creates, to the light of human conscience and the air of national opinion before it can be cured." See Washington, ed., *Testament of Hope*, 295.

Critical to this understanding of subversive civility is the practice of love or what King called "excessive altruism."[65] Excessive altruism is concretely expressed in acts of sympathy. It is to be distinguished from acts of pity that are general in application; rather sympathy is concerned with particularity. "Sympathy," writes King, "is fellow feeling for the person in need—his pain, agony and burdens." Sympathetic concern does not do something *for* others; rather it does something *with* others. It is only in this respect that the dignity and self-worth of others are preserved. Excessive altruism, therefore, goes beyond deontological decrees, universality as a criterion for duty, and uncritical compliance to law; it goes "the second mile." Therefore, it cannot be enforced by external decrees, but is motivated by unenforceable, self-imposed sanctions.

King makes a distinction between enforceable and non-enforceable obligations. Enforceable obligations refer to moral demands (rules, laws, and statues) that are externally imposed, while unenforceable obligations refer to the inner sanctions of persons, which are self-imposed. Unenforceable laws "concern inner attitudes, genuine person-to-person relations, and expressions of compassion which law books cannot regulate and jails cannot rectify."[66] Enforceable obligations are human laws that insure justice; unenforceable obligations belong to a higher law, rooted in the moral order of the cosmos, and they produce love.[67] Although behavior can be regulated by external decrees, King's view of civility as "excessive altruism" cannot be legislated. This was the logic of his argument against the limits of desegregation as an enforceable demand and integration as an unenforceable demand. "Desegregation will break down the legal barriers and bring men together physically, but something must touch the hearts and souls of men so that they come together spiritually because it is natural and right."[68]

Finally, King's brand of subversive civility was rooted in a profound sense of spirituality and a "searching ethical awareness."[69] Religion, for

65. King, *Strength to Love*, 32.

66. King, *Strength to Love*, 33.

67. King, *Strength to Love*, 33.

68. King, "The Ethical Demands of Integration," in Washington, ed., *Testament of Hope*, 124.

69. Howard Thurman makes this observation in his eulogy of Martin Luther King Jr. He stated, "Always he spoke from within the context of his religious experience, giving voice to the ethical insight which sprang out of his profound brooding over the meaning of his Judeo-Christian heritage. And this was indeed his great contribution to our times. He was able to put at the center of his own personal religious experience a searching ethical awareness. Thus organized religion as we know it in our society found itself with its back against the wall. To condemn him, to reject him, was to reject the ethical insight of the faith it proclaimed. And this was new. Racial prejudice, segregation, and discrimination were not regarded by him as merely un-American, undemocratic, but as a mortal sin against God. For those who were religious it awakens guilt; for those who are merely superstitious it inspires fear. And it was this fear that

King, played a prominent role in sustaining the "negative peace" of the culture of conformity. In his "Letter from a Birmingham Jail," King challenged the white religious leadership to imitate the example of the early Christian church by becoming "disturbers of the peace" and "outside agitators." Black leadership was not exempt from King's scathing critique. Throughout his public career, King was a critic of the two extremes of emotionalism and classism that he felt plagued black church leadership. Some of King's severest critics were fellow black clergy and elites who saw him as a "disturber of the peace," especially in his decision to speak out against the Vietnam War.[70]

Leaders of the new century can take an important cue from King and the leaders of the modern civil rights movement. The call for a new kind of subversive civility is echoed from many corridors as war escalates and violent acts of injustice are perpetrated through laws that silently exclude and relegate entire peoples to the margins. How might leaders who stand at the intersection where worlds collide maintain a disciplined, yet disruptive movement of presence without succumbing to the temptation to become physically violent and self-destructive in the process? The lessons of subversive civility represented by King and the civil rights movement may well be the salvation of American democracy if we have the courage to experiment with new forms of nonviolent dissent and resistance.

COMMUNITY

Considerable work has already been done on King's concept of community.[71] I am most interested in the final years of King's life and ministry (1964–1968). Although beleaguered with controversy and sabotage, these years are the most crucial in understanding the maturation of his

pulled the trigger of the assassin's gun that took his life." See Fluker and Tumber, eds., *Strange Freedom*, 186.

70. King, *Strength to Love,* 56–66*;* King, "Letter from a Birmingham Jail," and "A Time to Break Silence," in Washington, ed., *Testament of Hope*, 231–44; 289–302, and 497–504.

71. For Martin Luther King Jr., community is the ideal that serves as the goal of human existence and the norm for ethical judgment; it is the mutually cooperative and voluntary venture of persons in which they realize the solidarity of humanity by freely assuming responsibility for one another within the context of civil relations. Community provides the context for the sensuous articulation of the values of love, justice, and courage as dynamic and interrelated constructs. The search for community was the defining motif of Martin Luther King Jr.'s life and thought. From his early childhood until his death, there is a progression in his personal and intellectual understanding of the nature and goal of human existence, which he refers to as "the beloved community." The early development of the ideal of community in King reached its zenith in the march on Washington in 1963, but the following four and a half years proved to be a period in which his vision of community received its severest criticisms and challenges.

spiritual and intellectual growth in respect to community. It is in this period that one sees most clearly King's own transformed nonconformity in his wrestling with nonviolence as a means of achieving human community, his increased realization of the international implications of his vision of community, his understanding of the nature and role of conflict (especially his courageous stance against the Vietnam War), and the place of hope in the realization of human community.[72] In the remainder of our discussion, I will focus on his legacy of hope as a critical insight for transformed nonconformists in the twenty-first century.

TRANSFORMED NONCONFORMITY—THE LEGACY: HOPE AND COMMUNITY

The basis for the profound hope in King is found in the experience of transformed nonconformity. In his "Christian Sermon on Peace" (1967), King spoke of the disparity between his dream of 1963 and his personal nightmare that evolved over the following four years: "Yes, I am personally the victim of deferred dreams, of blasted hopes, but in spite of that I close today saying I still have a dream, because, you know, you can't give up on life. If you lose hope, somehow you lose that vitality that keeps life moving, you lose the courage to be, that quality to go on in spite of all. And so today I still have a dream."[73]

Faces tell stories and disclose mysteries of character and being. The final *face* of King is the one we most remember—the somber, distant, almost melancholic look—*a disfigured countenance that returns from the mountain.* No place in King is this face more vividly portrayed than in his bold excoriation of the Vietnam War and in his trials within the African American community around the political philosophy of black nationalism, articulated by Malcolm X. It is *the face of hope*. Professor James H. Cone suggests that Martin King's perspective on "racism, black empowerment and war led to a shift in emphasis and meaning regarding the themes of love, justice, and hope" which were operative concepts in his articulation of the beloved community.[74] The theme of hope, according to Cone, became "the shining center of Martin's thinking, revealing new interpretations of love and justice."[75] This shifting emphasis had significant implications for King's theological and spiritual perspectives surrounding the theological constructs of "exodus" and "exile." There is

72. Fluker, *They Looked for a City*, 120–28.

73. King, "A Christmas Sermon on Peace," in Washington, ed., *Testament of Hope*, 257.

74. Cone, *Martin and Malcolm and America*, 235.

75. Cone, *Martin and Malcolm and America*, 165 and 235.

evidence in the later King that there was a movement toward an "exilic" metaphor as a way of understanding the "shifting" epistemic grounds for the liberative claims for African Americans.

King's last speech is normally interpreted in light of the exodus paradigm. In that speech, King stands on the summit of the mountaintop and sees the "Promised Land." The "Promised Land" conjures up images of the conquest of Canaan, but a "shift" in lenses would offer a different reading. A closer examination of the substantive discourse in the speech reveals several levels of meaning. One is that King speaks out of a diasporic perspective. He begins his speech as a type of journey on which he takes a panoramic view of Western history. He calls his listeners to remember with him the long journey of Western civilization. He then locates himself in the latter half of the twentieth century in which there is a worldwide struggle for freedom. The exodus event is included as one instance in the long march of humanity toward freedom. The civil rights movement is situated in the broader context of a world movement that is taking place in America. This is a recurring theme throughout King's pilgrimage, beginning with his initial speech at Holt Baptist Church in 1955. The primary discursive note throughout the speech is the element of "hope." In the exile motif, the dominant existential category is "hope." What is the source and direction of this hope for King? A reading from within the exile paradigm favors the source of hope in the history of suffering peoples to create new meanings out of overwhelming oppression. The direction of the hope is toward a worldwide revolution. King viewed the strike of the garbage workers in Memphis as part of a worldwide struggle for equality and freedom. This line of thinking points toward an exilic existence within the United States in the hope for a global eruption of freedom.

Before his tragic death in April 1968, Martin Luther King Jr. reminded this nation that we no longer live in a small house, but rather we have inherited a world house of interrelatedness and interdependence. He suggested in clear and strident language that we must learn to live together as brothers and sisters or die apart as fools. During his latter years, King was acutely aware of the need for a broader interpretive framework for understanding what he perceived as a crucial passage in history. He wrote that "the civil rights movement in the United States is a special American phenomenon which must be understood in the light of American history and dealt with in terms of the American situation. But on another and more important level, what is happening in the United States today is a significant part of a world development."[76]

76. King, *Where Do We Go from Here?,* 169.

King further suggested that the struggles of African Americans must be understood in light of a "shifting" of the West's basic outlooks and philosophical presuppositions about "power." He argued that indeed

> We have inherited a large house, a great "world house" in which we have to live together—black and white, Easterner and Westerner, Gentile and Jew, Catholic and Protestant, Moslem and Hindu—a family unduly separated in ideas, culture and interest, who, because we can never again live apart, must learn somehow to live together with each other in peace. However deeply American Negroes are caught in the struggle to be at last home in our homeland of the United States, we cannot ignore the larger world house in which we are also dwellers. Equality with whites will not solve the problems of either whites or Negroes if it means equality in a world stricken by poverty and in a universe doomed to extinction by war.[77]

This dream of a "world house" has striking implications for the development of black church leaders as we prepare to meet the challenges of this century. Dr. King's prophetic insight of a global community is not quite the same as the "I Have a Dream" speech of 1963, of which many are so fond. That was a speech directed to the issue of the civil rights that African Americans had been denied. But the notion of a "world house" places the struggle within the context of liberation movements throughout the world. It implies that the freedom of African Americans, our human rights, is inextricably bound with yearnings and hopes of oppressed people everywhere. King often reminded us that "injustice anywhere is against justice everywhere."[78]

As we witness the shifting grounds of world change, leaders from historically marginalized communities must ask new questions about the nature and scope of our long, arduous journey on these shores. We must ask what does this new season of worldwide struggle mean for us, for this nation and the world? Who will lead? Dare we hope or must we conclude that we are at "the end of history?" King did not think we were at the end of history. King believed that what we are witnessing is a worldwide revolution that challenges the very foundations of Euro-Western hegemony. In his last public sentences, King said that he was pleased to live during this chaotic and precarious age because beyond the despair and hopelessness that abounded, he believed that this was a great moment for the united struggles of people throughout the world. King said:

77. King, *Where Do We Go from Here?*, 167.
78. Washington, ed., *Testament of Hope*, 290.

But I know, somehow, that only when it is dark enough, can you see the stars. And I see God working in this period of the twentieth century in a way that men, in some strange way, are responding—something is happening in our world. The masses of people are rising up. And wherever they are assembled today, whether they are in Johannesburg, South Africa; Nairobi, Kenya; Accra, Ghana; New York City; Atlanta, Georgia; Jackson, Mississippi; or Memphis, Tennessee—the cry is always the same—"We want to be free."[79]

79. King, "I See the Promised Land (3 April 1968)," in Washington, ed., *Testament of Hope*, 280.

10.

The Heart of a World Citizen: Martin Luther King Jr. as Social Mystic

BEVERLY J. LANZETTA

> I speak as a child of God and brother to the suffering poor of Vietnam. I speak for those whose land is being laid waste, whose homes are being destroyed, whose culture is being subverted. I speak for the poor of America who are paying the double price of smashed hopes at home and death and corruption in Vietnam. I speak as a citizen of the world, for the world as it stands aghast at the path we have taken.
>
> —Martin Luther King Jr.[1]

> By international consensus, Dr. King was a first citizen of the world. In the United States he was a main hope for a tortured nation.
>
> —Eugene Carson Blake[2]

Martin Luther King Jr. was a prophetic mystic-contemplative who brought the virtues of the interior life into the public sphere, in service of the dignity of all beings and the alleviation of racism, poverty, and war. There was nothing provincial or narrow about his focus; his heart was that of a global citizen, one who felt the pain of the world as his own and who dedicated his life to its eradication. This chapter situates King in the prophetic-mystical tradition, highlighting his role not only as a spiritual leader of the civil rights movement, but also as a spiritual master who taught movement followers and admirers around the world about an incarnational, engaged, and integrative practice of liberation.

1. Martin Luther King Jr., *The Trumpet of Conscience* (New York: Harper & Row, 1968; originally published in 1967), 31.

2. Quoted in Lerone Bennett Jr., *What Manner of Man: A Memorial Biography of Martin Luther King, Jr.* (New York: Pocket, 1968), 145.

In this sense, King belongs to the esteemed company of other spiritual giants of his century, including Abraham Joshua Heschel, Thomas Merton, Mahatma Gandhi, Howard Thurman, Dorothy Day, and Thich Nhat Hanh.

While rooted in black church theology of the American South, King forged a global spirituality that employed the oldest elements of spiritual discipline—transforming habits, developing virtues, and submitting to vows—in service of peace, applying principles and practices of the interior life to civil rights, and ultimately to global ends. Devoted to the southern black Baptist tradition, King also found meaning in the world's religions, and beyond tradition, having discovered that mystical desert outside religious structures. King's profound experience of the unity of life, exemplified in his vision of "the great World House," was the basis of his sensitivity to religious and cultural pluralism, and to his claim as "a citizen of the world."[3]

Like other votaries of peace, King struggled to live what he preached, confronting insecurity, hopelessness, doubt, guilt, and despair. His journey was one of ever-increasing awareness of his human weakness and God's presence in daily events: one who found in prayer a constant companion; who sought time alone, in silence, to be touched by divine love; who was called by God into the political arena and, ultimately, assassinated by a bullet, was felled by the violent injustice he gave his life to end. These personal trials enhance his stature as a prophet and God-filled person, whose heart cried out his grave longings for a world transformed. Prayer rolled off his soul like rain falling into the sea, effortlessly, spontaneously, dissolving bitterness or fear or conflict or pain in the waters of merciful love.

GLOBAL SPIRITUALITY

Martin Luther King Jr. forged a global spiritual vision and social mystic consciousness rare in the history of the world. His identification with the world's poor and the soul affliction caused by Jim Crow—a result of America's intransigent segregation culture—sensitized him to oppression and abuse inflicted on the disenfranchised. His commitment to the dignity of all persons, concern for the poor, and faith in nonviolence as a universal moral principle serve as one of the more stunning examples in modern history of an integrated, holistic consciousness. What stands out in the life of this modern mystic-prophet is his awareness of the poignancy of suffering and God's will toward its alleviation. Founded in

3. King, *Trumpet of Conscience,* 31.

the wisdom of his Christian heritage and that of other great world religions,[4] King actively sought the creation of a new spiritual possibility on Earth.

King had faith in and practiced a global spirituality for all humanity. Expanding the traditional notion of spirituality as a private, inner experience developed within a specific religious tradition, King incorporated the wisdom of the world's religions, issues of social justice, and an ecumenical and interfaith sensibility concerned for the fate of the world in his nonviolent campaigns. He recognized the emergence of a new planetary consciousness that signaled the birth of a common spirit and an awakening of humanity's capacity to rise above itself toward a more noble future. "We stand today," he wrote, "between two worlds, the dying old and the emerging new. . . . It is both historically and biologically true that there can be no birth or growth without birth and growing pains . . . , and so the tensions which we witness in the world today are indicative of the fact that a new world is being born and an old world is passing away."[5]

King also was acutely aware that humanity was struggling with the breakdown of old social paradigms, and the painful but necessary birth of a new world order of justice and freedom. In "The World House," he states:

> One of the great liabilities of history is that all too many people fail to remain awake through great periods of social change. Every society has its protectors of the status quo and its fraternities of the indifferent who are notorious for sleeping through revolutions. But today our very survival depends on our ability to stay awake, to adjust to new ideas, to remain vigilant and to face the challenge of change. The large house in which we live demands that we transform this worldwide neighborhood into a worldwide brotherhood.[6]

Here King stood in a tradition pioneered by a number of spiritual teachers who refused to separate their commitment to the life of the spirit from their engagement with the needs of humanity. As early as the 1920s, the French Jesuit and paleontologist Pierre Teilhard de Chardin

4. Martin Luther King Jr., *Where Do We Go from Here: Chaos or Community?* (Boston: Beacon, 1968; originally published in 1967), 190–91.

5. Martin Luther King Jr., "The Birth of a New Age" (11 August 1956), in Clayborne Carson et al., eds., *The Papers of Martin Luther King, Jr.: Birth of a New Age, December 1955–December 1956* (Berkeley: University of California Press, 1967), 3:340. Also see King's speech, "The Vision of a World Made New" (9 September 1954), in Clayborne Carson et al., eds., *The Papers of Martin Luther King, Jr.: Advocate of the Social Gospel, September 1948–March 1963* (Berkeley: University of California Press, 2007), 6:181–84.

6. King, *Where Do We Go from Here?*, 171.

(1881–1955) wrote about the humanization of the spirit on a planetary level, and clearly pointed to the vision contained in the term "global spirituality." For Teilhard, spirit is ultimate reality, and a spiritual outlook is an authentic outlook since all life is spiritual life or it is literally meaningless. "Beside the phenomena of heat, light, and the rest studied by physics," he wrote, "there is, just as real and *natural*, the *phenomenon of spirituality*." Understanding spirituality to be a higher state assumed by the very stuff of the universe—and not simply an individualistic, internal experience—he advocated for a "new mysticism" that combined active and contemplative modes in service of a "'mysticism of loving' . . . , of the dynamic, all-transforming fire of love, which radiates throughout the world" and sets it aflame.[7]

Certainly, Mohandas K. Gandhi was living a global spiritual vision in his identification with the citizens of India and their struggles to overcome poverty and colonialism. His commitment to religious "manyness," experiments in truth, and faith in self-sacrifice and nonviolence changed the political landscape of India and inspired nonviolent social activism around the world. Deeply rooted in his Hindu faith, and equally comfortable in the wisdom of the world's other religions, Gandhi centered his ashram life on the removal of caste distinctions, daily prayers drawn from Christian, Hindu, Muslim, and other sacred texts, performance of vows, and periods of solitary contemplation—all essential aspects of his service to God and humanity.

Other nonviolent pilgrims during King's lifetime include Howard Thurman's interfaith mysticism, Abraham Joshua Heschel's prophetic spirituality of pathos, the monastic vision of Thomas Merton, Dorothy Day's Catholic Worker movement, and Thich Nhat Hanh's nonviolent action against war. Each was devoted to the unification of our differences, offering their lives to the plight of refugees, racial injustice, soldiers in war, starving families, survivors of genocide, and other members of the human family whose dignity was debased by calculated violence or indifference.

Another thought-provoking expression of world spirituality is found in the book, *New Genesis: Shaping a Global Spirituality*. Robert Muller, former assistant secretary general of the United Nations, writes with passionate conviction concerning the need for a planetary vision of spiritual well-being for humanity as a whole.[8] While he cites advances in literacy and human rights as evidence of global bridge building, Muller

7. Ursula King, "The Phenomenon of Spirituality," in *The Spirit of One Earth: Reflections on Teilhard de Chardin and Global Spirituality* (New York: Paragon House, 1989), 65–82. Here one finds further analysis of Teilhard's unique understanding of the spirit.

8. Robert Muller, *New Genesis: Shaping a Global Spirituality* (New York: Image, 1984).

also laments "considerably less progress [has been made] on the moral, sentimental, and spiritual planes."[9] Fundamental questions of transcendence—Why am I on earth? What are the meaning and purpose of life?—are ignored in the world forums, and yet, according to Muller, are essential to develop the immense possibilities offered by the human heart and soul. "Where are the philosophers," he writes, "who have the courage to speak out for the whole human race?"[10]

Ursula King, professor emerita at the University of Bristol, United Kingdom, also has produced a distinguished body of literature on the spiritual implications of global thinking. "At the present critical time in human history," King concurs, "we have to pay particular attention to the deep need for spiritual well-being beyond the existing physical, mental, and moral needs of humankind. We have to ask ourselves: will questions of spiritual development one day become an integral part of our efforts to ensure global development towards peace and justice? What efforts do we at present devote toward developing the inner resources of human beings, their imagination, mind and heart, their power to love, care, and be compassionate as well as peaceful and happy?"[11]

Similarly, Krishna Sivaraman, Hindu theologian and professor emeritus at McMaster University, asserts that global spirituality "requires a worldliness, not an otherworldliness." That is, it is "a disposition to live in the world, singly or collectively, not for its own sake, not as a goal in itself worthy of pursuit as sufficient 'human end,' but as a means or medium to life 'in God,' . . . becoming truly aware, as never possible before, of the basic worth of all beings and one's kinship with them." "Spirit represents precisely that dimension which precludes the assertion of I as *against* you in any of its forms."[12]

As lived by Dr. King, global spirituality tempered the classical distinction between action and contemplation, transcendence and immanence, and the interior and exterior life. Moving away from the connotations associated with spirituality as a pessimistically, anti-material orientation, King retrieved spirituality in its more comprehensive sense as a relationship with God imbedded in a whole cultural, social, and religious orientation inseparable from the life of the community. Raising this notion

9. Muller, *New Genesis*, 15.

10. Muller, *New Genesis*, 19.

11. King, *Spirit of One Earth*, 3–4; Ursula King, *The Search for Spirituality: Our Global Quest for a Spiritual Life* (New York: Blue Bridge, 2008); and Ursula King, *Women and Spirituality: Voices of Protest and Promise* (University Park: Pennsylvania State University Press, 1993).

12. Krishna Sivaraman, introduction to *Hindu Spirituality: Vedas through Vedanta; and World Spirituality: An Encyclopedic History of the Religious Quest* (New York: Crossroad, 1989), xv–xvi.

up into a global context, the community becomes not a single, homogenous, group or religious tradition, but all human and non-human life forms. "I am absolutely convinced," King professed, "that God is not interested merely in the freedom of black men and brown men and yellow men. But God is interested in the freedom of the whole human race."[13]

"Clearly," writes Lewis V. Baldwin, "the concept of the *global* was not foreign to King. He envisioned a totally integrated world, undiminished and undeterred by human differences, and committed to the ethical norms of love, justice, equal opportunity, peace, and community."[14] Embracing the entire world as one beloved community, King sought answers to questions about worldwide poverty, racism, economic injustice, and war. As a philosopher and theologian, he recognized that economic and political considerations were only partial solutions to peace and justice. More important were the moral and ethical dimensions of global transformation, and the need for "a revolution of values to accompany the scientific and freedom revolutions engulfing the earth."[15] In these areas, as well as his commitment to interreligious fellowship and learning, King fought to free humanity from "a poverty of spirit," and to establish a spiritual foundation for his global vision.

The one element absent in the "global King," Baldwin concludes, "are penetrating critiques of the subordination and marginalization of women." While King championed the dignity of women and insisted they "must be respected as human beings and not treated as mere means . . . , he did not make the liberation of women a critical part of his global human rights agenda."[16] Like King, many of the civil rights activists of his era also were operating from a patriarchal mindset, and did not address sexism and the subordination of women. These omissions are especially egregious since "women outnumbered men as participants in the movement,"[17] and were instrumental in advancing the critical organizing and decision-making policies of the campaign.

In *My Life with Martin Luther King, Jr.*, Coretta Scott King noted: "'Martin had, throughout his life, an ambivalent attitude toward the role

13. Martin Luther King Jr., "The Three Dimensions of a Complete Life" (11 December 1960), in Clayborne Carson et al., eds., *The Papers of Martin Luther King, Jr.: Threshold of a New Decade, January 1959–December 1960* (Berkeley: University of California Press, 2000), 5:576.

14. Lewis V. Baldwin and Paul R. Dekar, eds.,*"In an Inescapable Network of Mutuality": Martin Luther King, Jr. and the Globalization of an Ethical Ideal* (Eugene, OR: Cascade, 2013), 5.

15. King, *Where Do We Go From Here?,* 186.

16. Baldwin and Dekar, eds., *"In an Inescapable Network of Mutuality,"* 15.

17. Linda T. Wynn, "Beyond Patriarchy: The Meaning of Martin Luther King, Jr. for the Women of the World," in Baldwin and Dekar, eds., *"In an Inescapable Network of Mutuality,"* 64.

of women. On the one hand, he believed that women are just as intelligent and capable as men," but "when it came to his own situation, he thought in terms of his wife being a homemaker and a mother for his children." "Coretta King . . . comprehended," declares Lynn T. Wynn, "that if the movement was to move forward and embrace all within the 'beloved community,' or the 'world house,'. . . its patriarchal structures had to be demolished."[18]

Although the lack of clarity on women's human rights has, to a certain extent, marred King's legacy, he, and other pioneers of a spiritual world community, radicalized and expanded the historical notion of spirituality, championing an orientation toward life that was (1) built on a mystical and contemplative foundation and applied to social and political situations; (2) concerned with the dignity and freedom of the soul; (3) inclusive of the wisdom of the world's religions; (4) employed the method of nonviolence and excessive love in waging peace; and (5) engaged with issues of injustice, including the effect of racism, poverty, nuclear war, and materialism on the sacredness of human and nonhuman life.[19]

The importance of a global spirituality that embraces the world in an ethic of love and divine concern is encapsulated in this passage from "The World House" as envisioned by King:

18. Coretta Scott King, *My Life with Martin Luther King, Jr.*, rev. ed. (New York: Henry Holt, 1993; originally published in 1969), 57–58; and Wynn, "Beyond Patriarchy," 73 and 75.

19. For further writings on a global spiritual vision, see Ewert Cousins, *Global Spirituality: The Meeting of Mystical Paths* (Madras, India: Radhakrishnan Institute for Advanced Study in Philosophy, University of Madras, 1985); Ewert Cousins, *Christ of the Twenty-First Century* (Rockport, MA: Element, 1992); Stephen Chase, ed., *Doors of Understanding: Conversations in Global Spirituality in Honor of Ewert Cousins* (Cincinatti, OH: Franciscan Press, 1997); Pierre Teilhard de Chardin, *Hymn of the Universe* (New York: Harper & Row, 1969); Pierre Teilhard de Chardin, *The Divine Milieu* (New York: Harper & Row, 1965); Mahatma Gandhi, *All Men Are Brothers: Autobiographical Reflections* (New York: Continuum, 1984); Mahatma, *Vows and Observances* (Berkeley: Berkeley Hills, 1999); Abraham Joshua Heschel, *The Prophets: An Introduction* (New York: Harper & Row, 1962); Abraham Joshua Heschel, *Man's Quest for God: Studies in Prayer and Symbolism* (New York: Charles Scribner's Sons, 1952); Abraham Joshua Heschel, *The Insecurity of Freedom: Essays on Human Existence* (New York: Farrar, Straus & Giroux, 1967); Harold Kasimow and Byron L. Sherwin, eds., *No Religion Is an Island: Abraham Joshua Heschel and Interreligious Dialogue* (Maryknoll, NY: Orbis, 1991); Beverly Lanzetta, *Emerging Heart: Global Spirituality and the Sacred* (Minneapolis: Fortress, 2007); Thomas Merton, *The Signs of Jonas* (New York: Harcourt Brace Jovanovich, 1979); Thomas Merton, *Conjectures of a Guilty Bystander* (New York: Image, 1968); Raimon Panikkar, *The Intra-Religious Dialogue* (New York: Paulist Press, 1999); Raimon Panikkar, *The Cosmotheandric Experience: Emerging Religious Consciousness* (Maryknoll, NY: Orbis, 1993); Howard Thurman, *The Luminous Darkness: A Personal Anatomy of Segregation and the Ground of Hope* (New York: Harper & Row, 1964); and Howard Thurman, *With Head and Heart: The Autobiography of Howard Thurman* (New York: Harcourt Brace, 1979).

> From time immemorial men have lived by the principle that "self-preservation is the first law of life." But this is a false assumption. I would say that other-preservation is the first law of life. It is the first law of life precisely because we cannot preserve self without being concerned about preserving other selves. . . . Self-concern without other-concern is like a tributary that has no outward flow to the ocean.[20]

KING AS SOCIAL MYSTIC

King is known throughout the world as the leader of the American civil rights movement, and a political hero. While aware of the deep religious foundation of his ministry, articles tend to neglect or ignore the mystical intention that guided his life's divine mission. King's experiences of God, beginning as a child and present throughout his life, were the motivating factors in, and the foundation of, his commitment to civil rights. The extent of humanity's deviation from love, which condoned and permitted slavery and segregation, poverty and war, awakened King to the realization that religious experience, and not philosophical thinking, was the basis of societal transformation. He was a social mystic, a person whose activism emerges from an intimate awareness of God's presence, coupled with a prophetic commitment to justice, and the intention to bring the divine possibility on Earth.

Over the course of history, saints and prophets have spoken out against injustice and have given their lives to help sufferers. We need look no further than Francis of Assisi, one of King's spiritual and intellectual sources,[21] to understand how deeply he identified with and felt the pain of the impoverished and disenfranchised, devoting his life to compassion for and healing of the poor. But in the twentieth century, a particular type of mystical engagement with the world, "social mysticism," became prominent on the world stage, and King embodied that to the fullest.

Social mysticism applies the deep experiences of faith to the struggle for dignity and human rights for all peoples. However, it does not refer simply to action for social change, but to awareness that this action is the fulfillment of a divine desire. Alton B. Pollard III comments: "Mystic-activism, therefore, is a praxis-orientation to the world which relies but in part—albeit a considerable part—on the political and intellectual argu-

20. King, *Where Do We Go from Here?,* 180.

21. Martin Luther King Jr., "On Accepting the St. Francis Peace Medal," *Peace* 1 (March 1964): 11–15; and Lewis V. Baldwin, *Never to Leave Us Alone: The Prayer Life of Martin Luther King, Jr.* (Minneapolis: Fortress, 2010), 3 and 105n10.

ments and dictates of society; the more demanding motive is located in the obligation engendered by religious experience."[22]

Like other concepts within humanity's spiritual heritage, mysticism is depicted in diverse and sometimes contradictory ways. Christian scholar Bernard McGinn describes mysticism as "the immediate consciousness of the presence of God," or ultimate reality, however named or defined. This experience takes place on a level of personality deeper than the consciousness of emotions, cognition, or psyche. As McGinn notes, mystics, regardless of religious lineage, "continue to affirm that their mode of access to God is radically different from that found in ordinary consciousness, even from the awareness of God gained through the usual religious activities of prayer, sacraments, and other rituals."[23]

At the same time, mystical experience is not confined to the realm of ecstatic experiences beyond the grasp of daily existence. It is based upon a kind of awareness whereby the person pays attention to glimpses and visions all around us of the oneness of reality. This passionate realization of the unity of life has been—across cultures and historical periods—the quintessential insight of the mystic.

The son, grandson, and great-grandson of southern Baptist pastors, steeped in the daily worship of the Savior of freedom and dignity, Martin Luther King Jr. developed a distinctive mystical understanding of the person. The philosophical basis of his social mysticism, experienced in nascent form during his childhood, was fleshed out during his college years. In time, he became a contemplative philosopher of "personalism," which was based on the idea that only personality, finite and infinite, is ultimately real. "It gave me," King wrote, "metaphysical and philosophical grounding for the idea of a personal God, and it gave me a metaphysical basis for the dignity and worth of all human personality."[24] In the sacred presence of each soul, King found the unity of consciousness, and the ultimate reality of the divine Person, working out a purpose in human society through the moral laws of the universe.

King's appropriation of personalism was uniquely his own, transformed by his commitment to the struggle for civil rights. He felt that the relationship between the sacred spark within each person and faith in God's plan for humanity was irrevocably tied to freedom from injustice.

22. Alton B. Pollard III, *Mysticism and Social Change: The Social Witness of Howard Thurman,* Martin Luther King Jr. Memorial Studies in Religion, Culture, and Social Development (New York: Peter Lang, 1992), 1.

23. Bernard McGinn, *The Foundations of Mysticism*, vol. 1, *The Presence of God: A History of Western Christian Mysticism* (New York: Crossroad, 1992), xix.

24. Martin Luther King Jr., *Stride toward Freedom: The Montgomery Story* (New York: Harper & Row, 1958), 100.

From the life of prayer, he forged "a thoroughly social activist personalism," writes Rufus Burrow, "that requires that one be relentlessly committed to acting against social injustice. . . . Indeed, King was truly the quintessential *social activist personalist*."[25]

While a doctoral student at Boston University School of Theology, King further expanded his philosophy of social activist mysticism from the local to the national and international arena. Introduced to Josiah Royce's term the "beloved community," which he identified with a "new world" of peace where human beings will live together as brothers and sisters, King later clarified the scope of his mission:

> If we all join together . . . we will be able to speed up the coming of a new world—a new world in which men will live together as brothers; a world in which men will beat their swords into ploughshares and their spears into pruning hooks; a world in which men will no longer take necessities from the masses to give luxuries to the classes; a world in which all men will respect the dignity and worth of all human personality.[26]

The social mystic approaches the world's injustices through the lens of the Divine. He or she is involved in a kind of messianic longing to see the world transformed, whereby the personal spiritual journey is transposed into the national and international realm. By this I mean that aspects of spiritual growth common across religions are worked out in the life and ministry of the social mystic. For example, in Christianity, the earliest occurrence of the stages of soul development is found in Dionysius the Areopagite, an anonymous fifth- or sixth-century monk. In *The Celestial Hierarchy,* Dionysius describes three stages of the spiritual journey—purgation, illumination, and union—that he understood to be complementary functions and successive activities. Later Christian writers expand his three-fold category, inserting additional stages, such as Saint John of the Cross's description of the "dark night," and Evelyn Underhill's five-fold path.[27]

In King, these stages of soul transformation were not only evident

25. Rufus Burrow Jr., "The King Type of Personalism," *Encounter* 73, no. 3 (2013): 4.

26. Quoted in James M. Washington, ed., *A Testament of Hope: The Essential Writings and Speeches of Martin Luther King, Jr.* (San Francisco: HarperCollins, 1986), 144.

27. Saint John of the Cross—sixteenth-century Christian mystic—inserts an additional stage between illumination and union—the "dark night"—which he describes as occurring in the soul, both in its relationship to the senses and to the spirit. The dark night is that anguishing process when the soul gives up its separate identity for a state of intimate union with God. See Evelyn Underhill, *Mysticism: A Study of the Nature and Development of Man's Spiritual Consciousness* (New York: New American Library, 1974), 1. Underhill outlines five stages of development: (1) Awakening or Conversion; (2) Self-Knowledge or Purgation; (3) Illumination; (4) Surrender or the Dark Night; (5) Union.

in his personal life, but also in the leadership or support he provided to civil rights campaigns at home and abroad. While he did not explicitly map his spiritual journey, in numerous writings, speeches, and prayers, King's pilgrimage of love and nonviolence clearly illustrates involvement in self-purification and compunction, divine illumination, personal and collective anguish or dark night, and the hope of union with God. He was a mystical presence—some considered him a holy presence—that showed the world how deep structures of religious consciousness could be applied to the resolution of social injustice. God "has placed within the very structure of this universe," he wrote, "certain absolute moral laws. We can neither defy nor break them."[28]

In general, King did not share with the public his personal prayer life, or his mystical experiences of God, except on rare occasions. One such instance took place during the Montgomery bus boycott, where King emerged as a confident leader of nonviolent activism. Privately, however, he was torn about being thrust into the national spotlight. It was on a late Friday night, January 27, 1956, when King, returning home from a long strategy session, received a hate-filled phone call threatening his life. He got out of bed, walked to his kitchen, and put on a pot of coffee. This was the scene he described in *Stride toward Freedom*, which is included here in its entirety:

> I was ready to give up. With my cup of coffee sitting untouched before me I tried to think of a way to move out of the picture without appearing a coward. In this state of exhaustion, when my courage had all but gone, I decided to take my problem to God. With my head in my hands, I bowed over the kitchen table and prayed aloud. The words I spoke to God that midnight are still vivid in my memory. "I am here taking a stand for what I believe is right. But now I am afraid. The people are looking to me for leadership, and if I stand before them without strength and courage, they too will falter. I am at the end of my powers. I have nothing left. I've come to the point where I can't face it alone."
>
> At that moment I experienced the presence of the Divine as I had never experienced Him before. It seemed as though I could hear the quiet assurance of an inner voice saying: "Stand up for righteousness, stand up for truth; and God will be at your side forever." Almost at once my fears began to go. My uncertainty disappeared. I was ready to face anything.[29]

28. Martin Luther King Jr., "Our God Is Able," in *Strength to Love* (Philadelphia: Fortress, 1981; originally published in 1963), 110.

29. Carson et al., eds., *Papers*, 6:533–34; Clayborne Carson and Peter Holloran, eds., *A Knock at Midnight: Inspiration from the Great Sermons of Reverend Martin Luther King, Jr.* (New York: Warner, 1998), 160–62; and King, *Stride toward Freedom,* 134–35.

This mystical event marked a distinguishing moment in King's life, establishing in his soul a new certainty. Like many spiritual journeys, King's profound experience of divine companionship was preceded by struggles with self-worth, fear, and doubt. The process of self-awareness and purification through suffering and sacrifice, which were central to his personal and social ministry, was given deeper credibility through the illumination of God's presence and the peace of the divine voice. It is precisely King's intimate contact with God that provided courage and strength, steering his life through greater successes and even more desolate periods, and challenging his resolve and forcing him to reaffirm the experience of never being alone. King's spiritual journey, up to the very moment of his martyrdom, moved along this ancient pattern, which was not linear or sequential, of purification, illumination, dark night, and union.

During the course of the following year and a half, after King's memorable encounter with the Divine, positive changes come to fruition: the US Supreme Court affirms the lower court opinion (Browder v. Gayle, November 13, 1956), declaring Alabama bus segregation laws unconstitutional; Montgomery City Bus Lines resumes services, now integrated, on all routes; King delivers his first national address at the Lincoln Memorial; and his first book, *Stride toward Freedom* is published in September 1958. However, during a signing of this new book at a bookstore in Harlem, King was stabbed by Izola Ware Curry. Rushed to Harlem Hospital, doctors successfully removed a seven-inch letter opener from his chest.

This attack and others on King and his family were not "a total surprise," he later wrote. "To believe in nonviolence does not mean that violence will not be inflicted on you. The believer in nonviolence is the person who . . . lives by the conviction that through his suffering and cross bearing, the social situation may be redeemed."[30] The deep well of faith from which King drew provided the resilience and hope that the "dawn of a new day was just around the horizon." Nonetheless, his near-death experience in Harlem clarified for him, once again, that a "climate of hatred and bitterness" was rampant in America:

> The pathetic aspect of the experience was not the injury to one individual. It demonstrated to me that a climate of hatred and bitterness so permeated areas of our nation that inevitably deeds of extreme violence must erupt. I saw its wider social significance. The lack of restraint upon violence in our society along with the defiance of law by men in high places cannot but

30. Martin Luther King Jr., *The Autobiography of Martin Luther King, Jr.*, ed. Clayborne Carson (New York: Grand Central, 2001), 119.

> result in an atmosphere which engenders desperate deeds. I was intensely impatient to get back to continue the work we all knew had to be done regardless of the cost.[31]

Dr. King lived with humility. He gathered strength from dependence on God and his constant prayer practice. He felt that his ability to be peaceful and calm during the attempt on his life was the result of divine companionship:

> If I demonstrated unusual calm during the recent attempt on my life, it was certainly not due to any extraordinary powers that I possess. Rather, it was due to the power of God working through me. Throughout this struggle for racial justice I have constantly asked God to remove all bitterness from my heart and to give me the strength and courage to face any disaster that came my way. This constant prayer life and feeling of dependence on God have given me the feeling that I have divine companionship in the struggle. I know no other way to explain it. It is the fact that in the midst of external tension, God can give an inner peace.[32]

In the months and years ahead, King would be subjected to further cruelty, despair, disbelief, and violence. He suffered through many anguishing moments, his soul torn apart as he sought the mountaintop, the dream of a beloved world community. Yet, despite whatever soul impasse or turmoil he experienced, he always turned to God and God's word in Scripture for inspiration in difficult times.

During the Birmingham protests in 1963, King was aware that he would be arrested if he continued the march. Team members wanted King to raise funds to help with the cost of bailing out already imprisoned protestors, and not subject himself to jail. "Everyone in the movement must lead a sacrificial life," he had said at St. James AME Church. I can't think of a better day than Good Friday for a move for freedom."[33] In the ensuing debate with members of SCLC, he had to rely on the inner voice, on God's instructions, for the right way forward. "I sat in the midst of the deepest quiet I have ever felt," King later wrote, "alone in that crowded room." Retreating to his bedroom to pray, he reemerged a half an hour later: "I don't know what will happen . . . where the money

31. King, *Autobiography*, 120.

32. Clayborne Carson et al., eds., *The Papers of Martin Luther King, Jr.: Symbol of the Movement, January 1957–December 1958* (Berkeley: University of California Press, 2000), 4:540; and King, *Autobiography*, 118–19.

33. Stewart Burns, *To the Mountaintop: Martin Luther King Jr.'s Mission to Save America 1955–1968* (San Francisco: HarperCollins, 2004), 167.

will come from. But I have to make a faith act . . . I have to go. I am going to march if I have to march by myself."[34]

Locked in solitary confinement at Birmingham City Jail, on Good Friday, April 12, 1963, how could he not compare his plight with that of his Saviour, and those other souls unjustly killed or imprisoned for truth? How would his soul suffer this affront to the God of peace, and to the terror that lay ahead? He later wrote, "You will never know the meaning of utter darkness until you have lain in such a dungeon, knowing that sunlight is streaming overhead and still seeing only darkness below."[35] But, perhaps most troubling, was the "suffocating self-reproach he conjured up" as he confronted his fears, and his "aching guilt for subjecting his wife and children, and parents, to the apparent inevitability of his death."[36]

King's religious life prepared him for the journey ahead. It inspired him to trust and depend on God completely and solely. His mystical experiences of divine illumination, and moments of union with God, confirmed again that the personal God of faith "does not leave us alone in our agonies and struggles," but instead, as he wrote, "seeks us in dark places and suffers with us and for us in our tragic prodigality":[37]

> In recent months I have also become more and more convinced of the reality of a personal God. . . . But in past years the idea of a personal God was little more than a metaphysical category which I found theologically and philosophically satisfying. Now it is a living reality that has been validated in the experience of everyday life. Perhaps the suffering, frustration, and agonizing moments which I have had to undergo . . . have drawn me closer to God. . . . I am convinced that the universe is under the control of a loving purpose and that in the struggle for righteousness man has cosmic companionship.[38]

Over time, prayer occupied the center of King's life. He sought silence and time alone to pour his heart out to God. He retreated for prayer-centered days and moments of secret communion with God. His soul reached out for strength to endure ridicule and hate, to not succumb to fear over threats to his life. King's emphasis on "prayer as silent language and as quiet contemplation and meditation," writes Lewis V. Baldwin,

34. Burns, *To the Mountaintop*, 168–69.
35. Burns, *To the Mountaintop*, 170.
36. Burns, *To the Mountaintop*, 170–71.
37. King, *Strength to Love*, 16.
38. King, *Strength to Love*, 154.

combined with nonviolent public activism to forge "a unique model of spirituality."[39]

In his days of silence, and intimate experiences of God's Presence, King was freed of separateness, discovering in the Spirit that nothing can divide us. In this mystical dimension, there was not a merely mental common denominator, or a false sense of oneness, but a more holistic awareness that perceived, along with the differences, the unitive energies on which differences rest. In this way, King was granted insight into the mysterious *oneness* that sustains and celebrates the dignity of all beings. All reality was interrelated, and human beings were essentially relational beings. In "The Letter from Birmingham Jail," King wrote: "We are caught in an inescapable network of mutuality, tied in a single garment of destiny. Whatever affects one directly, affects all indirectly."[40]

Remarking on King as "a model of holiness," Scott Hoffman asks: "Did King die for his God or for his race? . . . His struggle was for more than the right to sit on a bus, for more than the right to eat at a lunch counter, for more than the right to vote. King's struggle, the struggle of the civil rights movement, sought human dignity for all people, a fact he often made clear."[41]

King was more than a civil rights hero; he was a social mystic who felt God's pathos, suffering for all people the bullet that took his life. It is perhaps only after the moment of King's martyrdom that people were able to recognize that "many Americans determined that he died for more than a political movement, he died in witness to his faith."[42] In fact, his campaign was the outer garment of an inner cry for justice, the voice of God in his soul.

King's fierce spiritual commitment branded into global awareness the potency of contemplation engaged in the service of social change. Behind every tactic and victory in King's arsenal lay spiritual imperatives of silence, prayer, and self-sacrifice. Intertwined with African Americans' struggle for civil rights was his refusal to succumb to the trappings of social comfort or political expediency for the sake of suffering souls everywhere.

The international implications of his global vision is expressed in this prayer King gave while pastor of Montgomery's Dexter Avenue Baptist

39. Baldwin, *Never to Leave Us Alone*, 78–79.

40. Martin Luther King Jr., *Why We Can't Wait* (New York: The New American Library, 1963), 77.

41. Scott W. Hoffman, "Holy Martin: The Overlooked Canonization of Dr. Martin Luther King, Jr.," in *Religion and American Culture: A Journal of Interpretation* 10, no. 2 (Summer 2000): 142.

42. Hoffman, "Holy Martin," 142.

Church: "Keep us, we pray, in perfect peace, help us to walk together, pray together, sing together, and live together until that day when all God's children, Black, White, Red, and Yellow will rejoice in one common band of humanity in the Kingdom of our Lord and of our God, we pray. Amen."[43]

DIGNITY OF SOUL

Perhaps no time in recent history was more urgent than King's, when grassroots movements of the 1950s and 1960s—combating racism, war, poverty, and colonialism—were thrust into the consciousness of the world. It was King's acute awareness of humanity's pain that led him to identify with the social gospel and to expand its reach into the inner sanctum of person and community. To be effective and to live up to Jesus's message, religion could be neither solely concerned with transcendence—waiting for liberation in heaven—nor with social justice without addressing the implications of inequality for a person's spiritual life.

At the same time that large social, economic, and religious forces were freeing millions of people from the clutches of colonialism, King recognized a parallel process taking place in the inner life of the person. The outer, social work of civil rights and equal treatment under the law were undergirded by the even greater need for inner work, taking place in the depth of souls. As a pastor and religious leader, King felt that the dignity of African Americans, and the spiritual foundations of our common humanity, were dependent upon healing inner harm. He was acutely aware that it was truly not possible to conceive of the individual spiritual life in isolation from the fortunes and fates of humanity as a whole.

Concerned foremost with the health and dignity of souls, King understood that slavery had created the wounds of inferiority, and had led to paralysis and self-loathing in the black population. The end of slavery and segregation could not be achieved solely by decree or by force, but had to come from within, from the strength to love, coupled with concrete economic, societal, and psychological change. "Any religion," King wrote, "that professes to be concerned about the souls of men and is not concerned about the slums that damn them, the economic conditions that strangle them, and the social conditions that cripple them is a spiritually moribund religion awaiting burial."[44]

43. Martin Luther King Jr., *"Thou, Dear God": Prayers that Open Hearts and Spirits—The Reverend Dr. Martin Luther King, Jr.*, ed. Lewis V. Baldwin (Boston: Beacon, 2012), 146–47.

44. Martin Luther King Jr., "Pilgrimage to Nonviolence," in James M Washington, ed., *I*

One of King's significant contributions was his insistence that civil rights alone, without addressing the scarred souls of black people, would not revolutionize individuals and provide the strength to effect change. Thus, his attention, especially during the bus boycott in Montgomery, was on "remaking black souls as the route to the whole society's deliverance."[45] King declared:

> The Negro will only be free when he reaches down to the inner depths of his own being and signs with the pen and ink of assertive manhood his own emancipation proclamation. And, with a spirit straining toward true self-esteem, the Negro must boldly throw off the manacles of self-abnegation and say to himself and to the world, "I am somebody. I am a person. I am a man with dignity and honor . . . and this self-affirmation is the black man's need, made compelling by the white man's crimes against him."[46]

James Cone, *In Martin and Malcolm and America*, contended that the primacy of black religiosity was central in shaping "King's idea of God during his childhood, and it remained central to his perspective throughout his life."[47] Merging the suffering of the soul with the biblical narrative of the exodus was a unique feature of black church services, where the dignity of personhood was not solely an individual issue but also a cosmic issue of justice. Lewis Baldwin writes, "The concept of a personal God of infinite love and undiluted power 'who works through history for the salvation of His children' has always been central to the theology of the Black Church."[48]

King situated the civil rights struggle in the book of Exodus, an "effort to transfigure the participants into the biblical realm, in which actions have consequences for the divine plan of history."[49] This is the essence of the Hebraic-Christian faith—that God was concerned for humans and entered into history to assist them. In his 1957 Prayer Pilgrimage for Freedom address, King affirmed that the struggle for justice had "cos-

Have a Dream: Writings and Speeches that Changed the World (San Francisco: HarperCollins, 1986), 58.

45. Burns, *To the Mountaintop*, 110.

46. Martin Luther King Jr., "Where Do We Go From Here?," in Washington, ed., *I Have a Dream*, 171.

47. James H. Cone, *Martin and Malcolm and America: A Dream or a Nightmare?* (Maryknoll, NY: Orbis, 1991). Cited by Susannah Heschel, "Theological Affinities in the Writings of Abraham Joshua Heschel and Martin Luther King Jr." in *Conservative Judaism* 50, nos. 2–3 (1998): 128.

48. Heschel, "Theological Affinities," 138. Citation taken from Lewis V. Baldwin, "Martin Luther King, Jr., the Black Church, and the Black Messianic Vision," *The Journal of the Interdenominational Theological Center* 12, nos. 1–2 (Fall 1984/Spring 1985): 99.

49. Heschel, "Theological Affinities," 129.

mic companionship," and proclaimed that God was not "some Aristotelian 'unmoved mover' who merely contemplates upon Himself. He is not merely a self-knowing God, but another-loving God Who forever works through history for the establishment of His kingdom."[50]

The quest for justice advanced love and redemption on Earth and within the life of God, a tradition well-established in Jewish and Christian mysticism. King was Moses, leading black people from slavery and segregation to the promised land of equality and dignity. "Political activism is not simply history, but *Heilsgeschichte*, salvation history," writes Susannah Heschel, "occurring within the realm of God."[51] Thus, "to accept passively," King proclaimed, "an unjust system is to cooperate with that system. . . . Noncooperation with evil is as much a moral obligation as is cooperation with good."[52] Always, the person's "highest loyalty," he wrote, "is to God and not to the mores or folkways, the state or the nation, or any man-made institution."[53]

The spirituality of dignity that was so central to King's message "was drawn," according to C. Douglas Weaver, "from several sources."

> He cited the sacredness of every human being found in the Christian Scriptures and noted a parallel emphasis in Gandhi's concept of "non-injury" (ahimsa). He often quoted the slave spirituals and their sense of human worth in the eyes of God. King also frequently relied upon the influential "I/It . . . I/Thou" principle articulated by Jewish philosopher, Martin Buber. According to King, segregation was an I-It relationship. Jim Crow America treated African-Americans as things and degraded their worth as persons created in the image of God.[54]

The genius of Dr. King was that he understood that the oppression inflicted on generations of African Americans through the tragic sin of slavery and segregation was fundamentally a soul issue. There could be no freedom for his people until their souls were free from the crippling scars of oppression. The end of oppression had to come from within, from the forces of healing that could mend historical wounds, coupled with concrete physical change. "The freeing of each Negro soul would be the means of freeing the souls of all black folk. The Negro as full indi-

50. Martin Luther King Jr., "Give Us the Ballot" (17 May 1957), in Clayborne Carson et al., eds., *The Papers of Martin Luther King, Jr.: Symbol of the Movement, January 1957–December 1958* (Berkeley: University of California Press, 2000), 4:214.

51. Heschel, "Theological Affinities," 129.

52. King, *Stride toward Freedom*, 212.

53. King, *Strength to Love*, 140.

54. C. Douglas Weaver, "The Spirituality of Martin Luther King, Jr." in *Perspectives in Religious Studies* 31 (Spring 2004): 66. Also see Washington, ed., *Testament of Hope*, 119 and 293–94.

vidual would save the Negro as a full people. Each Negro was a potential messiah just as black people, like the Hebrew chosen people, were a collective messiah."[55]

King analyzed the deeper spiritual causes and consequences of oppression in black communities. In his "philosophy of self-liberation," civil oppression had its roots in soul oppression. What harmed a person's soul reverberates in his or her physical, emotional, and mental spheres, generating suffering in every area of life. Similarly, soul violations in the social realm had a direct impact on the health, dignity, and integrity of black people.

Awareness of the harm spiritual domination exerted on a person's dignity and self-worth—which undergirded the economic and social marginalization of blacks and their historical status as a permanent underclass in American society—was vitally necessary to reverse the effects of racism, and to activate the power of soul force. Integration was the social and political equivalent of healing the spiritual depth of humanity, especially through the transformation of soul suffering. "The tragedy of physical slavery . . . was that it gradually led to the paralysis of mental slavery. The Negro's mind and soul became enslaved."[56] King felt that "every person, though created in God's image, was cleaved by a jagged fault line between contending forces of good and evil. God was commanding humankind, especially black people, to pursue a messianic mission to fight the Devil and win the world back for God and goodness, which included cleansing each soul from inside out."[57]

The more I read of King's life, the more convinced I am that he held all forms of oppression to be fundamentally spiritual oppression; that is, acts of violence—overt or subtle—directed first and foremost at the divine core of a person's nature. Included within the category of spiritual oppression is anything that marginalizes, dominates, violates, humiliates, shames, diminishes, or silences a person's spirit. Violence against black persons, personal and structural, could be seen as nothing less than a desire to harm or destroy their unique and particular embodiment of God. King stated:

> The system of slavery and segregation caused many Negroes to feel that perhaps they were inferior. This is the ultimate tragedy of segregation. It not only harms one physically, but it injures one spiritually. It scars the soul and distorts the personality. It inflicts the segregator with a false sense of superiority while inflicting the segregated with a false sense of inferiority.

55. Burns, *To the Mountaintop*, 111.
56. Burns, *To the Mountaintop,* 110.
57. Burns, *To the Mountaintop,* 93.

> But through the forces of history something happened to the Negro. He came to feel . . . that the important thing about a man is not the color of his skin or the texture of his hair, but the texture and quality of the soul.[58]

These varied interactions of personal, societal, and institutional control over the lives of African Americans exerted their influence beyond external events to invade psyche and soul. Further, King understood that these abuses could not be resolved without recognizing how connected they were to cultural and religious devaluations of blacks as spiritually inferior to whites. The historic belief in the spiritual inferiority of black persons inevitably permeated the cultural imagination, and contributed to and fostered violent acts against them, as it most often remained unacknowledged and unnamed.

In attempting to eliminate these diverse forms of oppression, King directed his attention to political and religious powers that dominated, judged, or shamed, as violations of black people's moral dignity and spiritual rights. Even when blacks achieved success, prestige, or authority, there remained a deeper layer of racism embedded in the cultural and religious imagination that resisted extraction. In this attempt to conquer the inner life by unjust and injurious norms, true sins had been committed. King knew that unless the souls of black people were healed, access to the person's true self would always be an accommodation reflected back through the broken mirror of white privilege.[59]

A prophetic healer of souls, Dr. King articulated on a national and international scale a global, contemplative ethic, highlighting the ways in which systemic injustice robbed people of dignity and created wounds of inferiority and worthlessness. His aim in all of his campaigns was to restore the souls of black people—and that of all people marginalized and disenfranchised—in order to build the beloved community, an opportunity not only for blacks and whites to achieve levels of parity in education, work, and material comfort, but also, and most especially, to advance the Spirit's work on Earth. Integration was considered redemptive because it represented God's plan for a worldwide brotherhood and sisterhood. King remarked: "Whether we call it an unconscious process, an impersonal Brahman, or a Personal Being of matchless power and infinite love, there is a creative force in this universe that works to bring the disconnected aspects of reality into a harmonious whole."[60]

58. Quoted in Washington, ed., *Testament of Hope*, 85.

59. For further insight into spiritual oppression and spiritual rights, see Beverly J. Lanzetta, *Radical Wisdom: A Feminist Mystical Theology* (Minneapolis: Fortress, 2005), chaps. 4, 10, and 11.

60. King, *Stride toward Freedom*, 107.

More than a social issue, King's passion was forged by the mystical imperative to remove all that prevents God from coming to fullness in the life of the individual, a belief strongly held by King's friend and mentor, Howard Thurman:

> The mystic's concern with the imperative of social action is not merely to improve the condition of society. It is not merely to feed the hungry, not merely to relieve human suffering and human misery. If this were all, in and of itself, it would be important surely. But this is not all. The basic consideration has to do with the removal of all that prevents God from coming to . . . [fullness] in the "life of the individual. Whatever there is that blocks this, calls for action."[61]

A SPIRITUAL MOVEMENT

It is quite apparent that Dr. King approached the civil rights struggle and the quest for the alleviation of global suffering from a spiritual perspective. His clear intention was to generate a spiritual movement that would have a lasting impact on our nation's (and on the world's) self-understanding. He situated his ministry in biblical narratives of Moses's journey to the promised land, of Saint Paul's exhortations of bravery and love, and of the redemption of a suppressed, exiled people. A profound, mystical faith in the God of love permeated his every moment and called him to surrender in prayer to a similar fate as Jesus.

To understand King's legacy as primarily focused on spiritual transformation is to recognize his role as prophet and holy person. In his radical concern for all humanity, and in the singular importance he attributed to the life of prayer, he was a contemplative presence. For King, prayer was life, and prayer measured his life and also the movement he led.

King's was a mystical heart that felt the spiritual fractures tearing apart the soul of humanity and, as all "friends of God,"[62] suffered for it. It was his capacity for altruistic love that lent such power and credibility to his life's mission, and that demonstrated to a spiritually impoverished citizenry the miracle of God's presence in history. He wanted more for African Americans than civil rights; he wanted more for the poor than a job; he wanted more for the victims of war than the cessation of violence. What he wanted was a spiritual revolution in which the forces that generated racism, militarism, poverty, and violence would be immobi-

61. Howard Thurman, "Mysticism and Social Action," cited in Pollard, *Mysticism and Social Change*, 65.

62. Anonymous, "How the Friend of God Suffers," in *The Book of the Poor in Spirit: By a Friend of God*, ed. and trans. C. F. Kelley (New York: Harper & Brothers, n.d.), 229–51.

lized, weakened, and ultimately defeated by a world uprising of peace and love. He wanted redemption, even perhaps the erasure of the original sins we humans inflict on each other.

We see this spiritual commandment operable in humanity's heroes, those men and women who challenged the powers and principalities, igniting the moral fiber of the silent, oppressed ones. This was the path of Gandhi and Heschel, of Thich Nhat Hanh, Dorothy Day, and Thomas Merton, and also of King himself. From silence came speech; from solitude came commitment; from prayer came resolve; from mystical experience came excessive love. They had faith, as Teilhard de Chardin once remarked, "That the day will come when . . . we shall harness for God the energies of love. And, on that day, for the second time in the history of the world, man will have discovered fire."[63]

After spending these months with Dr. King's prayers and letters and inmost thoughts, I have come away with a belief that God sent Martin on Earth to lead humanity into a new era of religiously inspired spiritual and social transformation that includes all religions and all people. Even, I would add, to a new Christology and revelatory landscape. While based on his deep rootedness in the southern black church, King was nonetheless forging an ecumenical, interfaith, and universal path of salvation. He was demonstrating to the world the method (prayer, spiritual nonviolence, excessive love, vows, sacrifice, and self-suffering), the means (nonviolent social action, marches, rallies), and the goal (the world house, beloved community, and redemption from the sin of separateness). He was living a spiritual journey, showing others how to resist violence, temptation, and fear with love.

And, thus, instead of tracing King's concern for the poor, the world's religions, war, and so on—which is how I intended to end this chapter—I will concentrate on the spiritual nonviolence that informed each of these radically significant commitments, which have been documented by others, far better than I am able, in numerous tributes to him.

SPIRITUAL NONVIOLENCE

Dr. King had a keen sense of the fragileness and resilience of human communities, and the importance of a narrative able to unite divergent factions of the populace. He tapped into the river of wisdom that has guided religious leaders throughout history, especially in his recognition of the spiritual rights and dignity of the person.

63. Pierre Teilhard de Chardin, *Toward the Future*, trans. Rene Hague (New York: Harcourt Brace Jovanovich, 1975), 86–87.

King's ministry of justice and reconciliation was tied to the adaptation of Mahatma Gandhi's comprehensive praxis of nonviolence. Like Gandhi, King's involvement in civil rights emerged from personal experiences of discrimination within his ministering community, which led to the moral audacity to confront and rectify abuses of a person's God-given dignity. He drew inspiration not only from Christianity, but also from the phenomenal spiritual experiment unfolding across the great continent of India. In Mahatma Gandhi, King discovered a kindred soul.

King also understood nonviolent activism to derive power and efficacy from its theological foundation in divine love. It was never for social transformation without soul transformation. While "principled nonviolence" was based on moral values and "pragmatic nonviolence" rested on practical solutions, in almost all nonviolent campaigns these were interrelated paths.[64] However, King, like Gandhi and other social mystics, was especially concerned for the spiritual implications of nonviolence on the inner life of the person and her or his growth. For this reason, I modify the word "nonviolence," with "spiritual," to underscore the self-awareness and personal repentance that King recognized was critical in liberation movements.

Thus, nonviolence was not solely concerned with the negative impact of violence, but with what Gandhi called *satyagraha*—the "soul-force" that empowers the life-affirming strength and moral resilience necessary for the conversion of the human heart and the transformation of culture. It was this spiritual core of the person that provided the strength of character to resist dehumanizing violence in Gandhi and King's campaigns.

As the common element in all human cultures and traditions, King recognized that the spiritual dimension of life was intertwined with all other rights. For him, nonviolence provided a path and an interpretative framework to analyze our failure to prevent the severing and wounding of God's presence on Earth. It demanded an accounting of how human acts of violence tear at our hearts, lay waste to our souls, and lead us to the brink of despair. It asked how these travesties against the spirit of life contribute to our collective grief and afflict us in ways that even now the global community has yet to feel, name, or understand.

King realized that every advance in human dignity also involved the awareness and transformation of hidden states of consciousness that perpetuated acceptance or silence in the face of the inferior status of "the other." A vow of nonviolence led to growth in consciousness, which

64. Mary E. King, "Mohandas K. Gandhi and Martin Luther King, Jr.'s Bequest: Nonviolent Civil Resistance in a Globalized World," in Baldwin and Dekar, eds., *In an Inescapable Network of Mutuality*, 156.

in turn obligated the oppressed to combat the inferiority, self-hatred, or lack of self-worth that demoralized personal integrity and crushed one's ability to resist. Similarly, on the side of oppressors and those obligated to effect remedy, there must exist inner repentance, or coming to terms with the shame and sorrow one felt and the suffering and pain one had caused. This reconciliation also involved engagement with the spiritual depth of nonviolence.

As a fifteen-year-old student at Morehouse College, King first heard about Gandhi and the power of nonviolence. He was captivated by an assignment to read Henry David Thoreau's *On Civil Disobedience*, which was his "first intellectual contact with the theory of nonviolent resistance."[65] He was "deeply moved" by what he read and—along with further reading about Gandhi at Crozer Theological Seminary—ultimately became convinced that a philosophy based on agape love was his path. "As I delved deeper into the philosophy of Gandhi," King wrote, "my skepticism concerning the power of love gradually diminished, and I came to see for the first time . . . that the Christian doctrine of love operating through the Gandhian method of nonviolence was one of the most potent weapons available to oppressed people in their struggle for freedom."[66]

One of the contributions Gandhi made to King's life work was the offering of a global perspective on how nonviolent principles might be applied to the human condition. Reflecting on his service as spokesman for the Montgomery protest, King asserted that "my mind, consciously or unconsciously, was driven back to the Sermon on the Mount . . . , with its sublime teachings on love and the Gandhian method of nonviolent resistance. . . . Living through the actual experience of protest, nonviolence became more than a method which I gave intellectual assent; it became a commitment to a way of life."[67]

It was also during the Montgomery boycott that King noticed an inner transformation in the protesters:

> The struggle has produced a definite character development among Negroes. The Negro is more willing now to tell the truth about his attitude toward segregation. In the past, he often used deception as a technique for appeasing and soothing the white man. Now he is willing to stand up and speak more honestly. . . . There is an amazing lack of bitterness, a contagious spirit of warmth and friendliness. . . . Believing that a movement is

65. King, *Stride toward Freedom*, 91.

66. King, "Pilgrimage to Nonviolence," in Washington, ed., *I Have a Dream*, 59; and King, *Stride toward Freedom*, 96–97.

67. King, "Pilgrimage to Nonviolence," in Washington, ed., *I Have a Dream*, 59; King, *Autobiography,* 67; and King, *Stride toward Freedom,* 101.

> finally judged by its effect on the human beings associated with it, we are not discouraged by the problems that lie ahead.[68]

Nonviolence as social action was the outer manifestation of a mystical, contemplative state of consciousness that was itself the outer garment of an even deeper truth: reality moves in harmony with love. For King, nonviolence was not merely a cultural necessity or social form of protest, but the whole configuration in which life could be seen as it truly is, in its deepest dimensions. To translate nonviolence into the social sphere was to become a living practitioner of a spiritual path; and thus the journey toward nonviolence entailed not only inner growth, but also cooperation and reconciliation with members of the world's religions.

Dr. King was such an expansive, original thinker that it is not surprising to find the extent of his commitment to interfaith dialogue and ecumenical community. His fellowship with all men and women around the globe was based, as he put it, on "that force [of love] which all of the great religions have seen as the supreme unifying principle of life. Love is the key that unlocks the door which leads to ultimate reality. This Hindu-Moslem-Christian-Jewish-Buddhist belief about ultimate reality is beautifully summed up in the First Epistle of Saint John: 'Let us love one another: for love is of God.'"[69]

King developed a critical awareness of the integral unity that sustained life, and by which he abandoned any narrow sense of superiority of religion or person. Not only was God revealed in all religions, God also brought new or unexplored wisdom through other religions, King held: "There is a need for individual religions to realize that God has revealed Himself to all religions and there is some truth in all. And no religion can permit itself to be so arrogant that it fails to see that God has not left Himself without a witness, even though it may be in another religion."[70]

"Love and nonviolence were fundamentally Christian values for King," writes Eboo Patel, "but he learned to see them in new ways under the light of Thich Nhat Hanh's Buddhism and Gandhi's Hinduism. . . . They provided the light in which King could clearly see the rooms of love and nonviolence in the house of faith within him."[71] His spirituality

68. Martin Luther King Jr., "We Are Still Walking," *Liberation* (December 1956), cited by Mary Elizabeth King, "Mohandas K. Gandhi and Martin Luther King, Jr.'s Bequest," 173.

69. King, *Where Do We Go from Here?,* 190–91; and Washington, ed., *Testament of Hope*, 632.

70. Quoted in Martin Luther King Jr., *"In a Single Garment of Destiny": A Global Vision of Justice—Martin Luther King, Jr.*, ed. Lewis V. Baldwin (Boston: Beacon, 2012), 201 and 205.

71. Eboo Patel, "Martin Luther King Jr. and the Light of Other Faiths," *Crosscurrents* (1 September 2013): 275.

was radically inclusive of all people, "African American or white, rich or poor, American or Vietnamese."[72]

In his "Palm Sunday Sermon on Mohandas K. Gandhi," in March 1959, King offered a prayer underscoring the need for all faiths to work together to eliminate racism, poverty, and war.

> O God, our gracious Heavenly Father, we thank Thee for the fact that you have inspired men and women in all nations and in all cultures. We call you different names: some call Thee Allah; some call you Elohim; some call you Jehovah; some call you Brahma; some call you the Unmoved Mover; some call you the Archetectonic [sic] Good. But we know that these are all names for one and the same God, and we know you are one. And grant, O God, that we will . . . be able to establish here a kingdom of understanding, where men will live together as brothers and respect the dignity and worth of all human personality.[73]

No doubt, for these reasons, King developed deep friendships with other spiritual advocates of nonviolence. The distinguished Vietnamese Buddhist monk Thich Nhat Hanh, first wrote to Dr. King in 1965.

> I am sure that since you have been engaged in one of the hardest struggles for equality and human rights, you are among those who understand fully, and who share with all their hearts, the suffering of the Vietnamese people. The world's greatest humanists would not remain silent. . . . In writing to you, as a Buddhist, I profess my faith in love, in communion, and in the world's humanists, whose thought and attitudes should be the guide for all humankind.[74]

Hanh and King felt privileged to call each other friends, their souls joined as apostles of peace and nonviolence. Sharing a vision of world brotherhood and sisterhood, a planet free from suffering and injustice, I believe that had King lived, they would have pioneered a truly interfaith, mystical worldwide revolution.

"The moment I met Martin Luther King, Jr.," Hanh said, "I knew I was in the presence of a holy person. Not just his good work, but his very being was a source of inspiration for me."[75] Further, in an interview with bell hooks in 2000, Hanh described King as a "bodhisattva"—an enlightened being devoted to serving humanity: "Martin Luther King was among us as a brother, as a friend, as a leader. He was able to main-

72. Weaver, "The Spirituality of Martin Luther King, Jr.," 56.

73. King, *"Thou, Dear God,"* 45; and Carson et al., eds., *Papers*, 5:157.

74. Patel, "Martin Luther King Jr. and the Light of Other Faiths," 273.

75. "Thich Nhat Hanh and Martin Luther King's Dream Comes True in Mississippi," Plum Village, September 25, 2013, https://tinyurl.com/yc4ee788.

tain that love alive. When you touch him, you touch a bodhisattva, for his understanding and love was enough to hold everything to him."[76]

King also felt a deep, sympathetic resonance with rabbi and scholar Abraham Joshua Heschel. The photograph of them walking arm and arm during the march on Selma "has become an icon of American Jewish life, and of Black-Jewish relations."[77] Their bond was a religious one, stemming from their theological reading of the Bible, especially of the prophets, and "the nature of morality, of prayer, as well as the centrality of political commitments."[78] King wrote:

> In the struggle for human rights, as well as in the struggle for the upward march of our civilization, we have deep need for the partnership, fellowship and courage of our Jewish Brother. History will attest that the Hebrew prophets belong to all people. For, it has been their concepts of justice and equality which have become ideals for all races and civilizations. Today, we particularly need the Hebrew prophets because they taught that to love God was to love justice; that each human being has an inescapable obligation to denounce evil where he sees it and to defy a ruler who commands him to break the covenant.[79]

Heschel and King related to the personal God of pathos—one who suffered with humans and was concerned for justice and compassion, and was "the basis of the spiritual affinity between them."[80] Kindred souls, they shared similar values of love and compassion, as well as anguish and outrage over racism, violence, and the war in Southeast Asia.

Heschel's daughter, Susannah Heschel, notes three theological orientations they shared, evident in the "religious mood they evoked through their religious language." First, and most significant, was the spirituality that they taught, which was rooted in the emphasis King gave to the exodus narrative and in Heschel's theology of pathos found in the prophets. Second was their fundamental assumption of God's closeness to humanity, and of God's divine concern with the civil rights struggle; and third, they each spoke not as an "observer of society," but as prophets "for God, conveying a divine perspective."[81] Heschel's description of the nature of the prophet distills the heart-mission of these two men of God:

76. bell hooks, "Building a Community of Love: bell hooks and Thich Nhat Hanh," Plum Village, January 1, 2000, plumvillage.org/thich-nhat-hanh-interviews/interview-with-bell-hooks-january-1-2000/.

77. Heschel, "Theological Affinities," 126.

78. Heschel, "Theological Affinities," 128.

79. Martin Luther King Jr., "My Jewish Brother!," cited in King, *"In a Single Garment of Destiny,"* 206.

80. Heschel, "Theological Affinities," 127.

81. Heschel, "Theological Affinities," 130.

"The prophet is a man who feels fiercely. God has thrust a burden upon his soul, and he is bowed and stunned at man's fierce greed. . . . Prophecy is the voice that God has lent to the silent agony, a voice to the plundered poor, to the profaned riches of the world. It is a form of living, a crossing point of God and man. God is raging in the prophet's words."[82]

Along with Heschel and Hanh, King became a fierce critic of the Vietnamese War, maintaining that ending US involvement in Vietnam required fundamental spiritual changes in the hearts and minds of America's people, politicians, military, and government officials. Rather than promoting illegitimate regimes, unjust investments in developing nations, and assuming an arrogant role as "world teacher," King declared that compassion and a "radical revolution of values" were a necessary cure:

> Religion at its best has always sought to promote peace and good will among men. This is true of all of the great religions of the world. In their ethical systems, we find the love ethic standing at the center. This is true of Judaism, this is true of Christianity, this is true of Islam, of Hinduism and Buddhism, and if we go right through all the great religions of the world we find this central message of love and this idea of the need for peace, the need for understanding and the need for good will among men.[83]

Over and again, King affirmed the essential relationship between faith, justice, and political morality. His global mystical vision recognized that the entire community of humanity was immersed in a series of moral trials that could only be resolved through a spiritual conversion. His suffering over the Vietnam War, and other instances of global violence, indicated, as King wrote in *The Trumpet of Conscience,* that "our nation was on the wrong side of a world revolution," and that "we . . . must undergo a radical revolution of values."

> This business of burning human beings with napalm, of filling our nation's homes with orphans and widows, of injecting poisonous drugs of hate into the veins of peoples normally humane, of sending men home from dark and bloody battlefields physically handicapped and psychologically deranged, cannot be reconciled with wisdom, justice, and love. A nation that continues year after year to spend more money on military defense than on programs of social uplift is approaching spiritual doom.[84]

82. Abraham Joshua Heschel, *The Prophets: An Introduction* (New York: Harper & Row, 1962), 5.

83. King, *"In a Single Garment of Destiny,"* 204.

84. King, *Trumpet of Conscience*, 32–33; and King, *Where Do We Go from Here?,* 188.

King's intense moral outrage demonstrated to a people and a nation how to bear the anguish of violence and death. Experiencing despair, guilt, and doubt, as did his brothers and sisters in the movement, he did not succumb. He embraced God, listened for divine guidance, and gave himself away for a cause larger than his own. He compared his work to the "gospel of freedom" identified with Saint Paul:

> Just as the eighth century prophets left their little villages and carried their "thus saith the Lord" far beyond the boundaries of their hometowns; and just as the Apostle Paul left his little village of Tarsus and carried the gospel of Jesus Christ to practically every hamlet and city of the Graeco-Roman world, I too am compelled to carry the gospel of freedom beyond my particular hometown. Like Paul, I must constantly respond to the Macedonian call for aid.[85]

Any campaign designed to lift the oppression of one community required that it also expand beyond tribal and local concerns to include the universe of suffering beings. In his reflections on "the great World House," King says: "Deeply woven into the fiber of our religious tradition is the conviction that men are made in the image of God, and that they are souls of infinite metaphysical value. If we accept this as a profound moral fact, we cannot be content to see men hungry, to see men victimized with ill-health, when we have the means to help them."[86]

King's deep faith that God's love was real and concrete, that it was inclusive of the whole of creation, was "the organizing principle" of his thought.[87] The biblical injunction to love, shared by "all the world's major religions," is in essence the "supreme unifying principle of life,"[88] and the foundation of King's moral imperative. "Agape," King wrote, "is the love of God operating in the human heart. At this level, we love men not because we like them, nor because their ways appeal to us, nor even because they possess some type of divine spark; we love every man because God loves him. At this level, we love the person who does an evil deed, although we hate the deed he does."[89]

85. King, *Why We Can't Wait*, 77.

86. Quoted in Alex Ayres, ed., *The Wisdom of Martin Luther King, Jr.: An A-to-Z Guide to the Ideas and Ideals of the Great Civil Rights Leader* (New York: Penguin, 1993), 114.

87. Weaver, "The Spirituality of Martin Luther King, Jr.," 66.

88. King, *Where Do We Go from Here?*, 190; and Washington, ed., *Testament of Hope*, 242.

89. King, *Strength to Love*, 50.

"He lived and gave his life," writes Dwight N. Hopkins concerning King, "for the oppressed while building a coalition of poor African Americans, Asian Americans, European Americans, Latino(a)/Hispanic Americans, and Native Americans, the first stewards of the land."[90] His campaigns for justice were prophetic, expressing in sermons, writings, and prayers—and in his travels around the nation and the world—his anguish over racism, poverty, war, nuclear weapons, exploitation, and colonization. In these moments of despair, King found solace and hope in biblical wisdom:

> I think the Hebrew prophets are among us today because, although there are many pulpits that are empty while ministers physically occupy them, there are others from which the passion for justice and compassion for man is still heard. In the days to come, as the voices of sanity multiply, we will know that, across thousands of years of time, the prophet's message of truth and decency, brotherhood and peace, survives; that they are living in our time, to give hope to a tortured world that their promise of the Kingdom of God has not been lost to mankind.[91]

SUMMARY

Dr. King's global spiritual perspective was an affair of the heart that began deep within his soul, and was the active expression of God's call to love in a new way, to be more holy. I believe that his profound life and vision were dependent on the human capacity to love more, give more, and care more for the world. Illuminated in this way, his heart was enflamed by a divine longing to make our planet a place where love could flourish. His entire life's ministry was directed toward actualizing the promise of all the religions of the world—that we can achieve spiritual harmony on Earth.

King sacrificed himself as a prayer of healing for the historical sins and institutional oppressions of nations, cultures, and religions. He knew that only when we repent for hatred and violence, and seek a new and more positive path, will we have a "global" spirituality.

Dr. King devoted his life to meeting God face to face in the suffering of black Americans and of humans as a whole. The oneness of creation pierced the core of his being—the totality of human suffering experienced as his own. This mystical solidarity inspired him to extreme acts of altruistic love and self-sacrifice. He led the civil rights movement

90. Dwight N. Hopkins, "The Last Testament of Martin Luther King Jr.," *Theology Today* 65 (2008): 78.

91. King, "My Jewish Brother!," in King, *"In a Single Garment of Destiny,"* 207–8.

through the dark night of America's soul, to stand in the shadow of death, and emerge reunited with love. He taught the virtues and techniques of passing into the desert, of standing alone before God, baring one's body and soul to the potential violence of others. He led by example, giving his life for the justice he knew was divinely granted.

11.

A New Spirit Rising among Us? The Spirituality of Martin Luther King Jr. and the Spiritual Non-conformity of the Black Lives Matter Movement

MICHAEL BRANDON MCCORMACK

> The 1960s movement also had an innate respectability because our leaders often were heads of the black church, as well. Unfortunately, church and spirituality are not high priorities for Black Lives Matter, and the ethics of love, forgiveness and reconciliation that empowered black leaders such as King and Nelson Mandela in the successful quest to win over their oppressors are missing from this movement.
>
> —Rev. Barbara Reynolds[1]

> Perhaps a new spirit is rising among us. If it is, let us trace its movements well and pray that our own inner being may be sensitive to its guidance, for we are deeply in need of a new way beyond the darkness that seems so close around us.
>
> —Martin Luther King Jr.[2]

1. Barbara Reynolds, "I Was a Civil Rights Activist in the 1960s. But It's Hard for Me to Get Behind Black Lives Matter," *The Washington Post*, August 24, 2015, https://tinyurl.com/yajdvtch.

2. Martin Luther King Jr. "Beyond Vietnam: A Time to Break Silence," address given at the Riverside Church, New York City, April 4, 1967, https://tinyurl.com/y8leemc8.

A CRITICAL RESPONSE TO MARTIN LUTHER KING JR. AND THE BLACK LIVES MATTER MOVEMENT

In the current political context, this volume is bound to raise critical questions concerning the significance of the spirituality of Martin Luther King Jr. for public discourses surrounding the Black Lives Matter movement (BLM).[3] No doubt, the seeming irreverence of young people involved in, or identified with, Black Lives Matter consistently evokes some variation of the question, "But, what would MLK say about BLM?" Now, before venturing a response, we might imagine that King would engage in spirited exchanges with Black Lives Matter activists in a similar manner as he did with Stokely Carmichael and other advocates of the then-nascent Black Power movement. A careful reading of those exchanges might lead us to conclude that he would press them to consider the tactical wisdom of the connotations of their slogan of choice, though he would no doubt concur with its denotative meanings. King might also question some of their methods of public engagement. An equally careful reading, however, would remind us that he would likely understand, all too well, and empathize with their reasons for such potentially divisive discourse and practices.[4] Of course, if King were here with us in this moment, he would have been deeply disturbed by the tragic killings of Sandra Bland, Rekia Boyd, Renisha McBride, Trayvon Martin, Michael Brown, Tamir Rice, and countless others. Thus, he might be convinced that his prophesies concerning the "spiritual death" of the nation had come to pass and that indeed, "America *has* gone to hell."[5] More than fifty years after his own violent death, King's prayerful attunements to the liberating promptings of the spirit might lead him,

3. Black Lives Matter is referred to in many ways in public discourse. Oftentimes, Black Lives Matter is referred to as #BlackLivesMatter or #BLM. The use of the hashtag signifies the movement's significant use of social media platforms such as Facebook and Twitter. The origins of Black Lives Matter can be traced to Alicia Garza's Facebook post, "A love note to black people" following the death of Trayvon Martin. Throughout this chapter, I primarily use Black Lives Matter or BLM unless I am specifically referring to the work of the cofounders of #BlackLivesMatter—Opal Tometi, Alicia Garza, and Patrisse Cullors—or I am making a distinction between the grassroots activism that comes under the umbrella of Black Lives Matter and the popular or more social media–based representations of the movement. Occasionally, I will also use the alternative phrase, "the movement for black lives," which is often employed to signify the status of Black Lives Matter as the most recent manifestation of a more historic and ongoing black freedom struggle. For more on Black Lives Matter, see BlackLivesMatter.com.

4. See Martin Luther King Jr., *The Autobiography of Martin Luther King, Jr.*, ed. Clayborne Carson (New York: Grand Central, 1998), 314–23.

5. Martin Luther King Jr. had planned to deliver a sermon titled, "Why America May Go to Hell," on Sunday, April 7, 1968. Of course, that sermon was never delivered, as he was assassinated on April 4, 1968. See Cornel West, ed., *The Radical King: Martin Luther King, Jr.* (Boston: Beacon, 2015), ix, 245–52.

not to quietly kneel before militarized police, but instead to stand with young protesters who refuse to bow, shouting, "Black Lives Matter!" Of course, all of this is speculation.

Indeed, the framing of such questions presupposes and requires speculative responses. To be sure, this is not to trivialize the power of speculative imaginings. Yet, it is important to scrutinize such questions, as they often emerge from a desire to make strategic use of King's moral authority to evoke speculations that either chastise or affirm young activists. More often than not, there seems to be a desire for the former rather than the latter. In response to such questions, critics tend to deploy rhetorical strategies that discursively construct "the spirituality of Martin Luther King Jr." in order to discipline BLM activists for their perceived lack of morality, admonishing them to emulate their construction of his spirituality. Of course, such rhetorical strategies tend to presume that young activists must conform to constructions of "the spirituality of Martin Luther King Jr." without aberration, lest their own activism be considered to be deviant. As such, I will bracket such questions and speculations throughout this chapter and instead call attention to a different set of questions concerning how "the spirituality of Martin Luther King Jr." functions as a discursive construction among those attempting to influence public opinion on the morality and legitimacy of resurgent forms of black activism.

Along these lines, the questions that provoke my contribution to this volume demand neither a strictly historical, nor hermeneutical, approach to the subject at hand (though they engage these approaches, which have been ably demonstrated in previous chapters in this volume). Rather, they call for a more critical approach that scrutinizes the effects of such discursive constructions of "the spirituality of Martin Luther King Jr." within urgent public debates concerning the moral and sociopolitical status of vulnerable black youth involved in the contemporary movement for black lives. More specifically, I focus on the manner in which "spirituality," especially as it is ascribed to the Rev. Dr. Martin Luther King Jr., is deployed as a normative category, and used to mark moral and social distinctions between "respectability" and "deviance." Of particular concern, in this chapter, is the ways that discursive constructions of "the spirituality of Martin Luther King Jr." function rhetorically to (de)authorize the moral authority and political legitimacy of young activists identified with the Black Lives Matter movement.

Moreover, I trace how alternative uses of "spirituality" and "King," among younger activists, function rhetorically to disrupt taken-for-granted assumptions concerning the connections between "King," "spirituality," and a politics of (religious) "respectability." By disrupting such assumptions, I aim to clear the ground for alternative understandings of the significance of "the spirituality of Martin Luther King Jr." In so doing, I also intend to encourage continued research on how (dis)continuities with King's discourse and practice of "spirituality," in contemporary modes of activism, hold out potential for distinctive modes of resistance and resilience in the post–civil rights era.

Throughout the chapter, I draw upon the work of political theorist Cathy J. Cohen in order to show how discursive uses of normative categories, such as "spirituality," which are often uncritically ascribed to King and denied to black youth, function to diminish or establish the legitimacy of the youth-led movement for black lives. Cohen's provocative work on "the politics of deviance," encourages a shifted approach in African American Studies with regard to the theorization and articulation of the (limited) agency of the most vulnerable members of black communities.[6] The significance of her approach, for the purposes of this chapter, lies in her argument that "deviance" is often ascribed to intentional acts of nonconformity among the vulnerable (though not to similar acts among more privileged social groups), while ignoring possibilities that such acts could hold out potential for meaningful sociopolitical transformation. As such, Cohen *both* problematizes the use of "deviance" as a pejorative term used to critique the cultural and sociopolitical behaviors of the vulnerable and makes critical use of the term to call attention to the transformative potential of intentionally nonconformist (i.e., deviant) discourses and practices among the vulnerable.

Drawing upon Cohen's work, I not only problematize uncritical uses of "spirituality" and "King" to signify "deviance" or lack of "respectability," but I also point toward the transformative potential of young activists' intentional acts of nonconformity to reductionist accounts of "the spirituality of Martin Luther King Jr.," reified to emphasize, normalize, and prescribe a politics of patriarchal-hetero-normative-middle-class religious respectability. Subsequently, I argue that by taking seriously those discourses and practices among Black Lives Matter activists deemed to be deviant, we open space to reconsider the ongoing relevance of King's own nonconformity to institutionally prescribed notions

6. Here, we might consider the implications for African American *religious* and *theological* studies. Of course, this approach to the field of King studies might prove challenging, inasmuch as it would require a certain decentering of King. Nevertheless, such an approach might shed significant insight on how the experiences and perspectives of the most marginalized people in his era influenced the life and legacy of King. See Cathy J. Cohen, "Deviance as Resistance: A New Research Agenda for the Study of Black Politics," *DuBois Review: Social Science Research on Race* 1, no. 1 (March 2004): 27–45.

of "spirituality" and "respectability." Thus, by considering the transformative potential in the spiritual "deviance" of young activists identified with Black Lives Matter, we might open up possibilities for fresh insights into the "transformed nonconformity" of King's own spirituality and its ongoing potential to inspire radical change in the shifting sociopolitical terrain of the twenty-first century.

THE SPIRITUALITY OF MARTIN LUTHER KING JR. AND THE DEVIANCE OF BLACK LIVES MATTER

Rev. Barbara Reynolds's prominent opinion editorial, published in the *Washington Post,* serves as a poignant example of the ways that "the spirituality of Martin Luther King Jr." is deployed in public discourse as a rhetorical strategy to ascribe "respectability" to the activism of the civil rights generation, while ascribing "deviance" to a younger generation of activists identified with Black Lives Matter. On Rev. Reynolds's account, such deviance is evidenced by the abandonment of a legacy of "inherently respectable" activism, grounded in "church" and "spirituality" that was bequeathed to younger activists by the Rev. Dr. Martin Luther King Jr. and veterans of the civil rights movement.[7] Central to Reynolds's argument for this declension to deviance is an account of young activists' identifications with hip-hop culture (read: profane) and their counter-identifications with the institutional black church tradition (read: sacred).[8] As the argument goes, identifications with the former, rather than the latter, appear to be causal factors in the perceived lack of proper decorum among young activists.[9] In

7. Cohen, "Deviance as Resistance," 27–45. Here, it should be noted that "church" and "spirituality" are uncritically conflated, collapsing important and necessary distinctions between these two modes of black religious experience. Also see Reynolds, "I Was a Civil Rights Activist."

8. For further discussion of the association of hip-hop culture with the category of the "profane" over against the "sacred," see the emerging discourses on the study of religion and hip-hop. For example, see Monica Miller and Anthony Pinn eds., *The Hip Hop and Religion Reader* (New York: Routledge, 2014); Monica Miller, *Religion and Hip Hop* (New York: Routledge, 2013), esp. chap. 1, "Scapegoats, Boundaries, and Blame: The Civic Face of Hip-Hop Culture," 24–44; Su'ad Abdul Khabeer, *Muslim Cool: Race, Religion, and Hip Hop in the United States* (New York: New York University Press, 2016), see especially "Policing Music and the Facts of Blackness," 77–108, and "Conclusion: #BlackLivesMatter," 219–31.

9. For instance, in the iconic pictures that captured the Selma march, protestors can be seen in suits, kneeling to pray. Contrast this with young activists wearing jeans, T-shirts, bandanas and the like, blocking traffic or laying in the middle of the street for a "die in." In an article titled, "7 Ways #BlackLivesMatter Improves on the Civil Rights Movement," Mary Joyce makes the following argument, with regard to the contrasts in "decorum" between civil rights demonstrators and Black Lives Matter protesters. Joyce argues, "Black leaders of the 1960s were constrained in their sartorial aesthetics by the fact that they could not engage in mass self-broadcasts. They

her public sermonic discourse, "sagging pants that show their underwear," and the use of "profanity" function rhetorically as signifiers of the deviance of a younger generation of activists. As a more concrete example, Reynolds calls attention to younger activists' propensity to chant lyrics to Kendrick Lamar's "We Gon' Be Alright" (which are deemed to be "too harsh . . . nasty and misogynistic" for public demonstrations)[10] as opposed to the more "uplifting" civil rights anthem, "We Shall Overcome."[11] For Reynolds, and other critics of the contemporary movement for black lives, this shift in the public face of civil rights activism from the *respectable* "spirituality" of Martin Luther King Jr. to the *deviant* "profanity" of Black Lives Matter provokes a moment of *moral panic.*

Elsewhere, I have argued that the public (theological) discourse of black religious leaders has often reinforced the *moral panic* that surrounds black youth culture.[12] Here, I contend that rhetorical strategies deployed to ascribe "spirituality" to the tradition, or legacy, of Martin Luther King, while claiming that such "spirituality" is absent from Black Lives Matter, function within public discourse to diminish the moral and political status of already marginalized and vulnerable black youth. Thus, I argue that when critics, such as Rev. Reynolds, claim that black youth involved in contemporary modes of activism lack *respectability* due to their perceived *deviance* from "the spirituality of Martin Luther King Jr.,"

needed to appeal to the prejudices of the white liberal bourgeois media in order to get coverage for their struggle. The lacked the self-broadcast mechanisms of Twitter, Facebook, and cell phone video that have been so critical to BLM. . . . BLM activists do not need to accommodate white prejudice to gain a wider audience for their ideas, and they are refusing to do so." Mary Joyce, "7 Ways #BlackLivesMatter Improves on the Civil Rights Movement," MetaActivism, September 19, 2015, https://tinyurl.com/yca4bg95.

10. Of course, King himself lamented SNCC members' abandonment of the lyrics of "We Shall Overcome" in his discussion on the rise of the slogan "Black Power" within the civil rights movement. Apparently, like King himself, Reynolds's hearing was "not attuned to such bitterness," yet, unlike King, she fails to acknowledge that "in an atmosphere where acts of unpunished violence toward Negroes are a way of life," such bitterness should not come as a surprise. In other words, Reynolds's tone is far more dismissive than King's, who went to great lengths to hear and to empathize with younger activists. See King, *Autobiography*, 317.

11. Reynolds's claim depends upon a highly selective reading of the lyrical content of Lamar's "Alright," without a serious engagement with the reasons for its use during protests, or why and how it has become meaningful for activists involved in Black Lives Matter. More recent scholarship in (black) popular culture is critical of arguments that do not account for the meanings that young people themselves make of cultural products, such as hip-hop music. See, for instance, Michael P. Jeffries, *Thug Life: Race, Gender, and the Meaning of Hip-Hop* (Chicago: University of Chicago Press, 2011).

12. For a discussion on the definition of "moral panic," and its relationship to the public discourse of religious leaders, see Michael Brandon McCormack, "Black Churches, Moral Panic, and the Empowerment of Black Youth in the Era of Hip-Hop," in R. Drew Smith et al., eds., *Multiculturalism: Europe, Africa, and North America* (New York: Palgrave Macmillan, 2013), 251–64.

they wittingly or unwittingly lend their cultural capital as religious figures and/or civil rights veterans to public discourses that reify representations of black youth as morally deviant and socially dangerous. At this point, it is important to consider the work of political theorist Cathy J. Cohen, who reminds us, "We must all remember that the normative categories of 'respectable' and 'deviant' have significant political consequences beyond the academy in determining one's access to needed resources."[13] As Cohen has argued, too often, such discourses function to legitimate the increased surveillance, policing, incarceration, and even killing of those who are already vulnerable to various forms of sociopolitical violence.

Moreover, I take seriously Cohen's more normative argument that "observing and probing the agency of people who, understanding the expectations of the larger society and their communities, choose differently from what is prescribed must be the point from which we start to build a new research agenda for African American Studies."[14] Cohen argues for an approach to scholarship in African American Studies that centers the discourses and practices of "those most vulnerable in Black communities—those thought to be morally wanting by both dominant society and other indigenous group members."[15] At this point, Cohen is worth quoting at length. After detailing the discourse of "deviance" in much of the foundational literature in African American Studies in general, and the study of black politics in particular, Cohen writes:

> I offer their work as a lesson to us all about the instinctive move, even among some of our most dedicated and respected scholars, to judge and pathologize the lives of those must vulnerable in Black communities. At the root of such judgments sits an unexamined acceptance of normative standards of association, behavior, and even desire that limits our ability to respect the subjects under consideration and to explore their lived decisions with an eye toward its transformative and oppositional potential.[16]

With these theoretical and methodological perspectives in mind, let us consider the significance of a strong claim of nonconformity that emerged among younger activists, and that has been taken as evidence of *deviance* with reference to the *respectability* presumed to be inherent in "the spirituality of Martin Luther King Jr." In the opening lines of her opinion piece for the *Washington Post*, Rev. Reynolds seizes upon the angry rhetoric of St. Louis-based hip-hop artist and activist Tef

13. Cohen, "Deviance as Resistance," 42.
14. Cohen, "Deviance as Resistance," 42.
15. Cohen, "Deviance as Resistance," 29.
16. Cohen, "Deviance as Resistance," 37.

Poe: "This ain't your grandparents' civil rights movement!" These words were initially uttered in the midst of a contentious St. Louis community forum, held in the midst of weeks of defiant protest that erupted in the aftermath of the killing of Michael Brown in Ferguson, Missouri. Variations of this claim of counter-identification, "This ain't yo mamma's/daddy's civil rights movement," were subsequently popularized through Tef Poe's track, "War Cry," and were widely circulated among those identified with #BLM via social media and even T-shirts and other products of material culture.[17] For vulnerable black youth involved in BLM activism, this defiant pronouncement captured the sense of frustration, and indeed rage, that many young people felt toward the perceived failure of an older generation—and clergy in particular—to demonstrate solidarity with young protestors in the streets of Ferguson.

In an interview segment titled, "Faith after Ferguson," for *Heart and Soul*, on *BBC World Service*, Tef Poe describes his initial rage and resentment with the black church, for what he perceived to be its failure to "show up" during the initial stages of the protests in Ferguson.[18] Moreover, his critique extended to the at best ambiguous, and at worst complicit, relationship between black clergy and the militarized police force, over against protestors, during ongoing demonstrations. Indeed, the clergy, a religious leadership class that Rev. Reynolds invests with an "inherent respectability," were among those whom Tef Poe, and those who identified with his sentiments, indicted, challenging them to "Get off your ass and join us!"[19] To those clergy disinclined to "join" young activists, the message was clear, "Get out of the way!"

For Rev. Reynolds, Tef Poe's brash assertion, rooted in the deviance of hip-hop culture, is emblematic of the "generation gap that afflicts civil rights activism, and the struggle it is going to take to overcome it."[20]

17. Indeed, young activists could be seen on the front lines of many demonstrations wearing T-shirts with one version or another of this mantra printed on the front. See for instance a popular image of Rahiel Tesfamariam, founder of *Urban Cusp* magazine, marching with Rev. Starsky Wilson and Rev. Traci Blackmon. While the two clergy persons are adorned with clerical vestments, Tesfamariam, a graduate of Yale Divinity School, is wearing blue jeans and a black T-shirt emblazoned with Tef Poe's words, "This ain't yo mamma's civil rights movement."

18. Matt Wells, "Faith after Ferguson," *BBC News*, https://tinyurl.com/y7gm8pmv.

19. In an article for the *Huffington Post*, Rev. Nelson B. Rivers III takes particular umbrage with statements such as Tef Poe's that are critical of the clergy. Rev. Rivers insists, "We aren't enemies, we're on the same side. You shouldn't be speaking about preachers in the church as though they're your enemies, that's insulting and disrespectful." Nevertheless, Rev. Rivers's position was to remain in dialogue with his critics rather than allowing his perspective to foreclose further conversation. As a result, Rivers notes: "Where we didn't agree, we're now able to have a conversation." See, Antonia Blumberg and Carol Kurvilla, "How the Black Lives Matter Changed the Church," *Huffington Post*, August 8, 2015, https://tinyurl.com/y7lo3byw.

20. Reynolds, "I Was a Civil Rights Activist."

Tef Poe, cofounder of the millennial activist group, Hands Up United, might well agree with Reynolds concerning such a "generation gap," though the two would likely disagree sharply on "the struggle it is going to take to overcome it."[21] Yet, critics who position themselves on either side of this perceived "generation gap" might readily agree that the gap is defined, in large part, by conformity or nonconformity to a politics of black middle-class religious respectability. Moreover, they might agree that this politics of respectability is assumed to be the very *essence* of legitimate civil rights activism, and best exemplified by "the spirituality of Martin Luther King Jr."[22] No doubt, it is the irreverent rejection of this politics of respectability that provokes Rev. Reynolds's admonishment of the youth-led BLM movement and confirms her perception of their deviance.

If we take Cathy Cohen's work seriously, however, the "deviance" of, "This ain't your grandparents/mamma's/daddy's civil rights movement!" can be heard as an articulation of intentional *defiance* of, and nonconformity to, institutionally prescribed forms of religious respectability. Indeed, Tef Poe's pronouncement seems to be remarkably consistent with Cohen's argument: "It just might be that after devoting so much of our energy to the unfulfilled promise of access through respectability, a politics of deviance, with a focus on the transformative potential of deviant practices, might be a more viable strategy for radically improving the lives and possibilities of those most vulnerable in Black communities."[23] Thus, for Tef Poe and many younger activists within the movement, it is precisely this preoccupation with religious respectability

21. For more information on Hands Up United (HUU), see HandsUpUnited.org.

22. In an interview for the online feminist site ForHarriet.com, historian Evelyn Brooks Higginbotham responds to Kimberly Foster's query as to whether the complexity of Higginbotham's work on the politics of respectability in *Righteous Discontent: The Women's Movement in the Black Baptist Church, 1880–1920* has been lost on critics of respectability. Higginbotham adds clarity to the historical deployment of respectability politics by black church women in the late nineteenth and early twentieth centuries. Her argument, in the ForHarriet.com article, concerning the contemporary significance of respectability within discourses surrounding the Black Lives Matter movement does not adequately address the types of critiques that Cohen raises in "Deviance as Resistance." While Higginbotham's main concern seems to be issues of "character" and "moral authority," she does not call into question the social construction of such morality, rooted in white middle-class norms and values, nor does she interrogate the contemporary power relations involved in demonstrating respectability. Cohen does not dismiss the significance of Higginbotham's work in her article. Indeed, she insists that critics not trivialize the historical significance of political strategies of respectability. Nevertheless, Cohen critiques the assimilationist underpinnings of this strategy and calls for greater attention to the oppositional practices and transformative possibilities of those who choose to position themselves against or outside of dominant norms and expectations of social behavior. See Kimberly Foster and Evelyn Brooks Higginbotham, "Wrestling with Respectability in the Age of #BlackLivesMatter: A Dialogue," *For Harriet*, October 13, 2015, https://tinyurl.com/ybxzwedb.

23. Cohen, "Deviance as Resistance," 30.

that must be rejected if the aims of black liberation are to be achieved in post–civil rights America.[24] Activists have stated, in no uncertain terms, that arguments for respectability, rooted in "the idea that black people must demonstrate their value by assimilating to the respectability norms of the white bourgeoisie," are "anathema to BLM."[25] As such, "Respectability will not save us!" has become something of a mantra among a number of activists identified with BLM, while more strident (read: deviant) voices within the movement have provocatively declared, "Fuck your respectability politics!"[26]

THE SPIRITUALITY OF MARTIN LUTHER KING JR. AND BLACK LIVES MATTER'S DEFIANCE OF RELIGIOUS RESPECTABILITY

Yet, it must be insisted at this point that a rejection of religious respectability among young activists is not necessarily tantamount to a rejection of "spirituality," or even "the spirituality of Martin Luther King Jr." Here, I turn to the public discourse of Rev. Osagyefo Uhuru Sekou, an activist-clergyman with deep ties to the Black Lives Matter movement, in order to analyze alternative uses of "spirituality" and "King" in public discourse surrounding the nascent movement. Rather than deploying "spirituality" as a *normative* (or normativizing) category, with reference to King, I argue that Sekou uses "spirituality" as a *transgressive* category in order to disrupt associations between King and respectability, and between BLM and deviance. Rev. Sekou's more transgressive approach can be observed in his own rhetorical appeal to the defiant words of Tef Poe. While both ministers turn to Tef Poe as a source for their respective arguments, Rev. Sekou deploys the activist hip-hop artist's words in markedly different ways than Rev. Reynolds.

In an interview with *The Chicago Reporter*, Sekou argues for a more transgressive interpretation of Tef Poe's claim of nonconformity. For Sekou, Tef Poe's claim can be interpreted to mean that the emerging social movement, which centers the issues and concerns of those marginalized folks who are most directly impacted by contemporary forms of anti-black violence, "[Is] not going to be black people marching in suits and cufflinks. It's going to be rageful. . . . It's going to be angry. It

24. See Cornel West and Rev. Osagyefo Sekou, "And the Young Ones Shall Lead Them: The Ferguson Rebellion and the Crisis in Black Leadership," *Ebony*, October 2, 2014, https://tinyurl.com/yc9oxwtp.

25. See Joyce, "7 Ways."

26. Joyce, "7 Ways."

has tattoos. It's queer. It's primarily women-led."[27] In a more provocative variation on this claim, Rev. Sekou uses King as a rhetorical strategy to drive home his sermonic point, "Martin Luther King ain't coming back. Get over it. It won't look like the civil rights movement. It's angry. It's profane. If you're more concerned about young people using profanity than about the profane conditions they live in, there's something wrong with you."[28] However, Sekou insists that this is not a rejection of "spirituality" per se, or even "King,"[29] but rather a claim that the "spirituality" of this movement is being reimagined by young, poor, female, queer, tattooed, and angry activists who have been deemed to be among the deviant vis-à-vis those who Cohen describes as "on the march toward black middle-class respectability."[30]

For Cohen, those who have not exhibited the proper degree of respectable blackness have suffered from a "secondary marginalization," whereby they have been pushed to the edges of already marginalized black communities.[31] Cohen describes the ways that such "secondary marginalization" often involves alienation (though not necessarily a total break) from communal institutions—including churches and families—and the (limited, but nevertheless significant) resources that such institutions afford, "which also jeopardizes the formal standing of already marginalized individuals in relation to the state."[32] In her more recent work, Cohen extends her analysis of vulnerable individuals within black communities "with little access to and protection from dominant power" to discuss the particularly devastating effects that such marginalization

27. Yuri Han, "Leaving the Pulpit for the Streets of Ferguson," *The Chicago Reporter* (2 February 2015), chicagoreporter.com/leaving-the-pulpit-for-the-streets-of-ferguson/.

28. See Sarah van Gelder, "Rev. Sekou on Today's Civil Rights Leaders: 'I Take My Orders from 23-Year-Old Queer Women,'" *YES!*, July 22, 2015, https://tinyurl.com/nmznyzo.

29. Evidence for Rev. Sekou's claim can be found, in part, on the album art for Tef Poe's album, *War Machine III*. On the front of the album, Tef Poe is pictured laying in a bed, smoking what appears to be marijuana, with a gun lying across his abdomen and a bottle of Hennessy next to the trigger. At the same time, however, he is surrounded by an array of objects, including a copy of Tupac Shakur's book of poetry, *The Rose That Grew from Concrete*, Elijah Muhammad's *Message to the Black Man*, *The Holy Bible*, and a dated copy of a biography of Martin Luther King Jr. A closer inspection of Tef Poe's bodily adornment also reveals what appears to be a gold "Jesus Piece" pendant hanging from his necklace, and a large tattoo of King on his left bicep. Moreover, the initial track on the album opens with a sampling of Rev. Sekou leading a group of activists in the singing of "This Little Light of Mine" in Ferguson. Throughout the album, there are also several references to African American religious and spiritual traditions—albeit used in seemingly deviant ways. This all lends credence to Sekou's claim that a rejection of a politics of respectability, and even a thoroughgoing critique of the black church and its leadership, does not necessarily entail a rejection of "King" or "spirituality."

30. Cohen, "Deviance as Resistance," 42.

31. Cathy J. Cohen, *The Boundaries of Blackness: AIDS and the Breakdown of Black Politics* (Chicago: University of Chicago Press, 1999).

32. Cohen, "Deviance as Resistance," 37.

has upon black youth.[33] In her body of work, Cohen calls for an expansion of our understanding of "who constitutes black communities and [a reconstruction of] the boundaries of membership and identity."[34] At the same time, however, Cohen insists upon "highlight[ing] the agency of those on the outside, who choose outsider status, at least temporarily."[35]

Along these lines, Rev. Sekou argues for a reading of young people who have been marginalized from, or who *choose* to remain marginal to, black churches as those ideally positioned to claim and expand upon a more "authentic" understanding of the legacy, and indeed, "the spirituality of Martin Luther King Jr." In *Gods, Gays, and Guns: Essays on Religion and the Future of Democracy*, Rev. Sekou describes King's own increasing alienation from mainstream civil rights organizations, due to his nonconformist insistence upon "telling the truth of the ugliness of the American empire."[36] In this sense, Sekou's rhetorical strategy functions in ways that are consistent with Cohen's argument for the necessity of "[detailing] the work of power that constructs and disseminates the idea of outsider or deviant within and outside Black communities."[37] Thus, the spiritual legacy of Rev. Sekou's King represents an "outsider's legacy" that "used the hopes of an exiled people to transform American democracy," and we might add, to transform "the soul of America" in light of his view of its impending "spiritual death." As such, Rev. Sekou offers an account of the spirituality of King deemed to be consistent with, and empowering in light of, the "outsider" (read: deviant) status of many black youth involved in the Black Lives Matter movement.

In his 2017 Russell Lecture on Spiritual Life, delivered at Tufts University, Rev. Sekou expanded upon this line of thought by making transgressive use of the "spiritual" to position alienated black youth activists within the "prophetic tradition" of King. For Rev. Sekou, Tef Poe's "This is not your daddy's civil rights movement," can be understood with greater clarity by keeping firmly in mind the hip-hop and millennial generations' widespread use of the cliché, "I'm not religious, I'm spiritual."[38] However, in an essay titled, "Spiritual Not Religious," Sekou argues that for poor black youth in the hip-hop generation, this is no

33. Cohen, "Deviance as Resistance," 37. See also Cathy J. Cohen, *Democracy Remixed: Black Youth and the Future of American Politics* (New York: Oxford University Press, 2012).

34. Cohen, "Deviance as Resistance," 42.

35. Cohen, "Deviance as Resistance," 43.

36. Osagyefo Uhuru Sekou, *Gods, Gays, and Guns: Essays on Religion and the Future of Democracy* (Cambridge: Campbell & Cannon, 2011), 15.

37. Cohen, "Deviance as Resistance," 42.

38. Osagyefo Uhuru Sekou, "The Role of the Prophet in a Time of Monsters." This speech was delivered as the 2017 Russell Lecture on Spiritual Life at Tufts University (3 April 2017), chaplaincy.tufts.edu/blog/2017/03/07/russell-lecture-on-spiritual-life-2017/.

mere cliché, but rather a trenchant critique of what he refers to as "the sub-hegemony of the black church on religious discourse."[39] Nevertheless, Sekou argues that the seeming rejection of "religion" among younger activists is not necessarily to be taken at face value, but rather that it represents a response "to a popular construction of religion and not its prophetic heart."[40] Similarly, he argues that claims of counter-identification with an older generation are responses to "a popular construction of Martin Luther King's legacy and the civil rights movement and not it's prophetic edge. . . . They are not rejecting the prophetic edge, they are rejecting the lie that has been given to them."[41] Here, Sekou's use of the "prophetic edge" of the civil rights movement assumes that *this*, and *not* religious respectability, is the "essence" of both "the spirituality of Martin Luther King Jr." and the spirituality of young black activists who claim, "I'm not religious, I'm spiritual."[42] The essentialist underpinnings of Rev. Sekou's argument notwithstanding, his rhetorical use of "spirituality" is significant here, as it is deployed to disrupt taken-for-granted assumptions of respectability politics as the essence of "the spirituality of Martin Luther King Jr." More significantly, "spirituality" is deployed strategically to claim identification between King and young activists who are often deemed to be deviant for having rejected respectability.

Both Reynolds and Sekou make strategic use of "spirituality" and "King" in their public sermonic discourses. Both ministers also site Tef Poe's nonconformist claim of counter-identification in their arguments concerning the perceived "deviance" of Black Lives Matter, and contestations over the movement's relationship with the legacy of Dr. King. I argue that Rev. Reynolds deploys "spirituality" as a normat(-ivizing) category, used to position BLM activists in a morally estranged relationship to the respectability politics and the love ethic associated with King's legacy. By contrast, I hold that Rev. Sekou uses "spirituality" as a transgressive category in order to critique popular constructions of King, re-present King's radical politics within the (black) prophetic tradition, and to position young black activists within the trajectory of King's "outsider's legacy" of activism. In Sekou's estimation, poor urban black youth, who see themselves as alienated from black churches (whether such alienation is forced or chosen), are liberated to reimagine connections between their own struggles and "the spirituality of Martin Luther King Jr."

39. Sekou, *Gods, Gays, and Guns,* 52.
40. Sekou, "Role of the Prophet."
41. Sekou, "Role of the Prophet."
42. See also "Spiritual Not Religious," in Sekou, *Gods, Gays, and Guns*, 48–53.

THE SPIRITUALITY OF MARTIN LUTHER KING JR. AND THE SPIRITUAL NONCONFORMITY OF BLACK LIVES MATTER

Rev. Sekou's argument opens space for additional research on the intentionally nonconformist (read: deviant) conceptions and practices of spirituality within the Black Lives Matter movement, which are often ignored by critics of the movement. Such nonconformist and alternative framings of spirituality may be overlooked because critics assume that young activists, who are thought to be morally wanting, have rejected "religion" and/or "spirituality" altogether. Yet, the overlooking of such alternative discourses and practices can be attributed, at least in part, to the failure of religious practitioners and intellectuals alike to construct articulations of religion, theology, and/or spirituality that take seriously the experiences, perspectives, and voices of marginalized black youth.[43] More trenchantly, Rev. Sekou insists: "This is in part due [to] both the lack of value attributed to poor black and brown youth voices in the academy, the inability of the black church to relate to youth, and above all the sheer lack of courage among African American religious leaders and [others] to sit at the feet of young folks and engage them in [a] sustained way."[44] In Sekou's estimation, "Older African Americans and younger black folks with petite bourgeois sensibilities concerning youth," have simply failed to engage in potentially transformative dialogues with marginalized black youth concerning their understandings of, and sense of connections between, their own lived experiences, "spirituality," "the black church tradition," "activism," and "the legacy of Martin Luther King Jr."[45]

Yet, Sekou offers us more than a mere critique of the failures of black church leaders and black religious intellectuals. He raises challenging questions that deserve our attention. For Rev. Sekou, young, angry, queer, pregnant teenagers, gang members, those with "sagging pants that show their underwear," and other marginalized black youth, provoke urgent questions of, "Who has the right to engage in theological agency? Who has the right to authorize how we come to understand the sacred, divine, and notions of ultimate meaning?"[46] For the purposes of this volume, we might signify on Sekou's questions, asking such questions as, "Who has the right to authorize how we come to under-

43. Sekou, *God, Gays, and Guns*, 50.

44. Sekou, *God, Gays, and Guns*, 50.

45. Sekou, *God, Gays, and Guns*, 50.

46. Sekou, *God, Gays, and Guns*, 52–53.

stand what 'spirituality' is, who is publically identifiable as 'spiritual,' who stands in the tradition of the 'spirituality of Martin Luther King, Jr.' and more provocatively, who is authorized to challenge, critique, and/or expand upon the normative assumptions of that tradition?" I argue that by taking Cohen's argument seriously, we come to understand that those vulnerable young BLM activists, deemed to be "deviant" by those deeply invested in religious respectability, might offer us new insights on the transformative potential of a nonconformist approach to spirituality—an approach that was embodied, at least in part, by King, but critically evaluated and expanded upon by Black Lives Matter.

The constraints of this present volume do not allow for a thorough examination of the transformative potential of BLM's intentional acts of spiritual nonconformity. Yet, for the remainder of this chapter, I want to make a significant gesture in that direction, to be expanded upon in further research. Toward this end, I want to briefly highlight the use of "spirituality" and "King" in the public discourse and practice of Black Lives Matter activists. By focusing upon the ways that these younger activists reimagine connections between "spirituality," "the radical legacy of King," and contemporary modes of activism, I aim to offer a conclusion to this volume that provides fresh insights and inspires further research into the significance of "the spirituality of Martin Luther King Jr." in ongoing struggles for the revaluation of black lives.

In their piece for the *Huffington Post*, titled, "Celebrating MLK Day: Reclaiming Our Movement Legacy," Opal Tometi, Patrisse Cullors, and Alicia Garza articulate a position that both affirms and moves beyond Tef Poe's irreverent claim of counter-identification with the civil rights movement. Tometi, Cullors, and Garza observe: "This year, King's legacy is being thought of in the context of the #BlackLivesMatter movement which has spread like wildfire throughout the United States and around the world. Ignited by the killings of Islan Nettles, Mike Brown, Rekia Boyd, Oscar Grant, Trayvon Martin, Renisha McBride, Aiyana Jones, Jordan Davis and too many more by police and vigilantes, Dr. King's legacy and his work take on a different meaning in today's world."[47] As cofounders of #BlackLivesMatter, these three black women argue that though "the legacy of Dr. King has been largely sanitized, reconfigured, and appropriated to obscure his radical vision," they intend to assert their agency as young activists who are actively engaged in reimaging the "radical" legacy of King, as a defiant act of "reclamation,"

47. Opal Tometi, Alicia Garza, and Patrisse Cullors-Brignac, "Celebrating MLK Day: Reclaiming Our Movement Legacy," *Huffington Post* (18 January 2015), https://tinyurl.com/y9nj94r8 .

in the context of the contemporary movement. Thus, not only are they arguing that "Dr. King's legacy and his work *take on* a different meaning in today's world," they are asserting their agency in (critically and respectfully) *redefining* this legacy, including the legacy of "the spirituality of Martin Luther King Jr."

Throughout the piece, Tometi, Cullors, and Garza critique, reclaim, critique again, and ultimately expand upon the legacy of King, pressing King's legacy into the service of contemporary struggles for justice that have called forth #BlackLivesMatter. Their initial critique concerns the commodification of King's legacy, and its deployment by conservatives and liberals alike to obscure "his radical vision," or what Rev. Sekou refers to as its "prophetic edge." Their reclamation involves calling attention to the radicality of King's vision for his political and material context, but also includes an insistence upon the significance of both those who supported *and challenged* King in the development of that vision.[48] Thus, their subsequent critiques of King are rooted in claims for King's own openness to challenges to his idea(l)s, organizing strategies, and political tactics. On these grounds, the cofounders of #BlackLivesMatter pursue a rhetorical strategy that positions their activism within the legacy of King, while critiquing and expanding upon that legacy: "When we founded #BlackLivesMatter in 2013, we wanted to create a political space within and amongst our communities for activism that could stand firmly on the shoulders of movements that have come before us, such as the civil rights movement, while innovating on its strategies and approaches to finally centralize the leadership of those existing at the margins of our economy and our society."[49]

It is the last clause in the sentence above, however, that returns us to the significance of Cohen's theorization of "the politics of deviance" for the argument that I am making in this chapter. It is precisely this insistence upon "the leadership of those existing at the margins of our economy and our society" that echoes Cohen's call for research that centers the perspectives of those deemed to be "deviant" based upon their nonconformity to dominant norms of respectability. Indeed, Tometi, Cullors, and Garza lay bare the seeming "deviant" status of #BlackLives-Matter when they describe the movement as:

> [A] project started by three black women, two of whom are queer women and one who is a Nigerian-American. . . . Black trans people, Black queer people, Black immigrants, Black incarcerated people and formerly incarcerated people, Black millennials, Black women, low income Black people, and

48. Tometi, Garza, and Cullors-Brignac, "Celebrating MLK Day."
49. Tometi, Garza, and Cullors-Brignac, "Celebrating MLK Day."

> Black people with disabilities are at the front, exercising a new leadership that is bold, innovative, and radical.[50]

In this sense, Tometi, Cullors and Garza echo Tef Poe's claim, "This is not your grandparents' civil rights movement!" Moreover, they corroborate Tef's sentiment in his BBC interview, when he explains, "For once, you're not getting the most educated people on camera. You're getting the two-time felon with one more strike. . . . It's people who are finally so fed up that they don't know what this country should look like, . . . they don't know what the guidelines of that new relationship should be. They just know that we've been in a relationship with America that . . . it's not functioning."[51]

However, as I noted above, for critics of the movement, such as Rev. Reynolds, this shift in the public "face" of the movement provokes a moment of moral panic. In her *Washington Post* article, Reynolds opines that the demographics and aesthetics of #BLM render them a "motley-looking group."[52] This deviant characterization of #BLM is telling. No doubt, Cohen's work is instructive here as well. In "Deviance as Resistance," Cohen insists that the role of one's relationship to dominant power in constructing "the political" has often gone unexplained. As Cohen has argued, "It is, however, important to underscore, as critics of respectability remind us, the relative positioning necessary to prove that one is respectable and acceptable compared to other less fortunate 'souls' who compromise the excluded."[53]As such, Cohen argues for the necessity of "making visible all those who have been excluded from the middle-class march toward respectability."[54] And, it is precisely this work of making the excluded not only visible but privileging their voices that is at the center of Tometi's, Cullors's, and Garza's concerns.

For these cofounders of #BlackLivesMatter, such a shift in the public face and voice of the movement has important political implications-namely a more inclusive movement that resists the concentration of power in the hands of a few respectable black male charismatic leaders—often clergy.[55] Moreover, this shift promises clarified understandings of the effects of state-sanctioned violence upon *all citizens*, by centering the experiences of those vulnerable black folks at the margins, who are most directly impacted by such violence. For these activists, clarified

50. Tometi, Garza, and Cullors-Brignac, "Celebrating MLK Day."

51. Quoted in Wells, "Faith after Ferguson."

52. Reynolds, "I Was a Civil Rights Activist."

53. Cohen, "Deviance as Resistance," 37.

54. Cohen, "Deviance as Resistance," 40.

55. For an extensive critique of black charismatic leadership, see Erica R. Edwards, *Charisma and the Fictions of Black Leadership* (Minneapolis: University of Minnesota Press, 2012).

understanding of the effects of contemporary modes of state-sanctioned violence is understood to be the basis for revised and expanded strategies and tactics for resistance and resilience. Yet, for Tometi, Cullors, and Garza, such a shift is no rejection of King, but rather this shift opens radically transformative possibilities for realizing the fullness of King's radical vision. Indeed, Tometi, Cullors, and Garza do not credit political theorists, such as Cohen, for their "politics of deviance" at this point. Rather, their rhetorical strategy involves an invocation and alternative interpretation of King:

> Dr. King once said, "Whatever affects one directly, affects all indirectly. I can never be what I ought to be until you are what you ought to be. This is the interrelated structure of reality." And what we have learned from Dr. King's words and our current practice is that when a movement full of leaders from the margins gets underway, it makes the connections between social ills, it rejects the compromise and respectability politics of the past, and it opens up new political space for a radical vision of what this nation can truly become.[56]

While Tometi, Cullors, and Garza have been explicit about their efforts to "#ReclaimMLK" in terms of his radical *politics,* however, less explicit has been an insistence upon a reclamation of King's radical "spirituality."[57] Yet, while there may not be explicit references to "the spirituality of Martin Luther King Jr.," Patrisse Cullors has been as adamant as King about the "role of spirit" in the movement for black lives. As I will argue below, her account of the nonconformist spirituality of Black Lives Matter opens space for us to reconsider the influences on, and ongoing transformative potential of, King's radical discourse and practice of spirituality. At this point, however, it is important to take seriously BLM's deviations from the modes of spirituality most readily associated with King. As Hebah H. Farrag notes in an article for *Religion Dispatches,* "While the involvement of church groups and traditional religious leaders in various aspects of Black Lives Matter has been noted by news outlets, there is *another spirit* that animates the Black Lives Matter movement, one that has received little attention but is essential to a new

56. Tometi, Garza, and Cullors-Brignac, "Celebrating MLK Day."

57. Of course, many would assert that one cannot understand King's radical politics without taking account of his spirituality or religious commitments. For Cornel West, "The radical King was first and foremost a revolutionary Christian—a black Baptist minister and pastor whose intellectual genius and rhetorical power was deployed in the name of the Gospel of Jesus Christ. King understood this good news to be primarily radical love in freedom and radical freedom in love, a fallible enactment of the Beloved Community or finite embodiment of the Kingdom of God." See West, ed., *Radical King*, xv.

generation of civil rights activists (emphasis mine)."[58] It is this "another spirit" that I want to briefly explore below, as it may provide insights into the significance of the transformative potential of the spiritual "deviance" of Black Lives Matter.

To be sure, Patrisse Cullors regards spirituality as an integral component of the movement for black lives, even as she is careful to articulate (dis)continuities with institutionally prescribed understandings of spirituality, which in African American communities tend to presume commitments to the black church. For Cullors, the alternative modes of spirituality in #BLM are shaped, at least in part, by strained relationships between many younger activists and the black church. Echoing Cohen's theory of "secondary marginalization," Cullors describes how the respectability politics of the black church tradition has been alienating to large segments of the black community, and particularly poor black youth, women, and those who identify with the LGBTQ community. While King's spirituality was deeply informed by his intimacy and identification with the black church tradition, Cullors's does not share such intimacies or identifications. In an interview with Robert Ross, titled, "The Resilient World We're Building Now," Cullors explains:

> To be honest with you, so many of us in the Black Lives Matter movement have . . . been pushed out of the church, because many of us are queer and out. . . . The church has become very patriarchal for us as women, and so that's not necessarily where we have found our solace. And I think we have had to contend with that during this movement. How do we relate to the black church and how do we understand ourselves in relationship to the black church inside of this movement?[59]

In response to critics who insist that the movement falters because of its disconnection from black churches and its perceived lack of "spirituality," Cullors counters, "I think we think about it differently. But that hasn't stopped us from being deeply spiritual in this work."[60] Indeed, Cullors presents "spirituality" as an integral component of activist work with communities who have been directly impacted by disproportionate levels of policing and state violence.[61] Cullors insists, "In the last year and a half, from the black community in and of itself, as we say 'black lives

58. Hebah H. Farrag, "The Role of Spirit in the #BlackLivesMatter Movement: A Conversation with Activist and Artist Patrisse Cullors," *Religion Dispatches* (24 June 2015), https://tinyurl.com/ydakk3zr.

59. Patrisse Cullors and Robert Ross, "The Resilient World We're Building Now," *On Being with Krista Tippett*, February 18, 2016, https://tinyurl.com/y8qyz7f8.

60. Cullors and Ross, "Resilient World."

61. Farrag, "Role of Spirit."

matter,' you see the light that comes inside of people to the other communities that are like, 'I'm going to stand on the side of black lives.' You see people literally transforming. And that's a different type of work. And for me, that is a spiritual work. It's a healing work and we don't have it codified."[62]

Yet, the nonconformity or "deviance" of this spirituality can be seen not only in terms of its "extra-church" orientation (to invoke historian of religions Charles Long's useful phrase), but also in terms of its explicitly non-Christian practices. Cullors writes, "When we have actions of people . . . it's deeply spiritual. It's often led by opening prayer. Folks are usually sagging. We use a lot of indigenous practices. People build altars to the people who have passed. And so it's this moment to both stand face-to-face with law enforcement, but it's also this moment to be deeply reflective on the people who've been killed by the state and give them our honor."[63] By positioning nonconformist practices of spirituality in direct contrast to dominant normalized understandings of spirituality, young activists challenge not only state-sponsored violence against black bodies, but also hegemonic constructions of Christianity that are used to legitimate such violence and other forms of exclusionary practices that have positioned many of them in contested relationships with churches and the state.

Moreover, these alternative and African-derived practices of spirituality are deployed among Cullors and other BLM activists, not only as modes of *resistance*, but also of *resilience*. Through her Los Angeles–based grassroots organization, Dignity and Power Now (DPN), Cullors deploys practices such as "acupuncture, reiki, herbal tinctures and African and indigenous faith practice to bolster its justice work." Cullors's use of these non-Christian modes of spirituality is intended to attend to aspects of justice work that were unfortunately neglected among civil rights leaders such as King—and it could be argued, are still neglected in modes of black church-based activism. According to the DPN website (DignityandPowerNow.org), "This blend of spiritual practices helps activists impart meaning, heal grief and trauma, combat burn-out and encourage efficiency in their organization." Cullors describes her alternative approach to spirituality as a form of "healing-justice work" that is particularly attentive to the traumatization of victims of violence. DPN describes such work as "represent[ing] the front lines of new community development, founded on notions of self-care,

62. Cullors and Ross, "Resilient World."
63. Cullors and Ross, "Resilient World."

resilience, and transformative justice, and based in new conceptions of spirituality and activism."

Thus, as Cohen argues, with respect to politics proper, those who are reminded daily of their distance from the black church, and other communal and state-sponsored sites of power and authority, are often forced to reimagine and/or renegotiate their relationship to "spirituality" in ways that resonate with issues and experiences that affect their lives. For Cohen, such nonconformity to institutionally prescribed forms of spiritualty, performed by young, poor, female, queer, and/or otherwise marginalized activists, would constitute acts of defiance that might also be understood as intentional acts of deviance that can be mobilized for political resistance. Cullors would expand Cohen's argument to include not only political "resistance" but also "resilience." Cullors declares: "For me, seeking spirituality had a lot to do with trying to seek understanding about my conditions—how these conditions shape me in my everyday life and how do I understand them as part of a larger fight, a fight for my life. People's resilience, I think, is tied to their will to live, our will to survive, which is deeply spiritual. . . . The fight to save your life is a spiritual fight."[64]

And it is this "spirituality" of BLM's fight for the revaluation of black lives that is often overlooked. Yet, Cullors, like King, insists that spirituality radically affects the mode and manner of that fight. Indeed, Cullors echoes King's spiritual sensibilities when she argues, "It's not just about changing policies. It's not just about changing lives. It's about changing our culture and changing how we fight."[65] She goes on to insist, "We can change policies all day but if the fight to get there was full of trauma, was replicating oppressive dynamics, abusive dynamics, then what is the point?"[66] Hebah Ferrag concludes her article with a poignant observation that resonates with Cohen's insistence upon the transformative potential of the intentionally nonconformist practices of the "deviant." Here, Ferrag is worth quoting at length:

> The influence and involvement of black religious leaders in civil rights movements in the U.S. has been well noted. The Black church, along with the Nation of Islam and notable Black Muslims, have been fundamental to political advancements in the African American community. Yet, the discussion of faith-based involvement in the black civil rights movements remains (mostly) hetero-normative and almost exclusively male. As the black community grapples with the terrorism against it, the work of Patrisse Cullors and the Black Lives Matter movement expands the defi-

64. Quoted in Farrag, "Role of Spirit."
65. Quoted in Farrag, "Role of Spirit."
66. Quoted in Farrag, "Role of Spirit."

> nition of "faith-based," and offers alternate notions of faith, self-care and wellness as resistance to disrupt a martyr mentality and heal those within traumatized communities.[67]

At this point, it should be clear that for Cullors and many within the #BLM movement, seemingly "deviant" conceptions and practices of "spirituality" are grounded in a fundamental concern with recognizing, protecting, and enhancing the sacredness of black lives—*all black lives*—including those deemed to be beyond the boundaries of black middle-class respectability.

TOWARD A SPECULATIVE RESPONSE TO CRITICAL QUESTIONS CONCERNING THE SPIRITUALITY OF MARTIN LUTHER KING JR. AND THE MATTER OF RADICAL LOVE FOR BLACK LIVES

Here, the critical analysis of this chapter might finally open toward an argument for the most compelling connections between the spirituality embodied by King and its "deviant" expansions in Black Lives Matter. When Alicia Garza claimed, "Black Lives Matter affirms the lives of Black queer and trans folks, disabled folks, Black-undocumented folks, folks with records, women and all Black lives along the gender spectrum," this was an outworking of her original "a love note to black people" posted on Facebook following the killing of Trayvon Martin. Her "love note" ended with the words, "Black people. I love you. I love us. Our lives matter."[68] While the affirmations of the aforementioned nonconforming identifications with blackness exceed the respectability politics that undeniably shaped King's activism and spirituality, they are born of the same radical love that constitutes the very heart of King's legacy. Indeed, Cornel West argues in *The Radical King*, "there is no radical King without his commitment to radical love."[69]

If Cornel West is correct concerning the "radical love" of the "radical King," and that "this radical love of an intensely hated people is both liberating and contagious, just as this radical freedom of a thoroughly unfree people is both emancipating and infectious," then it should not be

67. Quoted in Farrag, "Role of Spirit."

68. See Alicia Garza, "A Herstory of the #BlackLivesMatter Movement," *The Feminist Wire* (7 October 2014), https://tinyurl.com/yd9vosqw. See also, "A Love Note to Our Folks: Alicia Garza on the Organizing of #BlackLivesMatter," *n 1*, January 20, 2015, https://tinyurl.com/ybcsusz4.

69. West, ed., *Radical King*, xvi.

surprising that Black Lives Matter activists have not only embraced this "radical love of an intensely hated people," but expanded this "ethos of collective black love" to include those previously deemed to be beyond the boundaries of black religious respectability.[70] Yet, critics have maintained that such an ethic of love is altogether absent from Black Lives Matter. For such critics, articulations of black rage over state-sponsored violence against black bodies is interpreted as a rejection of King's ethic of love, and for some, it is an outright expression of hate. Krista Tippett presses Patrisse Cullors on this point in an interview: "I know you hear this, and I also want to ask you with Black Lives Matter, they say, 'Where is the love?' . . . it's not just Black Lives Matter, but if rage is at the center, what is being created in terms of building a different world?" Cullors's response merits extensive quotation:

> Well, I disagree. It's both rage and love at the center of our work, I think. . . . And I think that—when we show up on the freeway, when we chain ourselves to each other, that's an act of love. That act of resistance is an act of love, that we will put our bodies on the line for our community and, really, for this country. In changing black lives, we change all lives, and I think that's the conversation that needs to be penetrated into folks, right? This conversation about black lives mattering is a conversation about all lives mattering, and I think that our work shows as such. When we have actions of people—have they ever been a part of a Black Lives Matter action—it's deeply spiritual.[71]

Thus, while Black Lives Matter may (rightly) insist, "This is not your grandparents' civil rights movement," and while there are undoubtedly sharp distinctions to be made between the modes and manners of King's activism and young people identified with BLM, nevertheless, to the degree that Black Lives Matter operates "from a place of deep love for black people," it has intentionally or unintentionally drawn upon the radical love inspired by King's spirituality. In so doing, they have made a compelling argument for the ongoing significance and transformative potential of "the spirituality of Martin Luther King Jr." And, even if this latter argument for the continuities between "the spirituality of Martin Luther King Jr." and Black Lives Matter is not finally convincing, it is worth remembering Cornel West's keen observation that even though King understood quite well that his southern middle-class religious respectability did not resonate with urban youth in the North, "King always extended his radical love to them—in a sincere and authen-

70. West, ed., *Radical King*, xv.
71. Cullors and Ross, "Resilient World."

tic way."[72] Perhaps, therein lies the most significant aspect of "the spirituality of Martin Luther King Jr." to be remembered and reclaimed for such a time as this.

As such, I conclude with a return to the speculative question that I intentionally bracketed at the beginning of the chapter, "But, what would MLK say about BLM?" With Cornel West, I am convinced that though he would recognize that his own religious respectability no longer resonates with many in this generation, "the spirituality of Martin Luther King Jr." would nevertheless lead him to engage BLM activists with a radical love and deep appreciation for their commitments to resistance and resilience in the face of virulently persistent anti-black racism, which he might be shocked to realize has remained so deeply entrenched, despite the most respectable efforts to uproot it. Now, King would likely challenge them as he did his own contemporaries in the civil rights movement who resorted to "vituperative language," exhorting them, "We don't need to curse anybody, we don't need to call them crackers, because they call us niggers."[73] Nevertheless, I suspect that he would also appreciate their own "deviant" version of his "transformed nonconformity," which has strengthened their resolve to engage in the spiritual fight for the rehumanization, revaluation, and revitalization of black lives—even those beyond the boundaries of black respectability.

And so, if I were to speculate on how "the spirituality of Martin Luther King Jr." might lead him to respond to Black Lives Matter, whatever else he might say, I would like to think that his radical love would lead him to acknowledge and appreciate the continuities and discontinuities between his spirituality and theirs. I suspect that his own experiences of being labeled as *treasonous* (read: deviant) for his spiritual nonconformity to dominant expectations of civil-religious American patriotism, due to his unpopular position on Vietnam, might lead him to empathize with the labeling of young BLM activists as *terrorists* (read: deviant) for their willingness to "break silence" around state-sponsored, militarized assaults on poor, black, bodies in these United States. As such, we might imagine that whatever else "the spirituality of Martin Luther King Jr." might lead him to say about BLM, he could at least see in it some partial fulfillment of his prophetic utterance: "Perhaps a new spirit is rising among us. If it is, let us trace its movements well and pray that our own inner being may be sensitive to its guidance, for we are deeply in need of a new

72. West, ed., *Radical King*, 4.

73. Martin Luther King Jr. "Transformed Non-Conformist," sermon delivered at Ebenezer Baptist Church, Atlanta, Georgia, January 16, 1966, https://tinyurl.com/y86cx78q.

way beyond the darkness that seems so close around us."[74] Of course, this is all speculation. But, dare we discount the power of such speculative imaginings concerning "the spirituality of Martin Luther King," which gave birth, not only to his final prophetic words concerning black lives, "We, as a people, will get to the promised land," *but also* the nonconformist jeremiad he planned to deliver to the nation, "America *May* Go to Hell"?[75]

74. Martin Luther King Jr. "Beyond Vietnam: A Time to Break Silence," address given at the Riverside Church, New York City (4 April 1967), https://tinyurl.com/y8leemc8.

75. This sermon, which King did not live to deliver at Atlanta's Ebenezer Baptist Church, is also known by the title, "America Too Is Going to Hell." King's brother A. D. actually preached the sermon for him at Ebenezer, the King's church home, the week after the assassination. For this account and more, see Coretta Scott King, *My Life with Martin Luther King, Jr.* (New York: Henry Holt, 1993; originally published in 1969), 292.

Afterword: Revived Again!

Sometimes I feel discouraged
And feel my work's in vain.
And then the Holy Spirit
Revives my soul again!

Martin Luther King Jr. left a legacy of justice-oriented spirituality, love and laughter, and engaged preaching, teaching, and scholarship. Thus, our annual celebrations of the man should never be limited to the mythic King, the construction of hagiographers' legends and idol seekers' dreams. King was a real person who experienced the mysteries of the divine and then translated those ineffable moments into sustained social action. The deep roots of King's spirituality kept him grounded, inspired his leadership, and continue to provide solace for those of us still on the journey.

Revives My Soul Again: The Spirituality of Martin Luther King, Jr. reclaims Martin Luther King Jr.'s spirituality and its importance to the ongoing struggle for justice everywhere. Notwithstanding its value as an academic and practical resource, this book offers spiritual encouragement and replenishment for those of us who have been in the struggle for justice most of our lives. King's spiritual example has been a part of my formation for as long as I can remember. As a young teen, I walked with my father in Selma during the second march. The experience shifted my life purpose from theater to teaching and activism. Later, as a young mother living in Atlanta, I observed the deep and complicated family ties that grounded King's spirituality.

As a professor living in Memphis, I was often overcome by the lingering essence of King's sacrifice that still permeates the atmosphere of the National Civil Rights Museum at the Lorraine Motel. And finally, as the president of a seminary in Minneapolis, I saw the rise of another generation of contemplative and spiritually "woke" Black Lives Matter activists. Although young activists sometimes reject the advice of past leaders, King's strategies and moral acuity have found good ground in the millennial generation. Today's activists are adapting elements of King's spirituality in new and creative ways.

Examples abound. Millennials' resistance to oppression is peaceful, but they refuse to abide by the rules of political correctness. Their leadership is grassroots and diverse like King's, but they are led by self-identified queer women, a leadership model that differs significantly from the male dominance of King's inner circle. Perspectives and strategies have changed, but the circumstances of the resistance, then and now, remain the same. When King led the resistance against America's system of apartheid, black people in America were not safe. Today as another generation takes to the streets, the same conditions prevail.

We are well into the twenty-first century, and black lives are endangered again. We need the Holy Spirit that inspired King's spiritual activism to revive our souls again. Ephesians 6:12 clearly identifies the spiritual nature of the battle for peace and justice: "For our struggle is not against enemies of blood and flesh, but against the rulers, against the authorities, against the cosmic powers of this present darkness, against the spiritual forces of evil in the heavenly places." King modeled dedication of body, soul, and spirit, sought the commitment of intersectional allies, and demonstrated the spiritual strength to continue the work even when he knew that it would not bear fruit during his lifetime.

I want to be clear that spiritual leadership does not presume perfection. King was as flawed as any of us, but his vulnerability and prophetic oratory encouraged African Americans to come out of the shadows of separate but unequal existence. In full view of a racially conflicted nation, black folk displayed their humanity and their spiritual maturity as they prepared to translate their yearning for freedom into the already/not yet beloved community.

Although the oft-stated objectives of the civil rights movement included integration and full acceptance in society, in retrospect, the agenda was the same as it is today: stop killing us. In response to this implied demand, gunshots rang out, King and others died, but the spiritually inspired dream lived on as a dormant hope. In the years that followed, we tried to consolidate gains and heighten personal achievement. To be truthful, we thought that the work was done, that despite the bloodshed, we had achieved our legal and educational goals. Accordingly, we dared to take deep breaths and to relax a little during the first black presidency.

In the aftermath of our well-earned complacency, we watched the resurgence of the alt-right, a new name for an old malignancy, and the continuing state-sanctioned murders of unarmed black people during traffic stops and on park benches. We didn't realize that although the work of the civil rights generation was righteous and brave, our goal of "integration" was utopian, justice work is intergenerational, and oppression is cyclical. Oppressors do not release captives because of our demands; instead, systemic racism's shape shifts and reappears in new and resilient forms.

Revives My Soul Again presents King as a spiritually awakened leader, whose example continues to inspire us. As psychologist Stephen Taylor notes, the elements of spiritual awakening include a strong sense of compassion, expanded horizons, and enhanced moral goals:

> For awakened individuals, justice and fairness are universal principles which transcend laws or conventions. They may even be willing to break laws if necessary, and even to potentially sacrifice their own well-being—perhaps even their lives—in order to uphold moral principles. This is why, throughout history, many of the world's great idealists and social reformers were spiritually developed individuals, such as Archbishop Desmond Tutu, Gandhi, Jesus, and possibly figures such as Martin Luther King and Nelson Mandela.[1]

Another generation is realizing that the issues are new, but the struggle is the same. We have gained great ground, but some of the ground gained is sinking sand. Still, we must stand, but where? Here, King's spiritual witness is helpful. It was King's multi-dimensional spirituality that allowed him to transcend culture, "stay woke," and interpret mountaintop visions. King challenged the status quo, and then passed the torch to another generation on the night before his assassination. He understood his role in the movement as one that transcended his life. It takes deep and abiding spiritual roots and practices to realize that one may not live to inherit the promises that one has seen by faith.

The end of the lyric from the title of this book is particularly meaningful, because we are told that just when we have become discouraged, the Holy Spirit revives our souls *again.* This is a journey, and we will get weary. King was weary and sometimes despondent because of the unrelenting attacks on his family, his activism, and his life. But no matter how many times he sojourned in the valley of the shadow of death, he feared

1. Steve Taylor, "Spiritual Activism," *Psychology Today*, June 24, 2016, https://tinyurl.com/ych352o4. See also Stephen Taylor, *The Leap: The Psychology of Spiritual Awakening* (Novato, CA: New World Library, 2017).

no evil. As he faced his earthly end, the Holy Spirit revived his soul *again* and he was able to give us one last vision of the future.

King reminds us that although black people are dying in the streets *again*, we cannot be discouraged as we struggle. This book and the spiritual life of Martin Luther King Jr. should remind us that we will be revived or awakened again. Stay woke if you can, beloved, but know that hypnotic cultural forces are humming lullabies of materialism, wealth for the wealthiest, and isolationism. So, if you succumb to reverie, do not worry, and remember the spiritual example of King and the many others who have followed. Know that death is not the end of life, because the Holy Spirit will revive your soul again and again and again.

Barbara A. Holmes
President Emerita
United Theological Seminary of the Twin Cities

Index